THE SOCIALIST SIXTIE

THE SOCIALIST SIXTIES

Crossing Borders in the Second World

Edited by Anne E. Gorsuch
and Diane P. Koenker

Indiana University Press

Bloomington and Indianapolis

This book is a publication of

Indiana University Press
601 North Morton Street
Bloomington, Indiana 47404–3797 USA

iupress.indiana.edu

Telephone orders   800–842–6796
Fax orders   812–855–7931

∞The paper used in this publication meets the minimum requirements of the American National Standard for Information Sciences—Permanence of Paper for Printed Library Materials, ANSI
Z39.48–1992.

Manufactured in the United States of America

Cataloging-in-Publication Data is available
from the Library of Congress.

ISBN 978-0-253-00929-6 (cloth)
ISBN 978-0-253-00937-1 (paper)
ISBN 978-0-253-00949-4 (ebook)

1 2 3 4 5 18 17 16 15 14 13

Contents

Acknowledgments

THIS VOLUME ORIGINATED at a conference held at the University of Illinois at Urbana-Champaign under the auspices of the Ralph and Ruth Fisher Forum of the Russian, East European, and Eurasian Center, 24–26 June 2010. We are very grateful to the Center, the College of Liberal Arts and Sciences, the School of Literatures, Cultures, and Linguistics, and the Office of International Programs and Studies for their generous funding. Thanks especially to Katrina Chester for programmatic and logistical support during the conference. We also wish to thank the conference participants, in addition to those whose papers are included here, for their lively and engaged comments on all of the papers, individually and together: James Brennan, Donna Buchanan, Christine Evans, Heather Gumbert, Padraic Kenney, Shawn Salmon, Mark Steinberg, Roshanna Sylvester, Christine Varga-Harris, and Eugénie Zvonkina.

THE SOCIALIST SIXTIES

Introduction

The Socialist 1960s in Global Perspective

Anne E. Gorsuch and Diane P. Koenker

THE 1960S HAVE reemerged in scholarly and popular culture as a protean moment of cultural revolution and social transformation, a generational shift through which age and seniority lost their authority, perhaps never to be regained. In Europe and the United States, civil rights, feminist, environmentalist, peace, and other movements drew in millions of participants. New media and cultural technologies emerged to circulate ideas and trends that provided the cultural substrata of these movements. The era also saw explosive urbanization in all parts of the globe that generated its own technological possibilities and spaces for cultural cross-fertilization, spurred by unprecedented human, technological, and cultural mobility. Revolution in Cuba and cultural revolution in China presented new models for transition and for the future. This was a time of world competition for the hegemony of two antagonistic systems—capitalism and socialism—but also of contest and competition within both systems. As a moment when decolonization created immense possibilities for political and social transformation throughout the world, the 1960s became the heyday of efforts from both the developed capitalist "First World" and the emerging socialist "Second World" to obtain the allegiance of and patronage over these newly liberated states and societies, the "Third World."[1] Against the backdrop of Cold War tension and the political violence that it spawned across the globe, the First and Second Worlds also engaged in peaceful contest to demonstrate the superiority of their systems and the certainty of their triumph. The 1960s, writ large, was a moment when the "orderedness" of these three worlds was arguably the most prominent in popular discourse and culture, and a moment when that order was contested and destabilized. The patterns that first emerged in the 1960s—cultural and political contest, identity politics, urbanization, youth movements, new patterns of mass consumption, the hegemony of popular over "high" culture as driven by new media—form the bases of today's discussions of globalization.

First World perspectives, particularly those of the United States, have dominated reconsiderations of the 1960s.[2] This volume seeks to use the Second World, socialist societies of the 1960s in the Soviet Union, Eastern Europe, and Cuba as the springboard from which to explore global interconnections and uncover new and perhaps surprising patterns of cultural cross-pollination. What did the 1960s look like from within communist systems? The avowed internationalism of their socialist ideology should have opened certain kinds of connections across borders, but how far? How might we periodize the era from a perspective other than one highlighting the Secret Speech, Sputnik, the Cuban Missile Crisis, and Prague? We must first consider whether *the 1960s* is a meaningful term of analysis for the experiences and transformations that took place within these communist societies. But we can do so only by considering interactions and influences, by rigorously exploring the kinds of transnational flows of information, cultural models, and ideas that may have linked events and processes across the capitalist-socialist divide. By examining the sixties from *inside* socialism and looking out, we can assess the directionality of these influences and also discern important discontinuities and differentiation. We must firmly reject any assumption of a hegemonic "sixties" culture that transcended national boundaries, while at the same time being motivated to uncover the kinds of global connections that were made possible by the social, cultural, and technological developments of the time.

In formulating our approach to the socialist sixties, we chose to focus on arenas that we believe to be most fruitful in identifying the balance between global integration and continuing political differentiation. Acknowledging the moment at the end of the 1950s in which these socialist societies became predominantly urban, we have identified the city as our primary unit of analysis. Cityscapes at the middle of the century appealed to contemporary social scientists as models of universalizing and global processes. Cities also served as arenas for the transmission of popular culture within them and among them. We then looked to those particular forms of popular culture that might most effectively lend themselves to transnational connections, whether through technology, political movements, or shared material culture. Within the realm of popular culture, we became most interested in media (including television, cinema, and popular music); material culture (including spaces and their uses as well as commodities); and leisure (including tourism and other activities, but also the very consumption of popular culture). We consider these three areas exemplary of the circulation of objects, images, sounds, and impressions on a level different from that of political programs, literature, and "fine arts," although we also acknowledge the ways in which the city helped to democratize "fine art" such as literature as well as to validate the cultural importance of popular music, sports, and television.

When Were the Socialist Sixties?

The essays in this book address a set of important and interrelated thematic commonalities, none more fundamental than the definition of the sixties as a historical period, its beginning and its end, its turning points and its greatest hits. We must first agree that there is a chronological commonality in order to test our expectations of cross-cultural influence and global phenomena. The precise dating of the "sixties" has generated its own scholarly debate. Few would accept a definition slavishly tied to the calendar, although this is the approach taken by Gerard DeGroot in *The Sixties Unplugged*, whose book is "the history of a decade, not of an idea. The Sixties is, strictly speaking, a period of 3,653 days sandwiched between the Fifties and the Seventies."[3] More commonly, historians acknowledge that the myriad processes and consequences of the sixties had origins earlier than 1 January 1960 and created trends that persisted after the decade's calendrical end. The editors of the journal *The Sixties* opt for a "long sixties," starting in 1954 and ending in 1975. They note that 1954 marked the beginning of the U.S. civil rights movement with the Supreme Court's decision *Brown v. Board of Education* and the Geneva Accords that legislated French withdrawal from Indochina, which led eventually to U.S. involvement in Vietnam. The year 1975 marked the withdrawal of U.S. forces from Southeast Asia and the decline of the social movements that the civil rights movement had catalyzed.[4] Arthur Marwick, who focuses on the rise of a conscious youth movement, also opts for a "long sixties" but begins with the more arbitrary date of 1958, marking the rise of a youth movement, its new musical forms, urbanization, automobility (interstate highways), and activism.[5]

Both periodizations are firmly anchored in a U.S.-centered or a West European–American frame of reference. Should a *global* sixties necessarily reflect those same markers? Periodization requires us to balance global trends and local particularities. For many historians, the prevailing ruling system matters more than chronology: the Chinese sixties, for example, is subsumed in the Maoist era of Chinese history (1949–76);[6] for historians of Cuba, the sixties are coterminous with the Cuban Revolution, beginning with the 1959 revolution that toppled the Batista regime. For many historians of the Soviet Union, the era of Khrushchev (1954–64), with its policies of the Thaw or "De-Stalinization," is a more meaningful period than one defined by chronological years. In their provocative work on the Soviet 1960s, Petr Vail' and Aleksandr Genis asserted their own definition of a limited sixties that began in the Soviet Union on 30 July 1961 with the publication of the new Communist Party Program and ended on 21 August 1968, when Soviet tanks invaded Czechoslovakia and put an end to socialism with a human face.[7] Certainly no periodization of the 1960s can *exclude* 1968, which emerges in this volume and elsewhere as a global moment of heartbreaking complexity.

The "socialist sixties," according to several of our authors, emerged in the throes of the fifties, and specifically the "Thaw." Polly Jones's chapter on the translation and transmission of Soviet literature in Britain and the United States—"The Thaw Goes International"—is firmly located in the internationalism of the Khrushchev era. For Nick Rutter, too, Khrushchev-era internationalism is key; in his chapter, "Look Left, Drive Right: Internationalisms at the 1968 World Youth Festival," Rutter sees the Moscow Youth Festival in 1957 as the opening act of a new outward-looking international socialist youth movement, the first of these youth festivals to embrace participation from nonsocialist youth and the precursor of festivals in nonsocialist capitals such as Helsinki and Vienna. Susan Reid also begins with the 1950s, even as her examination of Soviet consumerism moves well beyond it. In her chapter, "This Is Tomorrow! Becoming a Consumer in the Soviet Sixties," she links the rise of Soviet consumerism to broader postwar processes of affluent consumerism on which British artists fixed their gaze at the *This Is Tomorrow* exhibition of 1956. Soviet consumerism is also intimately linked, she argues, to the increase in the number of private apartments, a policy of the Soviet regime that took off in the mid-1950s. Rossen Djagalov also begins with the 1950s in his chapter "Guitar Poetry, Democratic Socialism, and the Limits of 1960s Internationalism," although he emphasizes the "long sixties," carrying his analysis into the early 1970s.

Other authors in this volume call our attention to divisions, highs, and lows, within the 1960s, much as Arthur Marwick describes the years 1964 to 1969 as the "high sixties," for reasons relating to capitalist societies' cultural revolutions. Lilya Kaganovsky takes a "long sixties" approach in her account of the use of memory in Soviet film, noting a turn toward more intimate and domestic themes starting as early as 1954 in her chapter, "Postmemory, Countermemory: Soviet Cinema of the 1960s." But she also describes a darker, more pessimistic turn in films after 1966, linking them with the growing pall cast on freedom of expression that came to be labeled "Stagnation," but also with a turn away from transnationalism. As with so much of the literature on the international sixties, 1968 is a "high" moment for many authors in this volume, even if the conclusions drawn sometimes differ from much of the literature about 1968 in North America and Western Europe. Christian Noack's account of the Soviet tourist song movement—"Songs from the Wood, Love from the Fields"—focuses on the emergence of the Grushin Song Festival in 1968, an outdoor event that continued through the 1970s and arose again in 1986. Despite the echoes of Woodstock, however, the timing of the festival's birth would seem to have little to do with the logics of protest or counterculture sweeping other parts of the world. Indeed, Noack notes a growing institutionalization of the tourist song movement in the second half of the 1960s, stemming from an increasing stratification of the freewheeling tourist and musical cultures. Rachel Applebaum also focuses on 1968 in her chapter exploring the limits of international understanding between Soviet tourists and Czechoslovak citizens during the Prague Spring. Nick Rutter finds a turning point in 1968, arguing that the failure of socialist youth and the West European New Left to find common cause at the Sofia World Youth Festival of 1968 signaled another shock to the Soviet-led international youth movement of the 1960s: in addition to Chinese and Cuban "ultra-leftism," Romanian nationalism, and the Prague Spring's liberalism, the festival now contended with a new "ultra-Left" from Western Europe. The significance of August 1968 for these socialist societies cannot be overestimated. Stephen Lovell, in his chapter "In Search of an Ending," calls August 1968 the end of the road of hopeful socialist progress and the beginning of the huge gulf that would divide official and unofficial culture. In Czechoslovakia, the period of "normalization" that followed the August invasion led to an official emphasis on domesticity and the quiet life, as Paulina Bren documents in her 2010 book *The Greengrocer and His TV: The Culture of Communism after the 1968 Prague Spring.*[8] In the Soviet Union, the gap between official and unofficial culture would underlie the notion of stagnation.

We should not be so quick, however, to accept that "stagnation" inevitably resulted from the imposition of the Brezhnev doctrine in Czechoslovakia. Socialist economies did not immediately plummet after 1968, and some of the themes of the sixties would persist well into the 1970s. Lewis Siegelbaum and Robert Edelman's chapters focus on the "late 1960s": for Siegelbaum in "Modernity Unbound: The New Soviet City of the Sixties," the construction of the modern city of Tol'iatti was a quintessential sixties project combining expert planning and rational design, but it did not begin until 1966 and its contours continued to be shaped well into the 1970s.[9] For Edelman, the moment of the withering of state authority came not in 1968 but in 1972, when the medium of television gave Soviet football fans a glimpse of world countercultures in hairstyles, fashion, and unruly fan behavior.[10] Thus the title of his chapter: "Playing Catch-Up: Soviet Media and Soccer Hooliganism, 1965–75."

Transnationalism or Globalization?

A second theme common to all of the chapters in this volume is transnationalism. Jeremi Suri, the author of an influential book on "global revolution" in the 1960s, describes 1968 in particular as a moment when "the entire world shook": "Across cultures," he argues, "people of all generations recognized the significance of the moment."[11] It should not surprise us that the two "socialist" examples Suri provides of this worldwide disturbance are Prague and the Chinese Cultural Revolution. The Prague Spring is the most common socialist reference for those looking to incorporate the socialist East into the international 1960s.[12] As Applebaum describes, Prague was the "unofficial capital of cosmopolitan activity—and 1960s culture—in [Eastern Europe]." During the springtime festivities of the Majáles in 1965, young people in Prague famously crowned the bearded beatnik Allen Ginsberg, king of May. For his coronation speech he clinked tiny cymbals while chanting a Buddhist hymn. Ginsberg was not alone in his visit to Prague. In 1966, about three-quarters of a million people visited Prague from the West.[13]

The flow of people and popular culture from capitalism to socialism, and the other way around, was not unique to Czechoslovakia among socialist countries, even if especially evident there. Cuba, as described by Anne Luke in her chapter "Listening to *los Beatles:* Being Young in 1960s Cuba," was also visited by Allen Ginsberg in 1965, and Cuban youth enjoyed listening to recordings of the Beatles, which, if still a clandestine pleasure, met with less official opposition than in many other socialist countries. The 1960s, we argue, ushered in a new era of human mobility, symbolized by the first manned space flight on 12 April 1961 by Yuri Gagarin, who was followed by numerous other cosmonauts and astronauts during the decade. On the ground, more prosaically, hundreds of thousands of earth dwellers continued to migrate from rural areas to the burgeoning cities. As Noack notes, it was in 1959 that the Soviet Union's urban population first surpassed the 50 percent mark, and cities served as the staging ground for much of the effervescence, contest, and experimentation of the global sixties, whether in or between Prague, Hanoi, Tol'iatti, Havana, or Dar es Salaam. This urban population was disproportionately young, and many of them were students, a point to which we will return. The higher standards of living associated with urbanization and economic development also fueled a boom in leisure travel, a kind of personal mobility, sometimes domestic, sometimes international, that facilitated the circulation of ideas and artifacts as well as people. If most of the tourists traveling between Czechoslovakia and the Soviet Union journeyed by rail, as explored by Applebaum, the development of passenger airliners accelerated the rate of tourist travel, which exploded around the world in the 1960s.[14] Soviet football teams and others could readily participate in European cup championships through this new mode of travel, even if their fans could follow the matches only at home on television. Air transportation changed the nature of tourism in Western Europe, making mass low-cost excursions to seaside destinations the new norm for Scandinavians, for example, and bringing thousands of middle-class tourists and backpacking American students alike to observe the cultural treasures of Western Europe and/or share countercultural experiences with *copains* and mates abroad.[15]

Domestic leisure travel in the Soviet Union and elsewhere also took off in the 1960s, creating new opportunities for exchanges of experience, songs, and perspectives. The number of tourists served by tourist bases and hotels grew tenfold during that decade (excluding untold numbers of "unorganized" tourists and vacationers who traveled without reservations).[16] Noack paints a collective portrait of the Soviet tourist on the road, with knapsack and guitar. "Tourism," he writes, "offered Soviet citizens a sphere that provided distance from the increasingly empty ritualism of state and party duties." The youth festivals discussed by Rutter were made possible as well by this new leisure mobility. If they did not lead to mutual understanding and camaraderie, as they certainly did not in Sofia in 1968, they nonetheless provided the opportunity for mutual observation and the expansion of horizons. Noack describes the growth of a particular kind of festival devoted to the tourist song, which began in 1968 and attracted as many as one hundred thousand people to listen and compete for amateur glory. The circulation of tourists led to the circulation of music, and especially of texts, in the form of the handwritten songbooks that tourists exchanged and in makeshift tape recordings as well.

Music and material goods, especially clothing, were the global products most likely to cross socialist borders, even if the latter sometimes crossed only as images to be reproduced with hard-won fabrics at home.[17] Everywhere, media—whether the reel-to-reel tape recorder, radio, film, or television—were a major way in which sights and sounds crossed ideological borders. Jones analyzes the explosion of print translations of Soviet fiction in the early 1960s, made possible by the new form of the paperback. Songs of the guitar poets circulated through tape recordings, as Djagalov notes, a more stable technological medium than the X-ray plates on which the earliest Soviet rock 'n' roll fans circulated this music from the West. Some of these cultural crossings, as Edelman suggests in his account of the unexpected transfer of soccer hooliganism from Western Europe to the Soviet Union, were unwanted by authorities. In other instances, however, previously condemned aspects of "Western" culture—fashionable clothing, urban cafés, light jazz—were domesticated and made acceptably socialist.[18]

Our focus on movement between the capitalist and socialist countries should not make us forget the vital importance of the circulation of goods, people, and information within and between socialist countries. We call particular attention in this respect to the chapter by João Gonçalves, "Sputnik Premiers in Havana," which explores the impact of the 1960 Soviet Exposition of Science, Technique and Culture in Havana. "Cubans had long been heavy consumers of American movies, music, food, sports, magazines, architectural styles, electric appliances, automobiles, urban planning, and information," Gonçalves writes. "The Soviet Exposition was the point at which items coming from the nearest mainland started being increasingly replaced by items of the same kind coming from the other side of the world." Gonçalves argues, taking off from anthropologist James Ferguson, that for Cuba a better metaphor than transnational "flows" might be a series of sometimes sudden "jumps" and "hops" of objects, people, and culture from, for example, the Soviet Union to Cuba. These "jumps" created "alternative circulation patterns" among countries in a "growing socialist world."

Much of the scholarly work on the 1960s as a global moment under capitalism is concerned with unofficial, global emancipatory movements. The focus is typically on cultural flows of countercultural style, music, or drugs, or political flows of anti-authoritarian protest between, for example, Berkeley and Paris.[19] In contrast, many of the contributions to this book focus on officially authorized forms of cross-cultural contact. Reid's and Siegelbaum's chapters on Soviet appliances and the new Soviet city respectively suggest that technology, architecture, and, broadly speaking, the aesthetics of modernity were especially likely to cross political borders, facilitated by the willing assistance of authorities. Soviet architects and urban planners in the 1960s "openly acknowledged 'points of contiguity' with ideas and projects elsewhere in the world," Siegelbaum argues. He observes that they, along with other professionals—"nuclear physicists and ballistics experts, obstetricians and sociologists, the designers of products rapidly filling up the apartments described by Susan Reid, members of dance companies, Olympic gymnastic squads, and the football teams discussed in Robert Edelman's contribution"—enjoyed a degree of professional autonomy that "encouraged the establishment of an essentially transnational set of standards and styles."[20]

This was also true for film. Officially authorized film festivals exposed socialist audiences to the new forms of experimental cinema originating in Italy and France in the postwar years, and a younger generation of directors, as Kaganovsky notes, adopted the new *auteur* style and made it their own. The Moscow Film Festival emerged as a biennial event in 1959, showing films from East and West and awarding its top prizes to films from the USSR, West Germany, Pakistan, Great Britain, and Czechoslovakia.[21] In the officialness of much of Soviet internationalism, the Soviet sixties did not differ in principle, if they did in degree, from earlier periods in Soviet history when delegations of professionals were allowed to travel abroad to capitalist countries to learn about a wide range of topics relating to technology but also to consumer culture ranging from paper plates to window decorations.[22] Until the late 1930s, the Soviet relationship to the West was cautious but not unreservedly hostile. Russia was eager to end the "international isolation in which the country found itself," Susan Solomon has argued elsewhere about public health professionals in the 1920s, and to "reclaim its place in the international arena."[23]

Socialist authorities did not encourage all forms of internationalism. Khrushchev's doctrine of peaceful coexistence enabled unprecedented international contact, even in contrast to earlier decades. In 1960, close to three hundred thousand tourists from capitalist countries visited the Soviet Union.[24] Soviet citizens also crossed international borders in record numbers.[25] In his memoir, Soviet intellectual Mikhail German describes encounters with the West (through language, culture, material items, personal encounters, and travel) as *the* defining experience of the Thaw.[26] But as Jones argues in her contribution to this volume, the politics of the Cold War still intruded everywhere, something she demonstrates in her discussion of Western reception of Soviet literature. Unprecedented openings were accompanied by continuing anxieties. As Jones argues, "The 'default' ideological setting of the Soviet leadership remained distrust of the West." The same held true for Britain and the United States. The politics of the Cold War also intervened in the guitar poetry Djagalov discusses. In contrast to the relaxed transnationalism of folkloric labor and protest songs in the 1930s, guitar poetry crossed borders with great difficulty in the 1960s. Its simultaneous expression in the Soviet Union, Germany, the United States, and Latin America (among others) should be attributed to a "simultaneity of feeling," not transcultural contact. Instead, Djagalov argues, the Cold War state, whether of a state socialist or a capitalist variety, prevented intimacy and rapprochement. The exceptions, importantly, were again Prague for a few months in 1968 and, as with so much in this volume, Cuba. Authorities also limited internationalism at the 1968 World Youth Festival in Bulgaria, as described by Rutter. Even as young people from around the world gathered in a supposed celebration of solidarity, authorities both Bulgarian and Soviet tried to control young Bulgarians' exposure to ideological countercurrents. Only 250 of approximately eight million Bulgarians were allowed to participate in seminars and forums at the festival. This was a far cry from Berkeley's freewheeling Summer of Love in 1967. It was also a far cry from Richard Ivan Jobs's description, in a recent article entitled "Youth Movements: Travel, Protest, and Europe in 1968," of a West European international youth identity, created in part through travel and mobility, that generated a "shared political culture across national boundaries." "An alternative community was developing," Jobs claims, "on the basis of informal interchanges and transnational cooperation."[27] Rutter argues otherwise, emphasizing the lack of communication and understanding between socialist youth situated on various points of the world Left.

As this suggests, if popular culture may have flowed across borders, politics did so much less easily. Jeremy Suri pointedly describes the political disruptions of 1968 as global, not as transnational. "Organizational ties between protesters across different societies were a minimal factor in these developments," Suri argues. Instead, "domestic conflicts grew from local conditions that, though unique in each case, produced a similar dynamic of rising expectations and attempted repressions."[28] Paulina Bren concurs in *The Greengrocer and His TV,* in which she argues that even in Prague cross-border understanding was limited by the "particularities of geography and political happenstance."[29] Visiting West German students were optimistic about the utopian possibilities of Marxism. Czech students, if committed to socialism, were all too familiar with the limits of Marxism as practiced. They found it difficult to understand, let alone agree with, the rigidly orthodox theories of West German leftists.

Suggestively, Bren's arguments about the limits of transnationalism stem from her study of television. Many forms of technology contributed to the acceleration of exchange of ideas and texts in the 1960s through the media of film, print, and sound recordings. Significantly, though, the advent of television, which did not become a staple appliance in socialist households until the end of the decade, tended more to restrict the circulation of ideas and images than to spread them.[30] With the exception of the televised soccer games that are the subject of Edelman's chapter, television served as a medium that reinforced national language communities rather than fostered global communities. For Czechoslovakia, Paulina Bren has analyzed the ways in which television serials reinforced the domestic norms preferred by the post-1968 regime.[31] Sabina Mihelj shows in this volume how watching Yugoslav television, an experience shared by millions but in the privacy of their homes, aimed to foster a sense of Yugoslav citizenship but increasingly reinforced subnational distinctions. Lovell goes so far as to suggest that the expansion of television marked the end of the Soviet sixties, creating a domestic community united around the common postmemory (in Kaganovsky's phrase) of the shared wartime experience, rejecting internationalism, and promoting a televised socialism in one country without allowing access to a wider world.

The contributions to this volume demonstrate that the socialist world was not a singular world, separate from what was happening elsewhere. But were the socialist sixties transnational, implying the circulation of information, organization, ideas, images, and people across borders? Or were they global, suggesting parallelism but not interpenetration? Our authors provide many examples of the former but emphasize the latter. This was in part because of the nature of socialist authoritarianism, but it was not only authorities—socialist but also capitalist—that challenged transnationalism and the universalism it implied. In his anthropology of late socialism, Alexei Yurchak encourages us to take seriously that by the 1960s, for "great numbers" of Soviet citizens, "many of the fundamental values, ideals, and realities of socialist life (such as equality, community, selflessness, altruism, friendship, ethical relations, safety, education, work, creativity, and concern for the future) were of genuine importance."[32] Anne Luke argues similarly that young Cubans could both love the music of the Beatles and believe in the Revolution. When applied to the socialist world, transnationalism has too often meant Americanization, with the implication that cross-border flows of everything from jazz to jeans led inexorably to popular disillusionment and the downfall of socialism.[33] This volume demonstrates instead that the Soviet, Czech, or Cuban citizen, like the American, French, or Canadian one, was discerning both about items and ideas at home and about those coming from abroad. If the socialist world became less exceptional in the 1960s, it did not necessarily become less socialist.

The World of Goods

Consumption was a preoccupation of both socialist and capitalist countries in the 1960s. In "The Politics of Privatization: Television Entertainment and the Yugoslav Sixties," Sabina Mihelj argues that during the sixties, "both east and west of the Iron Curtain, long-established fault lines of political struggle, tied to the alternative visions of modernity espoused by communism, liberalism, and fascism, gave way to issues of living standards and social welfare." Across the socialist East, "slowly but surely, average livelihoods were getting better, and it was becoming abundantly clear that both the domestic legitimacy and the international prestige of the socialist project, just like those of its capitalist rival, hinged increasingly on the quality of everyday life." Consumption was a site of Cold War competition over the "good life," the most famous example of which was the "kitchen debate" between Richard Nixon and Nikita Khrushchev at the 1959 American exhibition in Moscow about the relative merits of their economic systems. The exhibition launched the socialist sixties via a circulation of objects that brought East and West together materially, however different the meanings that were ascribed to them. For Reid and many observers of the Soviet 1960s, the exposition of American consumer culture marks a particularly significant juncture in the exchange of consumer products. The traveling exhibit drew thousands of Soviet visitors, ordinary people and experts, to catch a glimpse of alternative and wider consumer possibilities but also of a range of technology and design that expanded their imaginations. The appearance in Havana of the Soviet Exposition, the subject of Gonçalves's paper, similarly provoked admiration, curiosity, and opposition. The materiality of the exhibits, their size, and their presentation moved visitors in ways that two-dimensional printed texts or film could never do.

In socialist countries as well as capitalist ones, consumption was not only an international issue, of course. The "fundamental difference" between the Khrushchev era and the Stalinist one, Reid has argued in an earlier article about the "Khrushchev modern," was "the shift towards mass consumption and democratization of provision."[34] "The mood of the people and the productivity of their labor to a large extent depend on living conditions and good service," Khrushchev insisted at the Twenty-Second Party Congress in 1961.[35] The Soviet regime and the governments of most East European countries increasingly promoted consumer goods, even "luxury" goods, as emblems of socialist success. In Bulgaria, it was cigarettes "in their luxurious packaging and flavor variety" that were material evidence of the socialist "good life." The 1960s and early 1970s were, according to Mary Neuberger, the "golden years" for consumerism in Bulgaria.[36]

Still, socialist countries had some catching up to do. Elements of "consumer socialism" were evident in the early 1950s in Hungary,[37] and the East European countries of Poland, Czechoslovakia, and the German Democratic Republic (GDR) provided a cornucopia of consumer goods for tourists from the USSR throughout the 1950s and 1960s, even as these countries themselves struggled to recover from the war.[38] For contemporary Western observers at worlds' fairs and international expositions, however, Soviet goods in particular were thought not to have even made it into the sixties. Reid argues in her contribution to this volume that Cold War competition, but also a new "Soviet consumer consciousness," led Soviet specialists to pay more attention to the visual aspects of design, "drawing energetically both on Western expertise and on that of socialist Eastern Europe." East European experts in turn, often moved even closer to the West: Polish architects, for example, used Khrushchev-approved internationalism to justify publishing extensive articles about American architectural models while saying very little about Soviet design.[39]

If elements of socialist consumer culture were imported from the West—the international modernist conventions of urban planning or the sleek styling of refrigerators—socialist authorities, especially Soviet ones, forcefully maintained that their version was better. Sixties socialism was envisioned as an alternative modernity in which virtuous citizens would be cared for but not allowed to wallow in the hedonism of capitalist mass consumption. Khrushchev was eager, as György Péteri has argued, to "provide a workable way toward an *alternative* modernity" with "distinctly *socialist* characteristics."[40] Yurchak has explained the distinction as one between the positive, enriching traits of internationalism and the negative, undermining qualities of cosmopolitanism.[41] Appreciation for "aesthetic beauty, technological achievement, and the genius of the working people who created [bourgeois luxuries]" was to be encouraged.[42] The enthusiasm of the black marketeer for foreign clothing and culture was not.

For a brief moment in the "sixties," this "hybrid form of modernity," as David Crowley has called it, appeared promising, and not only to authorities.[43] An examination of popular Soviet response to the American National Exhibition in 1959 shows that not all viewers were "captured by the allure of America." "Many sought ways to define their difference from it, in terms and personae borrowed from Soviet public discourse," Reid has argued.[44] Socialist modernity was authoritative, open to learning from international models, and committed to satisfying needs and desires within the socialist framework. It was this model that the socialist Soviet Union hoped to export to the Third World.

Socialist modernity appears, however, to have been only provisionally successful, in part, György Péteri argues in a recent volume, because it was short-lived. If Khrushchev was eager to define a "socialist mode of consumption," those who followed him in the Soviet Union and throughout the socialist bloc largely abandoned Khrushchev's efforts, striving to imitate capitalist consumption but without the earlier ideology of socialist promise that made deficits seem justifiable.[45] Consumption, indeed the private sphere in general, increasingly became a site from which citizens could articulate—if sometimes only to themselves—opposition. In East Germany, some individuals made a political statement via their preference for wooden and earthenware products over the regime-trumpeted plastics. East German authorities marketed products made of plastic as a successful melding of "socialism, modernity, technology, and functionality." Oppositional consumers, in contrast, defined modernity as "tasteful," and "cultured," while rejecting plastics as *kitschig*.[46] Of course, the opposite was also true. East Germans who supported the system welcomed the abundance of new, inexpensive, plastic goods as evidence of progress. Either way, consumption, like so much of the sixties under socialism, was political.

Culture High and Low

Of all the transformations of the global 1960s, the challenge raised by popular culture to prevailing modes of dominant cultures remained the most enduring. In the sixties, popular culture became legitimate: a profit center for capitalist business and an area of expansion for official socialist institutions such as the Young Communist League (Komsomol). The triumph of popular culture also licensed a proliferation of canons and subcultures: no one canon could exert hegemony, a development perhaps appreciated later in the socialist world than elsewhere, as Jones suggests in her paper on the translation of Soviet literature to English-speaking audiences. But the quintessential form of sixties popular culture, of course, was music. Two of the papers in this volume address the phenomenon of guitar poetry, or bard poetry, which appeared to assume global proportions, as Djagalov explores. The appeal of guitar poetry and tourist songs, write Noack and Djagalov, was their simplicity and immediacy, "a structure of feeling," both in their musical forms and in the substance of the genre. Before the festivals and Komsomol sponsorship, Soviet tourist songs took place around the evening campfire, performed among friends, for friends, about friends. Such was the emotional power of the genre, as Noack argues, that the tourist songs are preserved and remembered to this day through a dense network of clubs and Internet sites.

On the other side of the socialist/capitalist divide, of course, folk music with its guitars was yielding to rock 'n' roll in forms that rapidly proliferated and conquered new audiences with their powerful rhythm and music, rendering the texts less important. Robert Edelman notes that by 1970 every department at Moscow State University sponsored its own beat group; along with the circulation of tourists, touring football players, and objects of Western consumer culture came recordings of Western music on disks and on tape. The reel-to-reel tape recorder was a ubiquitous feature of Soviet urban apartments, at least as depicted in the films of the period. The Beatles were officially disapproved of in Havana, Luke tells us, but sixties youth cultures sought out their global beat along with the more native *nueva trova*. Socialist rock 'n' roll gathered its greatest momentum after the 1960s, as a counterculture, perhaps, in opposition to the growing domesticity of the new post-1968 normalization regimes. The Komsomol would remain divided about whether to support or to marginalize rock 'n' roll bands in the Soviet Union.[47] In Czechoslovakia, the group Plastic People of the Universe emerged after 1968 in imitation of some of the more countercultural groups in the United States, including the Velvet Underground, only to incur the wrath of the normalizing regime and be driven into their own underground.[48] Socialist rock music seems to belong more to the history of the decline of socialism than to its global moment of the sixties.

Our contributors note that "popular culture" in these socialist societies generated opposition and resistance. Not only did the state seek to censor and to block manifestations of culture that challenged the prerogatives of authority, but ordinary people maintained their loyalty to a canon of authoritative and approved cultural forms. Polly Jones notes that Western critics found some glimmers of modernism in Aleksandr Solzhenitsyn's *One Day in the Life of Ivan Denisovich* but that some Soviet readers reacted with disgust and horror at the crude language and the celebration of unlettered people.[49] Rachel Applebaum writes that some Soviet tourists were shocked and repelled by the abstract art on display in state museums, by hippies in Prague, and by pictures of girls in miniskirts. Similarly, in Havana, miniskirts provoked public outrage. Popular culture shock also proved to be too much for Soviet tourists elsewhere in Eastern Europe, who refused to learn the twist from local Poles and taught their hosts Ukrainian folk dances instead.[50] A demonstration of the latest twist by Algerian tourists in Bulgaria caused similar offense: "The movements and gestures suggested something sexual," and the Soviets repaid the favor by performing another folk dance. "We let them know that we don't accept the bad aspects of Western culture." A German woman found Soviets like these "boring" and predicted that they too would eventually adopt contemporary dances that were now forbidden inside the USSR.[51] That sexuality and sexual identity did not occupy a central role in the 1968 Sofia conference likewise suggests that the socialist sixties were much more buttoned-down than their capitalist counterparts.

Who Made the Sixties?

The correspondence of the sixties with a generation of youth has become a commonplace in popular commentary. The demographic emergence of a postwar generation of young people, the expansion of institutions of higher education in which to train and empower them, and the resulting conflicts between generations are themes that run through scholarship on the sixties. Yet these papers also prompt us to take a more complicated approach to the question "Who made the sixties?" Socialist youth constituted a singular generation in the 1960s for many of the same demographic and economic reasons as in the First World: rising standards of living expanded access to higher education, providing young people with unstructured time, ideas, and ambition. Young people congregated in newly accessible spaces and participated in new forms of popular culture, such as the habitués of the Coppelia ice cream parlor in Havana that Anne Luke describes; amateur rock musicians in Moscow's universities, as witnessed by Edelman; or young tourists on Soviet roads, described by Noack. Young faces emerged on Soviet screens, most notably in the films analyzed by Kaganovsky, *Lenin's Guard* and *July Rain*, the faces of the future. Youth carried the banner of socialist internationalism across the World Youth Festivals of the 1950s and 1960s, the subject of Nick Rutter's chapter.

Socialist youth also confronted their generational others, as most explicitly analyzed by Kaganovsky, who argues that the key films of the 1960s confront the question of postmemory of the critical juncture of World War II by a generation too young to have direct memories and too privileged to readily empathize with the sacrifices of those who came before. Generational distinctions shaped the evolution of guitar poetry and the tourist song movement in complicated ways. The movement of singer-songwriters owed much to the tradition of political song championed by an international Left during the 1930s; Djagalov shows how this generation, epitomized by the American singer-songwriter Pete Seeger, became marginalized both by the rise of rock 'n' roll and by the indifference of official cultural promoters in socialist states.

Several of the chapters emphasize the importance of "youth" as a state project and the conflicts that this created between countercultural and official youth. The World Youth Festivals considered by Rutter offer the most explicit picture of the bureaucratized world of the Komsomol: the Moscow-based state youth organization controlled every aspect of the biennial youth festivals, from the invited participants to the political agendas. Officials themselves were far from young, but even their young lieutenants dutifully followed the prescribed line. Christian Noack offers some insight into why this might be so: the Komsomol had resources to support the cultural activities of youth, and some participants in the tourist song movement readily sought Komsomol sponsorship to gain access to festival venues and funds. Official youth organizations such as the Unión de Jóvenes Comunistas in Cuba, as Luke discusses, and the Free German Youth in the GDR, in Rutter's account, also sought to impose their own statist agendas over countercultural manifestations like marijuana use and political heterodoxy. Student youth even without official sponsorship might also disagree: as Gonçalves recounts, in the battle over Soviet influence in revolutionary Cuba it was anticommunist students who took to the squares to protest the Soviet Exposition in 1960. All of the chapters in this volume point to the complexity and plurality of "youth cultures" as well as to the conflict of generations.

The emphasis on youth in the 1960s has sometimes obscured the importance of other actors who became empowered by the movements, culture, and events of the decade. The net effect of mobility, demography, mass education, and economy appears also to have produced a generation of "ordinary people" who gained new agency in shaping the trends of the global sixties. Kaganovsky makes this point in showing the new subjects of the cinematic "New Wave" in Western Europe and in Soviet film: "Instead of monumentalism and the 'Grand Style,' sixties cinema gives us daily routine and intimate, domestic lives," she writes. Tourism, that quintessential leisure activity of the 1960s, also allowed ordinary people to engage in firsthand observation and even diplomacy. Socialist travelers throughout the East European bloc, as Applebaum points out, were expected to serve as everyday ambassadors, representing their country's politics and culture to their counterparts abroad. Expositions such as those discussed in Gonçalves's and Reid's papers likewise depended for their raison d'être on the participation of tens of thousands of exposition visitors and sought their comments and approbation. Cultural exchange was no longer restricted to touring ballet companies and high-profile musicians. Spectator sports also created publics out of ordinary people: as Edelman tells us, Soviet football fans became fanatics after observing how ordinary people at Nou Camp stadium in Barcelona supported their teams, with the manic disorder that became labeled football hooliganism. Soviet fans learned that they did not have to depend on official emblems of support and instead fashioned their own scarves and other symbols of team loyalty.

In these respects—the emphasis on youth cultures and on the democratization of daily life—these socialist societies joined in a global phenomenon. Our volume, however, offers a third answer to "Who made the sixties?" that on first glance seems to contradict the prevailing emphasis on the sixties as a challenge to authority. The chapters by Reid and Siegelbaum in particular suggest that it was also experts who made the socialist sixties: design professionals, urban planners, and sociologists, all employed in support of state projects. They include the editors who helped disseminate Soviet literature abroad and who monitored its reception, the subject of Jones's chapter. These were the intellectuals who styled themselves the "sixties generation," and "Children of the Twentieth Party Congress."[32] As Boris Kagarlitsky has argued, "The Soviet intelligentsia constantly criticized leadership. But that same leadership was supposed to become their main audience. . . . The movement was essentially elitist. The 'best minds' spoke and the rest listened."[53] These experts and intellectuals, now gray-ing, received new affirmation in the television serial that Stephen Lovell argues marked the end of the sixties, *Seventeen Moments of Spring*, a "characteristically 1970s blend of statist patriotism and cosmopolitanism."

We note the special role of the international Marxist journal *Problems of Peace and Socialism*, published in Prague starting in 1958. Its first editor, A. M. Rumiantsev, went on to found the Soviet school of sociology based at the Institute for Concrete Sociological Research. Another Prague editor, Boris Grushin, would return to Moscow to pioneer the practice of opinion polling from his center based at the newspaper *Komsomol'skaia pravda*. (Note the linkage between experts and the youth organization Komsomol.)[54] The influential Soviet rock critic Artemy Troitsky, as Applebaum tells us, spent his youth in Prague, where his parents worked for this journal, and it was this experience that sparked his enthusiasm for rock 'n' roll. The sixties, we argue, ushered in the heyday of "socialist modern," when educated professionals gained authority and opportunity to apply global concepts they were now permitted to study, in large part because of the circulation of objects and ideas that was also a part of this global moment in an expanding socialist world.

We have organized this volume around three main themes, although the chapters overlap among them and others. Our understanding of "socialist modern" emphasizes the utopian and forward-looking quality of the socialist sixties as a moment when socialist societies entered the world stage and claimed their right to inherit the mantle of the new. The sixties also marked a period in which these societies willingly and confidently engaged one another and the world outside, creating contact zones of mutual learning and emulation as well as conflict. And while serious literature and classical art forms continued to be produced, these socialist sixties, like their counterpart in the West, depended to a greater extent than ever before on popular culture and the media.

These do not exhaust the topics and possibilities for exploring the relationship of First, Second, and Third Worlds in the global 1960s. We hope, however, that this volume can help suggest some questions and themes to be pursued further. The interdisciplinarity of our contributors—anthropology, art history, literature, history, media studies—illustrates the fascination the sixties holds for many disciplines. Our authors, however, make scant reference to gender norms and the ways sixties movements did or not transform them. So too for sexuality, a major topic of study about the sixties in other places.[55] Nor do these chapters address the possibility of identity politics based on ethnic and other identities. Unequal power relations within the socialist bloc became manifest with the Soviet invasion of Czechoslovakia in August 1968; the question of whether these relations can be described as imperial and not fraternal deserves further exploration, particularly if extended to relations among Second and Third World nations. The place of China deserves more attention: the Sino-Soviet rift created two poles of allegiance for aspiring socialist states, and scholars would do well to explore how the themes of popular culture, expertise, and transnational flows affected these political movements.[56]

What have we learned by approaching the sixties from inside socialism and looking out? We see the limits of international solidarity and mutual understanding, the constraints posed by national interests and national rhetorics despite the cosmopolitan principles of international socialism. We see a remarkable conservatism among many of the actors, whether Komsomol officials in three-piece suits or kitchen-based bard singers who felt little solidarity with their counterparts abroad. But we also see the sources of what today has become a powerful nostalgia for the original promise of socialism. As Padraic Kenney said in his remarks at the conclusion of the conference that initiated this volume, "The sixties were the sweet spot of socialism," oriented toward the future; they were the heart of ordinary communism, communism as it was meant to be. Or as Shawn Salmon put it in her paper on the Soviet foreign tourist agency, Intourist, not included in this volume, the sixties represented "a return to the original promise of Soviet socialism: a system transparent and accessible to all, where the masses—not just the elite—were provided for; a world that celebrated mobility and welcomed outsiders, and a society that pushed ahead to the future in an effort to overcome its own backwardness."[57]

Notes

1. This term was coined by the French demographer Alfred Sauvy, "Trois mondes, une planête," *Observateur politique économique et littéraire*, no. 118 (14 August 1952): 5.

2. The literature on the sixties in the United States is immense. See, for example, Alexander Bloom and Wini Breines, eds.,*"Takin' It to the Streets": A Sixties Reader* (New York: Oxford University Press, 1995); David Farber, ed., *The Sixties: From Memory to History* (Chapel Hill: University of North Carolina Press, 1994); Todd Gitlin, *The Sixties: Years of Hope, Days of Rage* (New York: Bantam, 1987); Maurice Isserman and Michael Kazin, *America Divided: The Civil War of the 1960s* (New York: Oxford University Press, 2000); W. J. Rorabaugh, *Berkeley at War: The 1960s* (New York: Oxford University Press, 1989).

3. Gerard DeGroot, *The Sixties Unplugged* (Cambridge, MA: Harvard University Press, 2008), 1.

4. Jeremy Varon, Michael Foley, and John McMillian, "Time Is an Ocean: The Past and Future of the Sixties," *Sixties* 1, no. 1 (2008): 5.

5. Arthur Marwick, *The Sixties: Cultural Revolution in Britain, France, Italy, and the United States, c. 1958–1974* (Oxford: Oxford University Press, 1998), 5. Christopher Connery also opts for the long sixties marked by a "global explosion of world making" that included decolonization, anticapitalist revolt, counterculture, and new socialist political energies ranging from Mao's cultural revolution to the Prague Spring. Christopher Connery, "The End of the Sixties," *boundary 2* 36, no. 1 (March 2009): 184.

6. Our thanks to Jing Jing Chang on this point.

7. Petr Vail' and Aleksandr Genis, *60-e: Mir sovetskogo cheloveka*, 2nd corr. ed. (Moscow: Novoe literaturnoe obozrenie, 1998), 12, 310. For a different, also intimate retrospective on the Soviet sixties, see Leonid Parfenov, *Namedni: Nasha era, 1961–1970* (Moscow: KoLibri, 2009), and the accompanying TV series. For interviews with what historian Donald Raleigh calls the "Sputnik Generation," see Donald J. Raleigh, ed., *Russia's Sputnik Generation: Soviet Baby Boomers Talk about Their Lives* (Bloomington: Indiana University Press, 2006).

8. Paulina Bren, *The Greengrocer and His TV: The Culture of Communism after the 1968 Prague Spring* (Ithaca: Cornell University Press, 2010).

9. On the socialist city in the 1960s, see also Elke Beyer, "Planning for Mobility: Designing City Centers and New Towns in the USSR and GDR in the 1960s," and Brigitte Le Normand, "Automobility in Yugoslavia between Urban Planner, Market, and Motorist," both in *The Socialist Car: Automobility in the Eastern Bloc*, ed. Lewis H. Siegelbaum (Ithaca: Cornell University Press, 2011), 71–91 and 92–104 respectively.

10. See, similarly, William Risch, "Soviet 'Flower Children': Hippies and the Youth Counter-Culture in 1970s L'viv," *Journal of Contemporary History* 40, no. 3 (July 2005): 565–84.

11. Jeremi Suri, *Power and Protest: Global Revolution and the Power of Détente* (Cambridge, MA: Harvard University Press, 2002), 164. On the 1960s as a transnational moment, also see the series of articles "The International 1968," *American Historical Review* 114, nos. 1–2 (February and April 2009); Gerd-Rainer Horn, *The Spirit of '68: Rebellion in Western Europe and North America, 1956–1976* (Oxford: Oxford University Press, 2007); Padraic Kenney and Gerd-Rainer Horn, eds., *Transnational Moments of Change: Europe, 1945, 1968, 1989* (Lanham, MD: Rowman and Littlefield, 2004); Belinda Davis, W. Mausbach, M. Klimke, and C. MacDougall, eds., *Changing the World, Changing Oneself: Political Protest and Collective Identities in the 1960s/70s West Germany and U.S.* (New York: Berghahn Books, 2010); Ronald Fraser, *1968: A Student Generation in Revolt* (New York: Random House, 1988); Marwick, *Sixties*; and the references throughout.

12. See, for example, Jeremi Suri, *The Global Revolutions of 1968* (New York: Norton, 2007); Kenney and Horn, *Transnational Moments of Change*; Mark Kurlansky, *1968: The Year That Rocked the World* (New York: Ballantine, 2005); David Caute, *The Year of the Barricades: A Journey through 1968* (New York: Paladin, 1988); Carole Fink, Philipp Gassert, and Detlef Junker, eds., *1968: The World Transformed* (New York: Cambridge University Press, 1999). Two works that consider other East European countries are Martin Klimke and Joachim Scharloth, eds., *1968 in Europe: A History of Protest and Activism, 1956–1977* (New York: Palgrave, 2008), and Tony Judt, *Postwar: A History of Europe since 1945* (New York: Penguin, 2005), chs. 12 and 13. Vijay Prashad in *The Darker Nations: A People's History of the Third World* (New York: New Press, 2007) incorporates the Third World into a discussion of sixties transnationalism.

13. Kurlansky, *1968*, 32; Paulina Bren, "1968 East and West: Visions of Political Change and Student Protest from across the Iron Curtain," in Kenney and Horn, *Transnational Moments of Change*, 120; Czech television recorded the event. See "Allen Ginsberg zvolen králem Majáles v Praze," 1 May 1968, Vyprávěj, www.ceskatelevize.cz/porady/10266819072-vypravej/ve-stopach-doby/1965/allen-ginsberg-zvolen-kralem-majales-v-praze/, accessed 8 March 2011.

14. Pan Am's 1960 annual report described its new worldwide routes to Europe and Africa, South America, Australia, and the Middle East. George E. Burns, "The Jet Age Arrives," Pan Am Historical Foundation, www.panam.org/stories/70-the-jet-age-arrives.html, n.d., accessed 8 March 2011.

15. Thomas Kaiserfeld, "From Sightseeing to Sunbathing: Changing Traditions in Swedish Package Tours; from Edification by Bus to Relaxation by Airplane in the 1950s and 1960s," *Journal of Tourism History* 2, no. 3 (2010): 149–63; Christopher Endy, *Cold War Holidays: American Tourism in France* (Chapel Hill: University of North Carolina Press, 2004); Richard Ivan Jobs, "Youth Movements: Travel, Protest, and Europe in 1968," *American Historical Review* 114, no. 2 (April 2009): 376–404.

16. *Narodnoe khoziaistvo SSSR v 1974* (Moscow: Gosudarstvennoe statisticheskoe izdatel'stvo, 1975), 616–17; *Narodnoe khoziaistvo SSSR v 1975* (Moscow: Gosudarstvennoe statisticheskoe izdatel'stvo, 1976), 606–7; *Narodnoe khoziaistvo SSSR za 70 let: Iubileinyi statisticheskii ezhegodnik* (Moscow: Finansy i statistika, 1987), 602; G. P. Dolzhenko, *Istoriia turizma v dorevoliutsionnoi Rossii*

i SSSR (Rostov-na-Donu: Izdatel'stvo Rostovskogo universiteta, 1988), 154; "Turistskaia statistiska," *Turist*, no. 6 (1971): 14; Christian Noack, "Coping with the Tourist: Planned and 'Wild' Mass Tourism on the Soviet Black Sea Coast," in *Turizm: The Russian and East European Tourist under Capitalism and Socialism*, ed. Anne E. Gorsuch and Diane P. Koenker (Ithaca: Cornell University Press, 2006), 281–304.

17. Aleksei Kozlov, *Kozel na sakse* (Moscow: Vagrius, 1998); Sabrina Petra Ramet, ed., *Rocking the State: Rock Music and Politics in Eastern Europe and Russia* (Boulder, CO: Westview Press, 1994); Susan E. Reid and David Crowley, eds., *Style and Socialism: Modernity and Material Culture in Post-War Eastern Europe* (Oxford: Berg, 2000); S. Frederick Starr, *Red and Hot: The Fate of Jazz in the Soviet Union* (Oxford: Oxford University Press, 1983); Artemy Troitsky, *Back in the USSR: The True Story of Rock in Russia* (Boston: Faber and Faber, 1988); Sergei Zhuk, *Rock and Roll in the Rocket City: The West, Identity, and Ideology in Soviet Dniepropetrovsk, 1960–1985* (Baltimore: Johns Hopkins University Press, 2010).

18. Anne E. Gorsuch, "From Iron Curtain to Silver Screen," in *Imagining the West in Eastern Europe and the Soviet Union*, ed. György Péteri (Pittsburgh: University of Pittsburgh Press, 2010), 153–71.

19. See the works cited above; Jane Pavitt, *Fear and Fashion in the Cold War* (London: Victoria and Albert Museum, 2008); Axel Schildt and Detlef Siegfried, eds., *Between Marx and Coca-Cola: Youth Cultures in Changing European Societies* (New York: Oxford University Press, 2006).

20. So too for clothing. See Larissa Zakharova, "Dior in Moscow: A Taste for Luxury in Soviet Fashion under Khrushchev," in *Pleasures in Socialism: Leisure and Luxury in the Eastern Bloc*, ed. Susan E. Reid and David Crowley (Evanston: Northwestern University Press, 2010), 95–119.

21. "Moscow International Film Festival, 1959 Year," n.d., www.moscowfilmfestival.ru/miff32/eng/archives/?year=1959, accessed 8 March 2011.

22. Jukka Gronow, *Caviar with Champagne: Common Luxury and the Ideals of the Good Life in Stalin's Russia* (Oxford: Berg, 2003).

23. Susan Gross Solomon, "A Matter of 'Reach': Fact-Finding in Public Health in the Wake of World War I," in *Shifting Boundaries of Public Health: Europe in the Twentieth Century*, ed. Susan Gross Solomon, Lion Murard, and Patrick Zylberman (Rochester: University of Rochester Press, 2008), 233.

24. *Sovetskoe zazerkal'e: Inostrannyi turizm v SSSR v 1930–1980-e gody* (Moscow: Forum, 2007), 94.

25. Anne E. Gorsuch, *All This Is Your World: Soviet Tourism at Home and Abroad after Stalin* (Oxford: Oxford University Press, 2011).

26. Mikhail German, *Slozhnoe proshedshee: Passé composé* (St. Petersburg: Iskusstvo-SPb, 2000), 161, 233–34, 262, 264–65.

27. Jobs, "Youth Movements," 376–77, 378.

28. Suri, *Power and Protest*, 165. Padraic Kenney argues similarly that the protests of 1989 were more truly transnational than those of 1968. Padraic Kenney, "Borders Breached: The Transnational in Eastern Europe since Solidarity," *Journal of Modern European History* 8, no. 2 (2010): 179–95.

29. Bren, *Greengrocer and His TV*, 26.

30. Kristin Roth-Ey, *Moscow Prime Time: How the Soviet Union Built the Media Empire That Lost the Cultural Cold War* (Ithaca: Cornell University Press, 2011).

31. Bren, *Greengrocer and His TV*.

32. Alexei Yurchak, *Everything Was Forever, Until It Was No More: The Last Soviet Generation* (Princeton: Princeton University Press, 2006), 8.

33. Walter Hixson, *Parting the Curtain: Propaganda, Culture, and the Cold War, 1945–1961* (New York: St. Martin's Press, 1997); Harvey Cohen, *Duke Ellington's America* (Chicago: University of Chicago Press, 2010).

34. Susan E. Reid, "Khrushchev Modern: Agency and Modernization in the Soviet Home," *Cahiers du monde russe* 47, nos. 1–2 (January-June 2006): 232.

35. Nikita Khrushchev, "Report of the Central Committee of the 22nd Congress of the Communist Party of the Soviet Union," in *Documents of the 22nd Congress of the CPSU*, vol. 1 (New York: Cross Currents Press, 1961), http://archive.org/details/Documents OfThe22ndCongressOfTheCpsuVol1, 120.

36. Mary Neuberger, "Inhaling Luxury: Smoking and Anti-Smoking in Socialist Bulgaria, 1947–1989," in Péteri, *Imagining the West*, 241.

37. Mark Pittaway, "Stalinism, Working-Class Housing and Individual Autonomy: The Encouragement of Private House Building in Hungary's Mining Areas, 1950–54," in Reid and Crowley, *Style and Socialism*, 49–64.

38. Gorsuch, *All This Is Your World*, ch. 3.

39. David Crowley, "Paris or Moscow? Warsaw Architects and the Image of the Modern City in the 1950s," in Péteri, *Imagining the West*, 121–23.

40. György Péteri, "The Occident Within—or the Drive for Exceptionalism," *Kritika: Explorations in Russian and Eurasian History* 9, no. 4 (Fall 2008): 937, 934.

41. Yurchak, *Everything Was Forever*, 163.

42. Ibid., 169–75.

43. Crowley, "Paris or Moscow."

44. Susan E. Reid, "Who Will Beat Whom? Soviet Popular Reception of the American National Exhibition in Moscow, 1959," in Péteri, *Imagining the West*, 236.

45. György Péteri, "Introduction: The Oblique Coordinate Systems of Modern Identity," in Péteri, *Imagining the West*, 8–12.

46. Eli Rubin, "The Order of Substitutes: Plastic Consumer Goods in the *Volkswirtschaft* and Everyday Domestic Life in the GDR," in *Consuming Germany in the Cold War*, ed. David F. Crew (Oxford: Berg, 2003), 97, 108.

47. Gregory Kveberg, ""Moscow by Night: A History of Subculture, Music and Identity in the Soviet Union and Russia, 1977–2006" (PhD diss., University of Illinois, 2012), ch. 1. See also Troitsky, *Back in the USSR*, and Ramet, *Rocking the State*.

48. This is the theme of Tom Stoppard's 2006 play, *Rock 'n' Roll* (New York: Grove Press, 2007); Bren, *Greengrocer and His TV*, 53, 94.

49. Miriam Dobson, *Khrushchev's Cold Summer: Gulag Returnees, Crime, and the Fate of Reform after Stalin* (Ithaca: Cornell University Press, 2009), 214–22.

50. Reports of group leaders of tourist trips to Poland, 1963, in Gosudarstvennyi arkhiv Rossiiskoi Federatsii (hereafter GARF), f. 9520 (Trade Union Central Council on Tourism), op. 1, d. 597, ll. 5–6.

51. Reports of group leaders of tourist trips to Bulgaria, part 1, 1965, in GARF, f. 9520, op. 1, d. 866, l. 156; reports of group leaders of tourist trips to the GDR, 1962, in GARF, f. 9520, op. 1, d. 487, l. 24.

52. Vladislav Zubok, *Zhivago's Children: The Last Russian Intelligentsia* (Cambridge, MA: Harvard University Press, 2009).

53. Boris Kagarlitsky, "1960s East and West: The Nature of the Shestidesiatniki and the New Left," trans. William Nickell, *boundary 2* 36, no. 1 (March 2009): 98, 99.

54. *Rossiiskaia sotsiologiia shestidesiatykh godov v vospominaniiakh i dokumentakh*, ed. G. S. Batygin and S. F. Iarmoliuk (St. Petersburg: Institute sotsiologii RAN, 1999); B. A. Grushin, *Chetyre zhizni Rossii v zerkale oprosov obshchestvennogo mneniia: Epokha Brezhneva* (Moscow: Progress-Traditsiia, 2003). On the journal, see also Charles H. Fairbanks, "The Nature of the Beast," in *The Strange Death of Soviet Communism: A Postscript*, ed. Nikolas K. Gvosdev (New Brunswick, NJ: Transaction Publishers, 2008), 65; Yale Richmond, *Cultural Exchange and the Cold War: Raising the Iron Curtain* (University Park: Pennsylvania State University Press, 2003), 200.

55. For an example of what is possible for Eastern Europe in this respect, see Josie McLellan, *Love in the Time of Communism: Intimacy and Sexuality in the GDR* (Cambridge: Cambridge University Press, 2011).

56. On transnational exchanges in the socialist bloc in the 1950s, especially between the Soviet Union and China, see Austin Jersild, "The Soviet State as Imperial Scavenger: 'Catch Up and Surpass' in the Transnational Socialist Bloc, 1950–1960," *American Historical Review* 116, no. 1 (February 2011): 109–32.

57. Shawn Salmon, "Building Out: The Soviet Hotel in the 1960s," paper presented at the conference, "The Socialist 1960s: Popular Culture and the City in Global Perspective," University of Illinois, 24–26 June 2010, 41.

SOCIALIST MODERN

1 This Is Tomorrow!

Becoming a Consumer in the Soviet Sixties

Susan E. Reid

SUPPOSE THAT, AT the dawn of the 1960s, Soviet artist Aleksandr Laktionov had produced an updated remake of his well-known painting of 1952, *Moving into the New Apartment* (fig. 1.1), to reflect the hopes of the new decade: how might it have looked? In the intervening years Stalin had died and been denounced, the Cold War had entered a new phase of "peaceful competition," and, in 1957, the Khrushchev regime had launched its industrialized construction program to provide separate apartments not only for exemplary citizens like Laktionov's happy house-warmer but for all. Other measures promised further improvements in ordinary people's lives: enhanced services, more leisure time, and increased production of consumer goods to go in their new homes.[1] One change that Laktionov's sixties remake would surely have to reflect was that the ideal modern Soviet home was now widely envisaged as saturated with "labor-saving" technology and as already looking forward to the next generation of new improved devices. As *Izvestiia* proclaimed in 1959, with a dose of socialist realism: "Today many families have a washing machine, vacuum cleaner, and floor polisher. The majority of workers have a meat grinder, juicer, etc. But it would be much more convenient to combine them in a single 'domestic combine' [domashnii kombinat]."[2]

Despite these significant additions to the pile of possessions that marked Laktionov's family as modern, urbane citizens, his hypothetical 1962 remake probably would *not* have looked much like the collage that British pop artist Richard Hamilton made to publicize a London avant-garde art exhibition *This Is Tomorrow* in 1956. Entitled *Just What Is It That Makes Today's Homes So Different, So Appealing?*, the collage commented both on contemporary American consumer culture's self-representations

Figure 1.1. Aleksandr Laktionov, *Moving to the New Apartment*, 1952. Oil on canvas, 134 x 112 cm. Donetsk Regional Art Museum.

and on how the brave new world of mass consumption was seen from 1950s Britain, just emerging from postwar austerity.[3] Appropriating the visual style and iconography of American advertising and comics, Hamilton identified the shape of "Tomorrow" with the phenomena British writer and social critic J. B. Priestley in the previous year had labeled (more judgmentally) "admass."[4] "Tomorrow"—the sixties—would be a realm of images and styles; it would be overstuffed with mass consumer goods, pervaded by the media, and dominated by the entertainment industry. Domestic appliances—represented in Hamilton's image by television, a tape recorder, and a vacuum cleaner, cut out from an ad complete with hyperbolic strap line—appear as signature artifacts of postwar modernity alongside comics, the sexualized body, and canned food.

Why begin a chapter on Soviet consumer culture of the sixties with a British 1950s view of a chimerical Americanized "Tomorrow"? The title of this book, *The Socialist Sixties,* calls for a comparative, transnational perspective and a reconsideration of the system specificity of the term *sixties.* What does it mean to qualify it with the adjective *socialist,* producing a seemingly incongruous and even oxymoronic hybrid, *socialist sixties*? *Sixties* is not merely the chronological label for the decade between the 1950s and the 1970s; it evokes a whole nexus of concepts, images, values, and social phenomena that together constitute a new consumerist stage of modernity, generally identified with capitalism. When we say *sixties* in English we think of the affluent society, the never-had-it-so-good generation of growing mass consumerism, hedonism, and leisure, youth culture and style, and the iconic commodities of the consumer boom. Observing this culture as it emerged, Hamilton characterized it in 1957: "Popular (designed for a mass audience, Transient (short term solution), Expendable (easily forgotten), Low-Cost, Mass Produced, Young (aimed at youth), Witty, Sexy, Gimmicky, Glamorous, Big Business."[5] The term does not translate straightforwardly into Russian, however. For members of the Russian intelligentsia (both former Soviet and émigré), the term *shestidesiatniki* (sixties generation) traditionally references the critical intelligentsia of the 1860s and only secondarily its echoes in the intellectual ferment of the Thaw a century later. Both are characterized by high-minded seriousness and a self-defining ascetic disdain for material pleasures in favor of high culture and spiritual values. Thus there are cultural as well as systemic differences in the connotations of the term. The collocation *socialist sixties* invites us to consider how the socialist experience of late industrial modernity corresponds to or departs from paradigms that have been developed for understanding the Western, capitalist phenomenon, and thereby also to question the hegemony of a model of modernity defined in terms of occidental capitalism.

As with any such period, we can argue over the start and end dates.[6] In the USA, the sixties began in the mid-1950s, arriving not much later in Western Europe. Priestley coined his neologism *admass* in 1955.[7] This was also the turning point when major U.S. corporations definitively changed their marketing strategies, investing on an unprecedented scale in the visual aspects of design to induce people to spend—and keep on spending—their increasing incomes. While the rise of "merchandising"—creating a "new role for design in producing obsolescence and panic for status"—had begun already in the interwar period, as C. Wright Mills observed in 1958, it was in the postwar period that "the distributor becomes ascendant over both the consumer and the producer. . . . The salesman becomes paramount."[8] Consummating the innovations of the interwar period, such as the work of General Motors designer Harley

Earl, the mid-1950s brought, according to Thomas Hine, "sleek, powerful, finny low-priced cars and the emergence of a sexy, urgent new kind of popular music—rock and roll."[9] The product was henceforth designed as if it were an advertisement, selling not only itself but much more: a lifestyle and social status.[10] A new aesthetic of everyday life emerged, in which image, display, and the perfection of surface were paramount.[11] The attention to image entailed functionally redundant flourishes such as tailfins, which signified speed, fun, pleasure in consumption, hedonism, and luxury for all. Dubbing this "Populuxe," Hine explains: "'Populuxe' contains a thoroughly unnecessary 'e,' to give it class. That final embellishment of a practical and straightforward invention is what makes the word Populuxe, well, Populuxe."[12]

This was also the time when, in the capitalist West, industrial design was consolidated as a specialist practice with distinctive functions and methods. A vital role was played by professional designers and image makers in shaping the sixties. They branded the decade so powerfully that we are still in thrall to its self-styled image. As Dick Hebdige put it retrospectively, "From now on, the shape and look of things were to play an important part in aligning two potentially divergent interests: production for profit, and consumption for pleasure."[13] The sixties saw the realization of a longer process: "the intercession of the image between the consumer and the act of consumption."[14] For Jean Baudrillard, consumption not so much of the *use* value of goods as of their *sign* value was a defining characteristic of modern (and postmodern) life under capitalism.[15] Hamilton, reflecting on the emergent phenomena, uses the representations produced by commercial mass culture and their visual styles as the material of art—placing a world of signs, media images, and mass culture between the perceiving subject and nature—to represent the bombardment of visual images, packaging, advertising, hedonism, popular culture, glamour, sex.[16] Thus, in his collage, the canned ham, perched self-importantly on the coffee table like some modern fetish, represents not the nutrition value of the food it contains but its image and its sign value.

Sovuluxe or "an Oppressive Pile of Hardware"?

All this is surely poles apart from the Soviet material and visual culture of the 1960s, the concerns of Soviet planners, and the dour image of the USSR as viewed from the Western side of the Iron Curtain. If "the sixties" is a brand in itself, an image that comes between human consciousness and material existence, the image of the *Soviet* sixties is its opposite—*not* the Real Thing, *not* deserving the brand mark, with its connotations of swinging modernity, style, superabundance, sex, and fun. Could Populuxe have any place in the Soviet culture of goods and their presentation?

Not according to contemporary Western observers. When exposed in the international arena at expositions and world's fairs of the 1950s and 1960s, Soviet goods and their presentation were judged not to have made it into the sixties. Hamilton's associate, UK critic Lawrence Alloway, articulated the salient differences between socialist things and capitalist commodities, dismissing the USSR's presentation of material abundance at recent international exhibitions as "a spectacle with a message," over-loaded with "garrulous, cumulative weight, ungraspable profusion to convey pleni-tude."[17] At the Soviet Trade Fair in London 1961, "the rising level of consumption in the USSR was demonstrated clearly and repeatedly, but not entirely happily. Despite the fashion show, despite a modern flat hung over the model of a modern city, the exhibi-tion repeatedly failed to give a convincing image of the leisure in which the benefits of consumption are enjoyed."[18]

Merely to present an abundance of things was not enough, in Alloway's view; it was the extra, redundant flourishes that mattered—the "e" on "Populuxe," as Hine put it. Consumer goods represented for Alloway a baseline of civilized living, but sixties affluence required goods not only to use but to enjoy and desire, to fashion lifestyles, and to play with. Although the Soviet Union had placeholders for such items, it had missed the point of consumer goods: "The entertainment, the styling that goes with mass-produced consumer goods is part of their value and function. The Russians, how-ever, by denying themselves sophistication, just as they eschew advertising, reduced the fruits of peace to an oppressive pile of hardware in a bower of statistics."[19] In paying too little attention to the fun, fantasy, and magic that resided in styling, advertising, and packaging, Soviet consumer goods merely fulfilled a function, remaining utilitar-ian things, not objects of desire. The semiotics of consumer goods was still missing.[20]

Such views, mapping the opposition between sign value and use value onto the capitalism/socialism antithesis, are undoubtedly structured by Cold War polarities. These were projected conceptually onto goods and materials, supposing a First and a Second World of artifacts. While, from the Soviet perspective, capitalist commodities embodied excess, redundancy, and designed obsolescence, aiming to create "panic for status" and desires for unnecessary things, for Western observers the nature, circula-tion, and meanings of socialist goods were defined by shortage, uniformity, the bare satisfaction of basic need, and practices of repair and using up.[21]

Yet Alloway's criticisms cannot be discounted out of hand for systemic bias.[22] The dichotomy he outlined may be observed in relation to science fiction "houses of the future," such as the playful dwelling designed by Hamilton's colleagues Alison and Peter Smithson for the *Daily Mail* Ideal Home Exhibition in 1956, or Monsanto's plas-tic house installed at Disneyland, California (1957–68).[23] The Soviets also fantasized about polymer power and all-electric homes of the future and even built their own plastic house of the future in 1958.[24] But judging from photographs taken in 1963, the Soviet model was as dour and drab as Cold War stereotypes would have one expect. Fun, glamour, and mass entertainment were not its purpose; it was a serious scientific experiment for specialists to study, and the interior was furnished with sober, modern-ist good taste in the "contemporary style."[25]

While there *was*, of course, a pervasive image culture in the Soviet Union, its object, according to conventional wisdom, was to promote communism not com-modities, and rational consumption rather than consumerist lifestyles. Although ideological hostility toward the idea of fashion softened in the Khrushchev era, public rhetoric still vilified planned obsolescence and commodity fetishism as evils of capitalism and added to this a moral, aesthetic, and economic condemnation of "superfluity" (referring both to luxury and excess and to the Stalinist overemphasis on ornate facades and surface appearances at the expense of functionality).[26]

The systemic opposition is not the whole story, however. Not only did indigenous critics of burgeoning consumerism exist in the West (and not solely on the left), but attitudes were also changing among state bureaucracies and other authorities in the Soviet Union, partly as an effect of contact with international practices, which had increased significantly since the early 1950s. Some at least of the planners of the Soviet section at the 1958 Brussels World's Fair, for instance, were convinced that an emphasis on individual enjoyment of the fruits of progress, presented in a fun, dynamic, and engaging manner, was the best way to sell the Soviet "brand" abroad.[27] The shortcomings of finish and detailing, for which Western experts criticized Soviet consumer goods, were also recognized in the USSR. Beginning in the late 1950s, there were moves to develop new specialisms such as industrial or product design, drawing energetically both on Western expertise and on that of socialist Eastern Europe. The visual aspects of design, the aesthetics of commodities and packaging, marketing and branding, all became matters of concern in the 1960s.[28] When a new model of plastic house was developed in 1962, the so-called Leningrad House (designed by Lenproekt), it was an experimental transparent pod on a pedestal, with futuristic dwelling possibilities for transformation and interaction by the user—such as modular extension and a variable composition—and more than a nod to Monsanto. While increased international communication and competition may be part of the explanation for these shifts, I want to suggest that they also reflect a growing concern with the nature and interests of consumers, which played a part in the production of a modern form of consumption and new Soviet consumer consciousness. Albeit with a half decade's time lag, the Soviet Union was also entering the sixties.

To unsettle the binary order of things and open up questions about Soviet styling and marketing—about the attention to the surface design and image of consumer goods that would render them "objects of desire"—I follow Hamilton's lead in focusing on domestic appliances. The normalization of these new consumer durables that began to become available in the long Soviet sixties was part of the modernizing state's project to channel and direct the people's image of socialist modernity: to shape their horizons of expectation and actual lifestyles in ways that were considered commensurate with the USSR's position as an advanced industrial power and leader of the socialist world and which were expected to promote the attainment of full communism. But there were aspects of the styling of some appliances that transcended, eluded, or even contradicted the demands of rational socialist objects. Elsewhere I have attended to efforts, in the Khrushchev era, to shape demand in particular ways, focusing in particular on those that sought to *contain* demand within "rational" norms.[29] Here I turn, rather, to what I propose was a key development in the formation of a Soviet consumer culture in the sixties, beginning already under Khrushchev: the production of a need for new types of goods.

This chapter draws on research for a larger project about homemaking and becoming a consumer in the Soviet sixties, in which I use archival and published sources, both textual and visual, in combination with over seventy oral history interviews to excavate changing practices and attitudes toward homemaking, taste, and consumption.[30] The project examines the negotiations and accommodations between specialist discourses and practices and those of lay consumers and homemakers with regard to the new one-family apartments erected at speed on a mass scale beginning in the late 1950s: between the anonymous structures conceived by architects and planners and the agency of individuals who made home in them. The growing authority of specialists in determining the minutiae of everyday lives, which has been identified as one of modernity's hallmarks, is a significant part of the story of the Soviet sixties.[31] Here I focus on professional image makers and designers, but I also want to ask what part was played by ordinary consumers. In Western product design a vital role was recognized for consumer research: "Let the Consumer help," as Harold Van Doren, a leading first-generation industrial designer in the United States, put it in the 1954 edition of his manual for the new profession, *Industrial Design.*[32] The final section draws on appliance consumption biographies in the interview material to suggest answers to the question "Who made the Soviet sixties?"

I shall address three aspects: first, the meanings of appliances, both in contemporary authoritative discourse in the global Cold War context (the circulation of images "advertising" an appliance-enhanced lifestyle as a universally accessible socialist modernity) and as a way for the historian to trace social and cultural changes in consumption and living standards; second, the growing role of specialists, the professionalization of Soviet design and attention to styling matters and the Soviet "brand"; and finally, the need to create a need.

Why Appliances?

Appliances are of historical interest for what they tell us both about objective changes in living standards and about shifting cultural attitudes toward consumption. Durables consumption can serve as an economic measure of rising living standards and index of the increasing spending power of the Soviet populace. According to Engel's law of economics (ca. 1870), different types of commodities are affected in different ways by increases in disposable income: the balance of household expenditure shifts from the perishable—the contents of the refrigerator, which will be eaten up—to the durable: the refrigerator itself. In 1962 M. E. Ruban, analyzing changes in consumption patterns since 1940, found that this shift from food to durables was becoming apparent in the USSR, indicating the increased purchasing power of the Soviet public, as well as significant improvements in the supply of goods to the population.[33] Other foreign observers remarked on the signs of growing prosperity and consumption levels in the midsixties, as refrigerator production doubled in two years from 1964 to 1966 and consumer durables began to be acquired by most Soviet families.[34] Statistics indicate that appliances became a normal requirement for the modern Soviet home in the course of the long 1960s. In 1960, half of Soviet households still lacked basic durable goods, only 4 percent owned a refrigerator or washing machine, and 8 percent a TV. But the proportion of Soviet households with refrigerators grew rapidly over the next decade, rising to 11 percent in 1965 and 65 percent by 1975, while television ownership rose to 24 percent and then 74 percent in the same period.[35] A letter to the editors of *Ekonomicheskaia gazeta* at the end of 1962 reproduced the new, modernized image of a "typical" (in the socialist realist sense that it represented a desired tendency of development) Soviet lifestyle and implied a causal connection between the move to a new apartment and the modernizing process of becoming a consumer:

> Living conditions rise year by year, and, along with them, so do demands. Many receive new apartments to which not everyone takes along their domestic things that previously satisfied them, but often they try to acquire new furnishings. Going around town one can confirm that in every block there are many who have refrigerators, radios, televisions, washing machines, vacuum cleaners, and other items of primary necessity. . . . These items have firmly entered our everyday life and are already not considered to be luxury objects.[36]

The purchase of electrical household appliances had additional significance over and above that of nonfood durables consumption in general, because these were entirely new types of commodities for individual use in the home. It marked a change, rather than more of the same.[37] Marshall Goldman defined the significance of the shifts in 1968:

> The purchase of a washer or other appliances where there was none before is a major improvement. Many Soviet families have heretofore been living on a loaf-to-loaf basis; the bulk of their purchases have been for the purpose of sustaining life. Until the late 1950s there was little income left over for consumer goods of a more durable nature. Then the Soviet consumer's income increased so that he was able to spend money on products that generated enjoyment long after the initial purchase. Unlike a loaf of bread, a Soviet refrigerator provides consumptive pleasure for more than a few days. Thus an index of consumption which measures only current sales understates the enormous improvement that is taking place in the daily life of the Soviet consumer.[38]

The appearance of major appliances in people's homes thus marked a transition to a modern form of consumption and a qualitatively different lifestyle, associated with the purchase and accumulation of industrially produced consumer goods and, in Goldman's terms, with enduring "consumptive pleasure."[39]

This new lifestyle was also directly associated with the mass housing program launched in 1957, which provided millions of families with separate apartments with kitchens and "mod. cons." As the *Ekonomicheskaia gazeta* reader indicated, the move to new apartments figured in public discourse as a legitimate stimulant to consumption. The move also represented the modernization of living conditions in quite concrete ways: for many, a refrigerator and even more a washing machine was thinkable only after the move, since the housing they came from often lacked mains electricity or plumbing.[40]

Thus appliances are of special significance for the historian of this period. They also had meanings in contemporary public discourse. If, as Baudrillard proposes, it is a defining characteristic of consumer society that in buying an appliance one buys signs rather than functions, then a demonstrable shift in this direction—in the ways people account for their purchases and in the social meanings of their durables—could be a means to calibrate the Soviet transformation into a consumer culture, in which, I propose, the 1960s were the watershed.

It was the refrigerator that became the key symbol of a new, affluent lifestyle in Europe, beginning in the 1950s, combining in a single image the promise of abundance with technological modernity.[41] Hamilton used it in another work, *$he* (1958-61, Tate), where he conflated it with other objects of desire, whose visual language of advertising he also appropriated: the car, electric toaster, and reified pinup woman's body. According to Baudrillard's definition of consumer societies, the refrigerator was important not only for its chilling properties but for its position in a semiotic system representing consumer affluence. In the capitalist West, the purchase of this signifier, the refrigerator, invoked a whole lifestyle characterized by the consumption of images rather than objects and a whole constellation of meanings encompassed by supermarkets, suburban homes, televisions, and the family automobile.[42]

Domestic appliances were thus a key signifier of consumer society. They were also iconic images in the Cold War struggle over representations of modernity and mass prosperity, as was made clear by the "kitchen debate" between Richard Nixon and Nikita Khrushchev, which took place at the American National Exhibition in Moscow 1959 amid the "labor-saving" appliances of a lemon-yellow General Electric kitchen. In the less confrontational international climate of "peaceful coexistence," vacuum cleaners, refrigerators, televisions, and other appliances staked a claim for the advanced nature of state socialism and its ability to benefit ordinary people.[43] Both camps claimed that domestic technology could alleviate women's domestic drudgery and ascribed to it modernizing and liberating effects on the user, but the socialist bloc went further, claiming for it the power to promote a higher form of emancipation. In combination with expanded and improved services, appliances would help to free women from "kitchen slavery" for full self-realization in the public sphere, thereby enabling them to become fully rounded individuals and ultimately hastening the advent of communism.[44] Shortly after Whirlpool's futuristic "Miracle Kitchen" was seen at the American Exhibition complete with robotic "maid," the women's magazine *Rabotnitsa* (Woman Worker) published a cartoon where a man presents his wife with a domestic robot, a

Figure 1.2. Cartoon by M. Skobelev, A. Eliseev, and E. Vinogradov. "The Gift" [Podarok], *Rabotnitsa*, no. 12 (1959): inside back cover.

"housework aggregate" (*domrabochii agregat*) (fig. 1.2). The caption established a direct relation between space exploration and the quality of women's life, ending: "A joke? No. Rockets are flying. . . . We promise that these dreams will also soon come true!" Appliances were rockets for housewives, a gift to women for managing their double burden, whereby they too would have their share of the Space Age.

A shift took place in the symbols, style, and mode of circulation of representations of the good life during the 1960s. Prosperity and abundance were no longer represented by the cornucopia or sheaf of corn but by a large streamlined refrigerator, overflowing with processed foods (fig. 1.3).[45] The technological modernization of the iconography of the good life was complemented by a shift from oil painting toward the mass-reproducible medium of photography, with its rhetoric of documentary truth, presentness, and modernity—one reason why Laktionov would not have been a good choice of visual professional to define the image of the new prosperity of the Soviet sixties. Household encyclopedias and manuals displayed the latest range of Soviet appliances attended by smiling, well-turned-out women in poses similar to the stance of "affectionate genuflexion" that Hamilton identified in Western advertising (although the differences should also be noted, the Soviet ones being less youthful and seductive and displaying less naked flesh) (fig. 1.4).[46] Such imagery offered new modern identities to Soviet women and new models of domesticity.

A range of public discourses identified appliances in the home with cultured Soviet modernity and with social status. A satirical cartoon in a 1958 issue of *Krokodil* draws its humor and critical resonance from this context. It characterizes a corrupt manager as petit bourgeois by representing his material attributes. His office is more like a boudoir than a workspace, complete with chandeliers, potted palms, gilt mirrors, ornate furniture, and heavy drapes, but also with a large curvilinear ZIL refrigerator and a Ruban television set (the prestigious brands are named in the accompanying text). The manager justifies filling his office with luxury consumer goods and home comforts by appropriating the terms of authoritative discourse; it is required by his status, he says, "to keep in step with life. Furthermore, it sets an example to others; it is visual agitation for the cultured way of life." As a boss he is expected to be "an educator of good taste and good tone, a conductor of culture to the masses."[47]

That *Krokodil* could use the image of the refrigerator and television in this way (even if satirically) indicates that, however limited their actual penetration into homes in 1958, they had already accrued social meanings with broad enough currency among the magazine's readership. These meanings exceeded (or even contradicted) the use value of the machines; they were signs of being modern and "cultured." The cartoon also conveys acceptance of the idea that appliance acquisition was not a given; rather, it had to be modeled, advertised to others, to propagate the modern lifestyle—a point to which we return below.

Thus Soviet citizens were already living amid images of consumer goods and a corresponding lifestyle, which circulated even before the durables themselves entered

Figure 1.3. Soviet refrigerators. Illustration in *Tovarnyi slovar'*, ed. I. A. Pugachev, vol. 9 (Moscow: Gos. izdatel'stvo torgovoi literatury, 1961).

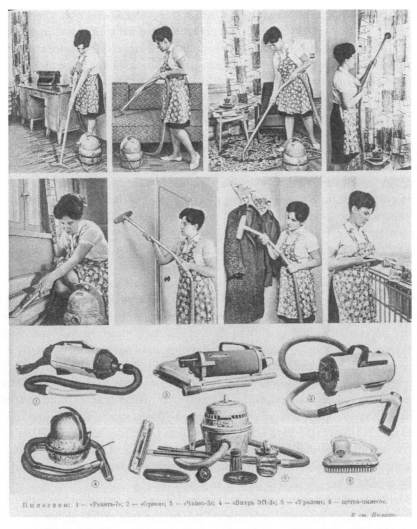

Figure 1.4. Women with vacuum cleaners. Illustration in *Kratkaia entsiklopediia domashnego khoziaistva* (Moscow: Bol'shaia sovetskaia entsiklopediia, 1966).

their homes and daily routines. Even as public discourse and visual culture propagated a consumption morality based on self-restraint, moderation, and the satisfaction of "rational" needs, and warned against acquisitiveness and commodity fetishism, specialists acknowledged that the definition of "rational consumption" was not fixed for all time and that the boundary between luxury and necessity could shift. As the *Ekonomicheskaia gazeta* reader above presented as a matter of course, consumer entitlement and rational consumption norms were dynamic; they would develop and become differentiated as the economy grew.[48] This potential for development had implications for two related sixties practices and new specialisms, more commonly identified with the capitalist West: market research—information gathering about consumer demand; and marketing—creating a need through design, image, branding, and associations with a desired lifestyle.

The Soviet Brand: Professionalization of Industrial Design

The rhetorical connotations of appliances that were produced in public discourse— associating Soviet *byt* with Space Age science, progress, and abundance—were reinforced, in some cases, by their visual appearance. We turn here to what Van Doren would call the "millinery" aspect of design or "styling" of the external appearance of these commodities—the aspect to which so much attention was paid in the West in the long sixties.[49]

In the Soviet Union industrial design was in its infancy and the term *dizain* was not yet used except to refer to foreign practice. The socialist culture of goods was differentiated rhetorically from the capitalist along systemic lines similar to those drawn by Alloway, but with the valences inverted. Thus a 1965 article accused: "Knowing the psychology of the consumer and his tastes and moods, [Western] firms often create an illusory impression of high quality in their products by means of their corresponding 'styling' [oformleniia]."[50] The purpose of styling, as of advertising, was to trick the consumer into buying unnecessary or poor-quality things, "speculating on his lack of expertise and human weakness."[51] While capitalist commodities deceived and let one down, Soviet products were rational and transparent. Their surfaces could be trusted to reflect their substance with no sleight of hand. "*Soviet* means durable and reliable [prochnyi]."[52] This was the Soviet "brand." And it seems to have been quite effective; in interviews in the mid-2000s many of my informants spoke of their Soviet appliances like trusty old friends, ascribing to them such characteristics as endurance and reliability, qualities they considered lacking in postsocialist goods.[53]

Market research began to occupy a range of Soviet specialists in the early 1960s, in association with economic reformism (indeed, the 1965 article above was a survey of Western approaches to market research). Its purpose was also differentiated: while in capitalist countries studies of consumer demand were all directed toward stimulating profit, under socialism their purpose was to support central planning and enable production to meet popular requirements more efficiently. Moreover, this was to be achieved, not by "blindly following the consumer, but by educating his aesthetic taste."[54] Whereas in the West the vulgar excesses that Populuxe epitomized were the result of pandering to popular desire for luxury, in the Soviet Union marketing and product design had a pedagogical, enlightenment role to play in the formation of the conscious, all-round Soviet person, developing his or her rational and aesthetic faculties.

The aesthetics of machines also became a matter of concern among Soviet specialists by 1960 as part of a reengagement with international modernist issues. Architects, artists, engineers, and philosophers debated such questions as "Can a machine be a work of art?" The design journal *Dekorativnoe iskusstvo SSSR* (Decorative Art of the USSR), founded in 1957, published many an article on this issue, printing one discussion of machine aesthetics under a photograph of the Soviet limousine, the ZIL-111, complete with tailfins.[55] Specialists took great interest in contemporary design education (both in the West and in Eastern Europe), and in its history, including excavating the theory and practice of the Russian constructivists and VKhUTEMAS, and of the Bauhaus.[56] They lobbied for industrial design (although it was not yet called this) to be recognized as a distinct discipline requiring specialist training and central institutions that would bestow professional accreditation and control standards, and for aesthetic experts to be more involved in production and given greater authority in factories.[57]

The emerging profession of Soviet design, or at least of its theoretical branch known as "technical aesthetics," was institutionalized with the formation of the All-Union Institute of Technical Aesthetics (VNIITE) by a Council of Ministers decree of 28 April 1962.[58] Discussions about product design, production aesthetics, industrial graphics, and the professionalization of the visual world of goods also went on in artists' organizations and government bodies.[59] The All-Union Institute of Assortment of Light Industry (VialegProm), set up under Gosplan USSR in 1944, along with special design bureaus for "industrial aesthetics," attended, in the late 1950s, to the branding *(markirovka)* of products and design of trademarks, packaging, and labels.[60] Foreign expertise on both sides of the Iron Curtain was also studied. In the socialist bloc, the German Democratic Republic was the acknowledged leader in branding, but Poland, Czechoslovakia, and Hungary had other important lessons to teach.[61] So did the West. The growing foreign exchanges of experts that were a feature of the late 1950s included architects, designers, and design education specialists, for example from Britain's Royal College of Art and Council of Industrial Design.[62] As Larissa Zakharova has also found with regard to Soviet fashion design in this period, the new professionals were anxious to prove themselves against international standards, which, for them, transcended the Cold War divide.[63]

Theoreticians of technical aesthetics also recognized the need to make appliances more attractive in appearance. Their stated reasons for attending to the aesthetics of appliances were system specific, based on Marxist materialist philosophy and on the close relation between ethical and aesthetic education in the formation of the future communist person (fig. 1.5). Attention to the aesthetics of the machine was not about selling goods through false claims to quality, nor about designing obsolescence so that the "panic for status" would force consumers to keep replacing their still functioning appliances. Rather, it was about enhancing the aesthetic level of the everyday material environment, for beauty would not only save the world but

Figure 1.5. Student design proposal for washing machine with spin dryer, in *Tekhnicheskaia estetika*, no. 10 (1965): 7.

educate the new person and help bring about communism. A well-designed handle on a spade made possible the all-round person envisaged by Marx, able to labor manually in the morning yet play the violin in the evening.[64] Domestic appliances had a specific role, for refrigerators or television sets would stand, permanently visible, in the home, and the aesthetics of the domestic interior were regarded as a major culture-building project of the Khrushchev era.[65]

Rationality and honesty—moral principles—were key to the socialist aesthetic, just as they were to Western modernism. "What is the beauty of appliances?" asked *Dekorativnoe iskusstvo*. Reporting in 1962 on the public reception of an exhibition of domestic appliances at VDNKh (the All-Union Exhibition of Economic Achievements), it distinguished among Soviet refrigerators on aesthetic grounds: the compact model, Sever', produced by the Moscow Gas Appliances factory; the Ukraina from Kiev, with its "convenient smooth external surface"; and "the famous Oka, object of many housewives' dreams." "But the greatest number of visitors are around the rotating stand of an apartment interior, in whose kitchen a wall-mounted refrigerator of the ZIL brand is installed. Here lies perhaps the answer to the question about the beauty of consumer goods. They should be maximally fit for purpose and minimally obtrusive."[66] A simple, modest, but commodious rectilinear box, the latest model of ZIL best answered this rationalist demand that form should follow function, with none of the redundant, attention-grabbing elaborations essential to Populuxe.[67]

The design of domestic appliances as well as of industrial machines was regularly discussed in VNIITE's specialist journal *Tekhnicheskaia estetika* (Technical Aesthetics). Typically, a 1965 report—presenting research conducted by VNIITE on Soviet-made vacuum cleaners—treated Soviet designs as part of an international continuum in which the merits of indigenous products were considered alongside those of foreign brands such as the Siemens Rapid (West Germany) or the British Electrolux.[68]

But not all was well in the kingdom of Soviet appliance production. The 1962 report in *Dekorativnoe iskusstvo* complained of the anachronistic form of some consumer durables, while a 1965 VNIITE study found problems in existing practice and identified contradictions in Soviet planning and production. It criticized the state standard (GOST) for vacuum cleaners for ignoring the basic requirements of technical aesthetics as well as other specifications that represented the "best world standards."[69] VNIITE also addressed matters of styling.[70] For styling and semiotics were not entirely absent from Soviet appliances, in spite of the continued insistence among aesthetic reformers that the guiding principles of the socialist manufactured object were rationality, economy, and fitness for purpose. Space iconography was widely used to represent the future of the Soviet home. As the punchline of the *Rabotnitsa* cartoon exemplified, domestic "woman-operated technology" to "help women" manage their domestic burden was associated metaphorically with the dream of space flight and its triumphant realization. The association between successes in space and on the home front was established through the styling as well as the naming of appliances. A woman could have her slice of the glories of the space age as she cleaned her home with a vacuum cleaner styled and named after a rocket (Raketa) or a planet (Saturnas) (fig. 1.6). Other appliances used the trope of harnessing nature's power, such as the vacuum cleaner Vikhr' (Whirlwind) or the refrigerators Sever' (North) and Sibir' (Siberia).[71] The ZIL, Rolls Royce of refrigerators, needed only to refer to the factory where it was produced.[72]

There was a contradiction, however. Although the new ZIL model praised in 1962 had gone rectilinear and rational, many Soviet fridges—such as the ZIL featured in the glossy multivolume *Tovarnyi slovar'* (Trade Dictionary) just the previous year—were still streamlined, a style intimately identified with American capitalism since the 1930s and possibly appropriated from the United States at that time along with the refrigeration technology (see fig. 1.3). Presented like a royal portrait, with a red carpet and plush curtains drawn back to unveil it, the bulbous fridge represented luxury and plenty with its applied aluminum script and a large handle that metaphorically equated its door with that of a car.[73] Other, lesser fridges also reproduced this streamlined style until the midsixties. Thus this stylistic materialization of capitalism entered millions of Soviet citizens' homes and found a place in their daily routines,

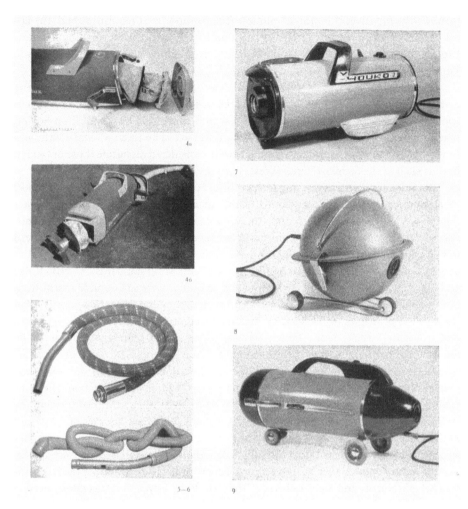

Figure 1.6. Styling of vacuum cleaners. Illustration in A. Kolosov, "O kachestve bytovykh elektropylesosov," *Tekhnicheskaia estetika,* no. 4 (1965): 16.

caressed and cared for every day. If material things shape consciousness, Soviet consumers received a dose of capitalist relations every time they opened the fridge door or ingested its contents.

VNIITE turned its critical scrutiny on such contradictions. The form of some Soviet vacuum cleaners demonstrated that "their creators strove to achieve a purely external similarity with their name" without reference to their functions and mechanisms. The "plastic" (sculptural) treatment of the Raketa imitated the form of a rocket, while the external detailing and body of the Chaika (Seagull) conveyed the idea of flight and dynamism; yet speed was hardly one of the salient properties of vacuum cleaners![74] VNI-ITE was not amused by such playful excesses. "The wholly unjustified styling [lit. 'form-creation'] in the production of such functional domestic appliances as vacuum cleaners leads to excessive expenditure of materials and complicates the technology of production. Thus nearly eight tons of metal a year are expended on the arrow-shaped decorations applied to the body of the Chaika."[75] The point of VNIITE's study was to impose rationalist, modernist principles and good taste. It condemned streamlining, and styling in general, on modernist, rational grounds. These norms corresponded to the moral-economic repudiation of excess and superficial aesthetic flourishes launched by Khrushchev in 1954 with regard to Stalinist architecture and extended by reformist aesthetic experts to all aspects of the material environment.[76] The beauty of socialist machines resided in a transparent relation between form and function.

In the capitalist West, the report emphasized, superficial differences between products enabled consumer goods to function as markers of distinction and social stratification. Yet in the Soviet Union, too, the range of vacuum cleaners currently in production was "irrationally large," according to the report, because it was not justified by any substantive differences among the available products. In their construction, mechanisms, and technical specifications there was little to distinguish the Buran (Snowstorm), Vikhr', Raketa, and Chaika. These models produced by different enterprises were set apart only by small variations in their external appearance. In the state socialist planned economy there was little point in competition between these brands, VNIITE admonished, since it merely wasted resources. Recommending rationalization, the VNIITE report rejected the play of difference and denied the importance of semiotics, fundamental to marketing in the West, which lay precisely in such distinctions.[77]

Such criticisms reveal tensions between different agencies and authorities responsible for durables production, indicating a split between intelligentsia theorists, working in central research institutes, and practitioners on the ground, dealing with localized situations in individual enterprises, and between aesthetic specialists and managers or trade specialists. The latter were concerned above all with fulfilling the plan and—following the Kosygin reforms of 1965—with turnover. Although VNIITE rhetorically identified its rationalist arguments with the superiority of socialist over capitalist goods, they were not unique to socialism. In the West, too, culturally powerful lobbies objected strongly to streamlining and Populuxe. Represented by the Council of Industrial Design in Great Britain and the Museum of Modern Art in the USA, they struggled for modernist good taste against what they saw as the excess, kitsch, and vulgarity of mass consumerism.[78] They, too, like the Soviet modernizers of the material environment, sought to define and propagate principles of "good design" and for similar reasons: to raise the level of popular taste and educate the masses to appreciate what the experts appreciated. Both rested on a kind of environmental determinism: the belief that good design improved users, while bad design corrupted not only their taste but also their morals. So the modernizers on both sides of the Iron Curtain had more in common with each other than with the peddlers of Populuxe.

Yet the very fact that styling already existed in Soviet production—even to be critiqued—requires explanation. Causes may include "uncritical assimilation" of foreign models, as well as tensions between blueprint and practice on the ground and the limits of the aesthetic specialists' authority.[79] In addition we need to know more about the work of designers embedded in enterprises, about the system of bonuses for bosses, including in defense sector enterprises, and about the implementation of Aleksei Kosygin's reforms in regard to appliance design and production.[80] As these reforms raised the importance, in assessing performance, of turnover rather than fulfillment of the production plan, factory bosses also had to get consumers to buy the goods. Thus we should also consider the role of the Soviet consumer and her "consumption junctions," to use Ruth Schwartz Cowan's term for the conjunction of conditions in which choices between competing technologies are made. Even though, under state socialism, resources were planned and allocated centrally, decisions about consumption were taken by individuals in their specific, located circumstances, in ways that eluded central planning.[81] In the USSR, too, it was not only specialists and elites who made the sixties, but also mass consumers.

Creating a Need, Producing Consumers

In the West the styling and allure of commodities was about creating a market, producing consumers to fit the product, and perpetually stimulating demand through "panic for status."[82] Could there possibly be any such image culture in the Soviet sixties? Surely it was neither necessary nor desirable in the socialist shortage economy; nor was the semiotics of social stratification through consumption to be encouraged.[83]

The circulation of images of the technologically saturated Soviet home and the modern Soviet *khoziaika* (housewife) operating domestic machines can certainly be explained by other reasons, including the demands of ideology and national prestige and their role in the Cold War competition over images of modernity. For the purpose of the Soviet Union's international standing it might suffice, however, to project the *image* of a Soviet appliance-enhanced lifestyle without necessarily investing in substantiating it on a mass scale: the "logic of models" that characterized Stalin-era consumer culture might continue undisturbed.[84]

However, the post-Stalin regime was also committed to achieving the actual penetration of technology into the homes of the masses as part of the project of achieving abundance and building communism in a period characterized by the party as one of "scientific-technological revolution." The mechanization of all forms of labor was part of the Soviet state's modernizing agenda. Appliance use in the home would develop scientific consciousness and free up women's time and energy for productive labor and social work.[85] That the penetration of technology was a priority is confirmed by investment in its production (even if inadequate) and by the assignment of production capacity in the military-defense sector to this effort.

This agenda—to get technology into everyday life—might explain increased production norms for appliances. But what need could there be in a shortage economy to promote the sale of consumer durables? If the things were produced and properly distributed, wouldn't they sell themselves? Why should design matter in what is assumed to have been a seller's market? Why should Soviet enterprises take the trouble and resources to brand and advertise their products? And why the range of product names, packaging, and logos? With regard to appliances, can the Cold War binaries have blinded us to a reason similar to the role of advertising in the West: the creation of a market? The production of needs is a question that is not usually asked in the Soviet context. Western commentators on the Soviet Union have traditionally focused on problems of shortage and failure to satisfy demand for consumer goods.[86] Like all consumer goods, domestic appliances were in short supply, hard to get hold of, and expensive. This was a shortage economy, and there could be no cause to cultivate the consumer or even to study demand and consumer psychology when state production capacity was unable even to meet existing needs.

As noted, however, while consumption within rational norms (that is, within limits attainable on a mass scale in the current state of production) was promoted, these norms were conceived as dynamic. Soviet economic theorists envisaged that, as the national economy grew, so would the population's rational needs and legitimate demands. The growth in demand for new types of goods, for higher-quality and more expensive consumer durables, was thus an important index of progress.[87] But in the early to mid-1960s appliances were unfamiliar and costly commodities in a culture where people possessed few manufactured goods and were only just emerging from what Goldman calls a "loaf-to-loaf existence." If it mattered to get technology into citizens' homes, it was necessary to persuade them to part with their small but increasing disposable income and to become consumers of these things.

The shortage paradigm assumes a permanent seller's market. There are indications, however, that Soviet economists did not share this confidence. Measures were introduced to stimulate demand for high-end durables. As early as 1959 the credit system for higher-priced goods was expanded to help make appliance acquisition possible.[88] Consumer behavior was also changing, as economists noted: some emerging elements of a buyers' market were observed as early as 1960, including shoppers' strikes and accumulations in warehouses of unwanted goods.[89] This situation engendered—or legitimated—new concern with studying consumer demand and with promotion and advertising, especially of expensive goods.[90] The so-called "Liberman economic reforms," discussed during the Thaw and introduced in part by Kosygin, after Khrushchev's ouster, proposed to make production more directly answerable and responsive to demand and thereby to make the consumer an agent in the rationalization and modernization of consumer goods production.[91] While terms such as *market forces* had to be tactfully avoided by using euphemisms such as *commodity-money relations*, already by the early to mid-1960s a more prominent role was ascribed to consumers and their choices as a driver of production, at the level of both planning (quantities and assortment) and design, and the 1965 reforms made turnover and profitability a performance indicator of enterprises.[92]

Significantly, VNIITE's first research projects included a market survey of domestic appliances (in collaboration with *Komsomol'skaia pravda*'s Institute of Public Opinion Research). It gathered and analyzed consumer opinions on small electrical appliances such as radios, televisions, and vacuum cleaners, attending particularly to the external appearance rather than the technical specifications.[93] An institute specifically dedicated to market research, the All-Union Scientific Research Institute for the Study of the Population's Demand for Consumer Goods and Market Prices *(kon"iunktura)* for Trade (or VNIIKS) was also established in 1965 under the USSR Ministry of Trade. This was a sixties institution par excellence, existing only from 1966 to 1972 and falling from favor after 1968, discredited along with the Kosygin reforms by association with the Prague Spring.[94]

The shortage paradigm also assumes that the need for appliances was already there, fully formed, and lurking unsatisfied: a "pent-up demand" as Goldman put it.[95] But that demand had first to be *produced*. The history of technology demonstrates that to achieve penetration a technology must not only be available but become necessary; a need must be created, whether for a luxury status symbol, or for a normal element of modern urban living. Appliances, like all technologies, are cultural artifacts, embedded in practices, habitus, attitudes, moral economies, and the circulation of images and meanings.[96] A range of values, often unconsciously held, come into play that might support acquisition or resist it: aspirations to modernity and attachment to novelty or resistance to change; notions of thrift and proper housewifery, gender roles and identities; desire for distinction or fear of standing out; culinary practices and ideas of national specificity; or handed-down perceptions of the physical effort required for a good wash.[97] A need for consumer durables was not an inevitable consequence determined by the possibility of that technology; it required also a cultural shift. As in the West, advertising and design had an acknowledged function to increase turnover, especially of higher-end goods.[98] Was styling also a means to embed the need for appliances by making the commodity an advertisement for itself?[99]

Becoming Consumers

In the USSR appliances came, in the course of the long 1960s, to be regarded as a normal need and even an entitlement. My informants' narratives of their appliance consumption in the decade following their move to new apartments around

1959–64 indicate how, at varying rates, refrigerators and washing machines came to seem first desirable, then normal, and were later upgraded or duplicated. But we shall look at two cases that show that this was no "whiggish inexorable succession of technologies"; it had to overcome resistance on various grounds.[100]

Ivan (b. 1910), a former army officer (and as such, relatively well off and enjoying privileged access to goods), had lived in Ukraine for two years before moving to Kaluga, where he and his wife received a separate apartment around 1960–61 in a block for officers. He tells the story of acquiring their first refrigerator, a ZIL:

> That was when I was still serving in the army. There was this officer from Moscow who went on leave. I say to him, "You know what—bring me back a refrigerator." That was in 1957. In January he came back from leave and sent it by rail. So . . . he arrived and we received it. Nobody had one yet in the town. They said, "Well, what do you need that for?" That was when we were in the Ukraine, it is hot there after all. I tell them what it is for, but it was winter, January. But then they saw what it was [he laughs] and started buying [them]. They also began—to buy, that is.

The year 1957, when Ivan ordered his refrigerator, was early in the history of Soviet appliance dissemination. Domestic refrigerators were hard to get hold of and in short supply, but it would be wrong to explain this difficulty entirely as a matter of "pent-up need." Even though the summers were hot in this Ukrainian town, there was no preexisting consciousness of a need for such equipment, according to Ivan. People continued to use the preindustrial cooling methods they were accustomed to, such as standing jars in cold water in the bathtub, or using deep cellars and the cavity between the external and internal walls or windowpanes (fig. 1.7).[101] Ivan's purchase was met with bafflement. However, exposure to this technology taught other residents to want refrigerators too.

Ivan played the role of a vanguard of demand. It is not perhaps coincidental that he was a military officer, implying a status and obligations similar to those of a party activist or Komsomol member. Just as the army and military-industrial complex (where most appliances were in fact produced) were a technological, modernizing force, Ivan saw himself as having a social duty to carry the torch of modernization.[102]

Statistics showing increasing penetration of appliances are corroborated in my informants' "consumption biographies," which also tell us how they experienced the material changes in their everyday lives and how these corresponded to changes in their sense of themselves. Their stories mark a shift—for which, as in Western Europe, the sixties are the decisive decade—from what Goldman calls "loaf-to-loaf" existence to the accumulation and replacement of appliances and other consumer durables, even before they are used up. Lewis Siegelbaum cites the prediction of writer Leonid Likhodeev: "Do you have a TV, do you have a refrigerator? So there will be a car."[103] My informants shared in this collective ascent of the Soviet

Figure 1.7. Traditional chilling methods, St. Petersburg, 2004. Photographer: Ekaterina Gerasimova, Everyday Aesthetics project.

consumer. One Kaluga woman tells about how she used to have only just enough money to pay for food on a day-by-day basis. In the course of the sixties, after moving into a new apartment, she, like many others, began to acquire appliances, starting with a television, then graduating to a vacuum cleaner, a refrigerator, a washing machine, a tape recorder, and, by the 1970s, a car.[104] Changing conceptions of what is necessary and what is excessive or extravagant luxury, which emerge clearly in my informants' accounts from their first appliance acquisition to the replacement, upgrading, and duplication of appliances, mark the passage toward a consumer culture.

The process was not, however, as inexorable as Likhodeev suggested, as if the first bite of the apple of appliance consumption "led" inevitably to further purchases. Once again the question "Who made the sixties?" requires us to consider the agency of the individual consumer and the nexus of conditions at the consumption junction. The acquisition of appliances remained a matter of choices and household priorities about how to dispose income or whether to cross moral or legal lines.[105] These choices began with the decision to prioritize the home over other spaces and objects of consumption, a choice that was conventionally gendered. Aleksandra, for example, tells how she had to make the down payment on their cooperative apartment behind her husband's back because he wanted to save up for a car.

Many of my interviewees recall their appliance consumption junctions in precise detail. Affordability and availability—price, spending power, and production levels—were clearly important considerations here, as were quality and benefit to their everyday lives. Legislation, sumptuary taxation or pricing categories, and the designation of certain goods as eligible for purchase on credit—all means by which the state sought to direct the consumption junction—also contributed to whether or when people would buy appliances and what they meant in the system of things (including whether they counted as luxuries or necessities).[106] But there were also social and cultural or ideological reasons why some technologies took hold faster than others and why some were never fully assimilated.[107]

While appliances entered the vocabulary and iconography of modern Soviet living, the line between legitimate needs and excessive desires was still contested in the Soviet sixties. In the 1950s, appliances had the aura of luxury (as we saw, as late as 1961, *Tovarnyi slovar'* was presenting the refrigerator as a VIP, giving it the red carpet treatment and associating it with a preindustrial luxury commodity, rugs).[108] During the long sixties its status slid from luxury to necessity, as the boundary between reasonable and excessive demands, rational and superfluous technologies, shifted, reflecting, in part, changes in the capacity of production.[109] That boundary remained uncertain, however, especially among older people. The elements of an emergent consumer culture were still in tension, in the 1960s, with pre–consumer society's handed-down sumptuary morality and valued practices of thrift, and with the intelligentsia's disdain for material comfort.[110] The sixties were a watershed, a period of struggle and negotiation between old and new cultures of consumption. My informants today often reveal continued adherence to aspects of pre–affluent society's morality of consumption, contrasting their own thrift and nonacquisitiveness favorably with that of a daughter-in-law representing the postsocialist present. In the 1960s, however, it was they who represented the young generation of new homemakers and fledgling consumers.

Technology choices were also a matter of gender and generational power relations within the household, subject to negotiations and power struggles over priorities. The acquisition of a television set was seen as a purchase for the household as a whole. Informants often say they got it "for the old people" or for the children.[111] Although most women in the Soviet Union worked and contributed to the household income, battles arose between the sexes and between generations over the choice of technology, and these revealed shifting attitudes toward appliance consumption. Rima, in Kazan', tells of how she and her husband came into conflict with the older generation, her parents-in-law, who lived in the same apartment. The younger couple wanted to buy labor-saving appliances. She relates her run-ins with her mother-in-law over the purchase of a vacuum cleaner, a relatively inexpensive and accessible appliance.

> Did you have a vacuum cleaner?
>
> Not yet at that time. No. . . . We only bought one probably in the seventies. What did we buy it for first? We began to redecorate the apartment ourselves. And it was inconvenient to use brushes, it takes a long time to paint, to whitewash. But we were told that it worked well to do it with a vacuum cleaner. And we bought a spherical vacuum cleaner. I think we also got that from Moscow, you couldn't get them here. And then we started to vacuum-clean. I remember there was a whole row over it here—that a woman doesn't work and goes and buys a vacuum cleaner to boot. That it is, after all, meant to save women's labor.[112]

Gender ideology (including a normative conception that good housekeeping, industriousness, and thrift are essential qualities of a good woman), generational differences, and resistance to the use of household finances to alleviate the younger woman's domestic labor played a part in this conflict. Although Rima worked, her mother-in-law evidently regarded her as spoilt and lazy and, in spite of widely circulating representations, also considered a vacuum cleaner unwarranted luxury rather than a necessary aid for a working woman. When they finally bought a vacuum cleaner in the 1970s it was already a "normal" item of Soviet household inventories, even if not yet readily available outside the metropolis. Even then, the primary purpose of the purchase was not to "save her domestic labor," in accordance with public discourse's rhetoric of liberating women from drudgery—meanings that Rima and her mother-in-law were evidently aware of—but to spray-paint the walls (a common use for Soviet vacuum cleaners but one that was scripted out in the West as the technology stabilized.)

Figure 1.8. Ivan's washing machine, Kaluga, 2005. Photographer: Alla Bolotova, Everyday Aesthetics project.

The purchase of a washing machine also met with resistance. They first bought a Volga 7, a cylindrical model (fig. 1.8). It wasn't exactly conducive to laziness: "You had to heat the water, then pour it in." But her mother-in-law objected: "She can do the wash herself, why does she need a washing machine?" Rima's story demonstrates the clash between the values of two generations within a single household. Rima and her husband desired a modern lifestyle with novelties and gadgets and new technologies, but "the old people wouldn't allow anything then. . . . We tried, if some novelty appeared, to buy it. Even if it was very difficult. If we had lived separately of course it would have been better. We could have bought anything. But as it was we had to ask permission. And she [mother-in-law] wouldn't agree. For whatever reason they were always opposed."

Moreover, the benefits of a washing machine were not convincing.[113] Ivan and his wife, although early persuaded of the need for a refrigerator, were more skeptical about the washing machine. It was she who resisted it. "Well, after all, that also involved manual labor, to wring it out is heavy." Ivan adds: "She kept refusing: 'Why? I'll do it all by hand.' But we said that it was necessary to make the transition [*perekhodit'*, i.e. to technology]." Ivan and his wife were not afraid of being seen as conspicuous consumers, as the refrigerator story above reveals; on the contrary, they seem to have enjoyed their status as the vanguard of modern consumption. His wife's resistance was at least to some extent due to the limitations of early Soviet washing machines and the quality of the wash; it was questionable how much or what kind of labor they saved, as they still had to be manually filled and drained of water and the heaviest part still had to be done by hand. Was the labor it saved even worth the space it took up in the small apartment?[114] Asked whether the manual wringer washing machine was convenient, Ivan's wife replies: "No. But we were young then and I was more or less healthy, so of course I was happy." More recently, however, they had replaced their old machine by a fully automatic one that did the whole process.

If it mattered to enterprises and state authorities to get appliances into people's lives and homes, then individuals had to be encouraged to choose technology. The adoption of technology by individual Soviet consumers was not a matter of pent-up need or inexorable progress determined by technological and scientific advances. Demand was produced in part through the actions and policies of the state's agents: through the development and increased production of technologies for the home, through their increased presence in everyday life, and through their representation in public culture as an inalienable attribute of the modern Soviet person, a necessity rather than a luxury. Did styling and branding also play a part in producing these meanings and overcoming resistance? Did refrigerators and vacuum cleaners perhaps need to change their image and become more functional and less luxurious in appearance before people like Rima's mother-in-law could be persuaded to adopt them? Did design professionals acknowledge this as part of their brief? Were appliances in the Soviet context just tools and nothing more, or was their primary function semiotic? If we can answer these questions we can begin both to define the role of modern industrial design in the USSR and to calibrate the Soviet transformation, somewhere between the 1960s and the 1980s, into a consumer culture and to answer the question "Who made the Soviet sixties?"

Published representations and oral history provide plentiful indications that appliance consumption carried social meanings. As noted, the styling of vacuum cleaners, identifying them with the Space Age, or that of refrigerators, associating them with automobiles, suggests that semiosis was not irrelevant, even in the planned economy. The currency of appliances as signs of status, affluence, or pull—even if they failed to fulfill their nominal function—was also part of contemporary visual culture. A cartoon in *Krokodil* showed a refrigerator on a balcony in the snow, pointing to its redundancy: it added nothing to the natural chilling effect of winter weather. Its only function was for show: it had been installed on the balcony to maximize its display and status value.[115]

From the point of view of state authorities and specialist agents (ideologues and image makers), household technologies were a necessary part of the image of modernity and prosperity. The reasons citizens might have for deciding to purchase a refrigerator may partly have coincided with these authoritative ones: it was seen as part of a modern lifestyle, conferring the social status associated with urbanity, and saving labor by making it no longer necessary to shop every day for perishables. But refrigerators had other, demotic meanings in excess of these official ones. They were part of the coping strategies for surviving the vagaries of distribution, thus cushioning households against the lapses of the state and giving them greater control over their food supply by allowing them to buy perishables in bulk if they appeared on sale and to store privately grown produce.[116] Reasons for buying appliances also varied according to status, education, income, and geography, and they changed in the course of the 1960s to the 1980s as Soviet consumer culture established itself. Desire for domestic technology still marked Rima, in the older generation's eyes, as lazy, selfish, and hankering after unwarranted luxury. But for Ivan, his Moscow refrigerator was associated with his social status as an officer and with his sense of himself as a force for progress and innovation; it represented his self-identification with the public values of the modernizing state. The corrupt, acquisitive factory manager lampooned in the *Krokodil* cartoon described above also invoked appliances' positive associations with modernity, culturedness, and social leadership to justify his accumulation of the latest consumer durables. For Rima's generation (or some of them) machines in the home represented convenience but also novelty, sensation, and status and projected their sense of themselves as resourceful, innovative, and modern. One novelty Rima and her husband did manage to get past the older generation was a television set. Not content with merely possessing a TV, they found a way to adapt it to watch in color, to the envy

Figure 1.9. Cohabitation of old and new refrigerators, Kazan', 2005. Photographer: Sofia Chuikina, Everyday Aesthetics project.

of their neighbors. Typically, this novelty had to be hunted down in Moscow and involved technical know-how; a kind of film of the same format as the screen had to be installed inside the set, which had then to be reassembled and retuned. But it was worth it: all their friends would come to their apartment to watch. "It caused a real sensation."[117]

Values, status, and social distinctions attached to having appliances in general, but some were more equal than others. Informants retrospectively identify certain types and brands of appliances as having been more "prestigious"—a Maiak record player, for example.[118] Certain technologies such as washing machines—expensive and hard to get—remained a sign of social status into the 1970s and also marked urban/rural distinctions.[119] In the early 1960s the acquisition was a first, but subsequently my informants began to replace their first models by newer or better ones. As they grew more prosperous and as appliances became more "normal" they drew finer distinctions, of the sort VNIITE would have dismissed as "irrational." Refrigerators were particularly important because of their large visual presence in the home, and certain brands were especially desirable, not solely because of their functional qualities and reliability, but also because of their appearance and social image. Nina D., trying to recall the name of her first refrigerator, dismissed the interviewer's suggestion that it might have been a ZIL, the beauty queen of Soviet refrigerators according to the 1962 report on the aesthetics of appliances cited above: "No that wasn't for the likes of us."[120] The fine superficial distinctions between brands, which VNIITE criticized as irrational in a planned economy, had become markers of social stratification.

To return to my initial question, then: Laktionov would probably have been the wrong choice of artist to commission for a sixties update of his domestic interior. A photographer or graphic designer would have been more in line with emerging tendencies in Soviet visual culture, with its emphasis on technological modernity. The style would also lack Hamilton's playful identification with the visual techniques of mass entertainment, advertising, and media, favoring rather the impression of sober documentary truth.[121] Nevertheless, some at least of the same symbols of Tomorrow would be bound to appear in a Soviet sixties version: the television and vacuum cleaner, joined perhaps by a ZIL refrigerator. Two decades later, it would include not one but two: an old curvilinear cream model, purchased in the 1960s, placed on top of a new, self-defrosting model (fig. 1.9).[122]

Notes

1. CPSU Central Committee and Council of Ministers Decree, "O razvitii zhilishchnogo stroitel'stva v SSSR (31 July 1957)," *Arkhitektura SSSR*, no. 9 (1957): 1–6; N. S. Khrushchev, *O kontrol'nykh tsifrakh razvitiia narodnogo khoziaistva SSSR na 1959–1965 gody* (Moscow: Politizdat, 1959), 50–59.

2. I. Izbarov, "Stoit podumat'!" *Izvestiia*, 26 July 1959; M. Aleksandrov, "Kto voz'metsia eto delat'?" *Izvestiia*, 19 July 1959.

3. *This Is Tomorrow* was a multimedia exhibition about art as a cultural process, conceived by Theo Crosby. On the Independent Group, see Anne Massey, *The Independent Group: Modernism and Mass Culture in Britain, 1945–59* (Manchester: Manchester University Press, 1995); David Robbins, ed., *The Independent Group: Postwar Britain and the Aesthetics of Plenty* (Cambridge, MA: MIT Press, 1990). The Hamilton collage can be viewed at Die Kunsthalle Tübingen, "Richard Hamilton: Just What Is It That Makes Today's Homes So Different, So Appealing?," www.kunsthalle-tuebingen.de/index.php?option=com_content&task=view&id=239&Itemid=8 9&catid=139.

4. J. B. Priestley, *Journey Down a Rainbow* (London: Heinemann-Cresset, 1955), 51.

5. Richard Hamilton, *Collected Words, 1953–82* (London: Thames and Hudson, 1982), 28; William R. Kaizen, "Richard Hamilton's Tabular Image," *October* 94 (Autumn 2000): 113–28.

6. Cf. Arthur Marwick, *The Sixties: Cultural Revolution in Britain, France, Italy, and the United States, c. 1958–c. 1974* (Oxford: Oxford University Press, 1998); Tony Judt, *Postwar: A History of Europe since 1945* (London: Pimlico, 2007), 338; Gian Piero Piretto, *1961: Il Sessantotto a Mosca* (Bergamo: Moretti e Vitali, 1998); Petr Vail' and Aleksandr Genis, *60-e: Mir sovetskogo cheloveka* (Ann Arbor, MI: Ardis, 1988). Alongside affluence, youth style, and consumerism, there are, of course, darker sides to the sixties, including mass population movements and rising racial tensions, as well as innovations in social organization and social movements. Marwick divides the "long 1960s" into three distinct subperiods, and in the Soviet case too there is good reason to treat 1968 as a turning point marking significant cultural changes.

7. *Admass* designated "the whole system of an increasing productivity, plus inflation, plus a rising standard of material living, plus high-pressure advertising and salesmanship, plus mass communications, plus cultural democracy and the creation of the mass mind, the mass man." Priestley, *Journey Down a Rainbow*, 51; Humphrey McQueen, *The Essence of Capitalism: The Origins of Our Future* (London: Black Rose Books, 2003), viii.

8. C. Wright Mills, "The Man in the Middle," *Industrial Design* 5, no. 11 (November 1958): 70, 72.

9. Thomas Hine, "Populuxe," extracted from *Populuxe* (New York: Alfred A. Knopf, 1987), in *The Design History Reader*, ed. R. Houze and G. Lees-Maffei (Oxford: Berg, 2010), 152.

10. Hine, *Populuxe*, 152; Dick Hebdige, "Object as Image: The Italian Scooter Cycle," extracted from his article of the same title in *Block* 5 (1981): 44–64, in Houze and Maffei, *Design History Reader*, 309; Daniel Boorstin, *The Image, or, What Happened to the American Dream* (London: Weidenfeld and Nicolson, 1961); Vance Packard, *The Hidden Persuaders* (London: Longman, 1957).

11. Hebdige, "Object as Image," 312; Mike Featherstone, "Postmodernism and the Aestheticization of Everyday Life," in *Modernity and Identity*, ed. S. Lash and J. Friedman (Oxford: Blackwell, 1992), 265–90.

12. Hine, *Populuxe*, 152. Design in the West had moved beyond the Populuxe aesthetic by the mid-1960s, but the emphasis on image remained.

13. Hebdige, "Object as Image," 309. C. Wright Mills critically defined the new designer's task: "By brand and trademark, slogan and package, color and form, he gives the commodity a fictitious individuality . . . confusing the consumer's choice and banalizing her sensibilities." Mills, "Man in the Middle," 73.

14. Hebdige, "Object as Image," 309–10.

15. Jean Baudrillard, *The System of Objects*, trans. James Benedict (London: Verso, 1996); Colin Campbell, "The Sociology of Consumption," in *Acknowledging Consumption*, ed. Daniel Miller (London: Routledge, 1995), 103–4.

16. The redundancy of images is epitomized by Charles and Ray Eames's multiscreen display *Glimpses of the USA* at the American National Exhibition in Moscow. See Beatriz Colomina, *Domesticity at War* (Cambridge, MA: MIT Press, 2007), 245 ff.

17. Lawrence Alloway, "USSR at Earl's Court: The Image," *Design* 154 (October 1961): 44–46. Like Hamilton, Alloway (1926–90) was a member of the Independent Group. He was author of an important study of pop art: *American Pop Art* (New York: Macmillan, 1974).

18. Alloway, "USSR at Earl's Court," 44–46.

19. Ibid., 45; Frederick C. Barghoorn, *The Soviet Cultural Offensive: The Role of Cultural Diplomacy in Soviet Foreign Policy* (Princeton: Princeton University Press, 1960), 88.

20. Soviet goods also lacked style and perfection of surface, according to another British design commentator, the industrial designer Frank Ashford, who described the display at Earl's Court as a "chaotic collection of poorly designed and, on the whole, badly produced articles." Frank Ashford, "USSR at Earl's Court: Products," *Design* 154 (October 1961): 47–49. See also Adrian Forty, *Objects of Desire: Design and Society since 1750* (London: Thames and Hudson, 1995).

21. Ferenc Fehér, Agnes Heller, and György Márkus, *Dictatorship over Needs* (Oxford: Basil Blackwell, 1983). For the ascription of ideology to technologies and materials, see Langdon Winner, "Do Artefacts Have Politics?" (1980), in *The Social Shaping of Technology,* ed. D. McKenzie and J. Wajcman (London: Open University Press, 1985); Ray Stokes, "Plastics and the New Society," in Reid and Crowley, *Style and Socialism Style and Socialism: Modernity and Material Culture in Post-War Eastern Europe,* ed. Susan E. Reid and David Crowley (Oxford: Berg, 2000), 65–80, and "In Search of the Socialist Artefact: Technology and Ideology in East Germany, 1945–1962," *German History* 15, no. 2 (1997): 221–39; Adrian Forty, "Cold War Concrete," in Kalm and Ruudi, *Constructed Happiness: Domestic Environment in the Cold War Era,* ed. Mart Kalm and Ingrid Ruudi (Tallinn: Estonian Academy of Arts, 2005) 28–45. On mentalities and practices associated with Soviet goods, see essays by Ol'ga Gurova, Galina Orlova, Ekaterina Gerasimova, and Sof'ia Chuikina, anthologized and translated in *Russian Studies in History* 48, no. 1 (2009). On efforts to define "socialist things" in the 1920s, see Christina Kiaer, *Imagine No Possessions: The Socialist Objects of Russian Constructivism* (Cambridge, MA: MIT Press, 2005).

22. Photographs and surviving objects indicate some justification. Eastern Europeans, even sympathetic ones, also found Soviet consumer goods backward, of poor quality, and lacking in taste. Report from representative of VOKS, Kuzmenko, "On Shortcomings of 'Moscow' Pavilion at Second Budapest Fair of Local Industries," 3 May 1958, in RGANI (Russian State Archive of Contemporary History), f. 5, op. 43, d. 23, ll. 66–68.

23. Lora Uinslou [Laura Winslow], "Novoe primenenie plastmass," *Amerika,* no. 48 (n.d.): 50–51; Stephen Phillips, "Plastics," in *Cold War Hothouses: Inventing Postwar Culture, from Cockpit to Playboy,* ed. Beatriz Colomina, Annmarie Brennan, and Jeannie Kim (New York: Princeton Architectural Press, 2004), 91–123; Raphaelle Saint-Pierre, "Happiness in French Houses of the Fifties," in *Constructed Happiness,* 130–43.

24. Experimental plastic house, 15 Shepeliuginskaia Street, Moscow, designed by the Institute of Plastics and Mosproekt, 1958: photograph M. Churakov, 1963, Shchusev Museum of Architecture, Moscow; Marietta Shaginian, *Zarubezhnye pis'ma* (1964; repr., Moscow: Sovetskii pisatel', 1977), 80–82.

25. On the contemporary style, see Iurii Gerchuk, "The Aesthetics of Everyday Life in the Khrushchev Thaw in the USSR (1954–64)," in *Style and Socialism,* 81–100; Susan E. Reid, "Destalinization and Taste, 1953–63," *Journal of Design History* 10, no. 21 (1997): 177–202; Susan E. Reid, "Communist Comfort: Socialist Modernism and the Making of Cosy Homes in the Khrushchev-Era Soviet Union," *Gender and History* 21, no. 3 (2009): 465–98.

26. Khrushchev's December 1954 condemnation of architectural "excesses" *(izlishestva)* and "building that was only for looking at" initially associated these faults with Stalinist practice, but their repudiation was extended into a general principle. N. S. Khrushchev, *O shirokom vnedrenii industrial'nykh metodov, uluchshenii kachestva i snizhenii stoimosti stroitel'stva . . . , 7 dekabria 1954 g.* (Moscow: Politizdat, 1955). On the status of fashion, see Larissa Zakharova, "Dior in Moscow: A Taste for Luxury in Soviet Fashion under Khrushchev," in *Pleasures in Socialism: Leisure and Luxury in the Eastern Bloc,* ed. David Crowley and Susan E. Reid (Evanston: Northwestern University Press, 2010), 95–119.

27. See Susan E. Reid, "The Soviet Pavilion at Brussels '58: Convergence, Conversion, Critical Assimilation, or Transculturation?" (Working Paper No. 62, Cold War International History Project, Woodrow Wilson International Center for Scholars, Washington, DC, December 2010).

28. For further discussion, see Susan E. Reid, "Khrushchev Modern," *Cahiers du monde russe* 47, nos. 1–2 (2006): 227–68. On Soviet design after Stalin, see Alexander Lavrentiev and Yuri Nasarov, *Russian Design: Traditions and Experiment, 1920–1990* (London: Academy Editions, 1995); Raymond Hutchings, *Soviet Science, Technology, Design: Interaction and Convergence* (London: Oxford University Press, 1976); Constantin Boym, *New Russian Design* (New York: Rizzoli, 1992). In Great Britain, similarly, efforts were under way to gain recognition of design as a separate discipline in the postwar period. See Judy Attfield, *Bringing Modernity Home: Writings on Popular Design and Material Culture* (Manchester: Manchester University Press, 2007).

29. Susan E. Reid, "Cold War in the Kitchen: Gender and Consumption in the Khrushchev Thaw," *Slavic Review* 61, no. 2 (2002): 211–52; George Breslauer, *Khrushchev and Brezhnev as Leaders: Building Authority in Soviet Politics* (London: Allen and Unwin, 1982), 139–40.

30. Susan E. Reid, "Everyday Aesthetics in the Modern Soviet Flat," forthcoming as *Khrushchev Modern: Making Oneself at Home and Becoming a Consumer in the Soviet 1960s* (working title), supported by the Leverhulme Trust and the Arts and Humanities Research Council.

31. Anthony Giddens, *The Consequences of Modernity* (Cambridge: Polity Press, 1991), 53, 83; Michel Foucault, "Governmentality," *Ideology and Consciousness* 6 (1979): 5–21. Specialists of various types gained influence in the Khrushchev era. See David Hoffmann, "European Modernity and Soviet Socialism," in *Russian Modernity: Politics, Knowledge, Practices,* ed. David Hoffmann and Yanni Kotsonis (Basingstoke: Macmillan Press, 2000), 246; H. Gordon Skilling and Franklyn Griffiths, eds., *Interest Groups in Soviet Politics* (Princeton: Princeton University Press, 1971); Breslauer, *Khrushchev and Brezhnev;* Peter Hauslohner, "Politics before Gorbachev: De-Stalinization and the Roots of Reform," in *The Soviet System in Crisis,* ed. Alexander Dallin and Gail W. Lapidus (Boulder, CO: Westview Press, 1991), 37–63.

32. Harold Van Doren, *Industrial Design: A Practical Guide to Product Design and Development,* 2nd ed. (New York: McGraw Hill, 1954), 271–92.

33. M. E. Ruban, "Private Consumption in the USSR: Changes in the Assortment of Goods, 1940–1959," *Soviet Studies* 13, no. 3 (January 1962): 244.

34. Marshall Goldman, *The Soviet Economy: Myth and Reality* (Englewood Cliffs, NJ: Prentice-Hall, 1968), 53 and table 4; Roger Skurski, *Soviet Marketing and Economic Development* (London: Macmillan, 1983), 5–6. Per capita consumption grew quite rapidly under Khrushchev, although it slowed down in the early 1960s. Philip Hanson, *The Consumer in the Soviet Economy* (London: Macmillan, 1968), and *The Rise and Fall of the Soviet Economy: An Economic History of the USSR from 1945* (London: Longman, 2003); Alec Nove, *An Economic History of the U.S.S.R.* (London: Allen Lane, 1970).

35. Jane Zavisca, "Consumer Inequalities and Regime Legitimacy in Late Soviet and Post-Soviet Russia" (PhD diss., University of California, Berkeley, 2005), 56; V. F. Maier, *Planirovanie*

sotsial'nogo razvitiia (Moscow: Izdatel'stvo MGU, 1988), 45; Lewis H. Siegelbaum, *Cars for Comrades: The Life of the Soviet Automobile* (Ithaca: Cornell University Press, 2008), 299 n. 82; David Lane, *Soviet Economy and Society* (New York: Blackwell, 1985), 58; Goldman, *Soviet Economy*, 54, table 4. By 1968 there were 27 million TV sets, 25 million washing machines, 13.7 million refrigerators, and 5.9 million vacuum cleaners for some sixty to seventy million households. Mervyn Matthews, *Class and Society in Soviet Russia* (London: Allen Lane, 1972), 84. For Western Europe, cf. Judt, *Postwar*, 338.

36. Letter to editors of *Ekonomicheskaia gazeta*, late 1962 or early 1963, forwarded to Gosplan, in "Initsiativnye predlozheniia i pis'ma trudiashchikhsia po proizvodstvu predmetov potrebleniia, 1963," in RGAE (Russian State Archive of the Economy), f. 4372, op. 65, d. 177.

37. Television was an exception, since it improved on the familiar technology of radio, which may partly explain the rapidity of its take-up. See Kristin Roth-Ey, "Mass Media and the Re-Making of Soviet Culture, 1950s–1960s" (PhD diss., Princeton University, 2003), 268–71, and "Finding a Home for Television in the USSR, 1950–1970," *Slavic Review* 66, no. 2 (2007): 278–306.

38. Goldman, *Soviet Economy*, 55.

39. Judt defines this shift to modern consumption: until the 1950s, most people did not shop or "consume" in the modern sense; they subsisted. This changed in the two decades after 1953 as wages and purchasing power grew and was felt most dramatically in the 1960s. Judt, *Postwar*, 338. We must beware, however, the fallacy of assuming that lack of wealth or abundance precludes sophisticated ideas about consumption. Paul Glennie, "Consumption within Historical Studies," in Miller, *Acknowledging Consumption*, 177.

40. Interviews gathered for my Everyday Aesthetics project (2004–7) indicate that television was sometimes acquired sooner, while the purchaser was still in communal accommodation. On living conditions, see Donald Filtzer, *The Hazards of Urban Life in Late Stalinist Russia: Health, Hygiene, and Living Standards, 1943–1953* (Cambridge: Cambridge University Press, 2011).

41. Reasons why the refrigerator most visibly indexed the mass rise in purchasing power and shift from subsistence to consumption in the modern sense are summarized by Judt, *Postwar*, 338–39.

42. Baudrillard, *System of Objects*; Don Slater, *Consumer Culture and Modernity* (Cambridge: Polity Press, 1997), 145–47. The issues in this section are explored further in David Crowley and Susan E. Reid, "Pleasures in Socialism?," in Crowley and Reid, *Pleasures in Socialism*, 3–51.

43. Raymond Stokes, *Constructing Socialism: Technology and Change in East Germany, 1945–1990* (Baltimore: Johns Hopkins University Press, 2000); Neue Gesellschaft für Bildende Kunst, *Wunderwirtschaft: DDR Konsumkultur in den 60er Jahren* (Cologne: Böhlau, 1996). See also Alfred Zauberman, *Industrial Progress in Poland, Czechoslovakia and East Germany, 1937–62* (Oxford: Oxford University Press, 1964); Katherine Pence, "Cold War Iceboxes: Competing Visions of Kitchen Politics in 1950s Divided Germany," unpublished paper for workshop "Kitchen Politics in the Cold War," convened by Ruth Oldenziel and Karin Zachmann, Deutsches Museum, Munich, 1–3 July 2005.

44. For the arguments, see Susan E. Reid, "The Khrushchev Kitchen: Domesticating the Scientific-Technological Revolution," *Journal of Contemporary History* 40, no. 2 (2005): 289–316.

45. The All-Union Agricultural Exhibition, at which such agricultural symbolism was ubiquitous, reopened in June 1959 as the All-Union Exhibition of Economic Achievements, VDNKh, rebranded to symbolize the Soviet Union's coming of age as an advanced industrial power. USSR Council of Ministers Decree No. 591, "Ob edinenii Vsesoiuznykh promyshlennoi sel'skokhoziaistvennoi i stroitel'noi vystavok v edinuiu Vystavku dostizhenii narodnogo khoziaistva SSSR" (28 May 1958), in RGAE/RGANTD (Russian State Archive of Science and Technology) (Samara), f. 127, introduction to op. 1.

46. The shift is exemplified by comparing the full-page spreads of vacuum cleaners in the 1959 edition of *Kratkaia entsiklopediia domashnego khoziaistva,* vol. 2 (Moscow: Bol'shaia sovetskaia entsiklopediia, 1959), plate facing 508–9, with that in the third edition (Moscow: Sovetskaia entsiklopediia, 1966). Cf. Richard Hamilton, "An Exposition of She," *Architectural Design* 32 (October 1962): 485–86; Pat Kirkham, ed., *The Gendered Object* (Manchester: Manchester University Press, 1996).

47. G. Kreslavskii, "Zolotoi chelovek," *Krokodil,* no. 23 (20 August 1958): 6.

48. For detail, see Reid, "Cold War in the Kitchen," 211–52; Reid, "Khrushchev Modern," 227–68.

49. Van Doren, *Industrial Design,* 17.

50. M. Subbotin (VNIITE), "Izuchenie zarubezhnymi firmami trebovanii potrebitelia," *Tekhnicheskaia estetika,* no. 4 (1965): 113; Victor Buchli, "Khrushchev, Modernism, and the Fight against *Petit-Bourgeois* Consciousness in the Soviet Home," *Journal of Design History* 10, no. 2 (1997): 161–76.

51. Subbotin, "Izuchenie zarubezhnymi firmami."

52. It was also to be beautiful. Khrushchev, *O kontrol'nykh tsifrakh,* 29; "Eto dlia vas, sovetskie liudi! Dobrotno i krasivo," *Izvestiia,* 17 October 1959; "Bol'she, dobrotnee, krasivee!" *Izvestiia,* 23 October 1959; "Dobrotnye, krasivye veshchi—v nash byt!" *Izvestiia,* 6 October 1959. On Soviet goods as trusty friends, see Ekaterina Degot', "Ot tovara k tovarishchu: k estetike nerynochnogo predmeta," *Logos,* nos. 5–6 (2000): 30; and essays by O. Gurova, E. Gerasimova, S. Chuikina, and G. Orlova in *Russian Studies in History* 48, no. 1 (2009).

53. In part this is a nostalgic reflection of these elderly people's experience of fundamental changes and present-day insecurity, expressed in the view that nothing can be depended upon anymore. Interviews for the Everyday Aesthetics project (Marina, Kaluga, 2006; Galina, Kaluga, 2005); cf. Olga Shevchenko, *Crisis and the Everyday in Postsocialist Moscow* (Bloomington: Indiana University Press, 2009) and "'In Case of Fire Emergency': Consumption, Security and the Meaning of Durables in a Transforming Society," *Journal of Consumer Culture* 2, no. 2 (2002): 147–70.

54. Subbotin, "Izuchenie zarubezhnymi firmami," 13; V. Shvili (VNIITE), "Chto daiut konkretno-sotsiologicheskie issledovaniia promyshlennosti i torgovle," *Tekhnicheskaia estetika,* no. 2 (1965): 2; for fuller discussion, see Reid, "Khrushchev Modern," 227–68.

55. See, e.g., the editorial, "Khudozhniku—dostoinoe mesto v promyshlennosti," *Dekorativnoe iskusstvo SSSR* (henceforth *DI*), no. 7 (1958): 17–22; Valentin Brodskii, "Forma avtomobilia," *DI,* no. 7 (1958): 23–29; I. Matsa, "Mozhet li mashina byt' proizvedeniem iskusstva," *DI,* no. 3 (1961); Iu. Gerchuk, "Mashina kak proizvedenie promyshlennogo iskusstva," *DI,* no. 2 (1962); Editorial, "K itogam diskussii: Mozhet li mashina byt' proizvedeniem iskusstva?" *DI,* no. 12 (1963): 22–25; V. Beletskaia, *Tekhnika i estetika* (Moscow: Profizdat, 1962); K. Kantor, "Novaia forma sviazi khudozhnika s promyshlennost'iu," *DI,* no. 11 (1963): 20–21; Iu. Solov'ev, "Nazrevshie voprosy tekhnicheskoi estetiki," *Kommunist,* no. 1 (1964): 122–24.

56. On VKhUTEMAS, see Sh. Boiko, "Kak gotoviat dizainery," *DI,* no. 10 (1964): 20–21; L. Pazhitnov, "Tvorcheskoe nasledie Baukhauza," *DI,* no. 7 (1962): 29–35 and no. 8 (1962): 16–21.

57. Terms such as *tekhnicheskaia estetika* (technical aesthetics) and *khudozhestvennoe konstruirovanie* (artistic construction) were used. Aleksandr Saltykov, Secretary of Board of USSR Artists' Union to CC Secretary E. Furtseva, "O sostoianii khudozhestvennoi raboty v promyshlennosti i o merakh po ee korennomu uluchsheniiu" (11 September 1958), in RGANI, f. 5, op. 36, d. 74, ll. 27–33; "SNKh SSSR: Upravlenie spetsializatsii i kooperirovaniia . . . 1964–65," in RGAE/RGANTD (Samara), f. 233, op. 3, d. 197, ll. 50–56. For further discussion, see Reid, "Destalinizatsiia and Taste," 177–202, and "Khrushchev Modern," 227–68.

58. USSR Council of Ministers Decree, "Ob uluchshenii kachestva produktsii mashinostroeniia i tovarov kul'turno-bytovogo naznacheniia putem vnedreniia metodov khudozhestvennogo konstruirovaniia," in *Resheniia partii i pravitel'stva po khoziaistvennym voprosam,* vol. 5, 1962–65 (Moscow: Politicheskaia literatura, 1968), 64–67. On VNIITE, see Hutchings, *Soviet Science, Technology, Design,* 147 and passim; Raymond Hutchings, "The Weakening of Ideological Influences," *Slavic Review* 27, no. 1 (1968): 71–84, and "Soviet Design: The Neglected Partner of Soviet Science and Technology," *Slavic Review* 37, no. 4 (1978): 567–83; Dmitry Azrikan, "VNIITE, Dinosaur of Totalitarianism or Plato's Academy of Design?" *Design Issues* 15, no. 3 (1999): 45–77.

59. Report of Upravlenie spetsializatsii i kooperirovaniia, in "SNKh SSSR," l. 64.

60. Report for 1959, "Organizatsiia raboty khudozh: Sovetov pri ViaLegProme," in RGAE/RGANTD (Samara), f. 400 (ViaLegProm), op. 3, d. 27, l. 21. ViaLegProm was mostly concerned with textiles and fashion. Report on work of Special Design Bureau of Mosgorsovnarkhoz, 1965, to develop "technical and industrial aesthetics," in RGAE/RGANTD (Samara), f. 233, op. 3, d. 197, ll. 97–99.

61. Report for 1959, "Organizatsiia raboty khudozh," l. 21; I. Sapfirova, "Promyshlenno-prikladnaia grafika," *Iskusstvo,* no. 7 (1959): 29–35. Articles in the GDR journal *Novaia reklama* were studied, on themes such as "Ob iskusstve sozdavat' khoroshie znaki," "Fabrichnye marki dolzhny zapomniatsia," and "Psikhologicheskoe vliianie fabrichnykh marok."

62. There were fruitful exchanges between UK and USSR design specialists. Paul Reilly, deputy director of COID, visited Moscow in 1957, where he met the future director of VNIITE, Iu. Solov'ev. Reports to UK Foreign Office, 18 and 21 October 1957, Public Records Office, Kew, BW2/532. Reilly was followed in autumn 1959 by Sir Robin Darwin, director of the Royal College of Art. "Robin Darvin v Moskve," *DI,* no. 12 (1959): 14. The USSR joined the ICSID (International Councils of Society of Industrial Design, founded in 1957) by 1968.

63. Zakharova, "Dior in Moscow," 95–119.

64. Karl Kantor, "Tekhnicheskaia estetika i proizvodstvennoe iskusstvo (O rabotakh Petra Tuchnogo)," *DI,* no. 9 (1960): 48–49; Karl Marx, *Economic-Philosophic Manuscripts of 1844,* in *Karl Marx: Selected Writings,* ed. David McLellan (Oxford: Oxford University Press, 1977), 82.

65. A. Dravkin, "Krasivoe sosedstvuet s nekrasivym," *DI,* no. 2 (1962): 36–37.

66. Ibid., 36–37.

67. Ibid., 36.

68. A. Kolosov, "O kachestve bytovykh elektropylesosov," *Tekhnicheskaia estetika,* no. 4 (1965): 15.

69. Dravkin, "Krasivoe sosedstvuet," 36–37.

70. Kolosov, "O kachestve," 14–16.

71. Dravkin, "Krasivoe sosedstvuet," 36.

72. Zavod imeni Likhacheva, the Likhachev Automobile Factory in Moscow.

73. *Tovarnyi slovar',* vol. 9, ed. I. A. Pugachev (Moscow: Gos. izdatel'stvo torgovoi literatury, 1961).

74. This may show awareness of Western critiques of streamlining, which Van Doren presented in order to repudiate: "'Why,' some critics say, 'should static objects be streamlined? Ridiculous!'" *Industrial Design,* 196.

75. Kolosov, "O kachestve," 15. Siemens's Rapid also associated the vacuum cleaner with speed. See also M. Shaposhnikov, "V Khar'kovskom khudozhestvennno-promyshlennom institute," *Tekhnicheskaia estetika,* no. 10 (1965): 6.

76. Khrushchev, *O shirokom vnedrenii industrial'nykh metodov;* Shaposhnikov, "V Khar'kovskom," 6.

77. Tomas Maldonado, future president of the International Council of Societies of Industrial Design (ICSID), had similarly proposed in 1961 that Soviet design had a potential advantage over design in capitalist societies: free from the framework of competition and the priority of merchandizing, it could address other tasks neglected in the West. Tomas Maldonado, "Notes on Communication," *Uppercase* 5 (1961), cited by Kenneth Frampton, "The Development of a Critical Theory," in *Ulm Design: The Morality of Objects*, ed. Herbert Lindinger (Cambridge, MA: MIT Press, 1991), 152. With thanks to Thomas Cubbin.

78. Attfield, *Bringing Modernity Home*; Clement Greenberg, "Avant-Garde and Kitsch," *Partisan Review* 6, no. 5 (1939), repr. in Clement Greenberg, *Art and Culture* (Boston: Beacon Press, 1961), 3–20.

79. VNIITE had limited success in getting its designs realized and recommendations adopted by industry. Lavrentiev and Nasarov, *Russian Design*, 95.

80. On defense sector consumer goods production, beginning ca. 1953, see Julian Cooper, "The Civilian Production of the Soviet Defence Industry," in *Technical Progress and Soviet Economic Development*, ed. R. Amann and J. Cooper (Oxford: Basil Blackwell, 1986), 31–50.

81. For the "consumption junction" in technology purchase, see Ruth Schwartz Cowan, "The Consumption Junction: A Proposal for Research Strategies in the Sociology of Technology," in *The Social Construction of Technological Systems*, ed. Wiebe Bijker, Thomas Hughes, and Trevor Pinch (Cambridge, MA: MIT Press, 1989), 261–80; Nelly Oudshoorn and Trevor Pinch, *How Users Matter: The Co-Construction of Users and Technology* (Cambridge, MA: MIT Press, 2003); Karin Zachmann, "A Socialist Consumption Junction: Debating the Mechanization of Housework in East Germany, 1956–1957," *Technology and Culture* 43, no. 1 (2002): 74.

82. Mills, "Man in the Middle," 70.

83. E.g., the Stiliagi youth subculture was condemned for its members' conspicuous consumption and deliberate effort to stand out and be different. See Mark Edele, "Strange Young Men in Stalin's Moscow: The Birth and Life of the Stiliagi, 1945–1953," *Jahrbücher für Geschichte Osteuropas* 50 (2002): 37–61.

84. Julie Hessler, "Cultured Trade: The Stalinist Turn towards Consumerism," in *Stalinism: New Directions*, ed. Sheila Fitzpatrick (London: Routledge, 2000), 182–209, and *A Social History of Soviet Trade: Trade Policy, Retail Practice, and Consumption, 1917–1953* (Princeton: Princeton University Press, 2004); Amy E. Randall, *The Soviet Dream World of Retail Trade and Consumption in the 1930s* (Basingstoke: Palgrave Macmillan, 2008).

85. N. S. Khrushchev, "Za dal'neishii pod'em proizvoditel'nykh sil strany, za tekhnicheskii progress vo vsekh otrasliakh narodnogo khoziaistva," CC CPSU Plenum, 29 June 1959, *Izvestiia*, 2 July 1959; "Programme of the CPSU" (XXI Party Congress, October 1961), in *Resolutions and Decisions*, vol. 4, *The Khrushchev Years, 1953–1964*, ed. Grey Hodnett (Toronto: University of Toronto Press, 1974), 252; R. Podol'nyi, "Tekhnika nastupaet," *Sem'ia i shkola*, no. 12 (1959): 10–11; A. Vul'f, "Protiv nedootsenki domovodstva," *Sem'ia i shkola*, no. 8 (1961): 47; L. Kaganov, "Tekhnika—kryl'ia semiletki," and S. Iofin, "Luchshe ispol'zovat' oborudovanie," *Mestnaia promyshlennost' i khudozhestvennye promysli*, no. 5 (1961): 3–6 and 7–8 respectively.

86. See, e.g., Charlotte Curtis, "The Way People Live," in *The Soviet Union: The Fifty Years*, ed. Harrison Salisbury (New York: Harcourt Brace and World, 1967), 41–42.

87. K. Skovoroda, "Zadachi dal'neishego uluchsheniia torgovogo obsluzhivaniia naseleniia," *Planovoe khoziaistvo*, no. 2 (1960): 43–53.

88. Procedures for installment sales were outlined in *Sovetskaia Rossiia*, 16 August 1959, 4. Several informants for the Everyday Aesthetics project say they bought "everything" on credit.

89. Skovoroda, "Zadachi," 43–53; V. Moiseev, R. Guz, and M. Khochinskii, "Nekhodovye tovary i ikh utsenka," *Sovetskaia torgovlia* (hereafter *ST*), no. 2 (1961): 41–42.

90. Skovoroda, "Zadachi." From 1954 the trade journal *Sovetskaia torgovlia* printed numerous discussions of how to study demand: see, e.g., I. Korzhenevskii, "Metody izucheniia sprosa naseleniia," *ST,* no. 5 (1954): 9–14; N. Kononov, "O metodakh opredeleniia potrebnosti v tovarakh," *ST,* no. 6 (1963): 5–11. Such discussions gathered new vigor and authority from 1963, appearing in the party theoretical organ: see, e.g., A. Struev, "Torgovlia i proizvodstvo," *Kommunist,* no. 16 (November 1964): 39–48. For Stalin-era antecedents, see Randall, *Soviet Dream World,* ch. 6.

91. Khrushchev endorsed the need for greater "consumer sovereignty" in *Pravda,* 15 December 1963; Breslauer, *Khrushchev and Brezhnev,* 100; Abraham Katz, *The Politics of Economic Reform in the Soviet Union* (New York: Praeger, 1973), 71; Jane Shapiro, "Soviet Consumer Policy in the 1970s," in *Soviet Politics in the Brezhnev Era,* ed. Donald Kelly (New York: Praeger, 1980), 104–28.

92. Katz, *Politics of Economic Reform,* ch. 5; Richard W. Judy, "The Economists," in Skilling and Griffiths, *Interest Groups,* 209–52; Nove, *Economic History,* 356–61; Hauslohner, "Politics before Gorbachev," 52; Basile Kerblay, "Les proposées de Liberman," *Cahiers du monde russe,* no. 3 (1963): 301–11; Hanson, *Rise and Fall,* 101–3; H. G. Skilling, *Czechoslovakia's Interrupted Revolution* (Princeton: Princeton University Press, 1976), 119–25. These arguments are elaborated in Reid, "Khrushchev Modern."

93. Shvili, "Chto daiut konkretno-sotsiologicheskie issledovaniia," 1–2.

94. VNIIKS: Vsesoiuznyi nauchno-issledovatel'skii institut po izucheniiu sprosa na tovary narodnogo potrebleniia i kon"iunkturu torgovli [All-Union Scientific Research Institute for the Study of the Population's Demand for Consumer Goods and Market Prices for Trade], in RGAE/RGANTD (Samara), f. 375, op. 1 and 2. The term *kon"iunktura* (market prices) was quickly dropped from its name, which was truncated to Vsesoiuznyi nauchno-issledovatel'skii institut po izucheniiu sprosa naseleniia na tovary narodnogo potrebleniia. In accordance with a 1965 decree, VNIIKS started work in 1966, charged with developing methods for study of the population's demands for consumer goods. Report of VNIIKS, 1966, in RGAE/RGANTD (Samara), f. 375, op. 1, d. 6, and f. 375, op. 1, d. 13, l. 14. Reforms proposing market socialism aroused fears that they would lead to ideological heresy and political reformism, especially since Soviet economic reformism had intellectual links with that in Poland (Włodzimierz Brus) and Czechoslovakia (Oto Šik).

95. Goldman, *Soviet Economy,* 53.

96. David E. Nye, *Electrifying America: Social Meanings of a New Technology, 1880–1940* (Cambridge, MA: MIT Press, 1990), 281; Mihaly Csikszentmihalyi and Eugene Rochberg-Halton, *The Meaning of Things: Domestic Symbols and the Self* (Cambridge: Cambridge University Press, 1981), 53; Robert Frost, "Machine Liberation: Inventing Housewives and Home Appliances in Interwar France," *French Historical Studies* 18 (1993): 109–30; Jennifer Loehlin, *From Rugs to Riches: Housework, Consumption and Modernity in Germany* (Oxford: Berg, 1999); Joy Parr, "Economics and Homes: Agency," in *Gender and Technology: A Reader,* ed. Nina Lerman, Ruth Oldenziel, and Arwen Mohun (Baltimore: Johns Hopkins University Press, 2003), 329–58; Elizabeth Shove and Dale Southerton, "Defrosting the Freezer: From Novelty to Convenience: A Narrative of Normalisation," *Journal of Material Culture* 5 (2001): 301–19; Sonia Livingstone, "The Meaning of Domestic Technologies," in *Consuming Technologies: Media and Information in Domestic Spaces,* ed. R. Silverstone and E. Hirsch (London: Routledge, 1992), 113–30.

97. Goldman, *Soviet Economy,* 51; Judt, *Postwar,* 338; Parr, "Economics and Homes."

98. I. Morshovich, "Magazinam—khoroshie vitriny," *ST,* no. 7 (1961): 60–64; Marshall Goldman, *Soviet Marketing: Distribution in a Controlled Economy* (New York: Free Press of Glencoe, 1963); Hanson, *Consumer in the Soviet Economy;* Philip Hanson, *Advertising and Socialism: The*

Nature and Extent of Consumer Advertising in the Soviet Union, Poland, Hungary and Yugoslavia (London: Macmillan, 1974).

99. Against this hypothesis we need to consider that appliances were not purchased from showrooms where they were displayed enticingly; often they were purchased unseen when an opportunity arose. However, photographs of the latest appliances were often published in the mass press.

100. Charlotte Curtis predicted, "All the signs indicate that once [the Soviet woman] gets her refrigerator, her vacuum cleaner, her automobile, and her dacha, she may reasonably be expected to think in terms of the air conditioners she is only beginning to hear about." Curtis, "Way People Live," 58. On the nonadoption of the automatic washing machine in 1950s Canada, see Parr, "Economics and Homes," 346; and on resistance to refrigerators in 1950s Western Europe, see Judt, *Postwar,* 338 n. 13.

101. My informants continued to use such methods complementing electrical chilling, even in the mid-2000s.

102. Ivan also served as a People's Court judge. Compare the Stalin-era "culture of models" whereby certain "leading" people such as Stakhanovites were marked out not only by their labor but by their advanced, "cultured" consumption. Hessler, "Cultured Trade."

103. Leonid Likhodeev, *Ia i moi avtomobil'* (Moscow: Sovetskii pisatel', 1972), 17–19, cited in Siegelbaum, *Cars for Comrades,* 299 n. 82.

104. The shifts were not limited to appliances; furniture also began to be acquired in the 1960s and then was replaced by new models in the 1970s as incomes, needs, and fashions changed.

105. Nye, *Electrifying America*; Roger Silverstone, Eric Hirsch, and David Morley, "Information and Communication Technologies and the Moral Economy of the Household," in Silverstone and Hirsch, *Consuming Technologies,* 15–31.

106. In the case of TV, penetration was important enough for measures to be taken to encourage purchase, such as removing it from the category of goods subject to luxury tax. Roth-Ey, "Mass Media," 22, 267–68. Cf. Ina Merkel, "Luxury in Socialism," in Crowley and Reid, *Pleasures in Socialism,* 53–70.

107. Many of my informants had vacuum cleaners, but they showed little attachment to them and complained that they were too heavy or noisy, and some said they never really used them.

108. *Tovarnyi slovar',* vol. 9.

109. See also Crowley and Reid, "Pleasures in Socialism?" 26–29.

110. Georgii Shakhnazarov, *Kommunizm i svoboda lichnosti* (Moscow: Molodaia gvardiia, 1960), 48; J. K. Gilison, *The Soviet Image of Utopia* (Baltimore: Johns Hopkins University Press, 1975), 173. There were also contradictions in authoritative discourse and practice. While appliances were promoted, Khrushchev had also expressed the suspicion of "mere gadgets" as frivolous superfluities when confronted by the appliances at the American Exhibition in 1959. "The Nixon-Khrushchev 'Kitchen Debate,'" *Everything,* April 26, 2000, http://everything2.com/node/515425.

111. Interviews for the Everyday Aesthetics project.

112. Interview for the Everyday Aesthetics project, Kazan', 2005.

113. Alix Holt, "Domestic Labour and Soviet Society," in *Home, School and Leisure in the Soviet Union,* ed. J. Brine, M. Perrie, and A. Sutton (London: George Allen and Unwin, 1980), 29–30. Some preferred to use public laundries, while women of lower income laundered manually at home. Matthews, *Class and Society,* 84; N. Lebina and A. Chistikov, *Obyvatel' i reformy: Kartiny povsednevnoi zhizni gorozhan* (St. Petersburg: Dmitrii Bulanin, 2003), 189. On resistance to automatics, cf. Slavenka Drakulic, *How We Survived Communism and Even Laughed* (New York: Harper Perennial, 1993), 43–54; Parr, "Economics and Homes."

114. Holt, "Domestic Labour," 29–30.

115. S. Kuz'min, "Kogda kholodil'nik 'Oka' ne rabotaet," *Krokodil'*, no. 25 (20 December 1959): 12.

116. Jane Zavisca, "Contesting Capitalism at the Post-Soviet Dacha," *Slavic Review* 62, no. 4 (2003): 803.

117. Rima, interview for the Everyday Aesthetics project, Kazan', 2005.

118. Samara informant 1, born ca. 1960, interview for the Everyday Aesthetics project.

119. Holt, "Domestic Labour," 31; Matthews, *Class and Society.*

120. Nina D., interview for the Everyday Aesthetics project, Kazan', 2005; Dravkin, "Krasivoe sosedstvuet," 36; Helen Watkins, "Beauty Queen, Bulletin Board and Browser: Rescripting the Refrigerator," *Gender, Place and Culture* 13, no. 2 (2006): 143–52.

121. The playful approach would be confined to the development of a Soviet form of pop art, "Sots art," in the "nonconformist" art world.

122. Interviews for the Everyday Aesthetics project; Shevchenko, "In Case of Fire Emergency"; Nicky Gregson, *Living with Things: Ridding, Accommodation, Dwelling* (Wantage: Sean Kingston, 2007); Jennifer Patico, *Consumption and Social Change in a Post-Soviet Middle Class* (Stanford: Stanford University Press, 2008).

2 Modernity Unbound

The New Soviet City of the Sixties

Lewis H. Siegelbaum

Unfortunately, far from everything planned for the seventies was realized, even ten years later. Perhaps they weren't first-order objectives . . . but without them, the district lost something in its spiritual development. I don't want to console myself with the thought that such is the fate of all our new "socialist cities"; anyway, that's a separate theme, large and instructive.

—S. P. Polikarpov, assistant director of VAZ

WHAT DISTINGUISHED THE Soviet cities of the sixties—not Soviet cities *in* the 1960s but the ones that were planned and created (more or less) ex nihilo during that decade? Did everyday life resemble that of other, older cities, did residents enjoy a better quality of life associated with everything being up-to-date and the product of the "scientific-technological revolution" then at its (rhetorical) zenith, or was there a darker side to these cities without pasts?

My essay addresses these questions by considering the middle Volga city of Tol'iatti, best known as the hometown of VAZ, the Volga Automobile Factory founded in 1966.[1] I use Tol'iatti as an example of how certain technological, ideological, and cultural processes came together in the 1960s to shape the lives of urban residents in succeeding decades. In doing so, I want to suggest a reading of the Soviet sixties in relation to what followed that decade alternative to the one that has tended to dominate the historiography. Well before Mikhail Gorbachev characterized the *longue durée* of Leonid Brezhnev's tenure as the "era of stagnation," leading Western scholars differentiated the years of Nikita Khrushchev's rule (1955–64) from those of his successors by employing the terms *reformism* and *conservatism,* with the "men of the sixties" (*shestidesiatniki*) to whom Khrushchev had looked for fresh ideas gradually—or not so gradually—being sidelined.[2] While clearly reflecting shifts in the configuration of the political hierarchy and quite possibly in other respects, this interpretation under-emphasizes certain continuities across the political regimes during the last decades of the Soviet Union's existence. It also begs at least two related questions central to this volume, namely when the Soviet sixties started (and, more to the point of this contribution, when they ended), and who/which groups defined the decade.

Commenting in 2000 on the material cultures of the former Soviet bloc countries, the architectural historian Catherine Cooke asserted that "these materialized manifestations always seemed more revealing and enduring descriptors of their attributes and tensions than the ephemera of properly 'political' analysis."[3] No less than material cultures, the built environment—what Soviet modernity looked like—was one of the continuities transcending the rise and demise of political leaders. In what follows, I argue that Tol'iatti's Avtograd district, built in the late 1960s and 1970s to accommodate VAZ's workers and their families, represented not the betrayal of the promise of Soviet modernity but rather its fulfillment. It is not clear what Stanislav Polikarpov had in mind by "everything planned for the seventies," but given that what actually results from plans drawn up by experts is never identical to those plans, Tol'iatti was far from notorious in this respect.[4] Arguing for an essential consistency between plan and realization does not, however, necessarily mean endorsing the project; on the contrary, by implicating the planning process in the lived reality of Tol'iatti I am trying to bring into relief the power as well as the limits of rule by experts, a dimension of the socialist sixties that hitherto has received little attention.

The rule by experts to which Tol'iatti and other Soviet new towns were subjected was part of a broad transnational trend in architecture and town planning that harkened back at least to the 1920s but gained new vitality from postwar technological advances that heightened the visibility of technical elites in both West and East and inspired notions of convergence between the two economic systems. If, as Henri Lefebvre argued around the time that the new Tol'iatti was taking shape, the USSR exhibited no architectural innovation of its own and no specifically socialist spaces, then the architectural principles governing its new town construction must have stemmed from the same or at least parallel impulses as those in the capitalist West.[5] Somewhat masked by the need to construct a narrative of Tol'iatti's specifically communist inspiration, this more heterodox approach to town planning potentially had greater application in the USSR than elsewhere because of the absence of private or other countervailing forces. Most of this essay is structured around the tensions between the Soviet communist specificities of Tol'iatti and its conformity to broader international modernist canons.

New and Newer Towns

New towns were hardly new in the 1960s. Kate Brown has noted that a primary means for creating the "stripped and ready to be remade anew" Soviet man was to relocate him, in many cases to newly built towns. She analogized one of them—northern Kazakhstan's Karaganda—to Billings, Montana. As in the United States, so in the USSR the technologies of steam-powered engines, irrigation systems, and telegraphic and telephonic communication enabled those in charge of them to replace indigenous peoples with European populations "sorted according to contrived understandings of race, class, and loyalty." Once the Soviet state became the principal agent of population movement in the 1930s, it no longer called such movement "migration" but rather "the process of the redistribution of the population," a process said to "reflect the growth of socialist productive strength and its new allocations."[6]

People allocated to such new towns as Zaporozh'e, Magnitogorsk, and Komsomol'sk-na-Amure were especially fortunate (so it was believed), for socialist productive strength made itself particularly evident at the enterprises that served as the towns' raison d'être. Not everyone who arrived came voluntarily, but as Thomas Lahusen demonstrated with respect to the writer Vasilii Azhaev, what was lacking in reality could be lacquered by socialist realism.[7] More uprooting and displacement occurred thanks to foreign invasion and occupation, and then in the 1950s the inauguration of a massive housing campaign. Indeed, a group of architects from Moscow University took it as axiomatic in their book *The Ideal Communist City* that "the development of socialist production requires, and will continue to require, the creation of new and ever more massive territorial-industrial complexes," adding that "it is bound to regroup vast populations at selected geographical points."[8]

Not all new towns were entirely new. A 1967 retrospective survey of town planning in the USSR pointed out that of the nine hundred or so founded between 1926 and 1966 only about a third could truly claim to be *novostroiki* (new projects), that is, built from scratch rather than as extensions or satellites of preexisting settlements.[9] This is only one way of distinguishing among new towns. Another is according to the kind of industry that they accommodated, or, more accurately, that accommodated them. Still other methods of categorization would be by size of population, location within the country, and period of planning and construction. Situating Tol'iatti within these matrices is complicated, not only because the urban sociologists and geographers who make such distinctions disagree—for example, about where to draw the line between *krupnye* (large) and *krupneishie* (the largest) cities, or whether the new cities of the 1950s and early 1960s represented a generation distinct from those that followed[10]—but also because Tol'iatti became a new town twice within the brief span of less than two decades. Between its founding as Stavropol' in 1737 and the early 1950s, it had served successively as a fortress, a grain depot and *uezd* seat, a minor river port, an object of contention during the Civil War, and a refuge for institutions evacuated from Moscow and Leningrad during World War II. The decision in 1950 to construct the Kuibyshev Hydroelectric Station by damming the Volga soon brought hundreds and then thousands of civil engineers, construction workers, and labor camp inmates to the area and doomed the original town to the fate of Atlantis. New rough-and-ready settlements with names such as Shliusovoi (Floodgates), Zhiguli Sea, and Port soon arose to house the construction crews and prisoner labor gangs. More substantial buildings went up in the village of Kuneevka, renamed Komsomol'sk in 1951, to accommodate the project's headquarters and personnel. Meanwhile, most residents of old Stavropol' were "redistributed" to higher ground about ten kilometers to the west, along with former dwellings, schools, and other institutions excepting churches. The authorities initially called the place Sotsgorod (Socialist City) before reverting to New Stavropol' (or simply New Town). Designed at first for a few thousand people, the town grew rapidly thanks to the nearby construction of synthetic rubber, phosphorous, and ammonia plants that took advantage of the abundant power generated by the hydroelectric station and insisted on pumping tons of noxious gases into the air for the residents to breathe. Four- and five-story apartment buildings, constructed with the prefabricated concrete exteriors that had become more or less standard throughout the USSR by this time, gave the city a rather monotonously colorless appearance. With its borders gradually expanded to encompass Komsomol'sk and other settlements, the new Stavropol' boasted a population of nearly eighty thousand by the census year of 1959.[11]

The second rebirth of the town—and the one to which the remainder of this essay will be devoted—occurred in 1966. Two years after the town's renaming in honor of Palmiro Togliatti, the deceased leader of the Italian Communist Party, the USSR Council of Ministers and the Communist Party's central committee announced that a car factory capable of producing six hundred thousand vehicles a year would be erected in Tol'iatti.[12] The presence of Kuibyshevgidrostroi, a large engineering-construction operation with a lot of recent experience in the area; the ample supply of electric power; lower transportation costs; and additional economic factors gave the city insuperable advantages over other possible sites. We need not dwell on this decision except to note that, characteristic of the prestige computers were beginning to enjoy in the Soviet sixties, it partially relied on a "special mathematical program" designed by the Academy of Sciences' Central Economics and Mathematics Institute (TsEMI) to come to precise determinations of those economic factors.[13]

But though considerably larger than its submerged predecessor, the Tol'iatti to which the computer gave the nod could not possibly accommodate the additional 250,000 people who would need to be housed (by 1975). The project required a newer new Tol'iatti, an *avtograd* (auto city) located within closer proximity to the factory. New Town thus got old very quickly. Because of its location between the Komsomol'sk and Avtograd districts, it became the Central District. The logic of the whole process, as summarized by a U.S. Department of Housing and Urban Development official who visited Tol'iatti and other Soviet new towns in the mid-1970s, was as follows: "First the decision is made to achieve a certain industrial production goal, then the location of the plants to achieve this goal is determined, and finally a new town site is selected."[14]

In this respect, VAZ and "its" town could be said to resemble previous projects. "We remember Magnitogorsk and Dneproges," an *Izvestiia* reporter wrote in 1979, "and today the history of our country is being written in steel and concrete at KamAZ and BAM. The Volga auto plant is a link in the chain of our industry." "It was like Magnitogorsk in its time, like Stalingrad Tractor, like ZIL," the longtime director of

Kuibyshevgidrostroi, Nikolai Semizorov, recalled in an interview many years later.[15] The analogies came easily to those who had been intimately involved in the construction of VAZ. But what about Tol'iatti, the town made new again by VAZ? The new Stavropol' had emerged from the waters dammed by the Kuibyshev hydroelectric station just as Zaporozh'e had from Dneproges, or Bratsk from its eponymous dam. Avtograd—or more formally, the auto factory district *(avtozavodskii raion)* of Tol'iatti—owed its existence to VAZ.[16] It represented a latter-day version of Nizhnii Novgorod's *avtozavodskii raion,* the original *avtograd,* site of the Gor'kii Automobile Factory (GAZ).[17] Tol'iatti's successive renewals, depending first on water power and then on auto power, served to connect it to the chain of Soviet new towns extending back to the 1920s. And just like these other once-upon-a-time "ideal communist cities," the new Tol'iatti would serve as a mechanism for transforming rural recruits into model urban residents, and as an outpost of the future communist society.[18]

Tol'iatti Modern

Yet no less important than connecting the new town to the heroic socialist chain of construction projects was to demonstrate its contemporaneity. Reflecting the ever-persistent march of Soviet progress, Avtograd also had to be different from—and *better* than—previous towns. "The new city will be grand . . . and we won't know any barracks," says a fictionalized version of Semizorov in a novel about Avtograd's construction.[19] Nor would there be any use of prison labor. Avtograd would differ in these respects not only from Magnitogorsk, with its tents, earthen dugouts, and large numbers of coerced laborers, but from many other new towns of the past, including the Tol'iatti that the power station produced. The absence of barracks and prison labor would mark the new district as a product of the post-Stalin era, a city planned in accordance with available resources including computer technology, and built in a more humane manner, as befitting a modern socialist society.

But one might question the extent to which Tol'iatti was a specifically Soviet or communist-inspired city. Its intended transformational functions, for example, echoed those of the unsocialist city of Brasília. The construction of Brasília, as James Holston noted, was intended to be "the means to forge a new national identity" by transforming the image of its builders, the *candangos,* from those "without qualities, without culture, vagabond[s], lower-class, lowbrow" to people from the interior or just "the common man."[20] For James Scott, whose dyspeptic analysis owes much to Holston's book, Brasília was the quintessential "high-modernist city," whose construction Brazilian president Juscelino Kubitschek sought to use "to transform the candangos into the proletarian heroes of the new nation."[21]

As for living in the new Tol'iatti, prospective residents could look forward to conditions rarely if anywhere experienced in the USSR, and this too resembled the conception of Brasília "as a city of the future, a city of development" that "made no reference to the habits, traditions, and practices of Brazil's past or of its great cities."[22] In the above-cited novel, a fictionalized Polikarpov emphasizes the future city's fulfillment of personal and familial as distinct from collective needs. He describes it as a *gorod-etalon* (model city), a term he defines as follows:

> Very simply, it's a city where people will live comfortably and happily, where there will be no crowding—neither on the streets, nor in apartments, nor in the stores. And it will be beautiful—everywhere. It will be a city in which one can go by foot from one end to the other in an hour and do everything a person normally does: earn a living, pick up the kids from kindergarten, get a ticket to the sports palace or the cinema, have a look at the polyclinic, call on one's mother-in-law, rest in a pro-phylactorium, make necessary purchases, order a table in a restaurant for Saturday, go on a yacht, swim in a pool, take a new novel off the shelves of the library. . . . This is not some pipe dream but an iron-clad reality of engineering.[23]

Or at least of town planning. So, let's take a look at the plan developed by a team of architects and engineers from the housing and town planning divisions of the Central Scientific Research and Design Institute under the direction of Boris Rubanenko and Viacheslav Shkvarikov.[24] As described by Rubanenko in 1970, the plan envisioned "the creation of a large modern city on an empty site in a very short time." It called for a linear approach to town planning, one suggested by the contours of the shoreline of the Zhiguli Sea formed by the damming of the Volga, but also by one of the principal elements of modernist aesthetics. The town would stretch from east to west in parallel strips or zones beginning at the water's edge and proceeding through parkland, the residential zone, and the industrial zone containing the VAZ complex. Broad boule-vards, some as wide as six hundred meters, would separate residential from industrial zones and would carry mostly bus traffic to and from the factory entrance efficiently and safely.[25]

The entire project was governed by the principle of recursion.[26] During the first phase of the plan (1968–71), four districts would be built, each of which would be divided by diagonal boulevards into *mikroraiony* (microdistricts). A hierarchical or "stepped" system of services, differentiated according to frequency of use, would enable residents of a housing block consisting of three thousand to five thousand people to fulfill their everyday needs (e.g., child care, basic foodstuffs, service bureau) within a radius of 150 meters. Residents of a microdistrict, numbering twelve thousand, could expect to travel no more than four hundred to five hundred meters to go to school, obtain house-hold goods, attend events at a local club, go to the hairdresser, eat in a cafeteria, and so on. More episodic visits to the cinema, restaurant, cosmetics store, dress shop, post office, savings bank, or large food store could be made by an entire district's twenty to twenty-five thousand residents without traveling more than one to one and a half kilo-meters. Finally, the entire new town would contain specialized shops, restaurants with "exotic cuisine," a theater, a concert hall, a train station, an outdoor market, a sports stadium, a hospital, and a city council headquarters at a distance of no more than five kilometers for any resident.[27]

The idea of a hierarchical system of services appeared already in urban planning of the mid-1930s, and Mark B. Smith has identified the microdistrict as the most significant feature of Khrushchev's housing program from the 1950s.[28] Two architectural principles distinguished the general plan for Avtograd from earlier projects. First, it relied exclusively on geometric abstraction. The varying sizes of the residential structures—five, nine, twelve, and sixteen stories—and their distribution throughout each microdistrict were dictated by geometric proportionality. Even the people who appeared in the drawings looked geometric. Second, it turned away from the street, situating social interaction within the enclosed areas of the microdistricts. Whether dormitories intended for single people or multiroom apartments to be inhabited by families, the residential structures would contain various dispensaries, services, and recreational facilities that "would not require residents to go out onto the streets."[29]

In these ways too Avtograd would reproduce international modernist conventions. The separation of the functions of automobile traffic and pedestrian movement was a cardinal principle of Le Corbusier's architectural thinking, vigorously applied in his design for the Punjabi city of Chandigarh. As for Brasília, a Corbusier-inspired city, the basic housing unit, the *superquadra,* "embodie[d] the fundamental modernist ideas of autonomy and community in residential organization crystallized into architectural form by Soviet and Western European architects"; in other words, it was the microdistrict by another name. The city was to have "no streets in the sense of public gathering places; . . . only roads and highways to be used exclusively by motorized traffic." Brasília thus became, in the words of its residents, a city where "there are no people in the streets," a city that "lacks the bustle of street life."[30]

Finally, the plan conformed to *both* international modernism *and* standard Soviet practice by prescribing a uniformity of facades, building materials, and construction techniques. The facades of Brasília (to refer to that city again) contained no variation in modeling, size, scale, ornament, or materials that would indicate status variations: "Each block is strictly geometric and egalitarian. Nothing distinguishes the exterior of one apartment from another."[31] While this may have made the new capital exceptional in the Brazilian context, it was absolutely standard elsewhere. If, as sociologist John Urry has written, the automobile was the "quintessential manufactured object produced . . . within 20th-century capitalism," then the Second World equivalent would be the large prefabricated ferroconcrete panels that covered the facades of apartment buildings erected throughout the USSR and the rest of Eastern Europe from the 1950s until well into the 1980s.[32] In Tol'iatti, the authors of the plan boasted, *tipizatsiia*—the use of various sizes and shapes of prefabricated "large-panel" components—would reach a new scale, creating hitherto unimaginable opportunities for industrial methods of construction.[33] Nowhere else would a brand-new city of ferroconcrete panels be built on such a scale. Tol'iatti in other words got closer than any other Soviet city to realizing the dream of a modern, rationalized agglomeration of citizens with homogenized, standardized social institutions and patterns of daily life.

The keywords used by Rubanenko to describe the design for the new city—*simple, organic, harmonious, hygienic, geometric,* and *contemporary/modern*—figured in others' descriptions as well.[34] Not for nothing was the architectural team awarded a national prize for its general scheme, which was made "mandatory course material for generations of architecture students in the Soviet Union and the GDR." The fact that Avtograd appeared as one of two exemplary new towns in a 1970 jubilee issue of the journal *Dekorativnoe iskusstvo* signified to architecture critic Aleksandr Vysokovskii its "membership in the premiere class of Soviet architecture." Along with Moscow's revised general plan of 1971, Avtograd represented, in the words of architectural historian Elke Beyer, "official approval of a definitive model for the modern Soviet city."[35]

Rule by Experts?

Less extravagant in its claims to promote the communist future than during the Khrushchev era, this approach to urban planning drew at least as much for its inspiration on Western models as on the Soviet functional urbanism (a.k.a. constructivism) of the late 1920s.[36] Although the full-blown rehabilitation of constructivism that the Moscow Section of the Union of Architects heralded in the early 1960s never happened, Soviet architects openly acknowledged "points of contiguity" with ideas and projects elsewhere in the world.[37] These included *inter alia* Polish and French sociologists' proposed cures for urban-induced anomie; the British garden city, new town, and satellite city movements; Michel Ragon's *Les cités de l'avenir,* a Russian edition of which appeared in 1969; Konstantinos Doxiadis's "science" of human settlement *(ekistics);* and above all, Le Corbusier's "world-renowned" apartment blocks (L'Unité d'Habitation in Marseille; La Maison Radieuse in Nantes), and plans for Chandigarh.[38]

We know that Western architectural literature was available, if not throughout the entire country, then in key institutions in Moscow and other cities, and that Soviet architects and town planners maintained a "business-like interest" in foreign experience.[39] In what Marija Dremaite cites as instances of "quiet modernism," architects and designers from the Baltic republics and Leningrad met with their counterparts in Finland and adapted to satellite city and new town projects designs from places like the garden city of Tapiola and Toulouse-Le Mirail (in France). For Dremaite this signified that contrary to the image of the Soviet architect "as a submissive instrument in the hands of the political system . . . architects, designers and planners were quite influential and had no other models or aspirations than those of Western Europe."[40] The line extending from VKhUTEMAS and other Soviet constructivist schools to the Bauhaus in the 1920s, through Le Corbusier's Athens Charter for the Congrès Internationaux d'Architecture Moderne (CIAM IV, 1933) and the application of CIAM's principles in Chandigarh, Brasília, and elsewhere back to Soviet new town planners of the 1960s was neither straight nor unbroken. But analogous to the heroic socialist chain that linked Tol'iatti to earlier Soviet construction projects, it helps situate this and other new town projects of the 1960s within the conceptual framework of the utopian or "high-modernist" city.

How, given repeated assertions of systemic difference and incompatibility, was such explicit acknowledgment of indebtedness to bourgeois architects and town planners possible? Convergence theory, which emerged among Western social scientists during the 1960s, can provide some insight, for one of the things that impressed Pitirim Sorokin, Marion Levy, John Kenneth Galbraith, Alfred G. Meyer, and other proponents was the rise of new technocratic elites and the increased reliance within "mature industrial society" on pragmatic and scientific methods to solve social issues or "tasks."[41] To be sure, Soviet commentators repeatedly rejected the notion of *systemic* convergence, although they did concede that technologies and administrative structures were transferable.[42] What I am suggesting is that this concession was not insignificant. Indeed, it—the relative autonomy of the technical—underpinned much of what was propagated at the time as the scientific-technological revolution.[43] Just as VAZ's "hyperfactory" would represent the latest word in integrated production based on the adoption of Fiat auto technology, so Tol'iatti's Avtograd would exemplify the best principles of urban planning, whatever or wherever their inspiration.[44] Ideologists regarded both projects as essentially technical.

In this respect architects like Rubanenko and Skvarikov resembled other "specialists"—nuclear physicists and ballistics experts, obstetricians and sociologists, the designers of products rapidly filling up the apartments described by Susan Reid, members of dance companies, Olympic gymnastic squads, and the football teams discussed in Robert Edelman's contribution—whose application of their skills earned the USSR international plaudits. These (and undoubtedly other) cases bore out convergence theorists' arguments, for the heightened public visibility and professional autonomy enjoyed by the Soviet scientific-technical elite encouraged the establishment of an essentially transnational set of standards and styles. Whether one should go so far as many convergence theorists did to interpret their increasing prominence as evidence of the growing power of the Soviet "technostructure" is another matter. Even if their work had profound effects on the Soviet public, helping to redefine the "Soviet way of life," their rule was limited to the provision of technical services, as Andrei Sakharov (himself a passionate advocate of convergence) and other experts who strayed into political dissidence found out.[45]

Convergence theorists' projections of the two vectors meeting at some not-so-distant point in any case proved illusory. While the Soviet vector would continue along the modernist-industrial path, Western capitalism was about to veer off in another direction, away from Fordism and toward more "disorganized" technologies resulting in time-space compression.[46] In the meantime, the French Marxist social geographer Henri Lefebvre propounded another version of convergence, arguing that in terms of conceptions of space it had essentially already occurred in the 1920s. Whether in the communist East or the capitalist West, the principles governing the "production of space" were the same: "technicist, scientific, and intellectualized." Even though this approach pioneered by the Bauhaus and Le Corbusier "was looked upon at the time as both rational and revolutionary . . . it was tailor-made for the state—whether of the state-capitalist or the state-socialist variety." Its characteristic feature—the fracturing of space via "the cult of rectitude in the sense of right angles and straight lines"—represented a fair description of the new Tol'iatti.[47]

Inhabiting Tol'iatti

By 1972, when Avtograd officially became a *raion* (district) of Tol'iatti, 118,000 people were registered as living there. They occupied 3,000,000 square meters of living space, sent their children to ten schools and sixteen kindergartens, and shopped at six commercial centers.[48] By September 1974, the population had risen to 150,000, and an additional two schools, four kindergartens, and one shopping center along with a new cinema and polyclinic had opened to accommodate the increased demand. Over the next two years the district added 267,000 square meters of living space, a new stadium seating 27,000, and an indoor sports palace along with diverse other facilities. Local authorities projected construction of an additional 200,000 square meters of living space by 1980 to accommodate an expected total population of 250,000.[49] But no matter how much was built, it was never sufficient. As of February 1976, 30,000 VAZ workers were waiting for apartments in Avtograd, and the *raion*'s kindergartens lacked spaces for 18,000 children. More than two years later, over 1,000 families were occupying living space of less than 4 square meters per person.[50]

The reason was simple enough: celebrated as a model city that had attracted the youngest population in the country, Avtograd was a Soviet company town par excellence. The French urban sociologist Pierre Merlin has noted with respect to the USSR as a whole that "the modalities of financing . . . all construction (which entailed dwellings as well as public facilities) [we]re assured by the ministry corresponding to the principal activity of the city. In the estimates," he added, "one did not make distinctions among the industrial complex, the residential districts, and public buildings."[51] But VAZ did. Assuming responsibility for all questions concerning the erection of housing and sociocultural structures, VAZ, like every other Soviet enterprise since the dawn of the putative planned economy, consistently gave priority to material production even while it hired workers in excess of planned targets.

As for consumer services, commercial and cultural outlets were reported in 1976 to be meeting only 25 to 30 percent of demand.[52] In this way too Avtograd conformed to the general pattern of urban forms and infrastructure described by geographer Thomas Poulsen. "Although theoretically," Poulsen wrote in 1980, "shops, restaurants, and cultural facilities for the self-contained residential unit are to be built simultaneously with the housing itself, there is characteristically a lag of four to five years before these elements are provided, if at all. All agencies are beset by the fact that they do not have enough funds to do everything they would like, and consumer services too often appear the most expendable."[53] Unlike their counterparts in many other new microdistricts sprouting on the edges of towns, Avtograd's residents did not have long commutes to work. But the inadequacies of the *raion*'s consumer services placed an enormous burden on those of New Town/Central and Komsomol'sk as well as the entire city's transportation system. In other respects—vistas exuding "Kafkaesque anomie," little if any spontaneous street life, and sensory deprivation—the bleak depiction of late Soviet new towns and microdistricts offered by Blair Ruble seems to fit Avtograd too.[54]

All of this produced what one local commentator characterizes as "a typical new town cultural environment." The team of Moscow-based historians that produced a history of VAZ assert that coexisting within this environment were two subcultures, each connected to a sociologically defined group: the white-collar workforce that came to Tol'iatti from large industrial centers with advanced skills and received apartments more or less straightaway, and primarily young, recently married or still unmarried migrants from the countryside who, like Brazil's *candangos*, occupied less skilled positions and had to scramble for accommodation and other resources. The first subculture—with its emphasis on self-expression, pursuit of fine arts, and sports participation—is the one VAZ liked to project about its employees and resembles what one might find in "many other enterprises throughout the country." The second the authors describe as "the other side of life in Tol'iatti," where the "turbid waters of drunkenness, fights, knifings [and] primitive leisure washed over the workers' quarters and dormitories."[55]

One is tempted to interpret this second subculture as endemic to occupancy in hurriedly built high-rise apartments. But, as demonstrated by another large microdistrict of superblocks erected at the same time as Avtograd but halfway around the globe, not all such structures have bred this assortment of antisocial behaviors. Co-op City, built by the nonprofit United Housing Foundation on landfill along the Hutchinson River in the Baychester section of the Bronx, and containing a population of some fifty-five thousand, looks from a distance like Avtograd and other Soviet high-rise projects. It has "the same stark, modernist architecture, the same lonesome spaces between the buildings, same walkways, same benches." Yet, founded in the spirit of socialism and cooperative progressivism by trade unionists who in some cases had emigrated from tsarist Russia as children, it differed from the start in the diversity of generations and types of employment of its residents, their sense of a shared ownership, and, above all, their participation in the governance of where they lived. They do not just occupy "living space" parceled out in square meters; rather, as described by one Co-op City official, they inhabit "a safe, viable community."[56]

According to Ruble, the research of sociologists and demographers helped expose the social inadequacies of microdistricts built throughout the Soviet Union, thereby serving as a surrogate index of consumer demand.[57] Like the architects and engineers whose imaginations their criticisms sometimes helped to tame, Soviet urban sociologists were experiencing a "golden age" in the late sixties and early seventies.[58] But Boris Grigor'evich Remizov, the sociologist in Evgenii Astakhov's novel set in the Tol'iatti of the early 1970s, is hypercritical. He wonders why Avtograd's construction takes longer than Bratsk's did. He *predicts* that the new residents will become dissatisfied with their living conditions, especially the youngest age group (ages seventeen through twenty-five), and when the writer-journalist hero of the novel, Ivan Pavlovich Tveritin, describes the residents as "all workers," he begs to differ: "They are all peasants. Pea-s-ants! You think that yesterday's kolkhoz lad will become a representative of the working class? Nothing of the sort! He remains a peasant by the very construction of his psyche." Remizov himself is a Muscovite who inevitably pines for the capital.[59]

Remizov is a foil not only for Tveritin, who studied architecture and had aspirations of designing part of the Kuibyshev Hydroelectric Station, but also for the collective heroes of the novel, "the communists—workers, engineers, party leaders who shouldered the most difficult burdens during those first three or so years." The novel, which appeared in 1979, desperately tries to evoke the narrative of heroic socialist construction, but a certain defensiveness in what became of Tol'iatti creeps into its evocation. This is particularly so in statements made by Nikolai Kharitonovich Obolonkov, formerly party leader at Kuibyshevgidrostroi and then city party first secretary. Astakhov has him rejecting the characterization of young cities as unoriginal and featureless by asserting that "before our eyes a new side of Tol'iatti is being born, where the residential part complements the architectural style of the industrial zone. Both in fact form a single, impressive whole; this is without exaggeration a monument raised by our architects to the era of developed socialism." He also responds to the complaint—memorialized in *An Irony of Fate*, the El'dar Riazanov comedic film from 1975—that it is impossible to distinguish one Soviet city from another by remarking: "No two cities are alike, just as no two rivers are alike. . . . One often hears that in the past twenty years mass housing construction has used only two or three types of designs and that as a result the new microdistricts resemble each other. Many in fact do lack a vertical profile and are monotonous to look at. . . . The microdistricts are alike, but the character of the cities, their internal essence and style, are different, and the attentive person always knows one from the other." As for Tol'iatti in particular, "Its popularity especially among youth, headlong growth, combination of modern buildings, and massive stands of primeval pine forest distinguish it from equally sized cities."[60]

If Astakhov's novel represents a heavy-handed attempt to promote local pride by drawing on elements of both the heroic socialist and the cosmopolitan modernist narratives about new towns, then another Tol'iatti novel, published in 1994, reflects a more somber attitude about the unbounded modernity of the city. Set for the most part in 1982 during the waning days of the Brezhnev era, Vasilii Volochilov's *Avtograd* tells of the gathering storm of declining productivity and morale, failure to recruit a sufficient number of workers for the line, and the runaway theft of vehicles and parts at VAZ. It is also about the rescue of a Soviet officer in Afghanistan; dropouts ("hippies") who inhabit the fishing communities along the Volga; and a budding romance between Larisa, a visiting Moscow reporter who has gone incognito by donning overalls to work on the assembly line, and Viktor Venedov, the line's boss. In an early scene, Viktor visits his mother and ailing father, who still live in the house where he was raised in Morkvashi, on the south shore of the

Zhiguli Sea opposite Tol'iatti. There, with a Proustian joy he greedily takes in the sounds and smells of his childhood—the flapping of the rooster's wings and its hearty crowing, the jingling of the slop pail that his mother carries out to Mashka the pig, the aroma of the wood-burning stove that his father could not bring himself to throw away and that made his mother's borscht taste that much better. The sense that Morkvashi is a world about to disappear, that living this close to nature has become increasingly rare, is palpable.[61]

Viktor's visit gives his father, Petr Grigor'evich, the opportunity to unburden himself. A veteran of the hydroelectric project, Petr Grigor'evich expresses deep regret about his failure to appreciate what the dam destroyed: "the fish, the meadows, the lakes and the old river beds, even the cities that disappeared under the water." He then asks for forgiveness from the river ("Matushka") and the people displaced from their homes.[62] Two weeks later they return to the same site, and the father returns to the same theme so redolent of the Village Prose movement of the 1960s and 1970s and so much in contrast with both the triumphalist communist narrative of construction and the urban modernism of the architectural journals. He asks for Mother Nature's forgiveness as he glances first toward Tol'iatti, "calm and triumphant" across the reservoir/sea, and then toward the Zhiguli Hills, scarred by explosives that extracted the materials used in the production of the large concrete panels. He also tells Viktor that his son's work at VAZ is "evil" because it promotes automobile dependence, a "narcotic" that is poisoning the atmosphere and, who knows, "might be the beginning of the degradation of humanity."[63]

The old city (Stavropol') buried under the water haunts the novel. One character refers to the legend that at low tide one can catch a glimpse of the Troitskii church.[64] The features of the new city—specifically, that portion of it that gives the novel its title—receive surprisingly little attention, perhaps because Avtograd is intended to be a metonym for Soviet power in its last, declining decades. The generic quality of the microdistricts—their lack of a specific connection to this particular part of the country—encourages this abstraction. Besides, VAZ is where the action is. Still, the occasional arch comment makes its way into the text, as in the following passage, in which Larisa, being dropped off by Viktor at the dormitory, says: "Do you know what I think of when I approach these colossal structures? I think that people lose any sense of themselves, become small insects, nonentities, actually nobody. Perhaps the builders specially built them with this subtext so that everyone living here and everyone entering them is turned into a slave deprived of any rights and vested with the obligation only to work."

"Not quite, Larisa," Viktor replies, echoing Astakhov's Obolonkov. "These buildings were constructed with a view toward the future," because every year more and more people are accommodated and the merit of the architects is that they foresaw this.

"Just try living here and associating [poobshchaites'] with people," Larisa retorts. "Especially in the evenings when you sit in your room and are afraid to go out to the street because you're never sure what the gangs of guys want from you. Do you think that all us girls will give themselves to these guys because we are bursting with love? No, it's fear, the most elemental fear of being beaten, clamped down somewhere, and finally raped."[65]

Whether Tol'iatti had "lost something in its spiritual development" and succumbed to "the fate of all our new 'socialist cities,'" as VAZ's assistant director, Stanislav Polikarpov, insisted it had, is at least debatable. One could argue in postmodernist fashion that the gangs of guys roving the streets and interior spaces of the city's microdistricts had desterilized a sterile modernist environment, engaging in what Michel de Certeau has called the "secondary production hidden in the process of utilization."[66] But this would only make Tol'iatti's environment indistinguishable from the projects and mean streets of the bourgeois cities of the West. As a new Soviet city of the sixties, Tol'iatti bore the promise of a departure from older patterns of urban life, of a new beginning—modernity unbound. At the same time, it also inspired among those invested in the grandiose project of heroic socialist construction thoughts of recapturing the spirit that at least in their minds had animated previous projects, thereby knitting them to earlier generations. But the trouble was that as the product of Soviet urban planning of the 1960s—which itself owed a great deal to Western avatars—Tol'iatti could not provide a better, more democratic version of urban living under socialism. Rather, it reproduced on an even larger scale some of the least appealing aspects of high-rise urban living. Obviously, before there could be a Soviet "sixties" there had to be a Soviet fifties. But perhaps the "separate theme, large and instructive," that Polikarpov could not acknowledge was that the dreams of the Soviet sixties did produce the lived experience of the Soviet seventies.

Notes

The chapter epigraph is from A. Shavrin, ed., *VAZ: Stranitsy istorii, 1991–1996*, 5 vols. (Tol'iatti: AVTOVAZ, 1997), 1:44. Polikarpov was reflecting back from the perspective of the mid-1990s.

1. The official name of the enterprise changed several times. Generally, it was known as VAZ in the Soviet period and as AVTOVAZ (or AvtoVAZ) after 1991. For the sake of consistency, I use VAZ in the text.

2. The locus classicus of this historiography is probably *The Soviet Union since Stalin*, ed. Stephen F. Cohen, Alexander Rabinowitch, and Robert Sharlet (Bloomington: Indiana University Press, 1980). See in particular Stephen F. Cohen, "The Friends and Foes of Change: Reformism and Conservatism in the Soviet Union," 17: "The overthrow of Khrushchev in October 1964 . . . ushered in . . . a far-reaching conservative reaction, which brought an end to major reform, and even some counterreform in most areas of Soviet society." For a recent variant by a former Soviet dissident who identifies with the New Left, see Boris Kagarlitsky, "The 1960s East and West: The Nature of the *Shestidesiatniki* and the New Left," *boundary 2* 36, no. 1 (2009): 95–104.

3. Catherine Cooke, preface to *Style and Socialism: Modernity and Material Culture in Post-War Eastern Europe*, ed. Susan E. Reid and David Crowley (Oxford: Berg, 2000), vii.

4. See R. A. French, "The Individuality of the Soviet City," in *The Socialist City: Spatial Structure and Urban Policy*, ed. R. A. French and F. E. Ian Hamilton (Chichester: John Wiley and Sons, 1979), 74: "It is extremely doubtful if a single town in the U.S.S.R. today conforms precisely to the ideal model of the Soviet urban planners." Cf. James C. Scott, *Seeing Like a State: How Certain Schemes to Improve the Human Condition Have Failed* (New Haven: Yale University Press, 1998), 117: "No utopian city gets built precisely as designed by its prophet-architect."

5. Henri Lefebvre, *The Production of Space*, trans. Donald Nicholson-Smith (Oxford: Blackwell, 1991), 53–55.

6. Kate Brown, "Gridded Lives: Why Kazakhstan and Montana Are Nearly the Same Place," *American Historical Review* 106, no. 1 (February 2001): 22–23, and *A Biography of No Place: From Ethnic Borderland to Soviet Heartland* (Cambridge, MA: Harvard University Press, 2003), 83, 115–16.

7. Thomas Lahusen, *How Life Writes the Book: Real Socialism and Socialist Realism in Stalin's Russia* (Ithaca: Cornell University Press, 1997). See also Marina Kuz'mina, *Komsomol'sk-na-Amure: Legendy, mify, i real'nost'* (Komsomol'sk-na-Amure: "Memorial," 2002).

8. Alexei Gutnov et al., *The Ideal Communist City*, trans. Renee Neu Watkins (New York: Braziller, 1971), 7. The book was translated from *Idee per la citta communista*, the Italian version published in Milan in 1968. According to Pierre Merlin, professor at Paris I–Sorbonne and president of the French Institute of Urbanism, more than a thousand new towns had been built in the USSR accommodating more than forty million people—a quarter of the urban population of the entire country. Pierre Merlin, "Les villes nouvelles d'URSS," in *From Garden City to Urban Reconstruction: New Towns in Perspective*, ed. Pierre Merlin and Michel Sudarskis (The Hague: INTA/AIVN, 1991), 89.

9. M. V. Posokhin et al., eds., *Gradostroitel'stvo SSSR, 1917–1967* (Moscow: Izd.lit. po stroi, 1967), 317.

10. Chauncy D. Harris, *Cities of the Soviet Union: Studies in Their Functions, Size, Density, and Growth* (Chicago: Rand McNally, 1970), 54–115; V. A. Vorotilov, ed., *Krupnyi gorod: Problemy i tendentsii razvitiia* (Leningrad: Nauka, 1988), 3–4. For a recent overview of approaches to cities in communist Eastern Europe (primarily the GDR and the Soviet Union), see Thomas M. Bohn [Tomas M. Bon], "'Sotsialisticheskii gorod' ili 'Evropeiskii gorod': Urbanizatsiia i ruralizatsiia v vostochnoi Evrope," *Rossiiskaia istoriia*, no. 1 (2009): 65–76.

11. See I. A. Prokhorenko, "Zhilishchno-grazhdanskoe stroitel'stvo v period vozvedeniia Volzhskoi GES im. V. I. Lenina (1950–1958 gg.)," in *Istoriia OAO "Avtovaz": Uroki, problemy, sovremennost'. Materialy I Vserossiiskoi nauchnoi konferentsii, 26–27 noiabria 2003 g.*, ed. A. E. Livshits and P. A. Nakhmanovich (Tol'iatti: AVTOVAZ, TGU, 2003), 176–78.

12. For a compilation of documents and commentary about the Fiat agreement, see A. E. Stepanov, ed., *Kolesa Rossii. Poslednee delo Valletty: Rozhdenie proekta FIAT-SSSR glazami zarubezhnoi pressy (po materialam Istoricheskogo arkhiva AO <FIAT>)* (Tol'iatti: AVTOVAZ, 2007). The awarding to Tol'iatti of a factory dependent on Fiat technical assistance apparently had nothing to do with its name. Quite the contrary. As Stepanov writes (with some exaggeration) elsewhere, "Such are the ironies of history that while Pal'miro Tol'iatti tried to ruin FIAT, the eighty-six-year-old president of FIAT Vittorio Valletta built a giant automobile factory in the city bearing the name of his ideological enemy." Aleksandr Stepanov, *Neskuchnaia kniga: Vvedenie v korporativnuiu istoriiu AVTOVAZa* (Tol'iatti: AVTOVAZ, 2008), 28.

13. Asked decades later whether the decision was the first of its kind to depend on a computer, Polikarpov replied, "In principle, yes, although the last word remained with the Politburo." See A. Shavrin, ed., *VAZ: Stranitsy istorii, 1991–1996*, 5 vols. (Tol'iatti: AVTOVAZ, 1997), 1:42. Intense lobbying efforts by regional party officials helped too. See S. V. Zhuravlev et al., *AVTOVAZ mezhdu proshlym i budushchem: Istoriia volzhskogo avtomobil'nogo zavoda, 1966–2005* (Moscow: RAGS, 2006), 52–54.

14. Jack A. Underhill, *New Soviet Towns: Housing and National Urban Growth Policy* (Washington, DC: U.S. Department of Housing and Urban Development, 1976), 8. See also N. Baranov, *Osnovy sovetskogo gradostroitel'sva*, vol. 3 (Moscow: Stroiizdat, 1967), 26–32.

15. V. Ia. Romaniuk, *VAZ-sem'ia rabochaia* (Kuibyshev: Kuibyshevskoe Knizh. Izd, 1979), 4–5; Shavrin, *VAZ*, 1:53. KamAZ is the name of the giant truck factory at Naberezhnye Chelny; BAM is the acronym for Baikal-Amur Mainline, the railroad built north of the Trans-Siberian in the 1970s and 1980s.

16. Iu. M. Bogomolova, a research fellow at Tol'iatti's historical museum, had it right when she referred to Avtograd as VAZ's "satellite." See her "'Avtograd'-Sputnik volzhskogo avtomobil'nogo zavoda," in Livshits and Nakhmanovich, *Istoriia OAO "Avtovaz*," 179.

17. See Lewis H. Siegelbaum, *Cars for Comrades: The Life of the Soviet Automobile* (Ithaca: Cornell University Press, 2008), 45–50.

18. See *Pravda*, 25 September 1968, 2; 26 September 1968, 2; 16 March 1969, 2; 17 March 1969, 2; 3 June 1970, 2; 11 June 1970, 3.

19. Evgenii Astakhov, *Pravo na biografiiu* (Moscow: Izd. Pol. Lit., 1979), 57–58. Semizorov is the hero of Astakhov's *Put' k dal'nei vershine* (Moscow: Sovremennik, 1976), which was about the building of the hydroelectric station. On the absence of barracks, see also I. M. Popova, "Proektirovanie novogo zhilogo raiona v g. Tol'iatti i ego osobennosti," in Livshits and Nakhmanovich, *Istoriia OAO "Avtovaz,"* 192; and V. M. Pravosud, "Rol' i znachenie sotsial'noi politiki VAZa kak gradoobrazuiushchego predpriiatiia. Uroki, problemy, sovremennost'," in Livshits and Nakhmanovich, *Istoriia OAO "Avtovaz,"* 249–50.

20. James Holston, *The Modernist City: An Anthropological Critique of Brasília* (Chicago: University of Chicago Press, 1989), 206–10.

21. Scott, *Seeing Like a State*, 129. Oscar Niemeyer, the chief architect for Brasília and a longtime member of the Brazilian Communist Party, was the mirror image of Rubanenko et al. (see below) in that, according to Holston, he rejected calls for a more "social architecture" in line with his Marxist beliefs in favor of "formal and technical innovations." See Holston, *Modernist City*, 88.

22. Scott, *Seeing Like a State*, 119.

23. Astakhov, *Pravo na biografiiu*, 23, 36.

24. Rubanenko was head of the housing division and Shkvarikov of town planning. Both were in their late fifties and had considerable practical experience dating back to the 1930s.

25. The linear principle also governed the new Naberezhnye Chelny, designed by a team led by Rubanenko. See Esther Meier, "On the Streets of a Truck-Building City: Naberezhnye Chelny in the Brezhnev Era," in *The Socialist Car: Automobility in the Eastern Bloc*, ed. Lewis H. Siegelbaum (Ithaca: Cornell University Press, 2011), 105–23. Meier traces the origins of the linear city model back to Arturo Soría y Mata, a Spanish urban planner active in the late nineteenth century.

26. "Novye goroda," *Dekorativnoe iskusstvo*, no. 4 (1970): 15–16. Half of this article is devoted to Tol'iatti and consists of an interview with Rubanenko.

27. B. R. Rubanenko, A. S. Obraztsov, and M. K. Savel'ev, *Gorod Tol'iatti: General'nyi plan novoi chasti goroda, proekt I ocheredi stroitel'stva (1968–1971 gg.)* (Tol'iatti: TsNIPI, 1968); I read this version of the plan in the Togliatti State Archive (TGA), also known as Upravlenie po delam arkhivov g. Tol'iatti, f. R-17 (Main Office of Architecture and Urban Planning of the Executive Committee of the Togliatti City Soviet), where it was catalogued as op. 1, d. 287b. For a general discussion of the application of recursion in town planning, see V. Shkvarikov, "Teoreticheskie osnovy formirovaniia sovetskogo goroda," *Arkhitektura SSSR*, no. 2 (1968): 3–6.

28. Mark B. Smith, *Property of Communists: The Urban Housing Program from Stalin to Khrushchev* (DeKalb: Northern Illinois University Press, 2010), 43, 116–21.

29. Ia. I. Myshkovskii, *Zhilishcha raznykh epokh* (Moscow: Stroiizdat, 1975), 50.

30. Ravi Kalia, *Chandigarh: In Search of an Identity* (Carbondale: Southern Illinois University Press, 1987), 106–7; Scott, *Seeing Like a State*, 121; Holston, *Modernist City*, 105, 165–66.

31. Scott, *Seeing Like a State*, 127.

32. John Urry, "The 'System' of Automobility," in *Automobilities*, ed. Mike Featherstone, Nigel Thrift, and John Urry (London: Sage Publications, 2005), 25. See also Kristin Ross, *Fast Cars, Clean Bodies: Decolonization and the Reordering of French Culture* (Cambridge, MA: M.I.T. Press, 1996), 19: "The car *is* the commodity form as such in the twentieth century."

33. Rubanenko, Obraztsov, and Savel'ev, *Gorod Tol'iatti*, 30. On the development of prefabricated panel construction in the USSR, see Smith, *Property of Communists*, 114. For a critical assessment of the use of *tipizatsiia*, see Blair A. Ruble, "From *khrushcheby* to *korobki*," in *Russian Housing in the Modern Age: Design and Social History*, ed. William Craft Brumfield and Blair A. Ruble (Cambridge: Cambridge University Press, 1993), 248–50.

34. See, for example, Yevgenii Ruzhnikov, "A New Town on the Volga," *Architect and Building News*, 22 May 1969, 61–62; V. Adamovich and V. Aronson, "Meditsinskii gorodok v Tol'iatti," *Arkhitektura SSSR*, no. 7 (1971): 16–18.

35. Elke Beyer, "Planning for Mobility: Designing City Centers and New Towns in the USSR and the GDR in the 1960s," in Siegelbaum, *Socialist Car*, 71, 88; Aleksandr Vysokovskii, *Stillborn Environments: The New Soviet Town of the 1960s and Urban Life in Russia Today*, Kennan Institute for Advanced Russian Studies Occasional Paper No. 261 (Washington, DC: Woodrow Wilson Center, 1995), 10. The other new town cited was Zelenograd, built on the outskirts of Moscow.

36. Stephen V. Bittner, "Remembering the Avant-Garde: Moscow Architects and the 'Rehabilitation' of Constructivism, 1961–64," *Kritika* 2, no. 3 (2001): 553–76. See also his *The Many Lives of Khrushchev's Thaw: Experience and Memory in Moscow's Arbat* (Ithaca: Cornell University Press, 2008), 120–40.

37. N. Osterman, "O zhilishche budushchego," *Arkhitektura SSSR*, no. 6 (1967): 30. Osterman was chief architect of the Novye Cheremushki housing project of the late 1950s.

38. L. Kogan, "Urbanizatsiia—Obshchenie—Mikroraion," *Arkhitektura SSSR*, no. 4 (1967): 39–43; Osterman, "O zhilishche budushchego," 30; V. Kazarinova and N. Romm, "Modulor: Le Korbiuz'e v teorii i na praktike," *Arkhitektura SSSR*, no. 8 (1968): 39–43; M. G. Barkhin, *Gorod, 1945–1970: Praktika, proekty, teoriia* (Moscow: Stroiizdat, 1974), 176.

39. Beyer, "Planning for Mobility," 121–23.

40. Marija Dremaite, "Soviet Industrialization of Housing Technologies in the Context of International Modernism" (Working Paper No. 2009_2, Tensions of Europe/Inventing Europe, April 2009, provided to the author), 11–13.

41. See P. A. Sorokin, "Mutual Convergence of the United States and the USSR to the Mixed Sociocultural Type," *International Journal of Comparative Sociology*, no. 1 (1960): 143–76; Marion Levy Jr., *Modernization and the Structure of Societies* (Princeton: Princeton University Press, 1966); J. K. Galbraith, *The New Industrial State* (Boston: Houghton Mifflin, 1967); Alfred G. Meyer, "Theories of Convergence," in *Change in Communist Systems*, ed. Chalmers Johnson (Stanford: Stanford University Press, 1970), 313–42.

42. On Soviet reactions to convergence theory, see Donald R. Kelley, "The Soviet Debate on the Convergence of the American and Soviet Systems," *Polity*, 6, no. 2 (1973): 174–96.

43. For analyses of the massive literature on this subject, see Arnold Buchholz, "The Scientific-Technological Revolution (STR) and Soviet Ideology," *Studies in Soviet Thought* 30 (1985): 337–46; Erik P. Hoffmann and Robbin F. Laird, *Technocratic Socialism: The Soviet Union in the Advanced Industrial Era* (Durham: Duke University Press, 1985), 112–20.

44. *Hyperfactory* is a term I borrow from N. Ia. Shrikh, a VAZ retiree. See his "Osobennosti proektirovaniia, stroitel'stva i razvitiia volzhskogo avtomobil'nogo zavoda," in Livshits and Nakhmanovich, *Istoriia OAO "Avtovaz,"* 134.

45. For Sakharov, according to his recent biographer, convergence "would be the closest thing to an idée fixe in the years" after 1968 when he first mentioned it in print. Jay Bergman, *Meeting the Demands of Reason: The Life and Thought of Andrei Sakharov* (Ithaca: Cornell University Press, 2009), 148.

46. Charles S. Maier, "Consigning the Twentieth Century to History: Alternative Narratives for the Modern Era," *American Historical Review* 105, no. 3 (June 2000): 807–31; Scott Lash and John Urry, *The End of Organized Capitalism* (Madison: University of Wisconsin Press, 1987); David Harvey, *The Condition of Postmodernity: An Enquiry into the Origins of Cultural Change* (Oxford: Blackwell, 1990).

47. Lefebvre, *Production of Space*, 43, 53–55, 124, 303–8. For an alternative interpretation emphasizing the evangelical thrust of post–World War I modernist urban planning, see Iain Boyd Whyte, ed., *Modernism and the Spirit of the City* (London: Routledge, 2003), 1–31.

48. Bogomolova, "'Avtograd'-Sputnik," 181.

49. See Zhuravlev, *AVTOVAZ mezhdu proshlym i budushchem*, 151. For more population data, see Siegelbaum, *Cars for Comrades*, 104–5.

50. Zhuravlev, *AVTOVAZ mezhdu proshlym i budushchem*, 151.

51. Merlin, "Villes nouvelles d'URSS," 96.

52. Zhuravlev, *AVTOVAZ mezhdu proshlym i budushchem*, 151. The source—a letter sent to Mikhail Suslov by the secretary of Tol'iatti's party committee *(gorkom)*, VAZ's general director, and another delegate to the party's Twenty-Fifth Congress—does not indicate how demand for services was determined. The letter is in TGA, f. R-352, op. 2, d. 591, ll. 18–19. Seven years later, in 1983, fulfillment of demand for services (by a population that had doubled in the interim) had risen to a reported 60 percent. Bogomolova, "'Avtograd'-Sputnik," 179–81.

53. Thomas M. Poulsen, "Urban Forms and Infrastructure in the Soviet Union," in *Soviet Housing and Urban Design*, ed. Steven A. Grant (Washington, DC: Woodrow Wilson Center, U.S. Government Printing Center, 1980), 16.

54. Ruble, "From *khrushcheby* to *korobki*," 250–51. A graduate student at Tol'iatti State University wrote that the "lack of decorative sculptural forms [and] cozy corners deprives the city's atmosphere of warmth and humanity." See Popova, "Proektirovanie novogo zhilogo raiona," 194.

55. Bogomolova, "'Avtograd'-Sputnik," 181; Zhuravlev, *AVTOVAZ mezhdu proshlym i budushchem*, 155. Theft (from VAZ) was another dimension of the subculture. On its dimensions, see the memo from N. A. Shchelokov, minister of internal affairs, to VAZ officials, June 1981, in *Shagi derznovenii*, ed. A. E. Stepanov (Tol'iatti: OAO "AVTOVAZ," 2006), 523–25, and Siegelbaum, *Cars for Comrades*, 107, 114.

56. Ian Frazier, "Utopia, the Bronx: Co-op City and Its People," *New Yorker*, 26 June 2006, 54–65. My awareness of Co-op City's potential for comparison has been enhanced by Ari Sammartino of Oberlin College, who is working on a project entitled "Freedomland: Mass Housing and Urban Crisis in New York and East Berlin, 1965–2000." For an autobiographical account of growing up in Co-op City, see Michael J. Agovino, *Bookmaker: A Memoir of Money, Luck, and Family from the Utopian Outskirts of New York City* (New York: Harper, 2008).

57. Ruble, "From *khrushcheby* to *korobki*," 251–54.

58. For a retrospective account by one of its practitioners, see Vladimir Shlapentokh, *The Politics of Sociology in the Soviet Union* (Boulder, CO: Westview Press, 1987), 22–55, 157–62. On urban sociology, see O. Ianitskii, "Sotsiologiia goroda," in *Sotsiologiia v Rossii*, ed. V. A. Iadov (Moscow: Institut sotsiologii RAN, 1998), 150–59. For a collection of relevant documents, see *Sotsiologiia i Vlast', 1969–1972, Dokumenty*, vol. 2, ed. G. V. Osipov et al. (Moscow: Akademiia, 2001); see also the sub-bibliography of sociological studies entitled "Social Structure of the City: The Issue of Housing," in Mervyn Matthews's *Soviet Sociology, 1964–75: A Bibliography* (New York: Praeger, 1978), 61–65.

59. Astakhov, *Pravo na biografiiu*, 62–63, 70.

60. Ibid., 294–95, 303, 304.

61. V. P. Volochilov, *Avtograd: Roman* (Samara: Samarskoe knizhnoe iz-vo, 1994), 9.

62. Ibid., 17–21. On the ecological damage to the Volga resulting from the dam, see P. S. Kabytov and G. A. Romanova, "Razvitie promyshlennogo potentsiala Kuibyshevskogo regiona v 1955–1965 gg.," in *Istoriia OAO "Avtovaz": Uroki, problemy, sovremennost'. Materialy II Vserossiiskoi nauchnoi konferentsii, 26–27 oktiabria 2005 g.*, ed. R. G. Pikhoia (Tol'iatti: AVTOVAZ, 2005), 125–27.

63. Volochilov, *Avtograd*, 61–62. On Village Prose, see Kathleen F. Parthé, *Russian Village Prose: The Radiant Past* (Princeton: Princeton University Press, 1992); and V. Akimov, *Chelovek i vremia: Putevaia proza: Otkrytiia i uroki* (Moscow: Sov. pisatel', 1986). For a classic study of the larger theme of the contrast between the city and the countryside in literature, see Raymond Williams, *The Country and the City* (London: Chatto and Windus, 1973).

64. Volochilov, *Avtograd*, 139–40.

65. Ibid., 171–72.

66. Michel de Certeau, *The Practice of Everyday Life* (Berkeley: University of California Press, 1984), xiii.

3 Sputnik Premiers in Havana

A Historical Ethnography
of the 1960 Soviet Exposition

João Felipe Gonçalves

CUBA TODAY ABOUNDS in reminders of the strong connection it once had with the Soviet Union and socialist Eastern Europe. Throughout the island, Hungarian buses shuttle the staff of many work centers; Soviet air conditioners make the summer heat more bearable; Ladas and *polaquitos* (Poland-made Fiats) are a common sight in the streets. Socialist housing estates dot Cuban urban landscapes, and Soviet references are present in the names of places such as Havana's vast Parque Lenin and small Seriozha store. Movie theaters often hold Eastern European film festivals, and Russian or Russian-inspired names are part of the ordinary repertoire of Cuban first names. In Cuban homes, libraries, and used bookstores, bookshelves boast publications such as guidebooks to East Germany and coffee table books on Bulgarian art. Cubans raised before 1990 remember their childhoods as a time in which they watched Russian cartoons and ate Bulgarian cabbage. More than that, thousands of them spent years as students or employees in Eastern Europe and the Soviet Union, and many more cultivate fond memories of their tourism or work trips to the former socialist bloc.[1]

These examples point to the fact that life in socialist Cuba has been deeply shaped by connections to the distant world area where state socialism first flourished. Obvious as this point might seem, its importance has typically been overlooked in analyses of socialism in Cuba. Because of the island's geographical location, its similarities and ties with other Latin American countries, and the canonical contours of area studies, Cuba has mostly been studied within the Latin American context.[2] There is nothing inherently wrong with this perspective, but because of its one-sidedness it has tended to obscure important and influential links the country has had with other world areas.

This tendency has been partly corrected by scholars who have examined the cultural connections between pre-1959 Cuba and the United States, but a similar effort remains to be made in relation to the socialist bloc, which for decades represented much of the island's exchanges with the rest of the world.[3] Recent works on Cuba have begun a comparative dialogue with theories of socialism and postsocialism, but they have focused on how these theories can illuminate the Cuban case and vice versa, rather than on links and exchanges between Cuba and other socialist areas.[4]

As a modest contribution to the analysis of those connections, this chapter focuses on a foundational event that took place in Havana in February 1960: the Soviet Exposition of Science, Technique and Culture. This exposition—which predated the official adoption of socialism in Cuba by more than a year—represented the first major contact of the Cuban public with Soviet culture. It brought to the island Soviet goods as diverse as clothing items, domestic appliances, magazines, cameras, drinks, and cars. It acquainted Cubans with Soviet cinema, literature, and music; it showed visitors large models of places such as a nuclear plant and a high-technology airport; and it showcased replicas of a comfortable Soviet apartment and of Soviet artificial satellites. For most Havanans this was also the first opportunity to come into contact with actual Soviet people, such as the ninety experts that worked on the installation of the exhibits and the fifty-seven officials, security personnel, journalists, interpreters, flight crew, and artists that came for the dedication ceremony.[5] All this movement aroused much curiosity and controversy, and even physical fights among Cubans, who for the first time encountered a universe that would become an important part of their lives for the following few decades.

This crucial event is testimony to the importance of the 1960s for the establishment of a regular circulation of goods, people, and culture between Cuba and the Eurasian socialist bloc, especially the Soviet Union. In the two years following the revolutionary seizure of power, the ongoing debate on whether Cuba should take a socialist path was to a large extent a debate on the achievements and limitations of state socialism in the Soviet Union and Eastern Europe. The Soviet Exposition was a landmark in that debate, since it contributed to the polarization of Cubans between those who embraced and those who opposed state socialism, opening cleavages along the political and ideological fault lines that underlay Cuban society at the dawn of the 1960s. The Exposition and its repercussions show how growing ties with the socialist bloc contributed to Cuba's adoption of socialism, which in turn led to more and stronger ties with Eastern Europe and the USSR. The rise and consolidation of state socialism in Cuba throughout that decade was inherently linked to increasing exchanges with the center of the socialist world—a connection that would only intensify during the 1970s and 1980s, and the impacts of which one easily sees in Cuba today.[6]

This chapter thus claims that focusing on the links with the socialist world can help us better understand Cuban socialism. But it also argues that the reverse is equally true—that is, including Cuba as part and parcel of the socialist world can provide a more complex and accurate understanding of state socialism. Cuba's embrace of social-ism in the sixties was actually an important step in the expansion of state socialism to formerly colonized areas of the world during the Cold War. The rise of state social-ism in Cuba shared several features with processes that brought that system to newly independent nations. Although Cuba had formally been independent since 1902, the 1959 Revolution was predicated on the same ideals as those of the anticolonial struggle in Africa and Asia: national sovereignty, social justice, and development.[7] Not only did the Cuban rebels end a regime that had long been supported by the United States, but their struggle was framed as one against Cuba's decades-long economic and political dependence on its powerful neighbor.[8] When the regime declared itself socialist in 1961, it presented socialism as the only way to overcome imperialism and underdevel-opment. In the words of Marifeli Pérez-Stable, "Consolidating a nationalist revolution led Cuba to socialism."[9] In that sense, the Cuban Revolution is a link in a long chain: if it followed nations such as North Korea and North Vietnam, it also had an impact on the spread and consolidation of socialism in other new nations by giving greater validity to the idea that this system could lead to national sovereignty and modernity.

In this chapter I want to use the Soviet Exposition in Havana to explore three ana-lytical consequences of the expansion of state socialism into postcolonial areas during the Cold War. First, this expansion led to an unexpected circulation of goods, people, and information along new channels and across discontinuous world areas. Socialist culture was increasingly being produced and circulated far beyond Eastern Europe and the Soviet Union, and "the socialist world" was getting broader and more diverse. The Cuban case provides several examples: Cuban sugar became massively consumed in the USSR; a major Cuban song became popular in Vietnam; Cuban guerrillas became models for Angolan and Congolese fighters; a housing estate named Havanna was built in Budapest; Cuban films were shown in the GDR, Poland, and Czechoslova-kia; and Eastern European technicians and tourists roamed in Cuba alongside African and Latin American students.[10]

Second, the analysis of the transition to socialism in places such as Cuba cor-rects and moderates the current analytical emphasis on similarities and convergences between capitalism and socialism. Authors such as Susan Buck-Morss have argued that the opposition between the two systems conceals important commonalities: the ideology of mass sovereignty, the promise of industrial modernity, the affirmation of material progress and mass utopia.[11] Historians have pointed to further conver-gence between the two systems when the post-Stalinist era brought to older socialist countries a concern with consumption and material well-being.[12] I accept both argu-ments, but I believe that they need to be put into perspective. Although socialist and capitalistic ideologies did share many goals, they offered radically different means to achieve them. And as the debates and conflicts in postcolonial contexts make clear, for millions of people the crucial political question during the Cold War was precisely the choice between different means to national affirmation and modernity. Whether one emphasizes the similarities or the differences between socialism and capitalism depends largely on one's analytical goals. But the divergences, not the similarities, between the two systems were what mattered politically in Cold War contexts where the choice between them was still an open question.

Third, focusing on the adoption of state socialism in postcolonial settings such as Cuba refines our understanding of the relationship between socialism and nationalism. Because nationalist concerns and discourses were prominent during the events surrounding the collapse of socialism in the USSR and Eastern Europe, and because theorists have tended to see nationalism as fundamentally related to capitalism, scholars typically treat nationalism and state socialism as intrinsically antagonistic to each other. Even sophisticated analysts of nationalism in socialist contexts uncritically suppose a contradiction between the two phenomena. Against this view, the development of state socialism in postcolonial contexts reminds us that socialism has often been embraced as a way to national sovereignty and that in several empirical cases an intrinsically symbiotic relationship exists between nationalism and state socialism.

In what follows, I interpret the impact of the 1960 Soviet Exposition in Havana as a way to explore these three analytical points. After an overview of Cuba's transition to socialism, I describe the Exposition as an example of shifting circulation patterns related to the expansion of state socialism. After that, I discuss the reception of the Exposition in Cuba and the controversies and conflicts it created in order to analyze the ideological and discursive field of debate over the validity of socialism in Cuba. I will show how supporters of capitalism and socialism fought over the different means to achieve the shared valued goals of national development and sovereignty.

Cuba's Transition to Socialism

When the three-year-long armed struggle against dictator Fulgencio Batista ended successfully, on 1 January 1959, there was no claim that Cuba had experienced or was entering a socialist revolution. The revolutionaries, united mostly by the goal of overthrowing the dictator, had a broad and vague political program and enjoyed nearly universal support across all classes. And whereas the upper classes had mostly supported the revolutionaries, Cuban communists had participated only reluctantly and marginally in the struggle. The group that had led the rebellion—the 26 July Movement (M-26-7)—had a reformist platform, in the tradition of Latin American populism: import-substitution industrialization, economic diversification, limited agrarian reform, support of national capital, a social pact between capital and labor mediated by the state, and redistribution of wealth through labor rights and salary raises. Throughout 1959 and 1960 Fidel Castro, the charismatic leader of the M-26-7 and Cuba's de facto ruler, described Cuban industrialists as an important part of the revolutionary class alliance, repeatedly proclaiming that the Revolution was committed to social justice and anti-imperialism but was not communist.[13] He many times stated that the Cuban Revolution was neither capitalist nor communist, and he reaffirmed its nationalist character by saying, "It is its own kind of revolution. . . . This is a native Cuban revolution, as Cuban as our music, because each people has its distinctive music and its distinctive mentality." If the revolutionary government defended the poor, he said, it was because its ideology was "humanism," not communism: "Our revolution is humanistic because it humanizes man. This is what the capitalists democratically proclaim, but nonetheless they mercilessly sacrifice man, which is also done in the communist states."[14]

Nevertheless, on 16 April 1961, the same leader proclaimed to a feverish crowd in Havana that Cuba had made a socialist revolution, thus publicly acknowledging what was already evident by then: Cuba had become a socialist country. By that date, all industry and major commerce had become state owned; latifundia and foreign-owned rural property had been nationalized; urban real estate had been largely redistributed, much of it having been confiscated; all of the press was owned by the state; the opposition had been silenced; civil society associations had either disappeared or been integrated into a tight-knit state institutional apparatus. Most of Cuba's external commercial and financial ties were now with the socialist bloc, and the United States had imposed a commercial embargo on the island and had broken diplomatic relations with it.

It was throughout the years of 1959 and 1960, therefore, that Cuba experienced its real socialist revolution, a deep transformation of its economic, political, and social structures. This period also saw an actual class struggle in the country, with different sectors of the upper classes gradually uniting in opposition, the lower classes becoming the regime's major beneficiary and source of support, and the middle class splitting between supporters and opponents of the new policies. The radicalization process was mostly unplanned and improvised, following an escalation pattern in which the two poles of the Cold War played a crucial role. Besides internal class conflicts, Cuba was led to socialism by a crescendo produced by the interplay between a populist leadership, a hostile United States, and a supportive Soviet Union.

The first reformist measures taken by the new Cuban government were similar to those taken years earlier in countries like Argentina, Brazil, and Mexico, where they had met with little resistance by the United States. However, because the American economic, political, and military presence was much more significant and direct in Cuba than in those countries, as early as 1959 the United States responded with threats to the government's anti-imperialist rhetoric and to measures such as the institution of labor rights, wage raises, progressive taxation, and the first (moderate) agrarian and urban reforms. The United States talked of reducing its purchase of Cuban sugar and gave shelter to a growing number of exiles, even harboring and assisting sabotage operations that some of them conducted against Cuba. Every new progressive step the Cuban government took was met with greater support and demands from the working classes and greater resistance from the upper classes and the United States. This antagonism only led the Cuban government to further radicalization, especially when the USSR started giving signals of support.

In that regard, February 1960 was a crucial moment for the turn toward socialism. That month, the second most powerful man in the USSR, First Deputy Premier Anastas Mikoian, came to Cuba to personally dedicate the Soviet Exposition and stayed for a ten-day tour of the island. As a result of that visit, Cuba reestablished diplomatic relations with the USSR, signed a five-year trade agreement with that country, and obtained a $100 million credit to buy Soviet industrial equipment. This accelerated the snowball effect in which American retaliations, the rapprochement with the socialist bloc, and the radicalization of policies fed each other. Particularly important for this chapter is the fact that the first major links with the socialist bloc at the time of the Soviet Exposition contributed to the establishment of state socialism in Cuba, which in its turn would strengthen and expand the connections with the USSR and its allies.[15]

Until February 1960, despite the growing power of communists in the government and the inflamed public debates on whether Cuba was adopting or should adopt socialism as a system, reforms had been kept within a capitalist framework. After that month, though, when foreign refineries refused to process the newly bought Soviet oil, the Cuban state nationalized them—a step to which the United States responded by reducing the purchase of Cuban sugar. As a result, the socialist bloc started buying more Cuban sugar and Cuba expropriated more U.S. businesses on the island. This led the U.S. government to declare an economic embargo on Cuba in early October 1960, which was immediately followed by the first massive expropriation of Cuban-owned private property, including all major commerce and industry. With this move, Cuba effectively established a socialist economy. The United States reacted by breaking diplomatic relations with the country and secretly supporting the failed Bay of Pigs invasion, on the eve of which Fidel Castro announced the obvious—that Cuba had now accomplished a socialist revolution.[16]

The Soviet Exposition happened thus in a moment in which the new government explicitly denied any socialist orientation and had not gone beyond populist reforms within capitalism. But hostility from the United States was growing, and the most radical members of the government—like Che Guevara and the pre-1959 communists—were becoming more influential. Cubans were openly and heatedly debating the meaning of the term *revolution*. The celebration of this fetishized entity was nearly universal, and there was little public contestation that the Revolution and the nation were inextricably related: being against the Revolution meant being against Cuba's sovereignty. Louis A. Pérez Jr. described this as an "extraordinary enthusiasm for *la revolución,* and as ambiguously defined as it was, it could mean all things to all people. Aroused too was a powerful surge of nationalism, one summoned by the revolution and soon indistinguishable from it."[17] Those who disagreed on the identification between these two entities had to either keep silent or leave the country: "Unable to oppose the revolution, disaffected Cubans left by the tens of thousands."[18] However, the key question, which created deep antagonisms and open conflicts, was how that identification between nation and Revolution translated into concrete political terms. How radical was or should be the Revolution? Was socialism the culmination or the betrayal of the Revolution? Was socialism the safeguard of or a threat to national sovereignty? And given that counterrevolutionaries (now mostly exiled, killed, or imprisoned) accused the Revolution of being communist, could one be anticommunist and still remain a revolutionary?

These debates and conflicts took place among great collective effervescence. Excitement and movement permeated Cuba in the transitional period between 1959 and 1961: frequent protests and celebrations filled streets and plazas with unprecedented crowds; defense militias were formed and trained throughout the country; people passionately discussed politics in street corners and cafés.[19] Enemies and heroes were constructed everywhere. Pictures in the press graphically revealed Batista's horrible crimes, and angered crowds yelled in the streets demanding the shooting of individuals involved in the dictatorship (who were often executed without due trial).[20] In contrast, images of heroic guerrillas proliferated: their hypermasculine figures appeared in photographs sold in the streets, in films, on TV shows, on postage stamps, on windshield stickers, in literacy primers, and in advertisements for milk, department stores, clothes, and distributors of drinks.[21]

Movements of people took spectacular proportions from the very beginning of this period. When the dictatorship fell, revolutionaries led by Fidel Castro crossed the island in a six-hundred-mile motorcade, triumphantly greeted in every town between Santiago de Cuba and Havana.[22] And before the new exodus from the island took massive proportions, thousands returned to Cuba from the exile that they had suffered under Batista.[23] All new national ritual celebrations involved performative movement: May Day 1959 inaugurated the tradition of a massive parade in Havana, and the anniversary of the beginning of the Revolution (26 July) brought to the capital thousands of peasants sporting machetes and straw hats.[24] In April, Havanans flocked to the streets to clean and paint up buildings and streets, in a state-run operation establishing a custom of voluntary work that survives to this day.[25] Fidel Castro's speeches often brought an alleged one million frenzied people—or two-thirds of Havana's population—to the city's central plazas.[26]

The Soviet Union in Havana

The Soviet Exposition not only came to Cuba in a very effervescent time but also occupied a conspicuous central location: the Palace of Fine Arts in downtown Havana. This museum was surrounded by landmarks of great symbolic and political significance: it faced a small square across from which stood the Presidential Palace, and it was located only a few blocks away from the country's massive Capitol and from Havana's central plaza. Occupying two city blocks between the city's colonial core and its turn-of-the-century shopping district, the modernist building contrasts to this day with the surrounding older ornate edifices.[27] During the transition to socialism, this dense area, besides its customary heavy pedestrian traffic, often attracted massive crowds that flocked to its public spaces to attend patriotic rituals, political protests, and speeches by Fidel Castro.[28]

From its installation until its closing, the Soviet Exposition brought even more crowds to the area. Charging a ten-cent entrance fee, it was open to the public for nine to ten hours every day for three weeks, at the end of which it may have received one million visits.[29] By transforming one of Havana's most important public buildings into a showcase for Soviet achievements, the Exposition was one of the first decidedly socialist interventions in the city's landscape. It placed symbols of the distant socialist superpower in the very symbolic center of the Cuban capital. The main facade of the building was covered with a large Cuban flag next to giant letters composing the acronym URSS, and one of its sides sported a three-meter-high Soviet coat of arms. Passersby could admire Soviet automobiles on display outside the museum, while replicas of Sputnik I and III hung over the visitors' heads in its central courtyard.

Sputnik III—the official symbol of the event, widely reproduced in posters and advertisements—was apparently one of the public's favorite objects, together with other satellites and rocket capsules. The Exposition certainly presented the Soviet success in the space race as an important theme, but it also displayed a broad inventory of Soviet material culture. Often explained by educational panels, the items shown ranged from watches and music albums to a TV studio and remote-controlled tractors, through medical equipment and motorcycles. The exhibition grounds covered over ninety-five thousand square feet, distributed in sections such as "Agriculture," "Nuclear Energy in the Service of Peace," "Construction and Architecture," and "The Well-Being of the Soviet Man."

But this large exposition was not originally created to be displayed in Cuba. Part of a greater Khrushchev-era effort to impress the capitalist world, it came to Cuba only because it had been shown in 1959 in New York, where it was visited by the influential Cuban revolutionary Antonio Núñez Jiménez. It was he who, when the Cuban and Soviet governments started their first talks, proposed to Castro and a Soviet diplomat that the Exposition be brought to Havana after its upcoming display in Mexico City.[30]

Before coming to the Americas, though, the Exposition had been first designed as the Soviet Pavilion for the 1958 Brussels World Fair. In her detailed work on the planning of that pavilion, Susan Reid argues that it was the result of a compromise between different conceptions within Soviet bureaucracy of how to best represent and publicize the country to the West.[31] As such, the Soviet Pavilion in Brussels emphasized both production, machinery, and industry, on the one hand, and consumer goods, leisure, and rising living standards, on the other. This double focus signaled that, in addition to socialism's traditional concern with production and heavy industry, the Thaw brought a greater hybridity with capitalist ideals of material comfort and consumption. In both cases, according to Reid, the fundamental goal was to show the West that the socialist system allowed faster development than capitalism, that is, "to emphasize the distance traveled, the progress made since the revolution, and the pace of change."[32]

Since it was the contents of the Brussels Pavilion that came to Havana in 1960, the double focus examined by Reid in fact shaped the Soviet Exposition that Cubans saw. Heavy industry and energy production were represented by some machinery but mainly by automated models—like those of a steel plant, an offshore oil platform, a nuclear plant, and a factory of blocks for prefabricated housing. Miniature machines that reproduced larger machines, these models showed the marvels of Soviet industrialization and introduced Cubans to idealized socialist spaces of production. Other models reproduced cutting-edge means of transportation—like the world's largest passenger airplane and a nuclear-powered icebreaker—and spaces of nonmaterial production—such as a sports complex and Moscow State University. These models, which allowed Cubans to imagine socialist spaces before actually experiencing them, were considerably large, occupying entire rooms and containing structures the height of or even taller than the visitors. Therefore, this dreamworld of large three-dimensional reproductions allowed visitors to see vast spaces and machines in their entirety, from an external viewpoint, but still gave a sense of their grandness, presenting a miniature but monumental socialist world.[33]

In contrast, the representation of socialist consumption and living standards relied on portable commodities: rugs, radios and television sets, canned food, wines, vodkas, clothes (including exotic items like fur coats and hats), vacuum cleaners, refrigerators, tape recorders, perfumes, jewels, vases, cameras, calculators, automobiles, and even a machine that could transmit long-distance facsimiles. A life-size reproduction of a Soviet apartment gave Havanans a more organic idea of how these modern items could be integrated. And for affordable prices they could take home different Soviet consumer items: "books, magazines, stamps, cigarette cases, canned food, vodka; but what really attracts Cubans are the watches. How many have been sold? Thousands. And thousands more will be sold until none is left."[34]

Posters and reproductions of paintings were also sold, exemplifying the Exposition's emphasis on art. Although definitely less prominent than consumer goods and technical production, artwork did represent a third minor theme of the event. At the entrance to the exhibition, visitors were welcomed by a larger-than-life socialist-realist sculpture of a hammer-holding worker, behind which stood a mural representing Moscow architectural landmarks juxtaposed with the Havana seashore. A special "Art and Culture" section displayed pictures and informative panels on Soviet performative and visual arts, and scattered throughout the Exposition were screens showing excerpts of Soviet movies and sculptures representing categories of people, such as sportsmen and children, and individual figures like Leo Tolstoy.[35]

The Exposition also provided the occasion for several Soviet cultural events in Havana beyond the confines of the museum. Cuba's most important publication on the arts, *Lunes de Revolución* (Mondays of Revolution), published a special issue on the USSR and the Exposition, featuring pieces of Soviet literature, interviews with Soviet artists, and essays on Soviet culture.[36] And although Cubans had known classic Russian composers for decades, the Soviet Exposition allowed them a closer encounter with Soviet music. Composer Aram Khachaturian and violinist Leonid Kogan, among other Soviet musicians, gave at least three concerts in the week of the Exposition opening—including one performed for the workers who were building the new National Theater. Another concert, featuring exclusively songs by Khachaturian, had Mikoian and Cuban authorities in the audience, but free tickets had been distributed to the larger public and it was also broadcast on television.[37] Soviet movies were present in two of the most important theaters in the city on the occasion of the Exposition—one played Sergei Iutkevich's *Othello* for a week, and the other housed a two-week festival of Soviet cinema, screening classics like *Battleship Potemkin* and recent films like Ivan Pyr'ev's *The Idiot*.[38] Havana was home to an avid cinema public, but until then it had been heavily oriented toward Hollywood—and, to a lesser extent, Mexican—cinema. The Soviet Exposition was the occasion of Cuba's first exposure to a cinema that would soon become a centerpiece of its movie theaters.[39]

Of course, it was not only Soviet movies and contemporary music that came as a novelty to Havana in February 1960. The whole Soviet Exposition was a veritable shock exposure of Cubans to Soviet culture—especially (but not only) material culture. Journalist José Rivero wrote that, coming back from a trip to the United States that month, he encountered so many "Russian" things, events, and people that "I thought I had arrived, not in Havana, but in Moscow."[40] This was surely an exaggerated claim, but that the event bothered Rivero so much is a sign of its impact. What he did not know (but probably feared) was that the Exposition was the founding moment of the long familiarity that Cubans would develop throughout the following decade with Soviet objects, people, and media. With this event, a brave new material world arrived on Cuban shores.

Encapsulated in one building for three weeks one found a whole repertoire of things Soviet that soon became part of life in Cuba: cars, cameras, domestic appliances, heavy machinery, medical equipment, books, canned food.[41] Cubans also became acquainted on that occasion with less material items—like the metric system, Soviet cinema, and images of Soviet supremacy in space—that would become a naturalized part of the Cuban cultural horizon throughout the 1960s. Another novelty that came to stay was the juxtaposition of symbols of the two countries, a practice introduced in this event—as with the Cuban flag and the Soviet coat of arms on the museum's facades—that would become a standard motif for many years to come. Soviet ships like the one that brought the Exposition materials to Havana would also become a common sight at Havana's harbor. And the small flood of Soviet personnel that generated so much curiosity during the time of the Exposition was an announcement of the growing number of Soviet technicians, instructors, tourists, and bureaucrats that would soon arrive on the island.[42] In the next few years *los rusos* (the Russians) became a taken-for-granted part of the Cuban human landscape, as North Americans had been until then.[43]

The 1960 Soviet Exposition in Havana provides a good example of the new circulation of goods, people, and information brought about by the postwar expansion of socialism. As state socialism took root in noncontiguous areas of the globe, it changed traditional exchange patterns and created an alternative sphere of circulation that broadened, diversified, and intensified throughout the 1960s. Until the late 1950s, Cuba's material culture and cultural references were heavily influenced by models from the United States, partly thanks to frequent, easy, and fast transportation and communication by cable, air, and sea. Cubans had long been heavy consumers of American movies, music, food, sports, magazines, architectural styles, electric appliances, automobiles, urban planning, and information.[44] The Soviet Exposition was the point at which items coming from the nearest mainland started being increasingly replaced by items of the same kind coming from the other side of the world.[45]

Discussing late twentieth- and early twenty-first-century theories of globalization, anthropologist James Ferguson argues that the metaphor of "flows" predominantly used to describe global movements is inadequate because "movements of capital . . . jump from point to point, and huge regions are simply bypassed. Capital does not 'flow' . . . ; it hops, neatly skipping over most of what lies in between."[46] If we extend Ferguson's observation from capital to movements of goods, people, and information, it becomes particularly apt to describe movements created by the postwar expansion of state socialism to areas far away from Eastern Europe and the USSR. Especially in the 1960s, there was an increase and diversification of "jumps" and "hops" of objects, people, and culture in the growing socialist world, creating alternative circulation patterns that helped shape a diverse socialist culture throughout the decade.[47] Havana's Soviet Exposition is a prime example of the "hopping" character of many movements occurring in the socialist sixties. The decision of the young Cuban political leadership to invite the Soviets to bring their exposition to the island created a sudden arrival of objects and people from a distant land, constituting a jump that ended up being a crucial moment in the greater jump of socialist culture from Eurasia to Cuba.

Wonders of Soviet Modernity

And the Exposition was indeed a successful jump. Most seemed to agree with a female coffee street vendor who found the event "wonderful because it show[ed] us things we had never seen." The Cuban press was unanimous in describing the excitement of the crowds that flocked to the place for three weeks, coming even from distant provinces.[48] Cuba's most popular weekly, *Bohemia,* reported that the Exposition presented "an astonishing universe" of fantastic machines and that therefore "people's curiosity has no limits in the Soviet Exposition. Men and women, children, and elderly people of all social backgrounds elbow each other in front of the Russian displays with the avidity of those who contemplate a rare spectacle."[49]

Even opponents of socialism typically started their criticism of the Soviet presence in Havana with a caveat praising Soviet progress. A highly critical statement
by the Christian Democratic Movement, for instance, recognized "the technical and
scientific achievements of the Soviet Union."[50] The conservative newspaper *Diario de
la marina* (The Harbor Daily) lamented that the Exposition had created a "frenetic
enthusiasm" and had made Russia "fashionable in Cuba." But even while ferociously
attacking socialism for its despotism and atheism, the editorialist praised the Exposition and Soviet technical progress, or, more precisely, "Russian inventiveness industrially converted into peace machines and war machines."[51]

It is not by chance that these positive comments focused on machines. Much of
the exhibition—whether representing heavy industry, energy production, the space
race, or consumer goods—consisted of machines, which of all items caught the most
attention of visitors. More than that, judging from press reports, the machines often
mystified them. A visitor candidly confessed his bewilderment and difficulty in understanding the functioning of all those devices.[52] In a less self-conscious way, a journalist
showed his limited comprehension by describing an object only as "a machine with a
complicated mechanism that worked automatically though scientifically adapted buttons."[53] More than just a clumsy description, this sentence reveals a fascination with
machinery itself, in which its utility was less important than its magic mechanized
character.

Another writer sarcastically criticized the "emotional descriptions" of Soviet
"mechanical wonders" that he heard from friends who had visited the Exposition. They
marveled, he said, at things like "a strange device that turns around and blows air,"
"a weird four-wheeled moving vehicle," or "a square box which, when one presses an
automatic button, shows an image or a movie," not realizing the objects were simply
an electric fan, a car, and a television set.[54] Although these phrasings were probably
exaggerated, the author's complaint about the transformation of the banal into something unusual points to the fascination that the Exposition's world of machines seems
to have exerted over Cubans. In Havana, as in Brussels in 1958, the Soviets were successful in the mission to impress a Western public with their technical and industrial
progress. Even the staunchest anticommunists and critics of the event admitted that it
demonstrated the Soviet Union's high level of material development.

This was no small accomplishment, since at this time Cubans of all classes, especially in Havana, shared representations of modern living heavily based on the North
American commodities, styles, and ideals that permeated their everyday lives. In the
words of Louis A. Pérez Jr., who abundantly documented that phenomenon in the
prerevolutionary period, "Cubans acquired early the vanity of modernity.... The idea
of the modern was itself associated with material conditions and inevitably involved
vast numbers of Cubans in modern consumer culture."[55] And this sensibility had an
intrinsic relationship to Cuba's powerful northern neighbor: "A great many Cubans
committed themselves to the pursuit of a standard of living derived principally from

North American commodities. . . . Material well-being and moral contentment were intimately associated with the consumption of North American goods."[56]

Still, all sources are unanimous in describing the public's fascination with the machines that the Soviet Exposition displayed. This success in a city with such an Americanized experience of modernity corroborates and can be explained by theorizations on structural similarities between socialism and capitalism, as well as by narratives of growing convergence between the two systems in the Khrushchev era. Regarding the former, the common fascination with machinery and technical development shared by Soviet producers and Cuban consumers of the Exposition evidences the commonalities shared by socialism and capitalism as two faces of a single project of technical-industrial modernity. To use the words of Susan Buck-Morss—one of the best articulators of this now commonly accepted idea—the two systems are "variations of a common theme, the utopian dream that industrial modernity could and would provide happiness for the masses."[57] Without this shared vision of an industrial mass utopia, the machinery and industrial progress displayed in Havana could hardly have generated such excitement.

Similarly, another condition of possibility of this excitement was the consumer orientation taken by the central socialist countries after Stalinism. Susan Reid's statement about the Soviet Union could also be said of countries like Hungary and East Germany: "There is little question that the USSR became a mass consumer society in its last decades, and the late 1950s and 1960s were decisive years in the process by which Soviet citizens developed a sense of entitlement to consume."[58] Socialist expositions in the West were at the forefront of the expression of this new socialist consumerism and have thus been aptly described as "sites of convergence" or "hybridization."[59] Without such a focus on consumer goods, the Soviet Exposition might not have succeeded in a city like the Cuban capital, with its large and consolidated American-style consumer culture and with so many supermarkets, department stores, and car dealerships.[60] The Soviet Exposition might not have been so successful there if, besides Sputniks and automated models, it had not also shown convincing fans, cars, and television sets—and sold those watches that seem to have pleased Cubans so much.[61]

Defending the Revolution, Protesting Socialism

By impressing Cubans with Soviet development, the Exposition was to some extent a site of convergence between Cuban and Soviet ideals of modernity. But the event did not only meet with enthusiasm and praise; it also produced resistance and animosity and led to an open clash between different conceptions of how to reach industrial modernity. The event that allowed closer cultural and economic links between Cuba and the USSR also revealed political tensions and divisions on the island, inflaming the debate on the relationship between its revolution and socialism. This was best expressed by another editorial in *Diario de la marina,* which sarcastically thanked First Deputy Premier Mikoian for a visit and an exposition that had "clarified many things and delineated the [contending] fields"[62]—that is, those for and those against a socialist turn of the Revolution. Its repercussions led to an open—and eventually insurmountable—conflict between defenders and opponents of state socialism, which fed the escalation of events that resulted in full-fledged state socialism. Thus the analysis of the Exposition and its consequences requires us to put into perspective theories of similarities and convergences between socialism and capitalism. It reminds us that in the postcolonial world the sixties were a time of open conflict and choice between the two systems, a time when their differences, not their commonalities, had an urgent political relevance. To explore this point, I will first examine the events that surrounded the dedication of the Exposition.

Anastas Mikoian, the second man in the Soviet political hierarchy, arrived in Cuba on 4 February 1960. The following morning, he performed a protocol ritual act at what was then Havana's most important plaza, Parque Central, accompanied by top commanders of the Cuban Revolution and watched by a large crowd that filled the square. Like all foreigners coming to the country on an official state mission, he laid a wreath of flowers in front of the statue of José Martí, Cuba's foremost national hero. Mikoian then gave a short speech and left for another plaza located two blocks away, in front of the Palace of Fine Arts, to dedicate the Soviet Exposition. Hundreds of people expected him for the ceremony, and he joined major Cuban political figures, including ministers, communist intellectuals, leaders of key revolutionary organizations, and the mayor of Havana, on an open-air platform. The army band played the Cuban and Soviet anthems, but immediately after that gunshots were heard at a distance and policemen and soldiers started running. People started talking about some street fight and sabotage of the event, but the rumors were suffocated by shouts of *¡Viva Cuba Libre!* and the tunes of revolutionary anthems, which the band started playing to distract the crowd. Normalcy returned after some fifteen minutes when Fidel Castro arrived and was received by enthusiastic applause and cries of support. The ceremony was then resumed. Mikoian and the Cuban minister of trade gave speeches, the ribbon was officially cut, and the authorities visited the Exposition.[63]

The gunshots had in fact come from the nearby Parque Central. After Mikoian had left for the dedication ceremony, a number of college students—thirty or one hundred, according to different accounts—arrived at the Parque to protest the homage the Soviet leader had paid to Martí, which they called an offense to Cuba. They held handmade signs with sayings such as "Fidel saved Cuba and Mikoian wants to sink it" and "Neither U.S. imperialism nor Russian totalitarianism," and they shouted, "Long live the Revolution, down with communism!" and "Long live Fidel, down with Mikoian!" Some people who were on the plaza yelled back at the protesters, insulting them and calling them counterrevolutionaries and "Batista's henchmen." Unmoved, the protesters tried to remove the wreath of flowers that lay at the feet of Martí's statue—which represented a globe topped by a hammer and sickle—and to replace it with a wreath they had brought—in the shape of the Cuban flag—but were stopped by the police.

At this point some counterprotesters took the flag-shaped wreath from the students, stomped on it, and burned it. Photographers who were taking pictures were attacked and had their cameras broken, and several physical fights broke out in the area. The police started shooting into the air, and an intense shootout followed. As people ran in different directions and more police and army soldiers arrived from the dedication ceremony, some twenty students—several of them wounded—were arrested and taken to the nearest police station. A furious crowd followed them, shouting a catchphrase that had often been heard in Cuba since January 1959: *¡Paredón! ¡Paredón!* Literally meaning "Firing wall!," this was a demand that the protesters be executed. The crowd stayed outside the police station and kept shouting for nearly two hours. They stopped and dispersed only when the head of the National Police showed up, praised their defense of the Revolution, and guaranteed that the students would be prosecuted.[64] The arrested protesters were released the following day, but the affair was discussed for days in student associations, in labor unions, in the press, and in the streets.[65]

The incident in Parque Central was just the most dramatic and visible event in the ongoing heated debates about the Exposition and the validity of socialism. There was a consensual celebration of "the Revolution," which was so identified with the nation itself that describing oneself as nonrevolutionary (let alone counterrevolutionary) was no longer publicly defensible.[66] With the radicalization of policies and the rapprochement with the USSR, the question that agitated Cuba at the time was whether socialism was conducive or opposed to the major goals and values of the Revolution.

The students that protested in Parque Central represented one of the poles of the debate: they described themselves as both revolutionaries and anticommunists. After the conflict, many voices—including those of moderate newspapers like *Prensa libre* (Free Press)—rose in their defense and criticized the violent reaction to their act. And, although the students' vehemence was perhaps extreme, their basic position—for the Revolution and against communism—was shared by many Cubans, who criticized the Soviet Exposition for having imperialistic goals and showing only one side of socialism. This was the argument, for instance, of a *Prensa libre* editorial that stated, "The Revolution is one thing, and communism is another," adding that the two were in fact contradictory.[67] Others were more compromising, saying that it was fine for Cuba to house a Soviet exposition but that this should not be taken as a show of supporting socialism. A popular newsreel, *Noticuba*, complimented the Soviet "advancements" shown in the Exposition and observed that Cuba welcomed all well-intending foreigners but stressed that "the fact that a state, using its right to broaden its economic and commercial horizon, exhibits its products to another people in no way means that we have to incorporate this [state's] ideology. Let us see this event as a usual practice among free peoples, and nothing more." As if the message were not clear enough, the report was followed by an intertitle that read, "Don't fool yourselves, ladies and gentlemen: the Cuban Revolution is not communist."[68]

Actually, the official line of the government at this time was still that this was *not* a socialist revolution. However, its enthusiastic sponsorship and embrace of the Soviet Exposition and the new trade agreements with the USSR gave much strength to the idea that attacking socialism was equal to attacking the Revolution. From this time on, anticommunism was increasingly seen as a counterrevolutionary attitude. The Exposition also gave a new visibility and power to those who had been communists since before the Revolution. Communist intellectuals received much attention; they appeared on television, published articles, commented on the Exposition and on the USSR.[69] Less publicly, members of the old Communist Party (PSP) grew in influence within the government and in key organizations like the Central Organization of Cuban Trade Unions (CTC).[70] And, what is crucial for my purposes here, the debates on the Soviet Exposition boosted the discourse that associated socialism with two major goals of the Revolution: development and national sovereignty. In what follows, I will discuss how these two master themes structured the polarized debate on the value of socialism at the time.

National Sovereignty and Development

As I discussed above, the Exposition impressed Cubans by showing a high level of development in the USSR, recognized even by its fiercest critics. It is revealing that critics and enthusiasts alike often referred to the Exposition as one of "technical advancement" or "industrial progress," although this was only one of its official themes.[71] Proponents of socialism made an effort to make it clear that this "progress" was the product of the Soviet economic system and not of other factors. On several occasions the visiting Soviet officials repeated this claim, which was the main topic of Mikoian's speech at the dedication of the Exposition. He also emphasized the idea of fast development that, according to Susan Reid, the planners of Brussels' Soviet Pavilion had been keen on transmitting. Comparing the poverty and primitiveness of tsarist Russia to recent Soviet achievements, Mikoian stated in his speech that such a rapid change would have been impossible in capitalism, since it was due to the central planning and lack of exploitation that characterized socialism.[72] Days later, speaking on television, he said that the Cuban Revolution also would make Cuba recover all the time it had lost in its history.[73] He did not explicitly state that for that to happen Cuba had to adopt socialism, but his words at the dedication ceremony, if taken seriously, implied his hopes that Cuba too would quickly overcome its backwardness.

Soviet publicity efforts, especially the demonstration of fast progress, struck sensitive chords with Cubans because of their long-held anxieties about their underdevelopment. Overcoming sugar monoculture, industrializing the country, diversifying the economy, and eliminating poverty had long been the central political concerns of the Cuban public sphere, and the dominant historical narrative of prerevolutionary Cuba is one of failed attempts to achieve development.[74] For socialist-leaning Cubans, the Soviet Exposition showed that socialism was the fastest and safest solution to the problem of underdevelopment, and they spared no efforts to convey this idea. Communist essayist Juan Marinello, for instance, argued that admiring the Exposition entailed recognizing "the greatness inherent in socialism." Praising the economic, social, technical, and scientific successes of a nation that merely "forty-two years ago [was] sunk in the most complete ignorance and slavery," he expressed the hope that Cuba could experience a similar process. For him, only those who did not want "Cuba to be free and prosperous" denied the lessons to be taken from the Exposition.[75] Marinello's speech is an example of the intrinsically nationalistic character of the Cuban obsession with development: the goal was not just development but *national* development.

This economic nationalism translated as a great enthusiasm for the consumption of national products: before being expropriated, even multinational companies advertised their commodities as genuinely Cuban, and when the Soviet Exposition opened in Havana a mobile exhibition of Cuban products was touring the provinces aboard a sixty-five-car train in a campaign called Railroad Action.[76] The seduction that many Cubans saw in the Soviet Exposition, therefore, was not that those wonderful Soviet goods and machines could replace the American commodities they had been consuming for decades, or that Soviet products would become a staple of life in Cuba, as eventually happened. Rather, they hoped that Cuba could do what the USSR had done: diversify its economy, industrialize and modernize itself at a fast pace. More than just a stronger connection with the Soviet Union, admirers of socialism wanted Cuba to be *like* the Soviet Union. An agronomist expressed it poetically by telling how, when he visited the Exposition and saw the marvelous mechanization of *sovkhozes* and *kolkhozes*, "[his] imagination [left] the grounds of the Exposition and start[ed] wandering in the Cuban countryside," for which he dreamt of a similar future.[77] A retired blue-collar worker phrased it more broadly, saying that the Soviet Exposition should "encourage underdeveloped peoples to take the USSR as an example, for in forty-three years it had reached the vanguard of progress and culture."[78]

Given the combination of Cuba's centuries-old capitalist underdevelopment and the Exposition's efficacy in demonstrating stunning Soviet progress, it seemed hard at the time to counter the impression that socialism was the best and fastest road to development. Only on very few occasions did critics of socialism try to show that Soviet development did not translate into material well-being. This was done mainly through visual language, as in two photo collages published by *Bohemia* and the newspaper *Prensa libre* under titles that could be paraphrased as "what is missing in the Soviet Exposition," which showed pictures of shacks, beggars, and female hard labor in the USSR.[79] Most of the time, instead of denying Soviet development, Cuban opponents of socialism resorted to a repertoire of Cold War tropes to highlight what they framed as the costs of that development. The self-justification of one of the student protesters exemplifies that "freedom" and religion figured high among those tropes: he said that the protesters had demonstrated against the envoy of "a totalitarian, enslaving, and completely anti-Christian regime."[80] Not only did the protesters identify themselves as Catholic students, but also some of the voices that defended them had Christian affiliations and evoked religious reasons to attack a system "based on historical materialism, which denies the existence of God, the soul, and all the spiritual world."[81] Still, the prevailing discourse on the costs of Soviet development was based, not on religion, but on liberal-democratic conceptions of "freedom" being suppressed by "despotism." Even a religious-based political movement framed its opposition to socialism, not in religious terms, but as a rejection of "a progress that regresses to times of ignominy and subjugation," based on millions of murders committed by the "bloodiest tyranny in History."[82]

Critics of socialism could hardly portray that system as an impediment to development, but they invested heavily in the argument that socialism was inimical to the other great goal of the Cuban Revolution: national sovereignty. For most Cubans the revolutionary promise to make Cuba truly sovereign and independent meant putting an end to American imperialism, but critics of socialism tried to turn this enthusiastic anti-imperialism against the USSR. They repeatedly accused the Soviet Exposition of being part of a strategy to turn Cuba into another "satellite in Moscow's orbit," noting that "the hammer and sickle . . . have taken away the independence of so many countries."[83] For them, socialism would abort Cuba's dreams of national affirmation.

To make that point, "Hungary" became one of their favorite watchwords, reminding Cubans of that country's recent invasion by the Soviets. On the front page of *Prensa libre* on 6 February, surrounded by stories on the Exposition and next to a photo of Mikoian at Parque Central, a headline read, "Sixty more people executed in Hungary for involvement in the 1956 anti-Russian revolution."[84] Similarly, the above-mentioned photo montage in *Bohemia* showed pictures of tanks in front of damaged buildings in Budapest and of young Hungarians who resisted the Soviets.[85] And in a televised press conference a journalist disconcerted Mikoian by asking his opinion "on the Hungarian case."[86] All these frequent references to Hungary implied that if Cuba embraced socialism it would become, not a superpower like the USSR, but another subjugated peripheral nation.

That Cuba risked replacing one imperialism with another was the topic of a *Prensa libre* article titled "Neither 'cubans' [in English in the original] nor 'cubanski': *Cubanos*," which claimed, "We don't like being anybody's satellites." This text also largely used another common nationalist trope of the critics of the Soviet Exposition, the alleged radical cultural differences between "cold" Soviets and "warm" Cubans: "We prefer our sun, our palm trees; our feelings of love, tolerance, and friendship. Our spirituality. Our cheerfulness."[87] Days later, the same newspaper published a cartoon depicting a Cuban looking at a sign written in Russian and thinking, "They are weird even in writing!"[88] But it was not only the press that used nationalist arguments against the Soviet Exposition and socialism in general. Such arguments were the main rhetoric of the Parque Central protesters, one of whom described their act as a "citizen's duty of loyalty to our flag," accomplished by people who put Cuba "above their private interests and physical integrity." One of the signs they carried at the protest read, "We don't want either Guatemala or Hungary," protesting both U.S. and Soviet interventions in the internal affairs of smaller nations.[89] The students' public joint statement pointed out that while their opponents had betrayed Cuba by stomping on and burning its flag, they had honored it as a sign that the nation "wanted to make a revolution of its own, . . . very unique and distinct." They were clearly evoking Fidel Castro's authoritative nationalist statements to emphasize that the Cuban Revolution should not be of the same kind as the Russian.[90]

Socialism and Nationalism

This clear opposition between nationalism and state socialism would not surprise many theorists of either phenomenon. To this day, the old Marxist conception of nationalism as a bourgeois ideology remains largely influential among scholars, especially since Benedict Anderson located the roots of nationalism in "print capitalism."[91] Given the strong analytical association between capitalism and the nation-state, theorists have often assumed that the great "other" of capitalism—socialism—tends to be in conflict with nationalism. Susan Buck-Morss, for instance, made that assumption explicit when she contrasted "capitalist and socialist models of mass sovereignty," defining the former as "based on a political imaginary of mutually exclusive, potentially hostile nation-states," as opposed to the latter's "political imaginary of irreconcilably antagonistic, warring classes."[92]

This statement implies a dismissal of the historical existence of socialist nation-states that is absent from empirical studies of nationalism in socialist contexts, like John Borneman's and Katherine Verdery's.[93] But even these sophisticated analyses presuppose a tension between nationalism and state socialism. After examining the attempts by Romania's socialist state to promote nationalistic ideologies that would legitimize its rule, Verdery describes how Romanian socialism ended up capitulating to nationalism: "In this process the discourse of Marxism was not just indigenized: it was overthrown."[94] The problem of Verdery's narrative is that she offers no explanation why socialism was eroded by nationalism; she just takes for granted that they were in conflict.[95] Borneman's comparison of the two Cold War Germanies makes a similar argument, claiming that the Democratic Republic failed partly because the Federal Republic was more successful in making claims to nationhood. He attributes this to socialism's universalism and future orientation, which he sees as being in contradiction to nationalism's particularism and glorification of the past.[96] This stark opposition, though, is far from convincing, for it ignores both that state socialism has always involved some glorification of the past *and* that capitalism and liberal democracy are not any less universalistic than socialist ideologies.[97]

Focusing on a moment like Cuba at the eve of its socialist turn makes evident that the relationship between socialist and nationalistic discourses varies according to the historical context and that they may be intrinsically interconnected. In the arguments surrounding the Soviet Exposition, prosocialist actors were every bit as nationalistic as the antisocialists. In fact, the two sides fought on a single discursive field, in which progress and nationalism were the supreme agreed-upon values; their conflict was a dispute about what system was the best for national sovereignty and development.[98] I have already shown how the Soviet Exposition helped the defenders of socialism make their case regarding its value as a means to development. But what did they say to show that *they*—and not the detractors of socialism—had the nation on their side?

First, they argued that—to use the words of a left-leaning Catholic priest—"our first enemy is not Russia, but the United States."[99] Enthusiasts of socialism repeatedly reminded their compatriots that U.S. imperialism had always been the obstacle to Cuba's real independence and was still so.[100] In a reference to the frequent acts of sabotage conducted by Florida-based and U.S.-supported Cuban exiles, a cartoon on a front page of *Hoy* (Today)—the Communist Party's official newspaper—showed airplanes bombing sugarcane fields. The title of the drawing— "The North American 'Exposition'"—invited a comparison between U.S. and Soviet attitudes toward Cuba.[101]

American ghosts also haunted the Parque Central incident. Two American witnesses—a photographer and a journalist—were physically attacked by the counterprotesters, who accused them of being involved in the planning of the protest.[102] And several rumors accused U.S. interests of being behind the act—the cars that brought the protesters allegedly had stickers of American schools, and a Cuban who tried to photograph the incident was accused of being an agent of the United Fruit Company.[103] A telegram sent to the president of Cuba by the employees of a five-star hotel was more general: it accused all the protesters of being "agents of Yankee imperialism."[104]

Sometimes enthusiasts of socialism accused not only Americans but a broader foreign mobilization against Cuba—or, to quote a statement of a workers' organization, a "horrible international conspiracy against our nation."[105] This kind of plot was often mentioned in one of the most characteristic kinds of written pieces of this period—the *coletillas*, or post scripta that employees of opposition newspapers added to materials published by their employers, denouncing their counterrevolutionary character. In more than one newspaper, stories criticizing socialism or defending the Parque Central protesters were followed by *coletillas* that used exactly the same phrasing: "The journalists and graphic workers of this work center . . . express that the content [of the above] is biased and is part of the conspiracy against our fatherland."[106]

Contrasts of imperialist (especially American) plots to Soviet "friendship" were also abundant in these controversies. A female employee of an elite club said that at the Soviet Exposition one could "clearly see the difference between a brother country that extends its hand to us, that helps us and does us justice, and those who try to exploit us."[107] The discourse of friendship between the Cuban and the Soviet people—which would thrive in Cuba until the Gorbachev years—proliferated at the time of the Exposition, being present for instance in Mikoian's speech at the dedication of the event and in an article titled simply "Friendship," published by a major communist intellectual.[108] Framing the relationship with the United States as power-ridden and that with the USSR as one of equality and support, this discourse helped strengthen the idea that, while persistent alignment with the capitalist world meant the perpetuation of imperial subjection, proximity with the socialist world would be conducive to national affirmation.[109]

Actually, the very realization of the Soviet Exposition was often greeted as an act of sovereign self-affirmation against the United States. Speaking at the dedication ceremony, the Cuban minister of trade claimed that, by broadening Cuba's international relations and diversifying its markets, the exhibit contributed to guaranteeing Cuban sovereignty.[110] In a similar vein, three white-collar workers interviewed by *Hoy* emphasized that the Exposition helped overcome years of lies about the socialist world told by American press agencies, and the Union of Salespersons circulated a statement that declared that the Soviet mission to Cuba "ma[de] one feel that Cuba is really free, independent and sovereign."[111]

But perhaps no discourse boosted by the Soviet Exposition contributed more to the association between socialism and the nation than that which identified anticommunism with counterrevolution. Since anticommunists opposed the government's growing friendliness to the USSR and were associated with American interests that the Revolution had bravely fought, they were increasingly considered counterrevolutionaries. This explains the fierce reaction encountered by the Parque Central protesters: no matter how much they framed their act as against communism and for the Revolution, this made no sense to the zealous revolutionaries that attacked them. For the latter, protesting communism equaled protesting the Revolution. And, given the general agreement in Cuba at the time that the nation and the Revolution were one and the same, protesting the Revolution meant betraying the nation. Many worker and student organizations harshly criticized the anticommunist protest with that argument. For the tobacco workers of a provincial town, the perpetrators had been "manipulated by imperialism."[112] When the powerful Federation of University Students expelled the protesters from its files, it justified it with nationalist rhetoric: their counterrevolutionary act had been "a crime against the happiness of a people." And an official note issued by the CTC declared the protesters to be "bad Cubans; more than that, traitors of our history, of our Homeland and our glorious Revolution."[113]

These discourses exemplify that, besides the promise of development, nationalism was the major weapon that defenders of socialism used in this crucial turning point of Cuban history. After February 1960, as opponents of socialism were increasingly labeled "anti-Cubans," the framing of socialism as the royal road to national affirmation only grew stronger and more pervasive. Less than three months after the Soviet Exposition, all opposition newspapers were seized by the state, and the discourse that socialism was inimical to the nation disappeared from print. And while American hostilities, Soviet support, and the radicalization of the Revolution increasingly fed each other, the identification between socialism and nationalism became a predominant public discourse.

Aftermath: Postcolonial Socialism

The culmination of these events was the speech in which Fidel Castro announced the socialist character of the Cuban Revolution—which revealingly happened during the funeral of seven victims of bombardments launched by Cuban exiles with CIA support. Most of the speech—delivered at a major Havana street intersection on 16 April 1961—was a vivid attack on American imperialism, which the leader denounced as the basis of class exploitation in Cuba. As the attending crowd shouted, "Cuba, yes! Yankees, no!" Castro castigated "American millionaires" as those responsible for poverty in Cuba and described their Cuban allies as "mercenaries, worms sold to imperialism." It was only toward the end of the speech that he explicitly mentioned socialism, connecting it to anti-imperialism: "What they cannot forgive us for, is that we are under their noses and that we made a socialist revolution under the very noses of the United States!" From the day of this speech, there was no more alternative in Cuban public discourse—one was either a socialist or a traitor to the nation.[114]

Immediately before introducing that famous bombastic sentence, Fidel Castro's speech had been comparing the American aggression against Cuba to the most recent Soviet accomplishment: the first human journey to outer space. If Sputnik III had been a success during the Soviet Exposition, Castro now evoked Gagarin's expedition to compare "the Soviet deed to the imperialist deed; the joy, the strength, and the hope that the Soviet deed has meant for humankind, to the shame, disgust, and repugnance that the American deed has meant." As had been the case fourteen months before, U.S. imperialism was contrasted to Soviet benevolence. And one could see the trope of Cuban-Soviet friendship in the reaction of the public when Fidel first mentioned that the Cuban Revolution was socialist: they started shouting, "Fidel, Khrushchev, we are with you two."[115] Again, socialism and the Soviet Union were seen as the key allies of Cuban national affirmation.

This is a clear example of a historical situation in which, far from being in contradiction, state socialism and nationalism were in a symbiotic relationship—*pace* contemporary theorists of both phenomena. Cuba's socialism has been since the beginning (and remains to this day) what I would like to call a postcolonial socialism, one whose main ideological foundation lies in national affirmation against foreign domination. And in this Cuba was far from being alone. As former colonies embarked on nationalist projects in the context of the Cold War, it is comprehensible that several of them embraced socialism as a means to achieve nationalistic goals. After all, they were rebelling against capitalist metropolises, and colonialism had always been part and parcel of capitalist expansion.

But it is not only in the postcolonial world that socialism has had a mutually constitutive relationship with nationalism, and historians of the Soviet Union give several instances from the very center of the socialist world. Ronald Grigor Suny has argued that in some non-Russian republics, like Latvia and Georgia, socialism and nationalism were part of a single movement in the early Bolshevik period.[116] Furthermore, he demonstrated that even in republics where this did not happen initially, once Soviet power consolidated, it invested heavily in creating national traditions, territories, and bureaucracies, to the point that "the Soviet Union became the incubator of new nations."[117] According to Stephen Kotkin, in Russia too the embrace of socialism in the revolutionary period had a solid nationalistic basis: "Russia's obsession with socialism can also be understood in this light, for along with the desire for a strong country there existed . . . a widespread feeling that Russia had, or ought to have, a special mission. . . . Socialism promised to allow just that. Through socialism, Russia would industrialize, matching and eventually superseding the great powers economically and militarily while retaining a supposed moral superiority."[118]

Two decades later, under Stalin, national pride remained a powerful legitimation basis of the socialist state—as Sheila Fitzpatrick has shown, the idea that socialism would allow Russia to "catch up and overcome the West" was also a predominant discourse in the 1930s.[119] More than that, the examples brought up by Suny, Kotkin, and Fitzpatrick show that the very socialist promise of fast development had a strong nationalistic overtone. In Russia and other Soviet republics, the industrial progress promised by socialism was a *national* progress, a process of development that would bring the nation out of backwardness. In this regard, Cuban enthusiasts of socialism in the early 1960s were repeating a story that had taken place in the very country they took as their ideal. What Cubans saw in the Soviet Exposition was the possibility not of development tout court, but of *national* development. The great promise they saw in socialism was not just that of living in a magic world of machines, but that of making their nation overcome underdevelopment. Socialism for them would bring not only modernity but, through the overcoming of foreign dependency, a specifically *national* modernity.

To summarize, this historical ethnography of the events surrounding the 1960 Soviet Exposition in Havana points to a need to reformulate the scholarly understanding of similarities and differences, as well as convergences and divergences, between capitalism and socialism. First, while analyses of similarities and convergences between them have focused respectively on the utopias of industrial progress and mass consumption, it must be recognized that nationalism was another important shared ideological ground on which the two systems competed. The Cuban case reminds us that both of them were often embraced and presented as the correct path to national affirmation and that the very dreams of development were framed in nationalist terms.

Second, despite this common ideological basis of shared values and goals, one should not underestimate the fact that this was a common ground of *conflict,* in which what mattered were not the similarities but the differences between the two systems. In the historical moment when the centers of the First and Second Worlds seemed to stabilize and converge, for the decolonizing or postcolonial part of the world the choice between the two systems was still open. This meant real and serious conflict for people on the ground, who focused, not on the ideals they shared, but on the two radically different paths offered by capitalism and socialism. In Havana today some old Fords run on adapted Lada engines, but when Cubans first marveled at Soviet machines in February 1960 it was an alternative and superior way to modernity that some of them saw, with much hope, on the horizon of their nation.

Notes

1. This description is based on ethnographic research done over several visits to Cuba between 2001 and 2009, especially over twelve continuous months between March 2008 and February 2009. I want to express my gratitude to the Social Science Research Council for an International Dissertation Research Fellowship, which funded my research during that period, when I also conducted the archival research on which this chapter is based.

2. On the implications of the different ways in which Cuba may be located regionally by scholars, see Ariana Hernandez-Reguant, "Cuba's Alternative Geographies," *Journal of Latin American Anthropology* 10, no. 2 (2005): 275–313. I believe that Cuba's Latin Americanness is more widely accepted in academic circles than Hernandez-Reguant argues in her piece.

3. Classic works that have explored Cuba's cultural connections to the United States are Gerald E. Poyo, *"With All, and for the Good of All": The Emergence of Popular Nationalism in the Cuban Communities of the United States, 1848–1898* (Durham: Duke University Press, 1989); Gustavo Pérez-Firmat, *Life on the Hyphen: The Cuban-American Way* (Austin: University of Texas Press, 1994); and Louis A. Pérez Jr., *On Becoming Cuban: Identity, Nationality, and Culture* (New York: Ecco, 1999).

4. See, for instance, Sujatha Fernandes, *Cuba Represent! Cuban Arts, State Power, and the Making of New Revolutionary Cultures* (Durham: Duke University Press, 2006); and Amelia Rosenberg Weinreb, *Cuba in the Shadow of Change: Daily Life in the Twilight of the Revolution* (Gainesville: University Press of Florida, 2009).

5. For sources used in my description of the Exposition, see note 35. For the number of specialists involved in the installation of the Exposition, see Antonio Pequeño, "La Exposición Soviética en La Habana," *INRA* 2 (February 1960): 25; for the number of personnel coming to the dedication ceremony, see "Cordial bienvenida a Anastas Mikoyan," *Revolución*, 5 February 1960.

6. The period from the early 1970s to the mid-1980s was the heyday of Cuba's proximity with the USSR. Closer commercial and political ties between the two countries meant for Cuba a heavy dependency on Soviet credit subsidies, investments, and industrialized commodities. Also, on common agreement, the Soviets sold oil to Cuba at lower-than-market rates and bought Cuban sugar at higher-than-market prices. According to Louis A. Pérez Jr., "By the mid-1980s, Cuban export dependence on the Soviet Union had increased to 64 percent, while import dependence reached 62 percent." *Cuba: Between Reform and Revolution* (New York: Oxford University Press, 1988), 355. In this period Cuba's internal politics and economy were also reorganized according to Soviet models, or, in Richard Gott's strong terms, "in the Soviet image." *Cuba: A New History* (New Haven: Yale University Press, 2004), 243. For detailed accounts of the "Sovietization" of Cuba in the 1970s, see Jacques Lévesque, *The USSR and the Cuban Revolution: Soviet Ideological and Strategical Perspectives, 1959–1977*, trans. Deanna Drendel Leboeuf (New York: Praeger, 1978); Carmelo Mesa-Largo, *Cuba in the 1970s: Pragmatism and Institutionalization* (Albuquerque: University of New Mexico Press, 1978).

7. A classic critique of anticolonial nationalism as part of a modern project is Partha Chatterjee, *The Nation and Its Fragments: Colonial and Postcolonial Histories* (Princeton: Princeton University Press, 1993).

8. Cuban economic reliance on trade with the United States developed while the country was still under Spanish colonialism, which helps explain the last-minute American intervention in Cuba's war of independence in 1898, resulting in what became known as the Spanish-American War. After the war, economic dependence grew, and so did American political influence, beginning with four years of military occupation; see Louis A. Pérez Jr., *Cuba between Empires, 1878–1902* (Pittsburgh: University of Pittsburgh Press, 1983); Marial Iglesias, *A Cultural History of Cuba during the U.S. Occupation, 1898–1902* (Chapel Hill: University of North Carolina Press, 2011). Despite Cuba's formal independence in 1902, the Platt Amendment inscribed in its constitution gave the United States the formal right to intervene in Cuban politics—a right that was used several times, for example in the military occupation of 1906–9 and the armed intervention of 1917–22; see Louis A. Pérez Jr., *Cuba under the Platt Amendment, 1902–1934* (Pittsburgh: University of Pittsburgh Press, 1986). Although the Platt Amendment was abrogated in 1934, the United States continued playing an important role in Cuban politics until the Revolution, as documented by Jorge Domínguez, "Governing through Regulation and Distribution, 1933–1958," ch. 3 in *Cuba: Order and Revolution* (Cambridge, MA: Belknap Press, 1978). In economic terms, Cuba remained heavily dependent on the United States throughout the period. Unfavorable trade reciprocity treaties perpetuated Cuba's sugar monoculture, since the national economy was based on the export of sugar to the U.S. market and the import of a wide variety of American consumer goods, which saturated the Cuban market; see Oscar Zanetti, "El comercio exterior de la república neocolonial," in *Anuario de estudios cubanos*, vol. 1, *La república neocolonial*, ed. Juan Pérez de la Riva et al. (Havana: Instituto Cubano del Libro, Editorial de Ciencias Sociales, 1975). Foreign capital, especially American, controlled most areas of the Cuban economy, including transportation, utility services, mining, banking, and, most importantly, the production of sugar, as analyzed by Francisco López Segrera in *Cuba: Capitalismo dependiente y subdesarrollo, 1510–1959* (Mexico City: Diógenes, 1973).

9. Marifeli Pérez-Stable, *The Cuban Revolution: Origins, Course, and Legacy*, 2nd ed. (New York: Oxford University Press, 1999), 81.

10. Until its dissolution, the USSR remained the biggest importer of Cuban sugar; see Susan Eva Eckstein, *Back from the Future: Cuba under Castro*, 2nd ed. (New York: Routledge, 2003), 47, 91. The popularity of "Guantanamera" in Vietnam was personally communicated to me in June 2008 by Vietnamese students living in Havana, who claimed that they thought the song was Vietnamese until they moved to Cuba. On the Cuban participation in African revolutionary movements, see Carlos Moore, *Castro, the Blacks and Africa* (Los Angeles: UCLA Center for Afro-American Studies, 1988); Piero Gleijeses, *Conflicting Missions: Havana, Washington, and Africa, 1959–1976* (Chapel Hill: University of North Carolina Press, 2002). On Budapest's Havanna *lakótelep* (housing estate), built in 1977, see *Havanna Online Web*, editor-in-chief Márton Varga, www.havannalakotelep.hu/, accessed 15 March 2011. For a thorough list of the numerous awards received by Cubans in Eastern European and Soviet film festivals, sorted by film and director, see *El Portal del Cine Cubano*, Instituto Cubano del Arte e Industria Cinematográficos, www.cubacine.cu/, accessed 15 March 2011. The information on Eastern European tourists and African and Latin American students comes mainly from my ethnographic research, but some numbers are available. According to Louis A. Pérez Jr., "As many as seven thousand Soviet advisors worked in Cuba during the 1970s and 1980s." *Between Reform and Revolution*, 356. Susan Eckstein mentions that Cuba started providing scholarships to foreign students in 1977, and they numbered twenty-five thousand in 1989; out of the twenty-one thousand remaining in 1992, twelve thousand came from sub-Saharan Africa. *Back from the Future*, 178. For an ethnographic study of African students in Cuba, see Paul Ryer, "Between La Yuma and África: Locating the Color of Contemporary Cuba" (PhD diss., University of Chicago, 2006).

11. Susan Buck-Morss, *Dreamworld and Catastrophe: The Passing of Mass Utopia in East and West* (Cambridge, MA: MIT Press, 2002).

12. Two edited volumes that discuss consumption in the socialist bloc are Susan E. Reid and David Crowley, eds., *Style and Socialism: Modernity and Material Culture in Post-War Eastern Europe* (Oxford: Berg, 2000); David Crowley and Susan E. Reid, eds., *Pleasures in Socialism: Leisure and Luxury in the Eastern Bloc* (Evanston: Northwestern University Press, 2010). Two excellent documentaries that depict consumer culture in Hungary's "goulash socialism" in the 1960s and 1970s are *Budapest Retró*, dir. Gábor Zsigmond Papp (Budapest: ADS Service Kft., 1998), DVD, and *Budapest Retró II*, dir. Gábor Zsigmond Papp (Budapest: ADS Service Kft., 2003), DVD. See also Susan Reid's chapter in this volume.

13. In an interview in early 1959, for instance, when asked whether his fellow revolutionaries Raúl Castro and Ernesto Che Guevara were communists, as rumors had it, Fidel Castro affirmed that "the 26 July movement is one with radical ideas, but it is not a communist movement, and it differs basically from communism on a whole series of basic points. And those in the 26 July movement, both Raúl and Guevara, like all the others, are men who agree very closely with my political thinking, which is not communist thinking." Fidel Castro, "1959 Interview 27 February with Castro," *Castro Speech Data Base*, Latin American Network Information Center, University of Texas, http://lanic.utexas.edu/la/cb/cuba/castro.html. All translations from Spanish in this chapter are mine.

14. Fidel Castro, "1960 Interview Castro Press Conference," *Castro Speech Data Base*, Latin American Network Information Center, University of Texas, http://lanic.utexas.edu/la/cb/cuba/castro.html. Note that this interview was given on 21 May, which means that, three months after the Soviet Exposition, Fidel Castro was still criticizing state socialism.

15. On how the relationship of the Soviet Union to the Cuban Revolution evolved from reluctant pragmatic rapprochement to a full support that was crucial for the establishment of socialism on the island, see Lévesque, *USSR and the Cuban Revolution*, 13–25. According to Lévesque, Cuba in mid-1960 was "on the fringe of the socialist camp" (20).

16. My account of Cuba's transition to socialism is largely based on Hugh Thomas, *The Cuban Revolution* (New York: Harper and Row, 1977), 413–576; Jorge I. Domínguez, *Cuba: Order and Revolution* (Cambridge, MA: Belknap Press, 1978), 137–49, 191–210; and Pérez-Stable, *Cuban Revolution*, 61–81.

17. L. Pérez, *Between Reform and Revolution*, 315. Similarly, Marifeli Pérez-Stable saw in 1959 the birth of a triangular identification between "Fidel-*patria*-revolution" that "has since remained at the heart of politics in Cuba." *Cuban Revolution*, 10. Pérez-Stable's formulation does not mean that the leader simply imposed his definition of revolution. Until he declared the Revolution socialist, his definitions were broad enough to accommodate different conceptions of how radical the Revolution should be, which allowed for the heated debates that I describe. To a great extent the radicalization of the Revolution by its leader responded to popular demands. For Louis A. Pérez Jr., this growing interplay featured "improvisation from an exhilarated Fidel and impatience from an aroused population." *Between Reform and Revolution*, 319.

18. L. Pérez, *Between Reform and Revolution*, 335. According to María Cristina García, "From January 1, 1959, to October 22, 1962, approximately 248,070 Cubans emigrated to the United States." *Havana USA: Cuban Exiles and Cuban Americans in South Florida, 1959–1994* (Berkeley: University of California Press, 1996), 13. Although white Havanans were overrepresented in these early years of Cuban migration, most of these early exiles were *not* upper class or supporters of Batista, but members of the middle class who did not agree with the radicalization of the Revolution.

19. See Thomas, *Cuban Revolution*, 413–576; Domínguez, *Order and Revolution*, 137–49, 191–210; Pérez-Stable, *Cuban Revolution*, 61–81; L. Pérez, *Between Reform and Revolution*, 313–36.

20. Graphic images of people tortured and killed by the Batista regime can be found on page 11 of *Revolución*, 15 January 1959, and on page 1 of *Bohemia*, 13 March 1960. On the "several hundred" of executions that followed "perfunctory trials," see Gott, *New History*, 168.

21. An image of a street vendor selling pictures of revolutionaries can be found in *Lunes de Revolución*, 31 December 1959, 12. Several films reenacted scenes from the revolutionary struggle.

See, e.g., advertisement for "El gran recuento" (*Revolución*, 16 February 1959) and for "De la Sierra hasta hoy" (*Diario de la marina*, 29 January 1960). For the complaints of a television critic about the representation of bearded rebels dancing cha-cha in a prime-time show, which he found disrespectful, see "Imagen," *Revolución*, 16 April 1959. Less than a month after the toppling of Batista, a stamp was released representing a bearded revolutionary lifting his rifle; see "La Revolución en estampillas," *Revolución*, 20 January 1959. A photograph of a car boasting a sticker with the image of Fidel Castro can be found in *Prensa libre*, 3 February 1960. For images of revolutionaries in a literacy primer for adults, see *Aprendo a leer y escribir: Un ensayo para el aprendizaje de la lectura-escritura para los adultos* (Havana: Gobierno Revolucionario de la República de Cuba, 1959), 13, 15, 21, 31. Advertisements of the mentioned products and companies using images of revolutionaries can be found in the following issues of *Revolución*: 27 July 1959; 23 February 1959; 12 January 1959; 27 January 1959.

22. See several consecutive stories in *Revolución* and *Diario de la marina* between 1 and 9 January 1959.

23. I have not been able to find statistics about those who returned to Cuba from the United States, but nearly thirty thousand Cubans were living in South Florida by 1959 (García, *Havana USA*, 16). My own research has shown that many of them have returned to the island (João Felipe Gonçalves, "The City and the Nation: Monuments to José Martí and the Cubanization of Miami," unpublished manuscript, 2009).

24. On the first revolutionary May Day celebration, see "Primero de Mayo de la libertad—grandiosa demostración," *Revolución*, 2 May 1959; "Un Primero de Mayo libre," *Bohemia*, 10 May 1959, 72–75. On the 26 July celebrations, see "'Ha sido cumplida la voluntad del pueblo'—Fidel," *Revolución*, 27 July 1959; "Más de un millón de cubanos se congregó en la Plaza Cívica," *Revolución*, 27 July 1959, 11–14; "Guajiro, ¡esta es tu casa! ¡esta es tu Habana!," *Bohemia*, 26 July 1959, 32–34; "Más de un millón de cubanos se congregó en la Plaza Cívica el 26 de julio," *Bohemia*, 2 August 1959, 60–65.

25. "Brocha en mano fue iniciada 'La Habana se viste limpio,'" *Revolución*, 25 April 1959; a similar operation was held in October to paint the city's seashore promenade. "Pleno éxito obtiene la OTV en su primera jornada cívica," *Revolución*, 12 October 1959.

26. For massive rallies in front of the Presidential Palace that reportedly brought more than one million people to hear Fidel Castro speak, see, for instance, "A Palacio," *Revolución*, 21 January 1960; and "Más de un millón de cubanos reunidos para demostrar su respaldo a la Revolución," *Bohemia*, 1 November 1959, 98–101. Fidel also spoke in the celebration of 26 July 1959, mentioned in note 24. Perhaps the most spectacular crowd event in this period happened on 2 September 1960, when more than one million people filled the vast Plaza Cívica to approve, by hand raising, what became known as the First Declaration of Havana. A speech by Fidel Castro submitted to and approved by this "General People's Assembly," the declaration denounced American imperialism, framed the Cuban Revolution as part of Latin American liberation struggles, and announced measures such as the end of a military treaty with the United States and the reestablishment of diplomatic relations with China. "En la asamblea más grande del mundo, el pueblo decidió . . . ," *Revolución*, 3 September 1960; "Más de un millón de personas en la asamblea popular más grande del mundo," *Revolución*, 3 September 1960. Note that in 1960 Cuba had an estimated population of 6,797,000 inhabitants, of whom 1,463,000 were estimated to live in greater Havana. Susan Schroeder, *Cuba: A Handbook of Historical Statistics* (Boston: G. K. Hall, 1982), 41; B. R. Mitchell, *International Historical Statistics: The Americas, 1750–2005*, 6th ed. (New York: Palgrave Macmillan, 2007), 51.

27. For portrayals of this central part of Havana and its development, see Joseph L. Scarpaci, Roberto Segre, and Mario Coyula, *Havana: Two Faces of the Antillean Metropolis* (Chapel Hill: University of North Carolina Press, 2002); Dick Cluster and Rafael Hernández, *The History of Havana* (New York: Palgrave Macmillan, 2006).

28. Some of the massive public events of this period—like the May Day and 26 July celebrations—were held at the new Plaza Cívica (soon renamed Plaza de la Revolución), two miles away from Havana's downtown. That plaza would become the most important place for political rituals in socialist Cuba, but during the transitional period most major public events still took place downtown, in the vicinity of the Palace of Fine Arts. See note 26 for events featuring Fidel Castro speeches that took place in the area. Also, in April 1959 the area saw a parade on the occasion of the first volunteer painting drive, "Brocha en mano." In October 1959, the Parque Central housed an exhibition on education in Cuba, featuring a replica of a rural school, film screenings, and theater plays; *Revolución*, 1 October 1959. Early in 1960, in front of the Capitol, the government promoted daily open-air classes of military training for civilians; *Revolución*, 9 February 1960.

29. The basic visitor information can be found in the one-page advertisements for the Soviet Exposition published in the press (these ads, incidentally, were illustrated with an image of Sputnik III). See for instance the ad on page 80 of *Bohemia*, 14 February 1960. The estimated number of visitors might be exaggerated and was based on the amount of visitors it had received during its first week of operation. Still, considering Havana's population of around 1.5 million inhabitants, it is impressive that in one week the Exposition may have received over three hundred thousand visits. Mario Rodríguez S., "El público en la Exposición Soviética," *Bohemia*, 14 February 1960, 66. I could not locate an estimate of the number of visitors at the closing of the Exposition.

30. Jon Lee Anderson, *Che Guevara: A Revolutionary Life* (New York: Grove Press, 1997), 441–43. Antonio Núñez Jiménez was already an important geographer of Cuba when he joined the rebel forces, and he would become Cuba's minister of land reform in 1961. Antonio Núñez Jiménez, *En marcha con Fidel* (Habana: Letras Cubanas, 1982).

31. Susan E. Reid, "The Soviet Pavilion at Brussels '58: Convergence, Conversion, Critical Assimilation, or Transculturation?" (Working Paper No. 62, Cold War International History Project, Woodrow Wilson International Center for Scholars, Washington, DC, 2010), 16–18.

32. Ibid., 46.

33. From the perspective of Cubans who saw these models in the Exposition, they were not unlike the planned spaces so characteristic of socialist modernity: both were imagined before being a lived reality. On modern urban spatiality in the Soviet Union, see Lewis Siegelbaum's chapter in this volume.

34. Justina Álvarez, "Miles de relojes se venden todos los días en la Exposición . . . ," *Hoy*, 18 February 1960.

35. My description of the Exposition is based on all February 1960 issues of the magazines *Bohemia*, *INRA*, and *Lunes de Revolución*, and of the following newspapers: *Diario de la marina, Prensa libre, Hoy*, and *Revolución*. Those magazines were, respectively, Cuba's most read weekly, the organ of the National Institute of Land Reform, and Cuba's most respected publication on the arts. The newspapers were the ones with greatest circulation in Cuba and represent a range of political positions: *La marina* was a widely respected right-wing Catholic-leaning newspaper; *Prensa libre* defended a liberal-democratic outcome for the Revolution; *Hoy* and *Revolución* were the organs of the two most important organizations of the revolutionary government: the Communist Party (PSP) and the M-26-7, respectively. I also relied on an excerpt on the Soviet Exposition from the newsreel *Noticuba Bohemia* (Havana, 1960).

36. *Lunes de Revolución*, 8 February 1960, entire issue.

37. "Concierto extraordinario fue ofrecido a los trabajadores del Teatro Nacional de Cuba," *Hoy*, 4 February 1960, 1; advertisement of Kogan's recital in *Revolución*, 6 February 1960; "Clamoroso éxito de Jachaturian y Kogan," *Hoy*, 7 February 1960; advertisement for "Concierto popular en homenaje a la Revolución Cubana," *Hoy*, 7 February 1960.

38. These movies were heavily advertised in the progovernment and moderate newspapers. See, for instance, *Prensa libre*, 24 January 1960; *Revolución*, 8 February 1960; *Revolución* 10 February 1960; *Hoy* 11 February 1960.

39. According to the prime historian of Cuban film, cinema audiences in Cuba had grown throughout most of the 1950s, and in 1960 they reached "roughly 120 million admissions a year—represent[ing] a national average of about seventeen cinema visits per person in a year." Michael Chanan, *Cuban Cinema* (Minneapolis: University of Minnesota Press, 2004), 31. In the late fifties, he adds, "there were fifteen people for every cinema seat in Cuba" (87). Given the higher concentration of theaters in the capital, both averages must have been even higher in Havana. For the predominance of Hollywood and Mexican cinema in prerevolutionary Cuban theaters, see 72–78, 100.

In 1958, 57 percent of the films distributed in Cuba came from the United States, 14 percent from Mexico, 10 percent from Great Britain, and 6 percent from Italy. In 1960, despite the introduction of films from the USSR and Czechoslovakia, 44 percent of the movies shown in Cuba still came from the United States. Paulo Antonio Paranagua, ed., *Cinéma cubain* (Paris: Centre Georges Pompidou, 1990), 32–33. In 1961, the change was dramatic—only 4.7 percent of the new films shown in Cuba originated in the United States, against 25.8 percent coming from the Soviet Union and 29 percent from six other socialist nations. In 1974, 20 percent of the movies shown in Cuba came from the USSR, which indicates that Soviet cinema probably never came to dominate Cuban theaters as much as Hollywood once had. Schroeder, *Cuba*, 389.

40. José L. Rivero, "Las Flores que Martí quería," *Diario de la marina*, 6 February 1960.

41. My claim regarding the presence of these Soviet products in Cuba is mainly based on participant observation in Cuba and on my informants' narratives, but some aggregate numbers document it more abstractly. According to Louis A. Pérez Jr., from the early 1960s to the mid-1970s around 50 percent of Cuban imports came from the USSR, and that share reached 62 percent in the mid-1980s. *Between Reform and Revolution*, 354. Eastern European products were also pervasive in Cuba; as affirmed by Susan Eckstein, socialist European countries other than the USSR "were a vital source of key products, such as trucks, buses, electric generators, centrifuges for sugar mills, and spare parts." *Back from the Future*, 89.

42. I found few traces of informal encounters between Cubans and Soviets during the Exposition, but they certainly happened. On 17 February, for example, some Cuban women's associations held a festive gathering for two Soviet women who worked at the Exposition. Justina Álvarez, "Encuentro amistoso de mujeres soviéticas y madres cubanas," *Hoy*, 21 February 1960.

43. To this day, the presence of people from the former Soviet Union—commonly called "Russians"—is still strongly felt in Cuba. A shop in Havana with subsidized prices caters exclusively to "Russian" customers, although Cubans try to find imaginative ways to get access to *la tienda de los rusos* (the Russians' store). In October 2008 I witnessed the dedication of the Russian Orthodox Cathedral Our Lady of Kazan by the seashore in Havana's historical core. Soviet women married to Cuban men and living in the country are a recognized social category in Cubans' imagination, and this apparently has a real demographic grounding. The documentary *Soviéticas*, directed by Gustavo Pérez Fernández (Camagüey: TV Camagüey Producciones, 2006), focuses on the lives of seven such women living in a Cuban province. An estimated six thousand "Russians" and descendants live in the country ("Fomentan enseñanza del idioma ruso en Cuba," *El Nuevo Herald Online*, 12 February 2010, www.elnuevoherald.com/2010/02/12/652449/fomentan-ensenanza-del-idioma.html).

44. For an impressive demonstration of the heavy consumption of American goods, styles, and habits by prerevolutionary Cubans, see L. Pérez, *Becoming Cuban*.

45. Of course, this does not mean that cultural exchanges between Cuba and the West ceased to exist. Commodities, people, and cultural products coming from the capitalist world kept circulating on the island, even if sometimes they were not well regarded by the state. An important example from the sixties—the relevance of the Beatles for young Cubans—is analyzed in Anne Luke's contribution to this volume.

46. James Ferguson, *Global Shadows: Africa in the Neoliberal World Order* (Durham: Duke University Press, 2006), 37–38.

47. Interesting examples of socialist "jumps" can be found in this volume. See the important role played by the Vietnamese delegates in the 1968 Sofia World Youth Festival, analyzed by Nick Rutter, and the participation of Cubans and Chileans in the global socialist guitar poetry movement, discussed by Rossen Djagalov.

48. A delegation from Camagüey is mentioned in "Miles de personas visitan la Exposición Soviética," *Hoy*, 7 February 1960. Workers from Santiago are mentioned in "Trecientos obreros de Santiago de Cuba admiran la Exposición Soviética," *Hoy*, 17 February 1960. Individuals from Pinar del Río and Las Villas are mentioned by Álvarez, "Miles de relojes." Álvarez also mentions school groups visiting the Exposition.

49. Rodríguez S., "Público en la Exposición Soviética," 66. This politically moderate magazine cannot be suspected of partiality, as this approving story on the Exposition was followed by a critical photographic essay (which I discuss below) showing poverty in the USSR and the invasion of Hungary in 1956. "¡Lo que no trae la Exposición Soviética!," *Bohemia*, 14 February 1960, 70–71.

50. "Estímase que serán acusados de desorden público los detenidos," *Prensa libre*, 7 February 1960.

51. "Ante la exposición industrial rusa," *Diario de la marina*, 4 February 1960.

52. Pequeño, "Exposición Soviética," 26.

53. "Opiniones sobre la Exposición Soviética," *Hoy*, 7 February 1960.

54. Luis Mitjans, "La Exposición Soviética," *Prensa libre*, 10 February 1960.

55. L. Pérez, *Becoming Cuban*, 348.

56. Ibid., 345.

57. Buck-Morss, *Dreamworld and Catastrophe*, xiii–xiv.

58. Susan E. Reid, "Who Will Beat Whom? Soviet Popular Reception of the American National Exhibition in Moscow, 1959," *Kritika: Explorations in Russian and Eurasian History* 9, no. 4 (2008): 903.

59. Ibid., 13; György Péteri, "Sites of Convergence: The USSR and Communist Eastern Europe at International Fairs Abroad and at Home," *Journal of Contemporary History* 47, no. 1 (January 2012): 3–12.

60. On department stores in Havana, see Scarpaci, Segre, and Coyula, *Havana*, 127. On car consumption and usage and on supermarkets in Havana, see L. Pérez, *Becoming Cuban*, 336–43 and 365–66, respectively.

61. Despite great disparities between regions and social classes, Cuba in the late 1950s had remarkable consumption records for Latin American standards. According to Louis A. Pérez Jr., within the region "only Mexico and Brazil exceeded Cuba in the number of radios owned by individuals (one for every 6.5 inhabitants). The island ranked first in television sets (one per 25 inhabitants). . . . Cuba was first in telephones (1 to 38), newspapers (1 copy per 8 inhabitants), [and] private motor vehicles (1 to 40)." *Between Reform and Revolution*, 296.

62. "Gracias, señor Mikoyan," *Diario de la marina*, 13 February 1960.

63. "Inaugurada la Exposición Soviética," *Revolución*, 6 February 1960; "La feria rusia: Inauguróla Mikoyan," *Diario de la marina*, 6 February 1960; "Inaugurada la Exposición Soviética," *Diario de la marina*, 6 February 1960; "Inaugurada con la Exposición una nueva era de amistad entre Cuba y la URSS," *Hoy*, 6 February 1960; Celia Yaniz, "Exposición Soviética: Felicitó Mikoyan al gobierno y al pueblo de Cuba por su ley de reforma agraria," *Prensa libre*, 7 February 1960.

64. Although versions of the Parque Central incident diverged on some details, they all agreed on the basic events that I narrate here. "Agresión de los comunistas a estudiantes católicos cuando se disponían a honrar a Martí," *Diario de la marina*, 6 February 1960; "La provocación rosablanquista," *Hoy*, 6 February 1960; "Disparos en el Parque Central y en los alrededores del Palacio de Bellas Artes," *Prensa libre*, 6 February 1960; "Continúan detenidos los estudiantes acusados de alterar el orden público," *Prensa libre*, 7 February 1960; "Estímase que serán acusados."

65. As several quotes below exemplify, expressions of support and condemnation of the students by associations and trade unions flooded the newspapers. Most notably, a special session of the

Federation of University Students expelled the protesters from its ranks. "Acuerdos y declaraciones de la FEU," *Diario de la marina*, 7 February 1960; "Expulsan a los traidores," *Hoy*, 6 February 1960.

66. At this time, even most exiles in Miami described themselves as the real revolutionaries, accusing Fidel Castro and his allies of having "betrayed" the Revolution.

67. "Ni 'cubans' ni 'cubanski': Cubanos," *Prensa libre*, 9 February 1960.

68. *Noticuba Bohemia* (Havana, 1960), newsreel excerpt.

69. The poet Nicolás Guillén, for instance, participated in the opening of the Exposition wearing his Lenin Peace Prize, which he had won in 1954 under the original name of Stalin Peace Prize. A key figure in Cuba's literary history and a staunch communist for several decades, Guillén had just returned to Cuba after a long exile. "Opiniones sobre la Exposición." Examples of articles published by distinguished communist intellectuals at the time of the Exposition are "La Exposición Soviética," by Juan Marinello (*Hoy*, 7 February 1960), and "Amistad," by Carlos Rafael Rodríguez (*Hoy*, 6 February 1960). For more information on them, see notes 75 and 108, respectively. Marinello was featured in a major hourlong television talk show in the week in which the Exposition was opened. "Juan Marinello el lunes por el canal 12 de television," *Hoy*, 7 February 1960; "Vibrantes palabras de Juan Marinello por el canal 4 de TV," *Hoy*, 12 February 1960.

70. On the growth of the power of the old communists in the government, see Thomas, *Cuban Revolution*, 456–93. On the conflict between the M-26-7 and the Communist Party within the CTC, and on the eventual victory of the communists, see Pérez-Stable, *Cuban Revolution*, 70–74.

71. A sympathizer simply described the Exposition as "an exhibit of technical advancement." "Declaraciones de la FEU, la CTC y los sindicatos contra la provocación," *Hoy*, 7 February 1960. An editorial of *Diario de la marina* mentioned above referred to the event as one of "industrial progress." "Ante la exposición."

72. "Palabras de Anastas Mikoyan—Difícil camino hemos recorrido," *Revolución*, 6 February 1960. This narrative of successful fast development had been a central part of official Soviet discourse at least since the 1930s; Sheila Fitzpatrick has termed it the "Out of Backwardness" story. *Everyday Stalinism: Ordinary Life in Extraordinary Times; Soviet Russia in the 1930s* (New York: Oxford University Press, 1999), 9–10.

73. "El viceprimer ministro soviético en TV," *Revolución*, 13 February 1960.

74. See, for instance, Hugh Thomas, *Cuba: The Pursuit of Freedom* (London: Harper and Row, 1971); L. Pérez, *Between Reform and Revolution*; Pérez-Stable, *Cuban Revolution*.

75. Marinello, "Exposición Soviética." Marinello had been an active communist public intellectual since the 1920s. He had headed several important journals and been an active participant in the anti-imperialist and antifascist movements in Cuba. He became the rector of the University of Havana in 1962 and a member of the Council of State at its creation in 1976. See Trinidad Pérez and Pedro Simón, *Recopilación de textos sobre Juan Marinello* (Havana: Centro de Investigaciones Literarias and Casa de las Américas, 1979).

76. For instance, less than one month after the triumph of the revolutionaries, "Canada Dry de Cuba" ran an ad in which it declared itself "part of this generous [Cuban] people." *Revolución*, 28 January 1959. Another example of a foreign company selling itself as Cuban was in the advertisement for "The Trust Company of Cuba," which was depicted as "one of the world's greatest banks and the biggest Cuban bank." *Revolución*, 26 July 1959. Guinness beer was more modest—it was advertised, not as Cuban, but simply as "world-famous, just like Cuban sugar and tobacco." Advertisement in *Bohemia*, 8 November 1959, 99. In 1960, newspapers *Hoy* and *Revolución* often inserted miniadvertisements with the simple words "Consume Cuban products" in their pages, including in the middle of reports on the Soviet Exposition (e.g. *Hoy*, 7 February 1960) and next to advertisements of Soviet films (e.g. *Revolución*, 10 February 1960). The railroad exhibition of Cuban products had left Havana in November 1959, and by early February it was thought to have been seen by four hundred thousand people in seventeen towns. "Invitan Mikoyan a ver la exposición de

productos cubanos," *Hoy*, 7 February 1960; "El tren más largo e instructivo del mundo," *Bohemia*, 7 February 1960, 44–45, 95.

77. Pequeño, "Exposición Soviética," 27.

78. "Miles de personas."

79. "¡Lo que no trae la Exposición Soviética!," 70–71; "Estas son las fotografías que usted no encontrará en la Exposición rusa," *Prensa libre*, 14 February 1960. *Prensa libre* also published a cartoon depicting a ragged Soviet couple sweeping a dirty Red Square and lamenting, "Mikoian said in Havana that we have the right to retirement and inheritance and that we can buy cars, and we did not know anything about that!" "En la Plaza Roja," *Prensa libre*, 12 February 1960.

80. "Estímase que serán acusados," 11. Many have argued that the relative weakness of the Catholic Church in Cuba was one of the reasons for the success of a socialist revolution on the island. Louis A. Pérez Jr., for instance, stated that "the Catholic church was a negligible factor in national life." *Between Reform and Revolution*, 334. Thomas A. Tweed has aptly phrased the limited institutionalization of Cuban religiosity by saying that Cubans were relatively "unchurched." *Our Lady of the Exile: Diasporic Religion at a Cuban Catholic Shrine in Miami* (New York: Oxford University Press, 1997), 16–18.

81. These words are from a public statement by the rector of Villanueva University, Cuba's only Catholic University, where several of the Parque Central protesters studied. "Ejercieron un derecho cívico los estudiantes católicos en el acto del Parque Central," *Diario de la marina*, 9 February 1960. See also the declaration by the Federation of Students of Catholic Schools, "Somos anticomunistas por ser estudiantes católicos," *Diario de la marina*, 7 February 1960.

82. The quotation is from the declaration of the Christian Democratic Movement that I mentioned above. "Estímase que serán acusados."

83. "Ante la exposición," 1-A; "Ejercieron un derecho cívico."

84. "Ejecutadas sesenta personas más en Hungría por la revolución antirusa del año 1956," *Prensa libre*, 7 February 1960.

85. "¡Lo que no trae la Exposición Soviética!," 71.

86. After embarrassedly claiming that he did not know what the question referred to, Mikoian gave a series of angry answers, saying first that Hungary's democracy was superior to that of many countries and then that the journalist had no right to ask him such a question. "Mikoyan ante la prensa," *Prensa libre*, 16 February 1960.

87. "Ni 'cubans' ni 'cubanski.'"

88. "La Exposición Roja," *Prensa libre*, 16 February 1960.

89. "Estímase que serán acusados." The mention to Guatemala was a reference to the 1954 U.S.-orchestrated coup in that country that overthrew progressive president Jacobo Arbenz.

90. Ibid.

91. Benedict Anderson, *Imagined Communities: Reflections on the Origins and Spread of Nationalism*, rev. ed. (London: Verso, 1991). In fact, Anderson famously stated that his intellectual concern with the topic was sparked by the nationalistic conflicts between socialist states, which he saw as a sort of unexpected anomaly (xi).

92. Buck-Morss, *Dreamworld and Catastrophe*, 13.

93. Katherine Verdery, *National Ideology under State Socialism: Identity and Cultural Politics in Ceausescu's Romania* (Berkeley: University of California Press, 1995); John Borneman, *Belonging in the Two Berlins: Kin, State, Nation* (Cambridge: Cambridge University Press, 1992).

94. Verdery, *National Ideology*, 166. This phrasing shows that much of the misunderstanding about the relationship between socialism and nationalism comes from the reduction of the former to Marxism. Even within Marxism, it was mainly Western Marxism that posited that relationship in terms of conflict. Eastern versions of Marxism had a different view, as exemplified by the views of Lenin and Stalin on the subject. See Vladimir Il'ich Lenin, *Critical Remarks on the National*

Question: *The Right of Nations to Self-Determination* (Moscow: Progress, 1974); Joseph Stalin, *Marxism and the National-Colonial Question: A Collection of Articles and Speeches* (San Francisco: Proletarian Publishers, 1975).

95. At one point, she refers to the relationship between socialism and nationalism as a "battle." Verdery, *National Ideology*, 12.

96. Borneman, *Belonging*, 16, 31, 286–88, 290.

97. On the role of an imagined past in the construction of socialism, see, for instance, Verdery, *National Ideology*; Michael Burawoy and János Lukács, *The Radiant Past: Ideology and Reality in Hungary's Road to Capitalism* (Chicago: University of Chicago Press, 1994); and Kevin Platt and David Brandenberger, *Epic Revisionism: Russian History and Literature as Stalinist Propaganda* (Madison: University of Wisconsin Press, 2006). On the universal character implicit in all nationalisms, see Etienne Balibar, *We, the People of Europe? Reflections on Transnational Citizenship*, trans. James Swenson (Princeton: Princeton University Press, 2004); and Prasenjit Duara, *Rescuing History from the Nation: Questioning Narratives of Modern China* (Chicago: University of Chicago Press, 1995).

98. The third main rallying cry of the Cuban Revolution—social justice—was conspicuous by its absence in the debates surrounding the Soviet Exposition. Surprisingly, I could not locate one single instance in which it was explicitly invoked to defend socialism. Although it might have been subsumed implicitly in the concept of development, there is no clear indication of that in the sources. Actually, the few explicit allusions to social injustice came from those who wanted to show its persistence in the Soviet Union—see the photo collages and cartoon quoted in note 79.

99. "Declaraciones de la FEU."

100. On Cuba's dependency on the United States, see note 8.

101. "La 'Exposición' Norteamericana," *Hoy*, 9 February 1960.

102. "Agresión de los comunistas," 1-A, 2-A; "El agente yanki George St. Jones," *Hoy*, 6 February 1960.

103. "Autos ocupados," *Hoy*, 6 February 1960. "Detienen un agente de la United Fruit," *Hoy*, 6 February 1960. Although the United Fruit Company never gained in Cuba the importance and power that it had in Central America and Colombia, in prerevolutionary times it had large sugar production operations in northeastern Cuba (in the microregion, by the way, where both Batista and Castro came from). The company had become throughout Latin America a symbol of American imperialism, and in the 1950s it was engaged in a ferocious anticommunist campaign in the region. See Oscar Zanetti, "The United Fruit Company in Cuba," in *The Cuban Reader: History, Culture, Politics*, ed. Aviva Chomsky, Barry Carr, and Pamela Maria Smorkaloff (Durham: Duke University Press, 2003), 290–95.

104. "Trabajadores del Hotel Nacional condenan la provocación," *Hoy*, 6 February 1960. *Yanki* (Yankee) is commonly used throughout Latin America as a derogative term for "North American."

105. "Declaraciones de la FEU."

106. Postscriptum to "Estímase que serán acusados," 11; postscriptum to "Agresión de los comunistas."

107. "Miles de personas."

108. Rodríguez, "Amistad." Like Marinello, Rodríguez had been an active communist public intellectual since the 1920s. Unlike Marinello, he had been involved in formal politics long before the Revolution, having served as mayor of Camagüey in the 1920s and a minister during the first presidency of Fulgencio Batista (1942–44), with whom the communists were allies at the time. Rodríguez was one of the few members of the old Communist Party (PSP) to join the rebels of M-26-7. He became Cuba's most important economic planner in the 1960s and was a key actor in the process of alignment with the USSR. See Araceli García-Carranza and Josefina García-Carranza, *Biobibliografía de Carlos Rafael Rodríguez* (Havana: Letras Cubanas, 1987).

109. Rachel Appelbaum's contribution to this volume, focusing on the Soviet-Czechoslovak case, examines the complexities of the widely circulating notion of "friendship" between socialist nations.

110. Raúl Cepero Bonilla, "El discurso del Ministro de Comercio," *Hoy*, 6 February 1960.

111. "Miles de personas"; "Nuevas protestas por la provocación del Parque Central," *Hoy*, 9 February 1960.

112. "Nuevas protestas."

113. "Declaraciones de la FEU."

114. Fidel Castro Ruz, "Discurso pronunciado por Fidel Castro Ruz . . . el día 16 de abril de 1961," in *Discursos e intervenciones del Comandante en Jefe Fidel Castro Ruz, Presidente del Consejo de Estado de la República de Cuba*, Cuba.cu, Republic of Cuba, www.cuba.cu/gobierno/discursos/1961/esp/f160461e.html.

115. Ibid.

116. "Latvians, like Georgians, combined their ethnic and social grievances in a single, dominant socialist national movement." Ronald Grigor Suny, *The Revenge of the Past: Nationalism, Revolution and the Collapse of the Soviet Union* (Stanford: Stanford University Press, 1993), 57.

117. Ibid., 87. Of course, the irony that Suny analyzes is that these nations one day would rebel against the very central power that helped construct them. For works that developed Suny's ideas of a nation-building Soviet Union, see Terry Martin, *The Affirmative Action Empire: Nations and Nationalism in the Soviet Union, 1923–1939* (Ithaca: Cornell University Press, 2001); Francine Hirsch, *Empire of Nations: Ethnographic Knowledge and the Making of the Soviet Union* (Ithaca: Cornell University Press, 2005).

118. Stephen Kotkin, *Magnetic Mountain: Stalinism as Civilization* (Berkeley: University of California Press, 1995), 12.

119. Fitzpatrick, *Everyday Stalinism*, 9, 71, 184. Fitzpatrick quotes a Stakhanovite woman who saw her personal upward mobility as uniquely Soviet and superior to that experienced by some individuals in the West because she had risen "together with the people" (88). This statement once again connected national superiority to the socialist system.

Contact Zones

4 The Thaw Goes International

Soviet Literature in Translation and Transit in the 1960s

Polly Jones

"Is it snooty of me to insist that in most realms of art the West is, in the simplest sense, more advanced than the Communist East?"[1] This was the rhetorical question posed by Philip Toynbee in his review of Evgenii Evtushenko's autobiography for the English newspaper the *Observer* in summer 1963. For Toynbee, the gulf in literary quality between "them" (writers authorized for publication by the Soviet authorities) and "us" (writers published in democratic Europe and North America) remained unbridgeable. His critique reproduced the binaries of the Cold War in the literary realm; here was one contest of the "cultural cold war" in which West had trounced East.[2]

Yet this haughty, seemingly emphatic critique nonetheless raises some questions: How backward was Soviet literature? Which criteria were being used to judge backwardness? And why, if its quality was so low, was this work being translated and reviewed so prominently in a national newspaper? The answer, and the subject of this chapter, lies in the enormous changes to Soviet literature's role and reputation in its two principal English-language markets in the early 1960s. The period, and this year above all, saw a marked rise in the number of Soviet literary works translated into English and a sharp upswing in public awareness and consumption of Soviet literature in Britain and America, provoking publishers, critics, and readers to rethink its identity.[3] When Aleksandr Solzhenitsyn's *Ivan Denisovich*, published in 1963 in numerous translations and in huge print runs, became a best seller across Europe and North America, Soviet literature turned into a "sensation."[4] During the Khrushchev Thaw—and indeed because of the Thaw—literature authorized for publication in the Soviet Union was deemed more worthy of translation and more marketable to Western readers than it had been for the whole of the Stalin era, and perhaps since the end of the "Russia craze" spawned by the Silver Age.[5] Well before the end of the 1960s, however, the limits imposed domestically on the Thaw brought an end to this episode of Soviet literature's international fame and aborted its tentative ascent toward the "heights" of world literature.[6]

During this brief interval, though, the growth in translations' publication and marketing, often by increasingly powerful Western publishing houses (including Praeger, Penguin, and Dutton), made the texts a regular feature of discussion in the British and American press. The physical juxtaposition of reviews and advertisements for Soviet literature with those for works from the other "side" in the Cold War suggested that Soviet literature, like its place of origin, might be edging toward "peaceful coexistence" with the capitalist West. At the same time, the Sovietness of Soviet literature, its ideological functions and political controls, presented a substantial barrier to such normalization. Toynbee's stance on Evtushenko offered one resolution, reasserting traditional cultural and ideological hierarchies. The broader process of reception of the growing corpus of Soviet literature in translation, which this chapter will analyze, also offered other, less predictable outcomes, however. It generated a rich variety of interpretations of the literary texts themselves and provoked reflections on the Soviet Union and on the possibilities and limits of "coexistence" between East and West.

If, as we will argue, Soviet literature's coexistence with international literature was uncomfortable and precarious, this was partly due to the precariousness of the doctrine of "peaceful coexistence" framing the broader political context of the 1960s. Viewed through the prism of foreign policy, the Soviet 1960s lack a clear identity. The early 1960s, in fact, are largely agreed to represent a step backwards from the 1950s' waves of rapprochement, being marred by the Berlin crisis, the U-2 incident, and the extreme tensions of the Cuban Missile Crisis.[7] These unpredictable rises and falls in East-West tensions become more predictable if we pay greater attention to the ideological continuities across the post-Stalin period. As Vladislav Zubok has recently argued, the Khrushchev period preserved the "imperialist-revolutionary paradigm" because of ideological inertia, the presence of "Stalinists" in the leadership, Khrushchev's own utopian-messianic views on world politics, and the "ideological romance" of the Cuban Revolution.[8] The "default" ideological setting of the Soviet leadership thus remained distrust of the West and its intentions for the Eastern bloc.[9]

Meanwhile the expansion of cultural exchange, while driven by many factors (some of them genuinely internationalist in spirit), must partly be understood, as Nigel Gould-Davies and others have argued, as a relocation, rather than a reduction, of the ideological battles of the Cold War.[10] In this, literature was no exception. Increasing numbers of translations bolstered the regime's proclaimed commitment to opening up to the West and lent credibility to the increasing participation of Soviet writers in international creative organizations and cultural exchanges.[11] However, the simultaneous hostile actions of Soviet authorities toward Western literature and literary organizations, persisting (and even intensifying) in the 1960s and much reported abroad, confirmed to international observers that Soviet literature remained heavily politicized.[12]

Such Soviet attacks ran alongside the ongoing propaganda activities aiming to discredit the West and promote the Soviet cause, analyzed in recent Cold War scholarship.[13] Indeed, the Soviet authorities generally viewed literature, like other print culture, in messianic rather than "mutual" terms, although crucially they had only limited power to control either the production or the reception of texts abroad.[14] In trying to control Soviet literature's image during this period of unprecedented global transit, the Soviet authorities frequently resorted to Manichaean conceptualizations of politics and culture, which hampered the cultural cooperation that Soviet literature might otherwise have fostered.

Manichaean thinking was not exclusive to the Soviet side. Recent studies of Western propaganda and culture in the Cold War have argued that both Britain and America were slow to break with the medium and the message of anticommunism of the postwar period.[15] When "peaceful coexistence" became the new foreign policy watchword, some of the crudest criticism of the "red menace" was removed from anticommunist propaganda and press coverage of the Soviet Union, but distrust of the Soviet Union remained prevalent among both policy makers and opinion makers.[16] Some scholars of American politics of the 1960s have suggested that this anticommunism was so powerful as to represent the "other side of the sixties."[17] This scholarship's focus on the early years of the sixties, rather than the decade's more famous second half, and its emphasis on ideological division and distrust, helps make sense of the sometimes hostile and patronizing responses that greeted this new wave of Soviet literature during precisely this "other" subperiod of the sixties. At the same time, this process of reception was also shaped by the genuine hopes for peace, mutual understanding, and cultural exchange that characterized elite policy making but took even more powerful hold of the intelligentsia in the Soviet Union (turning the *shestidesiatniki* into a much-mythologized cohort), and in Europe and America, from the mid-1950s onwards.[18]

The role of literature in the Cold War has been largely overshadowed by the much greater interest in other forms of high culture (notably film, art, and ballet), as well as by the attention granted to Soviet and American competition over everyday life and domestic comfort.[19] The exportation of Soviet ballet to the West (as the regime's most "spectacular cultural manifestation"), and of the treasures of Western art and theater to Russia, reveals both sides of the Cold War competitively showcasing the best culture that they had to offer, while also opening the "faucet of friendship."[20] The growing (though still circumscribed) translation and consumption of European and American literature in the post-Stalinist Soviet Union has rightly been recognized as an important factor in opening up to the West.[21] Yet these studies of Western literature's penetration of the "Iron Curtain" largely omit what happened to literature in translation and transit in the other direction.[22] In fact, the fate of Soviet literature in the West fits less easily into this narrative of exporting cultural excellence: not only its "excellence" but also the nature of its exportation was much more complex.[23]

First, on both sides of the Iron Curtain, albeit in different ways, the question of how to define Soviet literature's "quality" was unclear: Should it be judged according to its style, its content, or its politics? Were Western and Soviet understandings of literature simply incompatible?[24] These questions were vexing to Soviet authorities, whose post-Stalinist domestic policy on literature stressed aesthetic innovation but also ideological conservatism (the latter reaffirmed in major statements by Khrushchev in 1957, 1960, and late 1962–early 1963).[25] These tensions in the new state aesthetic doctrine perhaps accounted for the relatively low profile granted to literature during the "cultural offensive," certainly compared to the written word's domestic prestige.

Western critics also granted Soviet literature a relatively low profile in the hierarchy of Soviet exports, although the early 1960s are important precisely because they saw literature briefly emerge as the most important "cultural" news story to come out of the Soviet Union. Nonetheless, the question of how to define its "excellence" in both objective and relative terms remained unresolved. Western publishers, finally, had to make a case for Western readers to read Soviet literature in translation, and this effort at persuasion often combined (albeit in very different ways from the Soviet authorities) politics with aesthetics, and normalization with exoticization. During translation, marketing, and reception, all sides worried about the "translatability" (in a nonlinguistic sense) of these texts into works with international appeal.

Meanwhile, the process by which these publishers came to release translations of Soviet literature was also hybrid: unlike the Soviet authorities' control over, say, a foreign tour of the Bolshoi ballet, Soviet literature could travel westwards via a variety of routes. Ironically, it was the Soviet authorities' refusal to join the international agreement on copyright that helped to "internationalize" Soviet literature during this time, allowing multiple editions of the same text to coexist and often to fuel greater media interest.[26] Of course, as previously, some post-Stalinist Soviet literature traveled abroad through familiar channels of book exportation, including Soviet publishing houses such as Progress and Soviet English-language journals, notably *Soviet Literature*. This journal did in fact translate most of the key Thaw works published in *Novyi mir*.[27] On the other hand, the journal also claimed that conservative narratives of de-Stalinization were equally worthy of translation, as indeed were any number of highly standardized works of socialist realism, making its canon of the Thaw different from the emerging Western canon.[28]

Translations also arrived on European and American bookshelves via "progressive" Western publishing houses and book clubs, and via mainstream publishers who had signed formal contracts with the Soviet book export ministry.[29] Such contracts were lucrative for the Soviet authorities (though not for the authors, whose royalties were withheld from them) and also granted them some control over the texts and paratexts of the editions.[30] For Western publishers, however, such contracts were of limited appeal, since there was nothing to prevent rival publishers from rushing out unauthorized versions of the same text, often (though not always) in more sensational-ist packaging. Indeed, this was exactly what happened with the most sensational Soviet text of the sixties, *Ivan Denisovich,* as well as with several other prose works caught up in the media frenzy surrounding it. With little legal redress to prevent these unau-thorized translations, the Soviet authorities could only monitor them and hope that "Soviet" versions would prove more popular. In this way, the American and European postwar "paperback revolution," and its attendant practices of marketing, intersected with the powerful but idiosyncratic Soviet publishing industry to produce and pro-mote an unprecedented variety of high-profile Soviet translations.[31]

What made this period unique, moreover, was the degree of crossover between Soviet and Western canons of works in translation. For a short while at least, as a comparison of *Soviet Literature, Publishers Weekly,* and the *Bookseller* demonstrates, Soviet and Western publishers could agree not only on the fact of Soviet literature's international interest but also on some of the works that would prove interesting. These different, but overlapping, canons of the new Soviet literature could advertise the more liberal and sophisticated Soviet Union (as the party hoped) or could take readers on a journey into a still very different culture and political system (as Western publishers generally, though not always, argued). On both sides, there was now a case to be made for reading Soviet literature itself, rather than only works that had been banned domestically or published abroad.[32] In this sense, the early 1960s was a time of both rapprochement and alienation between Soviet literature and the West, a time of discovery of some unexpected common ground but also of reassertion of difference and of barriers to cultural interaction. Soviet literature's anxious exportation during its "short 1960s" thus reveals both sides of this ambiguous period.[33]

"Not by Tractors Alone": Dudintsev as a New Soviet Literature?

In autumn 1957, an advertisement for "the BOOK that ROCKED RUSSIA" was splashed across the *Manchester Guardian*.[34] The book in question, Vladimir Dudintsev's *Not by Bread Alone,* was by far the most famous work of Soviet literature translated during the 1950s (Boris Pasternak's *Doctor Zhivago,* its translation rushed out in the West at approximately the same time as Dudintsev's English translation, was of course under-stood and marketed precisely in terms of its *non*-publication in the Soviet Union).[35] A realist (and in many ways, archetypally socialist realist) novel about an inventor, Lopatkin, and his struggles against the conservative Stalinist bureaucracy, embod-ied in the novel's arch-Stalinist villain, Drozdov, the work indeed "rocked" its home country far more than the Soviet authorities had anticipated when authorizing it for publication in 1956. Discussions of the novel had spiraled out of control, moving from criticism of Drozdov to vilification of "the Drozdovs" embedded throughout the Soviet system. Read in light of the alarming events unfolding in Hungary at the same time,

Dudintsev's novel and its subversive interpretations started to seem genuinely dangerous, and the author and his supporters were forced to recant. In this way, this symbol
of the post–Secret Speech Thaw quickly came to symbolize the domestic "Freeze" of
late 1956 and early 1957.[36]

By the time of this "Freeze," however, Dudintsev's novel had already seeped
abroad, its manuscript becoming all the more lucrative for foreign publishers in light
of the domestic scandal. When multiple translations of Dudintsev's text were published in the United Kingdom and the United States, the book was "already one of the
most talked of books of the year."[37] A flurry of contracts and lawsuits had accompanied the translation process, and these too were covered in detail in news sections.[38]
The foreign translation and publication of this transgressive novel in the 1950s served
as preparation for the wave of translated Soviet literature that would engulf Western
publishers in the next decade, allowing publishers and critics to hone their practices of
"marketing" Soviet literature and to begin to erect the interpretive framework for the
Thaw that would operate in the 1960s.

Publishers and critics above all urged readers to understand, and to share in, the
excitement and scandal that Dudintsev's novel had caused in the Soviet Union. The
domestic publication of "the novel that upsets the Kremlin" was a genuinely significant event in a society where literature was recapturing its role as a substitute public
sphere, the stormy reaction to it attesting to its decisive break with precedent.[39] Western readers were invited to put themselves in the place of their Soviet counterparts
and to imagine how explosive the novel must have felt compared with what came
before. The work was marketed and read as an index of political and social change,
orchestrated through literature but extending well beyond the usual literary sphere
of influence.

Another technique used to bring readers closer to the Soviet encounter with the
text was to suggest that the problems dramatized in the novel were "a fault not peculiar
to Russia."[40] Western readers might feel a sense of familiarity as they read about the
"vested interests," even the "universal human predicament," that the hero Lopatkin
was combating.[41] At the same time, the critical reception emphasized the productive
differences between the Soviet and foreign reading experiences. Unconstrained by
Soviet controls on public discussion, and unfettered by the Soviet mind-set, liberal
critics and their readers should be able to tease out the full implications of the novel,
including those not perceived by Dudintsev himself (whose "target, in fact, is far larger
than he seems to imagine," explained one British reader).[42] One review explicitly fore-
grounded the differences in "freedom" between Soviet and Western reading contexts:
"So pervasive is the evil and the intrigue that the reader may find it difficult to distinguish between the failings of communist officials and the failings of communism. The
non-Russian reader, in any case, is under no compulsion to make this distinction."[43]

The less ideologically constrained critics outside the Soviet Union came to a
critical consensus: the novel was "revolutionary."[44] They explained how "the novel

questions the basic structure of the system"; its revolutionary subtext made the novel "a delayed-action time bomb" within the Soviet context.[45] Western readers, though, could understand and experience its explosive impact directly and immediately.

It was this description of the novel as an explosive device that struck Dudintsev himself when presented with foreign translations of his work, replete with lurid quotations from critics.[46] Western publisher interest in the novel had overwhelmed the Soviet authorities almost as soon as the novel was serialized in *Novyi mir*. It was partly their anxiety about foreign press rumors about the book that shaped Soviet decision making on both its domestic and its foreign publication. The "false allegations" of a ban that had been made by the "reactionary press abroad" eventually left them with no choice but to issue a small print run of a book edition domestically.[47] Decision making on foreign editions was similarly constrained; rather than banning the work's export and thereby fueling "bourgeois" rumors about Soviet repression, the authorities had to try instead to control the form that it assumed as it traveled abroad. However, Soviet officials had only limited control over the rights to the novel, and although they sought to dominate the market with approved translations by "progressive" Western publishing houses, the lack of copyright meant that unauthorized translations quickly proliferated.[48]

As early as the end of 1956, Soviet officials also sought to "establish control over translations and the context of prefaces" as a way to control "bourgeois" interpretations of the text.[49] The preface that Dudintsev was compelled to write (or sign) was intended as a counterattack "speaking out against those who try to use his book to anti-Soviet ends."[50] However, when Western critics read this preface they either ignored it or construed it as a sign of the author's ongoing resistance and refusal to recant.[51] Further Kremlin-sponsored attempts to counteract the Western reception only led critics to repeat, and even to deepen, their criticisms of the Soviet system. The *Observer*'s Edward Crankshaw responded to Soviet attacks on his coverage of the novel, allegedly voiced by Dudintsev himself and broadcast on Moscow radio, by insisting yet again that "Soviet society, with its multiplicity of Drozdovs and the sort of philistinism pilloried in Mr Dudintsev's book, is moving not towards true communism, but towards something quite different."[52]

With the novel's status cemented as the "high point in the effort of Soviet writers to speak boldly and frankly about burning problems of their country," aesthetic considerations became decisively secondary.[53] "Not a great novel in its own right," with substantial "literary failings," Dudintsev's work nonetheless retained its historic significance.[54] Indeed, its uncompromisingly honest content could even be viewed as stylistically innovative, initiating a shift from socialist realism to a renewed commitment to "critical realism"; this tentative revival of the nineteenth-century Russian tradition was sufficient recommendation to Western readers.[55] There was, after all, only so much that one writer, and one "explosive" text, could do to detonate the edifice of Stalinist literature: "It is certainly not surprising," concluded one observer, "that the years of

Stalinist over-simplification have left marks on literature that cannot immediately be erased."[56]

However, there were isolated challenges to this willingness to overlook aesthetic backwardness in the new Soviet literature. In a single week in late 1957, two reviews of the novel appeared in the British press that took aim at the dominant critical paradigm, asking respectively, "What would it look like to anyone who read it purely as a novel?" and "What is it like, not as a document . . . but as a novel, nothing but a novel?"[57] One of the two pieces relentlessly advanced its stylistic critique, making no concessions to the novel's pioneering content. Dudintsev was accused of epitomizing "the theory of 'realism' as understood by western novelists in 1910" and of writing "with a doggedness that makes the English novels of that epoch . . . seem like gossamer." So "backward" was Dudintsev's style, in fact, that the Western appeal of *Not by Bread Alone* was almost unimaginable: "History has moved on; we are out of the epoch of 'realism' just as we are out of reach of the hobble skirt and the chain-driven motor car. No western writer could combine the energy and imaginative concentration of Dudintsev with his faithfulness to the literary theory of 40 years ago. It is one of those details that bring home just what it means to live in a world where clocks and calendars move at different speeds. In Russian fiction it is still 1910. Joyce, Proust, Kafka, Gide have not yet existed." Judged by the advanced standards of Western modernism, Dudintsev had failed: to drive the point home, the review ended: "As an example of literary art, its interest is very slight, and nothing is likely to be gained by not admitting it."[58] The other stylistically oriented review was more succinct and yet less categorical. "As a novel," it argued, Dudintsev's work was "not particularly good," hampered by naïveté, rigidity, and didacticism. Having admitted these flaws, though, the reviewer contended that in fact "its literary flaws don't matter tuppence." Like all but one of his fellow reviewers, he ultimately was "so exhilarated, so moved and heartened by the mere fact of this novel that reviewing standards cease to count." Readers must similarly suspend normal literary criteria: "You have to take Dudintsev," he breathlessly concluded, "you simply have to."[59]

Not by Bread Alone excited Western publishers and critics alike because it revealed that the Soviet Union had changed but also that it had stayed the same. Precisely because its publication and dissemination bridged the Thaw *and* the "Freeze" of the first year after the Secret Speech, the novel could appear to be both Soviet and dissident, symbolizing the truth-telling potential of the new Soviet literature, while also making such "progress" seem dangerously contingent on the whims of a largely unreconstructed party leadership. The benchmark of this progress was "freedom," but of content more than of style: for the time being, if Soviet literature had become more "realistic" about the Soviet system, it mattered little that the stylistic straitjacket of socialist realism had not yet loosened.

As Soviet literature expanded within Western publishing in the sixties, the fast-moving political currents of the domestic Thaw (analogous to those that had caused the rapid decline in Dudintsev's reputation) continued to provide Western publishers with a compelling and marketable narrative of dissent and to fuel tensions with Soviet authorities, who had wanted this literature to advertise the regime's commitment to liberalization.[60] However, in contrast to their reception of Dudintsev, Western critics in the 1960s became less inclined to indulge Soviet literature's stylistic "backwardness." While its truth telling might allow it to "converge" with Western liberalism, the resolute antimodernism of the Soviet novel made it fundamentally incongruous with hegemonic Western notions of "good literature." In this sense, Soviet and Western critics paradoxically came to an agreement about the fundamental "otherness" of Soviet socialist realism. For Soviet critics, Soviet literature's uniqueness lay in its participation in the "messianic" dissemination of the communist message worldwide. For "nonprogressive" Western critics, however, this politicization was precisely the problem. Ironically, though, their defense of aesthetic experimentation free of political interference became part of an intensely political debate about the links between artistic and political freedom, which echoed and developed in new directions other Cold War debates about the links between politics and art.[61]

Translating and Marketing Thaw Literature

The Soviet publication of *Ivan Denisovich* in late 1962 made headline news the world over; moreover, it was the only Soviet literary text whose translation itself became the object of frenzied front-page discussion the following year.[62] The dispute between two American publishers regarding the simultaneous publication of two translations of the text, only three months after its first Soviet appearance, briefly dominated headlines, and the translators' political biases and linguistic differences were discussed in most subsequent book reviews.[63] Such "races" and lawsuits between rival translations of other texts recurred in the months and years after Solzhenitsyn's advent into world literature.[64] Robert Conquest has observed of *Ivan Denisovich* that "the appearance of his work in English . . . was an enormously different phenomenon from the mere 'translation' of a 'writer' in the ordinary sense."[65] These multiple forms of translation were not, however, exclusive to Solzhenitsyn, though they may have been peculiarly intensive and complex in that case; they extended to the many other works of Soviet literature that appeared in English translation in the 1960s.[66] The first part of this process was the marketing of translations, which significantly reinflected the texts' meanings as they traveled out of their original context toward their new readers. This section will examine these practices as applied to a new wave of Soviet literary works, peaking in 1963, when Solzhenitsyn's *Ivan Denisovich* led the charge of Soviet literature onto British and American bookshelves. At this time, American and British readers also encountered translated works by Iurii Bondarev, Ivan Stadniuk, Il'ia Erenburg, Fedor Abramov, Konstantin Simonov, and Viktor Nekrasov. These were compared and contrasted with Solzhenitsyn's best seller, producing new understandings of Soviet literature and life, as examined in the following section.

There was no single technique for marketing Soviet literature: some publishers (especially those politically hostile to the Soviet system, such as Flegon Press) relied on political sensationalism, while others elided political differences in favor of the universal appeal of a slowly rehumanizing literary tradition. The appeal of Soviet literature now also partly rested upon the idea that the Soviet literary intelligentsia were becoming increasingly bold in their resistance to the regime and closer to Western standards of liberalism and that there were growing similarities between everyday life in the West and in the East because of the gradual liberalization and westernization of the Soviet Union.[67] Thus the marketing of the Thaw relied on a paradoxical notion of Soviet culture's alterity and similarity relative to the West.[68]

The "sensational" case for reading Soviet literature relied on the exoticization of the Soviet Union as a land of political controls and gross suffering at the hands of the state—a perspective on the USSR with a long pedigree in the West.[69] In the 1960s, what was novel was that Soviet literature itself was contributing to this image by dwelling on the evils of Stalinism. This perhaps explains why the crimson common to the Soviet flag and to Soviet victims' blood proved irresistible as a cover design to publishers across the political spectrum. Red capital letters, "etched as it were in blood," ran the length of the cover of the Soviet-authorized text of Ivan Stadniuk's *People Are Not Angels,* alarming the author when he first saw it.[70] The hammer and sickle dripped blood in the remarkably similar cover of Flegon Press's scandalously *un*authorized translation of Aleksandr Gorbatov's memoir of the Great Terror.[71]

However, the design of both authorized and unauthorized versions of Solzhenitsyn's *Ivan Denisovich* reflected a greater sense of restraint, perhaps intended to allude to the austere, laconic style of the text itself. While barbed wire snaked across the cover of the Kremlin-approved version of the text, the unabashedly unauthorized translation by Hayward and Hingley depicted only a disembodied knotted brow, the expression of the eyes suggesting both suffering and determination.[72] Both designs nevertheless prompted readers to view Ivan Denisovich as an everyman and the experience of incarceration as at least widespread, if not universal, in the Soviet Union.

The textual framing in prefaces, afterwords, and publisher "blurbs" and advertisements, as with Dudintsev, most often highlighted the circumstances of domestic publication, urging readers to place texts' "revelations" within the limited glasnost of de-Stalinization. Such contextualization also linked this literature to texts with which foreign audiences would be more familiar: news coverage of Soviet politics. From the start, therefore, this new wave of literature was tied to the "political tide table" and the "sociological" and "informational" functions that Rachel May identifies as persistent features of nineteenth- and twentieth-century Russian literature in translation.[73]

In the comparison drawn by the American publisher of Konstantin Simonov's war novel *The Living and the Dead,* for instance, the analogy between political and literary de-Stalinization seemed exact: "What Khrushchev's famous speech on Stalin's crimes and blunders has done to Soviet political life," it averred, "*Victims and Heroes* is likely to do to Soviet war literature."[74] The longer translator's preface emphasized that the novel was "the first in Soviet war literature" to ask probing questions about Stalinism, even if they were not "always answer[ed] candidly and convincingly." It conceded that, to Western readers, "it may seem incredible that Soviet readers could have had to wait until 1959 before a novel could appear in their country whose heroes were allowed to ask themselves and others the kinds of obvious questions that millions of Soviet men and women must have been asking since the 22nd of June 1941." However, it asked them to understand the different political and literary norms that governed Soviet culture and thereby to perceive Simonov as a genuine pioneer.[75]

The exhortation to appreciate the novelty of the content within the Soviet context and to forgive any incompleteness in "truth telling" also featured in the paratexts of editions of Solzhenitsyn's *Ivan Denisovich* and Gorbatov's memoir. Well known as the camps were in the West, they had domestically been smothered by a "blanket of silence . . . as thick as the snow over the world's greatest land-mass"; thus Solzhenitsyn's text, while officially sanctioned, had substantially disrupted the status quo, becoming a "runaway Soviet sensation."[76] Gorbatov's memoir was likewise pioneering because it was the "first such account to be published in the Soviet Union," its candor especially remarkable given that de-Stalinization had released only "facts half hinted at by . . . rulers . . . disjointed shreds of history that are clearly incomplete."[77] In this way, Soviet literature was doubly exotic, allowing readers insight not only into unimaginable suffering but into constraints on public expression that seemed bizarre, if not immoral, to inhabitants of Western democracies. As with Dudintsev's text, the domestic sensation caused by these texts' revelations was supposed to be echoed by a similarly sensational effect in the West. Solzhenitsyn's "revolutionary document" should cause "horror and revulsion" among its Western readers, and Gorbatov's memoir ought to be a "sensation,"[78] even though much fuller information about the Gulag and the Terror had already been circulating abroad for at least two decades prior to the Secret Speech.[79]

Continuing a technique used to market Dudintsev, publishers were also conscious of the need to present their authors and texts as transgressors of Soviet norms.[80] Stadniuk's novel was thus said to be "unusually critical," even "iconoclastic," toward the Soviet system.[81] Simonov's novel, its partial truth telling conceded by its translator, was nonetheless marketed as the most "startling" piece of Russian literature since *Doctor Zhivago*. Here the analogy with a famously unpublished novel suggested that the novel was more disobedient than its authorization for publication might suggest.[82] After *Ivan Denisovich* started to make waves abroad, it became one of the points of reference for subsequent Soviet literary texts, imbuing them with the aura of dissent, even though all the works in question were technically "permitted" publications. Fedor Abramov's novel about collectivization *Vokrug da okolo* was first marketed in the United Kingdom by Flegon Press under the title *One Day in the New Life*. The title, before it changed (to *The Dodgers*), was obviously intended to provoke associations with Solzhenitsyn's "shattering impact," but in fact the publishers went further still.

Their publicity claimed that Abramov's "startling" revelations about *this* day in Soviet life cast Ivan Denisovich's day into the shade.[83] Increasingly peripheral within their domestic context, Thaw works translated abroad participated in an escalating competition to be the most daring Soviet text of all.

For all the emphasis on novelty and dissent, there remained uncertainty regarding the well-informed Western reader's interest in these texts' political and social revelations; this led publishers and translators also to emphasize that these texts pointed to experiences and values shared across the Iron Curtain. The Soviet everyday life and moral dilemmas presented by Nekrasov and Bondarev were therefore "strangely familiar" and said to "differ little from [those] of Chelsea or Greenwich Village."[84] *Victims and Heroes,* meanwhile, showed shared values and goals in the past, reminding readers about erstwhile Soviet-Western cooperation during the "hot" combat that had preceded the Cold War.[85]

Although less powerful than the "exoticizing" discourse that often framed Soviet translations, these hints at convergence and coexistence demonstrate the unstable Western image not just of Soviet literature but of the Soviet Union itself as it shifted between peaceful coexistence and Cold War tensions. Indeed, the Soviet authorities themselves were inconsistent in their "coexistence" with Western framings of Soviet literature. In extreme cases, the mere fact of translation and marketing could so transform texts that the Soviet authorities blocked their return home, regularly confiscating "translations of books by Soviet writers with hostile prefaces and commentaries" at the Soviet border.[86]

Understanding or Condescension? British and American Critics on Soviet Literature

By the early 1960s, front-page coverage of "Mr. K" still far overshadowed that of any Soviet writer, but coverage of the cultural politics of the Thaw and of individual writers' works now appeared regularly in the news and arts sections of the British and American press.[87] Where Khrushchev would typically appear daily on page 1 or 2, goings-on in Soviet creative unions might be covered once or twice a month (rising to daily coverage in the front pages at times of intensive change, such as the late 1962 and early 1963 "Freeze").[88] Meanwhile, visits by Soviet writers (Evtushenko, Erenburg, and Tvardovskii were the most famous and frequent) to British or American shores would receive plentiful coverage, reflecting their growing celebrity outside the Soviet Union.[89] This news coverage of Soviet cultural politics not only fueled interest in individual Soviet literary texts but was often combined with it, as many reviews of translations were authored by newspapers' Moscow correspondents.

These journalists, observing the fitful advances and retreats in official tolerance of formal experimentation and "unvarnished" realism, were unanimous in their confusion. "It is the hardest thing to form a clear picture of the state of literature and the arts in the Soviet Union today," concluded one correspondent, typically, in early 1963.[90]

It was precisely the continuous shifts in the "temperature" of the Thaw that induced many observers to concentrate exclusively on thermometer readings; the political shifts were so minutely detailed and complex that a certain "nurseyness" was unavoidable.[91]

Frustration with this dominant Kremlinological approach to literature, epitomized by the *Observer*'s Edward Crankshaw and Oxford's Max Hayward, spilled over into open debate in late 1963, when the *New Statesman* called for "political overtones" to be of secondary importance. The piece occasioned an angry response from Crankshaw and a partial recantation by the author, A. Alvarez, who conceded that politics could never be dismissed from consideration.[92] Complaints about the "school of interpreters . . . growing up in the West which has started to apply the methods of sovietology to the literary scene" did little overall to diminish this school's dominance of the public debate, not least because this approach was very powerful in rapidly growing American and European Slavic departments.[93]

Thus, paradoxically, a story that should have been about the loosening of ties between writers and politicians found politics to be inescapable, perhaps even more so than in the Stalin era. Politics intruded everywhere: as the explanation of the state of Soviet literature at the start of the Thaw, its maturity stunted by years of Stalinist dogma, and as a factor in the current failure to "catch up with the West," its progress now hampered by Khrushchev's sporadic anti-Western and antiformalist outbursts. The most intensive phase of Soviet literature's translation and reception in the West coincided with the performance and aftereffects of the most notorious of these. Khrushchev's March 1963 speech on the arts was widely translated and disseminated abroad and confirmed to critics that "the restoration of normal cultural relations with the outside world has been postponed yet again" and that "the thaw hasn't really happened yet."[94]

The dominant press narrative of the Thaw thus viewed its hesitant progress as the result of the system's "default" ideological settings.[95] Analyses frequently pointed out that writers themselves had in fact progressed much further from Stalinist norms than the authorities, that "the movement of the Soviet intelligentsia towards Western ideas and interests" showed no signs of stopping.[96] However, this liberal teleology in writers' identities was only weakly reflected in what they were permitted to publish in the Soviet Union, and it was these permitted publications that constituted the bulk of what was translated in the early 1960s.[97] The degree of acceptable aesthetic primitivism and ideological conformity therefore remained contested in the reception of these works, although critics less interested in taking the political system's "temperature" generally insisted on imposing more objective standards of literary excellence.

By the late Khrushchev era, not a single translation of Soviet literature was overlooked by the UK and U.S. press organs surveyed here; every translated work had received at least a paragraph-long review, and many had received stand-alone coverage. Thus, in contrast to the breathless coverage of Dudintsev's "extraordinary" work in the 1950s, Soviet literature as a whole became the object of an ongoing process of reflection in the 1960s. Soviet literature never lost its Sovietness during this process, but many translated works provoked readers to rethink the balance between social-ism and realism in socialist realism. Critics highlighted the greater truthfulness with which Soviet writers were now describing the country's past and present, echoing the reception of Dudintsev's novel and still expressing a lingering sense of surprise that Soviet literature was capable of such frankness. Reviewers acclaimed Stadniuk for "not flinching from the whole brutal story" and Gorbatov for "pulling no punches."[98] By thus framing Soviet literature in terms of what it was *not* doing, reviewers emphasized these texts' rupture with expected practice.[99] Konstantin Simonov's novel showed the "horror . . . despair . . . sheer chaos" with "the realistic savagery of a frontline camera-man" and "could scarcely be more frank."[100]

To a much greater degree than the books' marketing, however, critics also empha-sized that which had been left unsaid; Soviet literature's habit of "distorting or thin-ning out the facts" died hard.[101] Simonov's novel contained "by no means the whole truth . . . a fraction of the chaos" and "does not assess all the ultimate horrors"; review-ers, often journalists or close observers of the Soviet Union, compared his account of the war with what they (and Simonov himself) had witnessed at the time and found it partial at best.[102] Meanwhile, Gorbatov, even when writing about his own life, was "less than candid" and was "selective" in what he revealed about the Great Terror; reviewers knew from decades of publicity about the purges that there was more to be said.[103] Even Solzhenitsyn's universally acclaimed breaking of the Soviet silence about the Gulag was incomplete, according to some. "Mr Solzhenitsyn told the truth, but not the whole truth," a fact that became increasingly apparent when his book was compared with other accounts of the Soviet Gulag long in print in the West.[104] While a sign of progress, then, *Ivan Denisovich* did not "go nearly far enough or deeply enough into the great national trauma," and consequently "the many-faceted tragedy that has affected every Soviet man, woman and child still awaits its writer."[105]

Little did reviewers know that these works in fact represented the high point of Soviet literature's confrontation of the "truth" and that even this limited glasnost would be quickly rescinded as the authorities deepened the "Freeze" imposed at the start of 1963. For the time being, Soviet literature was surely, but slowly, inching toward the "full story" that Western readers already knew or assumed to exist. This ongoing "backwardness" in coming forward with the whole truth was attributed both to state literary controls and to writers' own inability to be fully honest.[106]

There was, however, yet another constraint on Soviet literature's frankness explored during this process of reception, and here the dividing lines between Soviet and Western norms were less clear. Reviews often expressed an awareness, and a contempt, of socialist realism's insistence on a happy ending. Stadniuk's novel about collectivization was universally acclaimed for its brutal honesty about peasant suffer-ing but was often gently chided for its happy ending.[107] Even Solzhenitsyn's work did not escape such complaints, with Frank Kermode claiming that "it is in fact socialist realism, the authorities approved of it, because . . . the suffering, like the bureaucratic cruelty which caused it, is a thing of the past."[108] However, it was also recognized that this narrative convention was not exclusively Soviet; one review, of Viktor Nekrasov's *Kira*, pointed out that the novel's upbeat conclusion resembled the "painless sunrise" of the standard Hollywood happy ending.[109] Many Western reviewers also confirmed this point implicitly by giving their own reviews "happy endings" and making this optimism central to the "selling" of the works to the Western audience. Solzhenitsyn's narrative of the Gulag, "a difficult world for Americans to comprehend," nonetheless contained the necessary element of redemption:[110] "Americans can read it," the *New York Times* promised, "for its simple recital of man's inhumanity and man's courage to survive."[111] Many other reviews of *Ivan Denisovich* echoed this redemptive, even "triumphant," trajectory, and the tropes of hope, survival, and victory echoed in reviews of other works.[112]

Indeed, when first producing the texts, publishers had often made happy endings a selling point. Bondarev's bleak novel of postwar terror, *Silence,* was widely criticized by Soviet critics and readers for its lack of a happy ending, yet the American translation claimed that "the novel ends on a hopeful note."[113] And after a relentless enumeration of Soviet crimes, Hayward and Hingley ended their preface to *Ivan Denisovich* in an optimistic key: "Solzhenitsyn has succeeded," they insisted, "in strengthening our faith in the ultimate victory of civilized values over evil."[114] Even though the promise of outrage and horror was central to the sensational "case" for exporting these works to the West, redemption still had to form part of the reading experience.

While reflecting in this way on changes and continuities in socialist realism (and between Soviet and Western norms), critics also reflected on socialism more broadly. Solzhenitsyn's *Ivan Denisovich,* while exceptional in other ways, was not the most extreme text in this regard, as it was largely viewed as a critique of Stalinism rather than of socialism as a whole. Viewing its publication as a healing rather than damaging act, Western critics echoed the discourse that greeted (and facilitated) its Soviet publication, albeit with a more emphatic (and durable) endorsement of the depiction of Ivan's despair and humiliation.[115] In fact, *Soviet Literature* sought from the start to moderate Western praise for the text's tragic elements, translating and printing a survey of positive *and* negative Soviet perspectives on the work, even though at the time Soviet acclaim for the text was still dominant.[116]

Nonetheless, it was other, less famous texts that provoked the most sustained systemic critique and sounded the strongest echoes of Dudintsev's reception. Reading Simonov's novel, the *New York Times*'s erstwhile Moscow correspondent Harrison Salisbury found in it a devastating "indictment" of the "system as it really is."[117] The publication of Fedor Abramov's novel was "past understanding," as it was so "accusatory" that it must surely damage rather than heal the system.[118] In both cases, these Western responses elicited Soviet counterattacks reminiscent of those orchestrated during the saga of *Not by Bread Alone.* Simonov and Abramov, both placed under considerable party pressure, publicly refuted Western critics' interpretations of their works as systemic critiques, insisting that they were serving rather than attacking the party.[119]

Like Dudintsev's counterattacks, these Soviet claims had little effect on either the reception or the marketing of 1960s Soviet literature. In fact, reviews in the vein of Crankshaw and Salisbury proved irresistible for publishers, featuring prominently in the ongoing advertising of these texts.[120] The political and politicized content of Soviet novels was unavoidable, yet it was also a big part of the appeal of these works: critics could honestly acclaim the "lights of criticism that have been rising over the stagnant waters of Russian fiction."[121] This fiction now offered real insight into Soviet life and a real critique of the Soviet system, both points of appeal to audiences inhabiting the other side of the still robust ideological divide. Yet if the content of Soviet literature could now be somewhat more "realistic," the stylistic constraints of realism had not relaxed nearly as much, and the purely literary pleasures of Soviet literature were much more dubious. In contrast to Dudintsev's reception, Soviet literature's continued stylistic failings (relative to Western literary standards) became increasingly hard to excuse into the 1960s.

A great many reviews simply ignored stylistic considerations altogether, focusing exclusively on content, a possibly unintentional but still unmistakable slight. A few advanced cautious praise for an incremental amelioration in Soviet literary style. Usually this improvement was seen as a gradual resumption of Russian nineteenth-century realism rather than being compared with "the brilliance of the twenties," the peak of Russian literary experimentation, its closest approximation to Western modernism, and the last gasp of creative freedom before the imposition of state literary doctrine.[122] Viktor Nekrasov's works, including his novella *Kira*, had originally been marketed as realism rather than socialist realism: in prepublication advertising, the work appeared as "a psychological drama," attractive precisely because it was "without obtrusive noises from factory floor or party congress."[123] Critics' assessments continued this emphasis, hailing his work for "elud[ing] the preachy banalities of the official 'socialist realism'" and for reviving "this gentle humanist tradition, so typical of Russia."[124] Less "gentle" but equally "humanist" was Solzhenitsyn's novella, often inserted by both publishers and critics into the "great Russian tradition."[125] Aside from the obvious parallels with Dostoevskii's *House of the Dead*, the "Russianness" of *Ivan Denisovich* lay in the depiction of Shchukov, "a 'simple heart,' a beloved Russian type from Turgenev to Tolstoy," and of "a selection of Russian characters . . . which may astonish English readers."[126] Thaw literature could in this way be both familiar and "astonishing": the unique qualities that had originally recommended classic Russian literature to foreign readers now seemed to have been interrupted rather than killed off during the Soviet period.[127]

A few critics even saw in this resurrection of Russian literature's hallmarks of "decency and truthfulness with a moral edge" an improvement on present-day Western practice.[128] One review of *Victims and Heroes* found in it "something that now seems wholly Russian and almost entirely absent from western writing . . . the ability to render basic human emotions simply and in their full dignity."[129] Other critics also viewed Russian literature's revived commitment to solving "fundamental Russian conflicts" as its "whole allure" for Western readers.[130] In such comparisons, the "sincerity" that Vladimir Pomerantsev had demanded of Soviet literature at the start of the Thaw had developed to the point of outshining its Western counterpart, where "sincere" emotion and morality had become less fashionable in light of 1950s and 1960s counterculture.

While the realism of 1960s Soviet literature was welcomed as a partial return to Russian literature's traditions, the socialism of socialist realism still remained decisively marginal to its appeal. The idea that socialist realism's ideological commitment might be a point of appeal to the Western reader was relegated to the periphery of the debate, limited to the "progressive" press.[131] Negatively inflected, however, its ideological commitment in fact featured prominently in critiques that, at first sight, deliberately distanced art from politics. As in contemporary debates surrounding abstract art, these unflattering comparisons of Soviet literature with supposedly universal aesthetic standards reaffirmed "western notions of the essential connection between art, individual freedom, and western capitalist democracy."[132]

Critics who were not professional observers of Soviet politics for the most part evaluated Soviet texts in terms of the (supposedly universal) literary criteria of "subtlety" and formalism.[133] In so doing, they found that even the newest Soviet literature was irredeemably backward compared with the "modernist canon" that Western literary criticism was constructing at the time.[134] One review of Aksenov's *Starry Ticket* explained that the novel was "one of the new 'Russian' novels which are hopefully greeted in the West as a sign that they are really like the US after all." However, the novel's "massive moral simplicity" had quickly dashed such hopes.[135] Again, the fault lay less with writers than with systemic constraints, but Soviet literature still seemed "immature" relative to present Western literary practice, thanks to decades of ideological pressures.[136] Another response made this binary between Western and Soviet standards explicit, splitting its review of Evtushenko's *Precocious Autobiography* into two halves. In the first, the text appeared remarkably exciting by Soviet standards, but in the second, the text was slammed for its lack of contribution to the general understanding of an educated westerner, since it was "above all an *unsophisticated* book."[137] Finally, Frank Kermode's survey of Thaw literature in spring 1963 saw only a few Russian writers (Tarsis, Tertz, Pasternak) as capable of a "strong affirmation of the Russian right to the European tradition"—and all of them were restricted to samizdat even in this supposedly more liberal era. Only a wholesale "thaw" of political restrictions on literature, and total creative freedom, would allow a genuine "new literature" to flourish.[138]

Kermode's critique was deeply troubling to the Soviet authorities. Translations of more direct invective from Soviet critics and authors against his, and other Western critics', alleged distortions of Soviet literature were a regular feature of *Soviet Literature* even at the height of the Thaw in late 1962, and increasingly thereafter.[139] In responding to "anti-Soviet" readings of Soviet literature, the Soviet authorities unsurprisingly resorted not just to invective but also to censorship. An example of the latter was the frequent banning of Western literary criticism of the Thaw, on its attempted entry into the Soviet Union, by officials troubled by its "anti-Soviet" narrative of the Thaw as a time of growing dissent and formal experimentation.[140]

Alone among foreign translations of Soviet-published works, *Ivan Denisovich* both received and survived serious stylistic scrutiny. Measured against both his Soviet contemporaries and non-Soviet authors including Hemingway, Solzhenitsyn's achievement seemed objectively impressive: here was an exception, in terms of "maturity," to the backwardness of most Soviet literature.[141] What was unique in his text was the successful fusion of maximal realism with stylistic sophistication, and most critics did not seek to separate out these fused components.[142] Only isolated critics insisted that Solzhenitsyn's tour de force had to be scrutinized independently of its gigantic political and moral significance. Two reviewers tried to argue that the style was so laconic and spare as to be not only unostentatious but perhaps nonexistent—and insisted that this represented a failure to live up to the highest literary standards.[143]

Despite having been taken more seriously than his contemporaries on stylistic grounds, Solzhenitsyn later professed himself horrified that "*Ivan Denisovich* [was] seized on all over the world as a Khrushchevite political sensation" and was "vulgarized beyond all recognition, turned into crude propaganda."[144] In the overall reception of the new Soviet literature, stylistic criteria indeed proved less important than "truth telling" and political critique; the Thaw reproduced the traditional "bias towards information and away from art" typical of the longer-term reception of Russian culture in Britain and America.[145] Critics and publishers insisted on portraying texts' truth telling as a sensational act of rebellion or iconoclasm against the Soviet system; in fact, the Western reception of Soviet literature shared many tropes with its original domestic reception, which also endorsed, at least for a while, the truths being "exposed" in such works.

But these points in common between Soviet and Western ideas about Soviet literature were precarious. Even during the Thaw of the early 1960s, the domestic reputations of the principal writers translated into English—Ehrenburg, Nekrasov, Bondarev, Solzhenitsyn, Abramov, and Tvardovskii—were subject to dramatic reversals and perpetually insecure. At times, even the shortest intervals between domestic publication and foreign translation could be long enough to witness a writer's fall from grace; this, of course, only increased the sensational appeal of their works abroad.[146] When Soviet piecemeal attacks on individual deviations developed into an overall "freeze" and a definitive dissociation of Soviet literature from the "whole truth," in the early Brezhnev era, Soviet literature's international appeal started to wane. Increasingly, into the mid- and late 1960s, the "truth telling" that had made Soviet literature most appealing abroad could take place only outside Soviet literature, in the samizdat and tamizdat texts that came to dominate the Western market.[147]

Soviet literature's aesthetic appeal was even more precarious, and from an even earlier juncture of the 1960s. The demands for greater stylistic sophistication made by some Western critics exposed the formal limits of socialist realism and indeed provoked the Soviet authorities to reassert them, accentuating the differences between Soviet and Western literatures. These literary debates thus dramatized and reaffirmed the limits of ideological and cultural convergence between East and West. This was confirmed before the end of the Khrushchev era, when stylistically experimental translated stories were already being marketed as "dissonant"; the further slide into active "dissent" against Soviet formal criteria, a little later into the 1960s, was barely noticeable.[148]

The Thaw and its hesitant internationalization thus exposed the explicit and implicit assumptions and practices of the institutions involved in "translating" it to foreign audiences. Both the marketing and the critical reception of Soviet literature revolved around the discursive construction of the Soviet Union as "other" and "backward" relative to "Western" literary and political standards. However, Soviet literature's commercial success also depended on "selling" a narrative of Soviet liberalization and modernization—in short, westernization—to its readers. But when critics judged Soviet literature according to criteria of modernity and modernism, they consistently found that it fell short. Soviet literature's success in the West, based above all on the thrill of its newly "truthful" content rather than its sophisticated style, depended on a constant supply of sensational revelations. However, the domestic "freeze" of the Thaw rapidly drove such revelations into the underground, shifting foreign publishers' and readers' attention beyond the limits of Soviet literature by the end of the decade.

Notes

The author would like to thank the editors of this volume and the participants of the "Socialist Sixties" conference, and also Philip Bullock, Kristin Roth-Ey, and Gerry Smith, for their helpful comments on this piece.

1. Philip Toynbee, "Voice of Young Russia," review of *A Precocious Autobiography,* by Evgenii Evtushenko, *Observer,* 4 August 1963, 14. Cf. Toynbee's similarly dichotomous claim that "in this field, we are comparatively *haut* and they are comparatively *bas*"; Philip Toynbee, "A Soviet Novelist in Bohemia," review of *People and Life: Memoirs of 1891–1917,* by Ilya Ehrenburg, *Observer,* 3 September 1961, 25.

2. Expression drawn from, among other works, Frances Stonor Saunders, *The Cultural Cold War: The CIA and the World of Arts and Letters* (New York: New Press, 2000).

3. For a list of Soviet literature translated into English in the late 1950s and early 1960s, see Thomas Whitney, ed. and trans., *The New Writing in Russia* (Ann Arbor: University of Michigan Press, 1964), 382–412. David Engerman claims that "translations, anthologies and reportage on thaw literature abounded"; *Know Your Enemy: The Rise and Fall of America's Soviet Experts* (Oxford: Oxford University Press, 2009), 130. Rachel May by contrast asserts that "translations of Soviet (that is nondissident) prose of the 1950s–1970s are relatively few and far between" (*The Translator in the Text: On Reading Russian Literature in English* [Evanston: Northwestern University Press, 1994], 47), but this ignores the sudden intensification in the early 1960s.

4. On *Ivan Denisovich*'s print runs and sales figures, see "Rival Translations," *Bookseller,* 19 January 1963, 104; *Bookseller,* "One Day," 2 February 1963, 272; untitled report on print runs, *Publishers*

Weekly (hereafter *PW*), 7 January 1963, 48; ad for Praeger edition with information on print runs, *PW*, 7 January 1963, 51; double-page ad with information about print runs selling out, *PW*, 14 January 1963, 34–35; "Rival Versions of Russian Novel Go Down to the Wire," *PW*, 14 January 1963, 47–48; "Best Sellers of the Week," *PW*, 4 March 1963, 132 (first mention of *Ivan Denisovich* in "bestsellers" section; it remained there for several months); ad for Penguin edition, *Bookseller*, 29 June 1963, 69. The advertising campaign for the work was the biggest in Praeger's history (untitled report, *PW*, 7 January 1963, 48; Praeger ad, 14 January 1963, 51; double-page ad for Praeger edition, *PW*, 14 January 1963, 34–35). A CC ideology department 1963 report regarding the reception of *Ivan Denisovich* abroad also noted its "enormous print runs" in Russian State Archive of Contemporary History (Rossiiskii gosudarstvennyi arkhiv noveishei istorii, RGANI), f. 5, op. 55, d. 44, ll. 39, 40–51.

5. May, *Translator in the Text*, 42.

6. Compare with the tensions between Latin American literature's "revolutionary" identity and its place in the "autonomous world of international literary space." Russell Cobb, "Promoting Literature in the Most Dangerous Area in the World, the Cold War, the Boom and Mundo Nuevo," in *Pressing the Fight: Print, Propaganda and the Cold War*, ed. Greg Barnhisel and Catherine Turner (Amherst: University of Massachusetts Press, 2010), 231–50.

7. Lowell Schwartz emphasizes that 1960 "ushered in a new and highly dangerous period of the cold war." Lowell Schwartz, *Political Warfare against the Kremlin: US and British Propaganda Policy at the Beginning of the Cold War* (Basingstoke: Palgrave Macmillan, 2009), 190; cf. Walter Hixson, *Parting the Curtain: Propaganda, Culture and the Cold War* (New York: St. Martin's Press, 1997), esp. 219. Robert English points out that only Berlin in 1961 and Cuba in 1962 forced both sides to learn the "nuclear lesson" and make a "real turn in thinking about east-west relations." Robert English, *Russia and the Idea of the West: Gorbachev, Intellectuals and the End of the Cold War* (New York: Columbia University Press, 2000), 50, 57. John Andrew emphasizes that early 1960s anticommunism was linked to the crisis of confidence over late 1950s events, notably Sputnik and the Cuban Revolution. John A. Andrew III, *The Other Side of the Sixties: Young Americans for Freedom and the Rise of Conservative Politics* (New Brunswick: Rutgers University Press, 1997).

8. Vladislav Zubok, *A Failed Empire: The Soviet Union in the Cold War from Stalin to Gorbachev* (Chapel Hill: University of North Carolina Press, 2007); quotation from English, *Russia and the Idea*, 57.

9. Frederick Barghoorn deems the Soviet stance "inherently restrictionist." Frederick Barghoorn, *The Soviet Cultural Offensive: The Role of Cultural Diplomacy in Soviet Foreign Policy* (Westport, CT: Greenwood Press, 1976), 118.

10. Nigel Gould-Davies, "The Logic of Soviet Cultural Diplomacy," *Diplomatic History* 27 (2003): 193–214; Hixson calls this "cultural infiltration" (*Parting the Curtain*, passim). Hills argues that the "cultural front" was an integral part of the "general Cold War project to seek military, political and industrial dominance over the Soviet Union." Patricia Hills, "'Truth, Freedom, Perfection': Alfred Barr's *What Is Modern Painting?* as Cold War Rhetoric," in Barnhisel and Turner, *Pressing the Fight*, 251–75; see also their introduction to *Pressing the Fight*, esp. 3, and David Caute, *The Dancer Defects: The Struggle for Cultural Supremacy in the Cold War* (Oxford: Oxford University Press, 2003).

11. See, e.g., "What Khrushchev Told the Writers," *Observer*, 18 August 1963, 11; "Obespechit' iskusstvu budushchee," *Pravda*, 6 August 1963, 4; "Literatura sotsialisticheskogo realizma vsegda shla ruka ob ruku s revoliutsiei," 12 May 1963, 4.

12. See, e.g., "Mr Khrushchev on Literature," *Bookseller*, 13 April 1963, 1575; "Catalogues of Depravity," *Bookseller*, 10 August 1963, 1013; "Soviet Writers in New Break with the West," *Observer*, 1 March 1964, 2. For examples of Soviet statements on the irreconcilability of Western and Soviet literatures, see L. Sergeyev, "American Reviewers about Soviet Poets," *Soviet Literature*, no. 8 (1963): 147–49; M. Kuznetsov, "Irreconcilable Positions," *Soviet Literature*, no. 2 (1964): 133–42.

13. Barghoorn stresses "the negative mission of considerable significance" (*Soviet Cultural Offensive*, 12). Barnhisel and Turner stress that the Soviet Union was "busy with its own propaganda projects"

(introduction to *Pressing the Fight*, 15) and emphasize (as does the chapter by Christian Kanig, "Establishing a Beachhead: Literature and Reeducation in Occupied Germany, 1945–1949," in *Pressing the Fight*, 71–88) the massive power of the Soviet publishing industry. Martin Manning, "Impact of Propaganda Materials in Free World Countries," in Barnhisel and Turner, *Pressing the Fight*, 145–65, argues that there was a "shift to a soft approach" after 1954 but still significant production of anti-American propaganda.

14. Barghoorn concludes that, at the start of the 1960s, there was still a "predominance of messianism over mutuality" (*Soviet Cultural Offensive*, 336).

15. Schwartz, *Political Warfare*, 181–209; John Jenks, *British Propaganda and News Media in the Cold War* (Edinburgh: Edinburgh University Press, 2006).

16. Jenks describes the "pattern of reflexive anti-communism" (*British Propaganda*, 12), although he illustrates the modification of the "unrelenting polemical tone in a climate of improving Anglo-Soviet relations" (70; cf. 144). Cf. Schwartz, *Political Warfare*, 188; Henry T. Bernstein, *And None Afraid: Soviet-Western Suspicion and Trusting from Red October to Glasnost Dialogue* (Oxford: Baardwell, 1991). On images of the Soviet Union in popular culture, see, e.g., Tony Shaw, *British Cinema and the Cold War: The State, Propaganda and Consensus* (London: I. B. Tauris, 2006).

17. Andrew, *Other Side of the Sixties*, 5 and passim. Cf. Laura Jane Gifford, "The Education of a Cold War Conservative: Anti-Communist Literature of the 1950s and 1960s," in Barnhisel and Turner, *Pressing the Fight*, 50–67.

18. For a fascinating analysis of the differences between the *shestidesiatniki* and 1960s protest movements in the West, see Boris Kagarlitsky, "1960s East and West: The Nature of the *Shestidesiatniki* and the New Left," *boundary 2* 36, no. 1 (2009): 195–204. On hopes for rapprochement in the 1960s, see also English, *Russia and the Idea;* Vladislav Zubok, *Zhivago's Children: The Last Russian Intelligentsia* (Cambridge, MA: Harvard University Press, 2009); Petr Vail' and Aleksandr Genis, *60-e: Mir sovetskogo cheloveka* (Ann Arbor: Ardis, 1988); Yale Richmond, *Cultural Exchange and the Cold War: Raising the Iron Curtain* (University Park: Pennsylvania State University Press, 2003). Barnhisel and Turner, in their introduction to *Pressing the Fight*, argue that print culture is ideally suited to both cultural exchange and ideological contestation (2).

19. Caute, in *Dancer Defects*, and Barghoon, in *Soviet Cultural Offensive*, exclude post-Stalinist literature from their studies of the cultural Cold War. On the ideological battles over everyday life, see Hixson, *Parting the Curtain*, and especially the work of Susan Reid, including "Who Will Beat Whom? Soviet Popular Reception of the American National Exhibition in Moscow, 1959," *Kritika* 9, no. 4 (2008): 855–904, and her chapter in this volume. Barnhisel and Turner, *Pressing the Fight*, is an important recent corrective to the neglect of literature, though it too contains only one chapter on Soviet literature, and that from the Stalin period.

20. Quotations from Schwartz, *Political Warfare*, 190, and Barghoorn, *Soviet Cultural Offensive*, 52; cf. Hixson, *Parting the Curtain*, 159, and Caute, *Dancer Defects*.

21. See, e.g., Maurice Friedberg, *A Decade of Euphoria: Western Literature in Post-Stalin Russia* (Bloomington: Indiana University Press, 1977); English, *Russia and the Idea*, 60 ff.; Zubok, *Zhivago's Children*.

22. For Soviet complaints about the disproportion between Soviet translations of Western works and Western translations of Soviet works, see, e.g., untitled article, *Observer*, 29 January 1961, 20, and "Across the Gulf," *Observer*, 5 March 1961, 17.

23. On the reception of Soviet music in the West, which raised similar issues of aesthetic quality, see Pauline Fairclough, "The 'Old Shostakovich': Reception in the British Press," *Music and Letters* 88, no. 2 (May 2007): 266–96.

24. See note 12.

25. Priscilla Johnson, *Khrushchev and the Arts: The Politics of Soviet Culture, 1962–64* (Cambridge, MA.: MIT Press, 1965); M. Zezina, *Sovetskaia khudozhestvennaia intelligentsiia i vlast' v 1950-e i 1960-e gody* (Moscow: Dialog MGU, 1998).

26. For criticisms of the Soviet stance on copyright, and allusions to consequent lack of Soviet control over translations, see "Neck and Neck," *Times Literary Supplement* (hereafter *TLS*), 2 January 1963, 77; "US Publishers Discuss Copyright with the Russians," *Bookseller*, 26 January 1963: 174–76; "Russian Publishing Group Arrives for U.S. Tour," *PW*, 8 April 1963, 30.

27. For a very positive summary of *Novyi mir* in the early 1960s, see I. Pitlyar, "The Magazine Novyi mir," *Soviet Literature*, no. 1 (1963): 160–66.

28. Soviet authorities were also concerned at the "distortions" to the canon of Khrushchev-era literature in Eastern bloc countries, including Poland, where there was also more translation and discussion of "marginal" Thaw works and little interest in mainstream Soviet literature. State Committee on the Press report to the CC, in State Archive of the Russian Federation (Gosudarstvennyi arkhiv Rossiiskoi Federatsii, hereafter GARF), f. 9604, op. 1, d. 8, l. 55.

29. On book exports and *Mezhkniga*, see Barghoorn, *Soviet Cultural Offensive*, 166–69, and "A Report on Book Distribution in the Soviet Union," *PW*, 14 January 1963, 40–46. On book club publications, see, e.g., "The Russian View of Britain," *New Statesman* (hereafter *NS*), 5 July 1964, 9–10.

30. V. Dudintsev, *Mezhdu dvumia romanami* (St Petersburg: Zhurnal "Neva", 2000), 156–97; I. Stadniuk, *Ispoved' Stalinista* (Moscow: Patriot, 1993), 302. On changes to royalties arrangements later in 1960s, see Soviet Ministry of Foreign Trade report, March 1968, in RGANI, f. 5, op. 59, d. 56, ll. 309–10. On the Soviet authorities' limited success in controlling the form of authorized editions, see "Soviets Say Contract for Solzhenitsyn Novel Is Void," *PW*, 4 February 1963, 48.

31. Barnhisel and Turner, introduction to *Pressing the Fight*, 4–8 and passim; Kenneth C. Davis, *Two-Bit Culture: The Paperbacking of America* (New York: Mariner Books, 1984).

32. Several authors confuse unpublished and published literature, deeming Pasternak Soviet, for example (May, *Translator in the Text*, 46–47; Barnhisel and Turner, introduction to *Pressing the Fight*, 10). Tamizdat and émigré texts remained important for UK and U.S. publishers: on publication of translations of works by Valery Tarsis, for example, see report on publication of Tarsis's *The Bluebottle*, *PW*, 18 March 1963, 41.

33. Andrew argues for a perspective that encompasses "two sides to activism in the sixties," incorporating anticommunist, conservative activism as well as the more famous activism of the late 1960s (*Other Side of the Sixties*, 220).

34. *Manchester Guardian*, 4 October 1957, 4. The quotation in the section's title, "Not by Tractors Alone," is the title of a review in the *New York Times* (hereafter *NYT*), M. Futrell, "Not by Tractors Alone," 15 January 1958, 4.

35. See, e.g., "Russian Author Tried to Get Back Novel," *Times*, 16 November 1957, 6.

36. Zezina, *Sovetskaia khudozhestvennaia intelligentsiia*; Dudintsev, *Mezhdu dvumia romanami*.

37. N. Burger, "Books of the Times," *NYT*, 21 October 1957, 23.

38. L. Ingalls, "Soviet Attempts to Block a Book," *NYT*, 3 March 1957, 27; "Russian Book Due Here," *NYT*, 8 March 1957, 6; Thomas Whitney, "The Novel That Upsets the Kremlin," *NYT Magazine*, 24 March 1957, 9, 34–40; "Trials of a Lone Inventor," *Times*, 10 December 1956, 12; "Foreign Publication of a Novel," *Times*, 30 March 1957, 5; untitled article, *Times*, 7 May 1957, 10; "Lawsuit over Book," *Times*, 25 June 1957, 10; Dudintsev, *Mezhdu dvumia romanami*, 89–114.

39. Preface to V. Dudintsev, *Not by Bread Alone* (London: Hutchinson, 1957); cf. Whitney, "Novel That Upsets."

40. Burger, "Books of the Times," 23.

41. "The Fate of Innocence among Guilty Men," *Times*, 3 October 1957, 13; Burger, "Books of the Times," 23; Dudintsev, *Not by Bread Alone*.

42. "Fate of Innocence," 13.

43. Burger, "Books of the Times," 23.

44. Whitney, "Novel That Upsets."

45. M. Slonim, "At the Root of It All," *NYT*, 20 October 1957, BR3; E. Crankshaw, "A Russian Novelist's Time-Bomb," *Observer*, 17 February 1957, 13.

46. Dudintsev, *Mezhdu dvumia romanami*, 89–112.

47. CC Department of Culture report on Soviet book edition, in RGANI, f. 5, op. 36, d. 37, l. 1; cf. Dudintsev, *Mezhdu dvumia romanami*.

48. CC Department of Culture report on foreign editions of Dudintsev's novel, in RGANI, f. 5, op. 36, d. 18, l. 107.

49. Ibid., ll. 107–9.

50. Ibid., l. 107; Dudintsev, *Mezhdu dvumia romanami*, 108–14.

51. *Times*, 7 May 1957, 10; V. Zorza, "No Apologies from Dudintsev," *Manchester Guardian*, 7 May 1957, 7; Ingalls, "Soviet Attempts," 27; Whitney, "Novel That Upsets"; "Foreign Publication of a Novel," 5; "Lawsuit over Book," 10.

52. "Crankshaw and Dudintsev," *Observer*, 7 April 1957, 12 (radio coverage in "Dudintsev Reply to Crankshaw," *Observer*, 31 May 1957, 11).

53. Slonim, "At the Root," BR3.

54. Crankshaw, "Russian Novelist's Time-Bomb," 13; Slonim, "At the Root," BR3.

55. See preface to Dudintsev, *Not by Bread Alone*.

56. Futrell, "Not by Tractors Alone," 4.

57. Reviews of *Not by Bread Alone*, by Vladimir Dudintsev: J. Wain, "Halfway House," *Observer*, 6 October 1957, 14, and V. Johnson, "New Novels," *Manchester Guardian*, 1 October 1957, 4.

58. Wain, "Halfway House," 14.

59. V. Johnson, "New Novels."

60. See, e.g., State Press Committee reports on Western press, in GARF, f. 9604, op. 1, d. 16.

61. On such debates on abstract art, see Barnhisel and Turner, introduction to *Pressing the Fight* (esp. 24), and Hills, "Truth, Freedom, Perfection"; also Saunders, *Cultural Cold War*.

62. See, e.g., "Two Survivors," *Guardian*, 2 November 1962, 9; "Cultural Bickering," *NS*, 25 January 1963, 104.

63. H. Salisbury, "Books of the Times," *NYT*, 22 January 1963, 7; "Neck and Neck," 77; "Out in the Cold," *TLS*, 8 January 1963, 93; "House of the Dead," *TLS*, 1 February 1963, 3; "Rival Translations," *Bookseller*, 19 January 1963, 104; "Rival Translations," *Bookseller*, 2 February 1963, 244; "Mr Praeger and Some Others," *Bookseller*, 23 February 1963, 1086–89; "One Day," *Bookseller*, 2 March 1963; ad for Praeger edition, *PW*, 7 January 1963, 51; "Rival Versions," 47–48; "Three (at Least) Paperback Solzhenitsyns on the Market," *PW*, 25 February 1963, 38; Soviet internal communications about this rivalry between foreign translations, in RGANI, f. 5, op. 5, d. 44, ll. 39, 40–51.

64. E.g., between rival versions of Stadniuk's *People Are Not Angels* ("Unauthorised Translation," *Bookseller*, 17 August 1963, 1063; Stadniuk, *Ispoved' Stalinista*, 301), and of Abramov's *Vokrug da okolo* ("Another Russian Novel with Two U.S. Publishers," *PW*, 13 May 1963, 33).

65. Robert Conquest, "Solzhenitsyn in the British Media," 3–23, in *Solzhenitsyn in Exile*, ed. John B. Dunlop, Richard S. Haugh, and Michael Nicholson (Stanford, CA: Hoover Institution Press, 1985), 4.

66. For a detailed examination of the many different aspects of the translation process and the ways in which they can affect a text's meaning, see May, *Translator in the Text*, 1–10.

67. On moves toward democracy, see "Fiction from Moscow," *Observer*, 10 December 1961, 27; E. Crankshaw, "The Slow Dawning of Democracy," 14 January 1962, 10; I. Deutscher, "Tanks Are No Answer to This Kind of Crisis," 4 February 1962, 11.

68. Rachel May argues that a similar paradox governed, for example, the reception of Turgenev in nineteenth-century Britain and America (*Translator in the Text*, 25).

69. See, e.g., Jenks on prewar British press and its "propaganda-laced stories of purges, bloodshed, famine and despotism" (*British Propaganda*, 32).

70. I. Stadnyuk, *People Are Not Angels* (London: Mono Press, 1963); for author's reaction, see Stadniuk, *Ispoved' Stalinista*, 301.

71. A. V. Gorbatov, *Black Year* (London: Flegon Press, 1964).

72. Alexander Solzhenitsyn, *One Day in the Life of Ivan Denisovich*, trans. R. Parker (London: V. Gollancz, 1963), and *One Day in the Life of Ivan Denisovich*, trans. M. Hayward and R. Hingley (New York: Bantam, 1963). The eye image quickly became an iconic shorthand, used in advertising (e.g., Praeger edition ad, *PW*, 14 January 1963, 34–35).

73. May, *Translator in the Text*, 12, 17, 42, 45, and passim.

74. Preface to Simonov, *Victims and Heroes*.

75. Translator's preface by R. Ainztein, in ibid.

76. Translators' preface to Solzhenitsyn, *One Day in the Life of Ivan Denisovich*, trans. Hayward and Hingley; quotation from advertisement for hardback release, *Observer*, 17 February 1963, 5. Other references to the domestic "sensation" include M. Frankland, "Prison Camp View of Stalinism," *Observer*, 3 February 1963, 23; "The Inside Story of Life in a Stalinist Labour Camp," review of *One Day in the Life of Ivan Denisovitch*, by Aleksandr Solzhenitsyn, *Times*, 31 January 1963, 15; "A Lot Happened While We Were Away," *NYT*, 7 April 1963, BR1; M. Slonim, "The Challenge Was the Need to Stay Alive," *NYT*, 7 April 1963, BR4.

77. A. Gorbatov, *Years Off My Life* (London: W. W. Norton, 1965), 7–11.

78. Preface to Solzhenitsyn, *One Day*, trans. Hayward and Hingley.

79. See the particularly detailed evocations of the contrast between Western and Soviet public knowledge of Stalinism in introductions to Gorbatov, *Years Off My Life*, and the Hayward/Hingley translation of *Ivan Denisovich*.

80. Evtushenko was another Soviet writer whose "disobedience" and rebelliousness were often discussed in the press (e.g., "Soviet Poet Is Published Here," *NYT*, 27 September 1962, 34; H. Salisbury, "The Poets versus the Commissars," *NYT*, 11 August 1963, 329; "Yevtushenko Back Home, Defends the Twist," *Observer*, 27 May 1962, 1; "Yevtushenko Signs Off," *Observer*, 27 May 1962, 2; "My Russia," *Observer*, 27 May 1962, 21; "Yevtushenko," *Observer*, 3 June 1962, 14; "Poet and Party," *Observer*, 17 June 1962, 22), and cited in publishers' publicity (untitled brief report of publication of *A Precocious Autobiography*, *PW*, 22 April 1963, 33; ad for Dutton edition of *A Precocious Autobiography*, *PW*, 10 June 1963, 14).

81. "Unauthorised Translation," 1063; brief untitled report on Stadniuk, *PW*, 20 May 1963, 46 .

82. Double-page spread for Hutchinson edition of Simonov's *Victims and Heroes*, *Bookseller*, 27 April 1963, 1693. Further claims in reports on publication of Simonov's novel in translation that it was "extremely outspoken in its criticism" and that "its nature was obvious" immediately after publication in "Post-Stalin," *Bookseller*, 4 May 1963, 1791.

83. Ad for Flegon edition of Abramov's *One Day in the New Life*, *Bookseller*, 6 April 1963, 1555; brief report on publication of Abramov's text, *PW*, 1 April 1963, 42; ad for Praeger edition of *One Day in the New Life*, *PW*, 13 May 1963, 6. According to Max Hayward's preface, Solzhenitsyn and Abramov both had carried de-Stalinization "far beyond the terms of reference" of the party's critique. Fedor Abramov, *The Dodgers* (London: Flegon Press, 1963); "New Fiction," *Times*, 11 July 1963, 13, calls it "the exact opposite of what we expect of a Soviet novel."

84. Preface to V. Nekrassov, *Kira* (London: Cresset Press, 1963); frontispiece of Y. Bondarev, *Silence: A Novel of Post-War Russia* (London: Chapman and Hall, 1965); cf. teenagers in Aksenov's *Starry Ticket* advertised as having "a lot in common with their American counterparts" ("Forecast of Paperbacks," *PW*, 13 May 1963, 59).

85. Preface to Simonov, *Victims and Heroes*.

86. For State Committee on the Press reports to this effect, see State Committee on the Press reports to the CC, in GARF, f. 9604, op. 1, d. 8, ll. 6–11, 55–67, 109–31, 50–57; and GARF, f. 9604, op. 1, d. 21, ll. 6, 53–58. For more evidence of anxiety about the changes in meaning generated by prefaces, making published literature look dissident, see KGB reporting on Munich edition preface to Bykov's *Mertvym ne bol'no*, in RGANI, f. 5, op. 58, d. 45, ll. 60–62.

87. The publications reviewed for this section were the *Observer*, the *Guardian*, the *Times* (London), the *New Statesman*, the *Times Literary Supplement*, the *New York Times*, and *Survey*.

88. "Abstract Warning for Soviet Writers," *Observer*, 9 December 1962, 3; "Khrushchev Tightens Grip on Artists," *Observer*, 23 December 1962, 1; E. Crankshaw, "Art v. Politics in Russia," *Observer*, 3 February 1963, 26; "Prison Camp Author Is Attacked," *Observer*, 3 March 1963, 9; "Stronger Attacks on Russian Writers," *Observer*, 17 March 1963, 2; E. Crankshaw, "Moving Away from Hell," review of *One Day in the Life of Ivan Denisovich*, by Alexander Solzhenitzyn, *Observer*, 29 December 1963, 21; "Cultural Bickering," 104; "Khrushchev and the Eggheads," *NS*, 15 March 1963, 342; K. Karol, "The Pen and the Sword," *NS*, 21 June 1963, 926.

89. See, e.g., "View of an Old Revolutionary," *Guardian*, 17 May 1960, 7; "After the Angry Poet—the Happy Grandfather," *Observer*, 20 May 1962, 3; "Lovely English Fog," 3 June 1962, 8. On Tvardovskii as an international ambassador, see, e.g., "Literatura sotsialistcheskogo realizma," *Pravda*, 12 May 1963, 4.

90. Quotation from Crankshaw, "Art v. Politics," 26; "Khrushchev Tightens Grip," 1; "Fresh Signs of the Thaw," 23 July 1961, 22.

91. "Stay at Home," *NS*, 5 July 1963, 16.

92. "St Antony and the Dragon," *NS*, 29 November 1963, 795–96; Crankshaw, "Moving Away from Hell," 21; "Soviet Writers," 5 January 1964, 24.

93. *TLS*, 1 April 1963, 234.

94. F. Kermode, "Novels of the Thaw," *NS*, 22 March 1963, 242–25; "Cultural Bickering," 104; Karol, "Pen and the Sword," 926; "The Long Talk," *TLS*, 19 April 1963, 265. Hills, "Truth, Freedom, Perfection," shows how U.S. art criticism was revised in the mid-1960s to include criticism of Khrushchev's 1962–63 outbursts (268).

95. Examples of cross-fertilization between press and scholarly accounts of the Thaw include Max Hayward's "Conflict and Change in Literature," *Survey*, no. 46 (January 1963): 9–22, and his later volume of conference proceedings (the cause of the Alvarez-Crankshaw dispute): *Literature and Revolution in Soviet Russia, 1917–62: A Symposium*, ed. Max Hayward and Leopold Labedz (London: Oxford University Press, 1963). This article examines scholarship on Soviet literature only to the extent that it intersected with the press, as here. An excellent recent study of scholarship is Engerman, *Know Your Enemy*, which views the 1950s and 1960s as crucial decades for the growth of American scholarship (albeit with significant "sociological" biases), as "the result of the post-sputnik language boom and the direct and indirect effects of the thaw" (152).

96. "Pawns in Moscow's Game," *Observer*, 17 November 1963, 11; cf. untitled article, *TLS*, 5 December 1963, 1002, and "Pasternak's Children," *Observer*, 5 May 1963, 10, which claims that a "Pasternakian intelligentsia" was taking root.

97. The "anti-Soviet" writers Abram Tertz and Valery Tarsis represent important exceptions, being widely translated and discussed in the West during this time.

98. H. Salisbury, "The General Survived," review of *Years Off My Life*, by A. Gorbatov, *NYT*, 28 February 1965, BR50; J. Daniel, "A Village in the Ukraine," review of *People Are Not Angels*, by Ivan Stadniuk, *Guardian*, 9 August 1963, 5.

99. "The Patriotic Corrupter," review of memoirs published in Russia by Il'ya Ehrenburg, *TLS*, 31 May 1963, 388.

100. "Quasi-Jew," review of *Victims and Heroes*, by Konstantin Simonov, *NS*, 28 June 1963, 981; "And Russia," review of *Victims and Heroes*, by Konstantin Simonov, *TLS*, 5 July 1963, 489.

101. "The Mask and the Face," review of *First Years of Revolution*, by Ilya Ehrenburg, *Observer*, 1 December 1962, 24.

102. "The Real Stalingrad Epic," review of *Victims and Heroes*, by Konstantin Simonov, *Observer*, 23 June 1963; H. Salisbury, "The People Endured," review of *Victims and Heroes*, by Konstantin Simonov, *NYT*, 14 October 1962, 284.

103. E. Litvinoff, "The General's Story," review of *Years Off My Life*, by A. Gorbatov, *Guardian*, 20 November 1964, 8.

104. No title, *TLS*, 20 September 1963, 702.

105. V. Zorza, "Story of the Stalinist Terror," review of *One Day in the Life of Ivan Denisovich*, by Aleksandr Solzhenitsyn, *Guardian*, 31 January 1963, 8.

106. Litvinoff, "General's Story," 8.

107. Untitled review of *People Are Not Angels*, by Ivan Stadniuk, *Times*, 24 October 1963, 16; untitled review of *People Are Not Angels*, by Ivan Stadniuk, *TLS*, 5 December 1963, 1017; Daniel, "Village in the Ukraine," 5.

108. Kermode, "Novels of the Thaw," 424–25.

109. P. Viereck, "Redemption through Self-Knowledge," review of *Kira*, by Viktor Nekrasov, *NYT*, 6 May 1962, 302.

110. Salisbury, "Books of the Times," 7 (on *Ivan Denisovich*).

111. Slonim, "Challenge," BR4.

112. "Inside Story," 15; cf. Zorza, "Story of the Stalinist Terror," 8; cf. L. Schapiro, "Bent Backs," review of *One Day in the Life of Ivan Denisovich*, by Aleksandr Solzhenitsyn, *NS*, 1 February 1963, 158–59; "General's Memoirs Describe Stalinist Inhumanities," *Times*, 15 May 1964, 11; Salisbury, "General Survived," BR50 (both on Gorbatov's *Years Off My Life*). Simonov's novel was easier to frame in terms of victory, since readers knew that the war had eventually been won ("Real Stalingrad Epic," 24).

113. Bondarev, *Silence*.

114. Solzhenitsyn, *One Day*.

115. Zorza, "Story of the Stalinist Terror," 8, claims the novel helped to "cleanse the soul of Russia." Cf. Slonim, "Challenge," BR4; "Inside Story," 15; Schapiro, "Bent Backs," 158–59.

116. "Soviet Critics on Alexander Solzhenitsyn," *Soviet Literature*, no. 9 (1963): 141–44. CC ideological department surveillance of Western criticism of *Ivan Denisovich* in 1963 saw the American criticism as the most important, with European critics largely following its lead (RGANI, f. 5, op. 55, d. 44, ll. 39, 40–51).

117. Salisbury, "People Endured," 284; cf. Salisbury on sequel, "Disasters in War Laid to Stalin's Purge of Army," *NYT*, 19 May 1964, 15.

118. E. Crankshaw, "Tragicomedy of Rural Russia," *Observer*, 7 July 1963, 22; "Down on the Dunghill," review of *Dodgers*, by Fedor Abramov, *NS*, 12 July 1963, 49–50.

119. K. Simonov, "In Spite of Common Sense," *Soviet Literature*, no. 7 (1963): 181–85; on Abramov, see "Rewriting His Book," *Bookseller*, 29 June 1963, 2263.

120. Ad for Simonov's *Victims and Heroes* on front page of issue, *TLS*, 28 June 1963.

121. A. Duchene, "Odds on the Novels," review of *Victims and Heroes*, by Konstantin Simonov, and *Dodgers*, by Fedor Abramov, *Guardian*, 12 July 1963, 7.

122. One anthology was described as "traditional in a nineteenth-century way": M. Slonim, "In Russia, at Long Last, It's Spring," review of *Stories from Modern Russia* anthology, *NYT*, 15 April 1962, BR1.

123. Brief, untitled report of Cresset Press publication of *Kira*, *Bookseller*, 2 February 1963, 329; Cresset Press ad for Nekrasov's *Kira*, *Bookseller*, 9 February 1963: 673.

124. Viereck, "Redemption through Self-Knowledge," 302; "Ordinary Russian Chaps," *TLS*, 1 February 1963, p. 3; "Party Line," *TLS*, 29 January 1963, 6.

125. Schapiro, "Bent Backs," 158–59. The Hayward/Hingley preface acclaims "that deep humanity that once made Russian literature so great in the eyes of the world."

126. Slonim, "Challenge," BR4; Frankland, "Prison Camp View," 23. The Dostoevskii parallel was prominent on the Penguin paperback back cover.

127. V. Phelps, "Literature in Russia," *Observer*, 17 September 1961, 29; "Stay at Home," 16. See May, *Translator in the Text*, on the appeal of Tolstoy and Turgenev in the late nineteenth century.

128. May uses these terms to describe late nineteenth-century British and American views of Russian literature (*Translator in the Text*, 21).

129. "Quasi-Jew."

130. "Stay at Home," 16.

131. See, e.g., Pat Sloan's article lambasting British literature's "angry young men" and acclaiming Soviet literature's political and moral commitment. Pat Sloan, "Literature Moral and A-moral," *Soviet Literature*, no. 6 (1962): 158–62.

132. Barnhisel and Turner, *Pressing the Fight*, and also Cobb, "Promoting Literature," on the politicized promotion of abstract art since "in contrast to Soviet painting it was neither representational or didactic" (236).

133. Cobb points to the Cold War promotion of modernism, or at most modernist "distortions" of realism, in order to distinguish clearly Western art from socialist realism ("Promoting Literature," 236).

134. Engerman, *Know Your Enemy*, 148.

135. F. Hope, "Jolly Good Fun in Moscow," review of *Starry Ticket*, by Vasilii Pavlovich Aksenov, *Observer*, 24 June 1962, 24.

136. "Stay at Home," 16.

137. Toynbee, "Voice of Young Russia," 14.

138. Kermode, "Novels of the Thaw," 424–25.

139. Following Kermode's *New Statesman* piece, the journal printed a rebuttal from a Soviet critic (Alexander Dymshits, "Tall Stories by Frank Kermode," *Soviet Literature*, no. 9 [1963]: 152–54); other articles in a similar vein include Sergei Surikov, "In Two Voices," *Soviet Literature*, no. 7 (1963): 186–87; Sergeyev, "American Reviewers"; Valentina Jacque, "Soviet Scholars on Modern American Literature and Scholarship," *Soviet Literature*, no. 10 (1963): 161–66; D. Dmitriev, "Literature Misused," *Soviet Literature*, no. 2 (1964): 144–48; T. Motyleva, "In a Bad Tradition," *Soviet Literature*, no. 5 (1964): 152–61. For discussion of the interest or tedium of *Soviet Literature*, in the wake of the spat between the journal and Kermode, see "Soviet Novels," *NS*, 5 April 1963, 489–90; "Soviet Novels," *NS*, 12 April 1963, 520.

140. State Committee on the Press report to the CC, ll. 6–11, 150–57; State Committee on the Press reports to the CC on Soviet literature's reception abroad in the 1960s, in State Press Committee reports on Western press, ll. 24–29, 129–378. See Engerman, *Know Your Enemy*, 129–52, on American Slavists' approaches to Russian and Soviet literature at this time.

141. Slonim, "Challenge," BR4.

142. Salisbury, "Books of the Times," 7; "Inside Story," 15. However, Crankshaw claims that "written clumsily and haltingly, it would still be an invaluable document." Crankshaw, "Moving Away from Hell," 21.

143. Kermode, "Novels of the Thaw," 424–25; Zorza, "Story of the Stalinist Terror," 8. Compare this combination of stylistic criticism and acclaim: "Though it is a thoroughly conventional piece of realistic writing, it is beautifully simple and direct" ("Ordeal by Fire," *New Yorker*, 29 April 1963, 168).

144. Aleksandr Solzhenitsyn, *The Oak and the Calf* (London: Collins/Fontana, 1980), 210, 292.

145. May, *Translator in the Text*, 46.

146. Ad for Flegon Press edition of Abramov's *One Day in the New Life*, *Bookseller*, 6 April 1963, 1555; ad for Praeger edition of same text, *PW*, 13 May 1963, 6.

147. Already before the end of the Khrushchev era, many of the writers in Western anthologies of the Thaw had come under attack, a fact that critics emphasized when reviewing them ("Triumph of the Pen," *NYT*, 13 September 1964, BR42; P. Toynbee, "Voices of Subversion," *Observer*, 19 July 1964, 22: reviews of Whitney's *New Writing in Russia* and *Half-Way to the Moon: New Writing from Russia*, ed. Patricia Blake and Max Hayward [Garden City, NY: Doubleday, 1965], respectively). On the growing proportion of unpublished literature in Western anthologies, see, e.g., the review of the anthology *For Freedom, Theirs and Ours*, ed. R. G. Davis-Poynter (New York: Stein and Day, 1969), "Making Free," *Guardian*, 20 December 1968, 7.

148. See, e.g., review of *Dissonant Voices in Soviet Literature*, ed. Patricia Blake and Max Hayward (New York: Pantheon, 1962), "Pen Stabs at the Monolith," *Guardian*, 30 April 1965, 9.

5 Guitar Poetry, Democratic Socialism, and the Limits of 1960s Internationalism

Rossen Djagalov

A Specter Is Haunting the World

During the 1960s new and curious figures were sighted simultaneously in different parts of the world. Whether *bardy* in the Soviet Union, *Liedermacher* in East and West Germany, *cantautori* in Italy or Latin America, *auteurs-compositeurs-interpreteurs* in France, or *singer-songwriters* in the USA, those figures brought together a new type of an audience to listen to their poetry, which they usually sang to the accompaniment of their own guitars. In every culture in which they appeared, they were deeply rooted in local poetic, musical, and performative traditions, yet everywhere their performance exhibited several fairly constant characteristics: a powerful potential to construct counterpublics; a critique of the state, whether of a state socialist or capitalist variety; and a tense relationship with the musical industries. These are the commonalities that place on the same plane such seemingly disparate and deeply national phenomena as the Russians Bulat Okudzhava and Vladimir Vysotskii, the Poles Jacek Kaczmarski and Edward Stachura, the Czech Karel Kryl, the Germans Wolf Biermann and Franz Josef Dagenhardt, the Frenchman Georges Brassens, the Italians Luigi Tenco and Fabrizio De Andre, the Cuban Carlos Puebla, the Chilean Victor Jara, and the Americans Pete Seeger, Phil Ochs, and the pre-electric Bob Dylan.

There is no single recognizable name for the international cultural formation represented by these performers. Many of them could be found under the "Bob Dylan of [insert the name of the country]" entry of *Wikipedia*. The absence of a single, international category to designate the phenomenon has meant that for the few Russians who know him Wolf Biermann is the "German Okudzhava" while in France Okudzhava goes by "the Russian Brassens." This is why this essay will adopt the term *guitar poetry,* coined by Gerald S. Smith in his pioneering study of the Soviet variant.[1] While offering equal distance from the different national varieties, it posits two fairly constant—and defining—features of the performance: the guitar and the poetry. The adoption of the term implicitly constitutes the enabling argument of this essay: despite the incredible variety of national inflections, these musics represented local instantiations of a single, international genre.[2]

By examining guitar poetry's relationship with its publics, we will demonstrate that this international genre was the foremost cultural expression of the social movements of the 1960s. The genre is also connected to the Left through its genealogy: Hanns Eisler's "fighting songs" *(Kampflieder)* of the 1930s provided a common source for the different national guitar poetries. Yet unlike Eisler's Popular Front repertoire, which achieved worldwide distribution, guitar poetry crossed borders with great difficulty, in a way that was symptomatic of 1960s social movements' larger inability to link up across ideological blocs and national boundaries. Reflecting the social movements of the 1960s, the national instantiations of guitar poetry remained homologous phenomena, caused by similar structures and inspired by a common imaginary, but lacking the transnational connections of their 1930s predecessors. Existing scholarship on the national variants of guitar poetry rarely mentions, let alone analyzes, the international dimensions of the genre.[3] In post-Soviet scholarship, for example, a nation-based perspective has resulted in guitar poetry's exclusive interpretation as an anti-Soviet (and with some slippage, anticommunist) cultural form that disappeared with the disappearance of the Soviet regime. Placing the genre in the international context of 1960s democratic socialism/socialism with a human face would, for example, allow us to revise its political valences and the time frame of the Soviet variant.

Finally, however, guitar poetry was more than a reflection or part of the social movements of the 1960s: it helped shape them. This symbiosis is confirmed by the simultaneous disappearance of guitar poetry and the social movements of the 1960s. In practically every national culture, the genre's move to the cultural periphery was accompanied by the rise of rock music, which better encoded the structures of feeling of the new social formations that replaced those of the 1960s.

Guitar Poetry Constructs Publics

Christian Noack's account of guitar poetry's social forms *(kompaniia, pokhod, slet)* in this volume illustrates guitar poetry's power to reconfigure public space, sociability, and discourse. Also in this volume, Anne Luke has detailed the way *nueva trova* performance in postrevolutionary Havana helped local youth claim urban spaces previously occupied by elite social clubs and establish an autonomous subculture. Indeed, everywhere guitar poetry was performed—in the intimate spaces of kitchens in Moscow or Berlin, in leftist youth theaters in Italy, in the stadiums of Latin America, on reel-to-reel tapes around the world—it helped construct veritable public spheres.[4] Jürgen Habermas's theoretical framework seems particularly helpful in analyzing the social role of this genre. His account of the rise of the public sphere in late eighteenth-century Western Europe on the basis of a set of shared cultural texts closely approximates the role of guitar poetry in catalyzing a critical public in the radically different national contexts in the 1960s.

Habermas's analysis of the construction of the public sphere also explains the evocative power of the first-person plural with which singer-songwriters addressed their audience, whether this was Bulat Okudzhava's famous "Let us take each other's hands, friends" ("Voz'memsia za ruki, druz'ia"), or Wolf Biermann's "We sit in the dark by the fire" ("Wir saßen am Feuer im Dunkeln"), or Pete Seeger's "We Shall Overcome."[5] That "we" was very different from and self-consciously oppositional to the type of collectivity that the post–World War II nation-state (whether of a "state socialist" or a "democratic" variety) promoted. It was not "we Russians," or "we Germans," or even "we oppositional students and intellectuals." Instead, "we" stood for a much more open and inclusive identity-in-the-making. Sometimes, to lend a particular emotional quality to their address, guitar poets resorted to the second-person plural "you." Pete Seeger's "Which Side Are You On?," which is both the title of the poem and its refrain, challenges listeners to take sides and take action. Aleksandr Galich's angry "you" in "Are you leaving? Then leave!" ("Uezzhaete? Uezzhaite!") serves to admonish his dissident friends for choosing exile and abandoning the struggle at home, positing his decision to remain as a self-sacrificial alternative:

Leave then!   Uezzhaite!
But I'll stay.   A ia ostanus'!
Someone must, despite all tiredness,   Kto-to dolzhen, prezrev ustalost'
Keep the graves of our dead.   Nashim mertvym berech' grobov.[6]

Those alternative "we's" or "you's" were also being constructed through print culture, yet guitar poetry enjoyed certain unique advantages in hosting the public sphere of democratic socialism of the 1960s. While print culture provided common texts for the creation of a public that sometimes overlapped with that of guitar poetry, its operational mechanisms were quite different. The act of reading, which incorporates the reader into a larger public, is a deeply private act characterized by an unequal relationship between author and reader. Unlike the unmediated, collective, and simultaneous experience of a live guitar poetry performance, the construction of a public sphere through print takes the additional step of discussing those texts; as imagined by Habermas, further discourse and arguments (in salons or cafés) are needed for the transformation of a literary public sphere into a political one. Guitar poetry's immediacy, its performative and participatory character, not only elevated it to the status of a privileged site for the leftist culture of the 1960s but also helped shape its social forms.

Habermas's notion of a public sphere can be helpful in explaining why guitar poetry proved an ideal host for the social formations of the 1960s, but it does not fully account for the ideological labor the genre actually performed. Mark Mattern's study of Chilean *nueva canción* helps concretize our understanding of that labor by distinguishing three functions of Chilean guitar poetry performance: (1) confrontation or protest, which contrasts the wrong and the right side of a particular issue and creates enduring ties among individuals committed to the latter; (2) deliberation, by which the musical practices serve to debate and examine the identity and commitments of their public or negotiate relations with other publics; and (3) a set of purely pragmatic functions that allows the public to promote "awareness of shared interests and to organize collaborative efforts to address them."[7] While these three functions do not exhaust the potentialities of guitar poetry, they provide a useful framework for describing guitar poetry's inter- and intrapublic communication and comparing them to its predecessors, especially the leftist musics of Europe's "Popular Front."

Guitar Poetry's Ancestry in the Musics of the Popular Front

Tracing guitar poetry's origins back to the political musics of the Popular Front not only confirms guitar poetry's leftist affinities but also allows us to contrast the two generations of leftist music and the respective social and cultural formations behind them. To concretize our discussion of Popular Front musics, we will distinguish two separate traditions: Hanns Eisler's modernist applied music *(angewandte Musik)* and the various national folklore songs of struggle and labor. Though better known now as Arnold Schoenberg's most illustrious student and Bertolt Brecht's leading composer, Eisler single-handedly developed a whole repertoire of political music. Previously, with the major exceptions of the "Marseillaise" and the "Internationale," most leftist songs had borrowed the musical templates of popular songs, Christian hymns, and even patriotic songs, replacing the lyrics with politically appropriate texts. By contrast, Eisler composed his fighting songs *(Kampflieder)* with the specific goal of providing the Berlin proletariat with a rhythm to march to on the streets.[8] After his exile in 1933, and during the antifascist struggles of the 1930s, these songs began to reach a more international audience, aided by the Spanish Civil War. Quick to respond to the Republican side's call for military music, Eisler spent a few months in Spain composing songs for the International Brigades. After the fall of the Spanish Republic, tens of thousands of volunteers from dozens of countries took those songs home or to further exile, translating and freely interpreting them, or sometimes singing them in the foreign languages in which they originally heard them. Those songs' mobilizing power was later tried and tested by the antifascist resistance movements during World War II.[9]

Even though his postwar musical production grew increasingly traditional, Eisler's was nonetheless a powerful international influence on the singer-songwriters of the 1960s: Wolf Biermann received his early musical and theatrical training in Brecht's Berliner Ensemble and to this day refers to Eisler as "Mein Meister"; Vysotskii's emergence as the leading Soviet singer-songwriter occurred during his years as an actor at Moscow's leading Brechtian theater, Teatr na Taganke; Pete Seeger came to know Eisler personally through his father, the pioneer of American ethnomusicology Charles Seeger, who not only was deeply influenced by Eisler's theories and compositions but also facilitated Eisler's immigration to the USA in the late 1930s. In Italy, the intense interest in Brecht's plays and drama theory in the late 1950s helped fuel the dramatic, poetic, and musical experimentation that accounts for the particularly close ties between guitar poetry and youth theater in Italy.[10] In their post-1959 search for revolutionary art forms, Cuban artists, and *nueva trova* performers in particular, looked to Brecht for inspiration.[11] Although by the late 1950s the cultural networks of the Popular Front had been dismantled and their Western publics diminished, Eisler's music and Brecht's performative practices provided the templates and styles common to the different national instantiations of 1960s guitar poetry.

The Popular Front musics also had a more national, folkloric dimension, influenced as they were by traditional folkloric labor and protest songs. The American case most dramatically illustrates those musics' uneasy coexistence with Eisler's modernist compositions. Second- and third-generation central and Eastern European migrants in New York and other East Coast cities (a major constituency of American leftist culture at the time) proved less than enthusiastic about the prospect of political "hillbilly" music. Nevertheless, largely thanks to the ethnomusicological work of John and Alan Lomax and Charles Seeger, the blues of Leadbelly and the topical songs of the Oklahoman Woody Guthrie as well the songs of other southern folk performers became common in union halls and other venues of the late Popular Front.[12] In North America, this folklore tradition proved much more influential for the 1960s musical tradition than Eisler's repertoire.

So too in South America, where in Chile, Violeta Parra, another living embodiment of the connection between the earlier Popular Front culture and the *nueva canción* music of the 1960s, drew much more heavily on local, Chilean musical folklore than on Eisler's internationalist repertoire.[13] Similarly, the founding father of the French *auteur-compositeur-interpreteur* tradition—Georges Brassens—began composing his songs during World War II on the templates of the traditional French *chanson*.[14] These and many other figures provided the all-important continuity between the leftist musical repertoire of the 1930s and early 1940s and the second leftist musical revival in the late 1950s and 1960s.

The genealogical continuities between the leftist marches of the 1930s and the guitar poetry of the 1960s should not obscure major differences between the musical cultures of the Old Left and that of "socialism with a human face," however. Most obviously, technological advances made it easier to record and reproduce live performances on reel-to-reel tape. The new sound-reproduction technologies facilitated a new culture of listening to political music in more private settings, which in turn helped shape a new form of sociability. Indeed, the performative differences between guitar poetry of the 1960s and the mass song of the 1930s are highly suggestive of the ideological differences between the two eras: the collective ethos and the marching rhythms of the 1930s working-class songs had given way to the highly lyrical voice of the solo guitar poet. The figure of the poet-composer-singer-guitar player was a 1960s innovation with no ancestry in the mass songs of the 1930s Left. Finally, Eisler's modernist compositions could rely on transnational political and cultural networks of the Communist Party and the Popular Front Left. Even if only briefly, Eisler presided over the Moscow-based International Music Bureau.[15] His repertoire traveled along such highly transnationalist and centralized networks, reaching most corners of the world with similarly leftist political formations.

Guitar Poetry—A National Story

Needless to say, these networks were not available for the generation of 1960s guitar poets, who had to rely largely on chance events and connections to hear their foreign peers' performance. Despite these occasional and powerful transnational exchanges, guitar poetry on either side of the Iron Curtain remained a much less cosmopolitan artistic form than the Popular Front–era musical repertoire. To some extent, purely immanent factors reduced the genre's mobility. The primacy accorded to the verbal in guitar poetry performance severely limited the genre's appeal to foreign audiences. In general, translating lyrics while preserving a musical template rarely works; no matter how great the quality of translation, the cultural references and humor, so central to the genre's effect, can rarely be conveyed adequately, while the need to match the musical to the poetic rhythm makes the translator's already difficult task even more difficult. If many of Eisler's marches were sung in numerous languages and reached truly international audiences, fewer guitar poems reached other cultures. The folkloric rootedness of the genre and the absence of a common internationalist musical core like Eisler's helped keep it rooted in national cultures.

Contributing to guitar poetry's largely national rather than international appeal were also factors extrinsic to the genre. As members of the cultural formations of democratic socialism of the 1960s, guitar poets—in the East and West—had grown up during the national purification operations of the late 1940s and 1950s, whether of an anticosmopolitan or an anticommunist variety. They lacked the transnational cultural networks of the Popular Front and the international communist movement. Most importantly, however, two fraught relations most impeded guitar poetry's transnational mobility: its relationship with the state, especially of the socialist variety, and above all, in the case of guitar poetry outside state socialism, its relationship with the music industry.

Guitar Poetry and the State

As Pete Seeger's biography illustrates, the existence of two distinct moments in the history of leftist music in the West—the 1930s and the 1960s—was a product not of intrinsic musical developments but rather of political forces that forced an interruption between the two. The paradigmatic movement artist, who came of age in the late 1930s, Seeger saw the pacifists who constituted much of his audience before World War II first dwindle and then, after Pearl Harbor, disappear. Similarly, his union songs, which had enjoyed considerable popularity in pre-1941 union halls, lost their appeal during the war era, with its social contract uniting government, employers, and unions.[16]

The end of the war did not bring back those listeners, as the war was followed by the McCarthy era, which decimated the remainder of Seeger's radical leftist publics. In addition to the dwindling audiences, many previously welcoming performance spaces or record companies lost their liking for political songs and musicians. In the course of their retrenchment, the political structures of the former Popular Front coalition, most notably the Communist Party, lost whatever energy or interest they had in supporting cultural initiatives. Not only did McCarthyism attack the publics and structures vital for the circulation of leftist musics; it also it struck at the musicians themselves. The mention of the Weavers in *Red Channels*, an anticommunist tract, not only shrank their audiences and distribution possibilities but attracted the FBI's attention to the band, causing it to disintegrate.[17] For many years, some of its members, including Seeger, had to devote much of their energies to legal proceedings. The People's Artists' Label, Seeger's initiative to provide support for political musicians, went bankrupt.[18]

While lacking equally dramatic episodes of state-led persecution, the history of guitar poetry in France, Germany, and Italy is also punctuated by the restrictions that states imposed on the genre. Operating under a strict code of censorship, TV and radio channels well throughout the 1960s proved quite reluctant to broadcast politically critical, and often distinctly unpuritanical, guitar poetry performances to broad audiences. The mass media were suspicious even of the most popular and universally acclaimed guitar poets, such as Brassens, whose repertoire included songs such as the humorous "La gorilla," about a gorilla who escapes from the zoo and satisfies its prodigious sexual appetite by ravishing a robed judge. The judge screams, showing little of the solemnity he exhibited earlier while issuing death sentences.[19]

A similarly demotic and often highly unpuritanical vocabulary distinguished Soviet bloc guitar poetry from the mainstream poetic tradition and rendered much of it unpublishable or unsuited for official performance spaces. At a time when such practices were unusual in poetry, Biermann engaged in sustained explorations of the lyrical I's sexuality ("The Stasi Ballad") and peppered his poems and their prefaces with scatological references ("Ballad of the Rotting Old Men").[20] Similarly, the final stanza of Aleksandr Galich's parodic poem "The Tentative Text of My Speech at a Tentative Conference of Socialist Bloc Historians, if Such a Conference Were to Take Place and if I Were Given the Honor to Deliver the Keynote Speech," playfully sets up a rhyme with "shit," without actually saying the word:

And this Marxist historical tool kit	I etot marksistskii podkhod k starine
Has long ago entered our country's lit.	Davno primeniaetsia k nashei strane
In our country it's proven a good fit.	On v nashei strane prigodilsia vpolne

And in your country it will be a good fit. I v vashei strane prigoditsia vpolne
Because we live in the same . . . *camp.* Poskol'ku vy tozhe v takom zhe *lagere,*
You'll find it an excellent fit! On vam prigoditsia vpolne![21]

In his oral rendition of the song, Galich pronounces the "ideological camp" *(lagere)* only after a slight pause and in an entirely different register, in gross violation of the poem's meter, further suggesting that the word is merely a cover.[22]

The history of guitar poetry in the Soviet bloc is one of many performers' constant encounters with state censorship, partly puritanical but primarily political; as such, there is no shortage of literature about those conflicts.[23] Suffice it here to provide a few dramatic examples of the results of this confrontation: after several years of living as a persona non grata, Galich was expelled from the Soviet Union in 1974 and spent the last three years of his life as an exile.[24] Beginning in 1965, Biermann was banned from performing in public and had his East German citizenship revoked while he was giving a concert in West Germany in 1977, causing a major confrontation between the East German state and its cultural producers who came out in his defense. Karel Kryl fled his native Czechoslovakia in 1969 to avoid the legal and other consequences he would have faced after the release of an album explicitly oppositional to the Soviet-led occupation.[25]

More often, however, guitar poetry enjoyed a liminal, semiofficial status, never particularly liked by Soviet bloc cultural bureaucracies for the uncontrollable public sphere it fostered and the near-impossibility of censoring highly improvised, oral performances but not explicitly forbidden either. In fact, the authorities were not sure what to do with guitar poetry, sometimes providing official venues for guitar poetry performance, in the hope of keeping it ideologically correct; at other times clamping down on concert organizers, guitar poets, and their audiences; and on still other occasions leaving it be. The interactions between state and genre in the Soviet bloc form such a decisive part of the latter's history that they have led the foremost historian of the Soviet *bardic song,* Andrei Krylov, to suggest that the genre would never have achieved its cultural centrality without official censorship. Oral performance was simply much more difficult to subject to censorship than written texts. Indeed, Krylov argues that censorship's disappearance in the late 1980s robbed the genre of the advantage it had enjoyed over print culture and ironically doomed it.[26]

The Cultural Borders of State Socialism

If the state functioned as a formidable obstacle to the popularization of guitar poetry within its borders, it proved even more effective at diminishing its transnational mobility. The cultural bureaucracies of state socialism, in particular, proved quite successful in preventing the cross-border passage of leftist cultures. In the rare instances when foreign cultural producers did cross the physical Iron Curtain, the cultural bureaucracies of the socialist state inserted themselves as mediators between local and foreign cultural producers, thereby producing another communicative barrier between the two. Few experienced the withering effects of such bureaucratic mistrust as poi-gnantly as Pete Seeger, who visited a number of socialist states during the world tours he undertook with his family in 1963–64 and 1971. Instead of letting him connect with his natural peers—the bards of Moscow—Seeger's Soviet hosts were quick to chan-nel him into taking a more innocuous ethnographic expedition to Crimea to collect musical folklore. Seeger did not take much prodding: always the salvage ethnographer, he eagerly set about visiting rural schools, collective farms, and folk music perfor-mances in the region.[27] On the other hand, the officialness of his concerts in Moscow and Novosibirsk ensured that Soviet guitar poets did not recognize him as one of their own. As a result, neither David Dunaway's authoritative biography of Seeger nor the Russian bards' memoirs mention any encounter.

Nor does Dunaway's *The Ballad of Pete Seeger* have anything to say about *nueva trova* music during his 1971 visit to Havana. What Dunaway discusses instead is Seeger's frustration with the VIP treatment he received, the luxury suite in the former Havana Hilton he lived in, the car with a chauffeur that mediated his contact with the Cuban people. The Seegers' experience of visiting North Vietnam was similarly constrained: "Despite requests to travel like fellow workers, not diplomats, they [the Seegers], were given a fancy car and a driver, who honked bicycles and pedestrians out of the way. Once, unable to communicate his discomfort to their driver, [Seeger] jumped out and walked alongside."[28] Ultimately, in Vietnam, he did have the opportunity to speak to people who were not part of his entourage. His music resonated a great deal with his audiences. By contrast, "China proved anti-climatic. Seeger gave only one major per-formance, a concert in Peking that he called one of his 'signal failures': 'They were so busy analyzing me that they couldn't join in one bit. Analyzing this song, analyzing that one . . . they didn't even tap their feet.'"[29] Indeed, every time he visited a state socialist country, Seeger, like so many other Western leftists before and after him, felt controlled by his hosts and alienated from the people he really wanted to address. Distrustful of both their own people and foreign sympathizers, the cultural bureaucracies of state socialism sought to avoid any uncontrolled contact between the two.

Official hosting of foreign cultural producers was only one of the ways in which the cultural bureaucracies of state socialism sterilized potentially fruitful contacts between cultural producers. As Daniil Granin's visit to Australia illustrates, even in the absence of immediate ideological supervision the boundaries between the ideolog-ical camps could still prevent unmediated communication between Soviet bloc artists and their Western peers. Though no bard himself, Granin was part of the 1960s milieu and author of some seminal texts of the Soviet Thaw. He knew the bards Vysotskii and Okudzhava personally. While in Sydney, he immediately thought of them when he heard the performances of local singer-songwriters such as Kevin Putch and Joseph John. But when asked by John whether they had anything similar in the USSR, Granin did not share his observation with the Australians. The question evoked in him the image of a major cultural bureaucrat unleashing a devastating critique of the fledgling genre. Reluctant to tell his Australian acquaintances the truth about guitar poetry's precarious status in the USSR—he was, after all, playing the role of a Soviet cultural ambassador,—but unwilling to lie, Granin limited himself to a "yes" and fell silent.[30]

Indeed, even in the rare cases when unmediated contact between guitar poets and audiences from different national traditions did take place, as it did during Wolf Biermann's unofficial visit to Moscow in 1970, the cultural Iron Curtain still stood in the way of genuine communication. It distanced cultural producers from each other's contexts and struggles. Biermann received an invitation to give an informal concert at Evgeniia Ginzburg's apartment, attended by Moscow's cultural elite: Ginzburg's son Vasilii Aksenov, Bella Akhmadulina, Lev Kopelev, Anatoli Naiman, Bulat Okudzhava, and others. In Naiman's account, the Russians were not enthralled. Biermann's voice seemed to them too piercing. The German *Liedermacher* struck the guests as too much of a licensed liberal, too careful in his critique of the East German regime. The fact that he was allowed to travel to Moscow was also held against him. Bella Akhmadulina expressed the displeasure Biermann had incurred among the audience most resolutely: "Better give the guitar to Bulat."[31]

Exactly what happened that evening is hard to say. We only have Naiman's highly subjective account, reconstructed with the help of his diaries. Nevertheless, the whole episode reads like a testament to the elite post-Stalinist intelligentsia's immense capacity to misread a situation, aesthetically and politically, a capacity that would only grow in time. At the time of the episode, Biermann was already banned from performing in public, under constant Stasi surveillance, and a subject of several condemnations in the East German public press; indeed, he had entered into a more open conflict with the authorities than any other person present in that room.[32] To dismiss him as a "convenient" opponent of the East German regime, as, according to Naiman's narrative, many people in Ginzburg's apartment did, was to demonstrate real ignorance of East German politics. What the audience—by that time increasingly anticommunist—was not equipped to recognize was Biermann's position as an antiregime communist. After 1968 especially, such a position must have sounded increasingly oxymoronic for the elite Russian intelligentsia.

In this respect, and not unlike the Soviet cultural bureaucracy, the Russian intelligentsia all too often transferred their political judgment onto the realm of aesthetics. There is a causal relationship behind this similarity: by defining official culture as its antagonist and main referent, the oppositional, post-Thaw, Soviet intelligentsia ended up adopting the logic and terms in which official culture was operating, with minus signs to be sure, but without changing the overall system of criteria. According to this logic, for example, someone with the wrong politics (Biermann) could not possibly have the right aesthetic qualities (his voice was too shrill). Such an objection could hardly have been based on unbiased aesthetic criteria: Biermann's timbre was no less hoarse or masculine than Vysotskii's, to which this public would have been much warmer.

As hopes for democratic reform within the Soviet bloc states faded with the suppression of the Prague Spring, the elite Soviet bloc intelligentsias, who competed with the official bureaucracy as to who would serve as a conduit and interpreter of foreign cultural production, grew increasingly suspicious of Western leftist cultural producers. The state socialist regimes' effort to cultivate relationships with them further discredited Western leftist singers in the eyes of a significant section of the oppositional intelligentsia. With the progressive growth of automatic anti-Soviet attitudes that characterized the liberal late-socialist intelligentsia, their attitudes to a Western artist were often determined by that artist's position vis-à-vis the Soviet Union. Dean Reed—the so-called Red Elvis, who had left the USA for East Germany after years of involvement in Latin American leftist politics—became a butt of popular jokes among the oppositional Soviet bloc intelligentsia, who showed little sympathy for the causes he was supporting (American withdrawal from Vietnam, a Popular Front Chile, a free Palestine), equating these causes with Soviet foreign policy.[33] Such attitudes extended even to leftists who had little to do with the Soviet bloc, such as the Chilean Victor Jara, who in the highly uncharitable characterization of a late/post-Soviet bard, Aleksandr Rozenbaum, was nothing more than a "bar musician from whom they made up a martyr."[34]

Guitar Poetry's International Forays

The Cold War state, whether of a state socialist or a capitalist variety, thus proved instrumental in keeping guitar poetry not only from reaching a broader national public but also from crossing boundaries. There were exceptions, of course, especially among the states that came the closest to the aspirations of 1960s democratic socialism. For a few months in 1968 in Czechoslovakia, improvised performances were openly encouraged. Similarly, in its first postrevolutionary decade, the Cuban government actively promoted its *nueva trova* musicians and even sought to popularize that musical culture throughout Latin America by broadcasting it internationally to other Latin American countries.

The commonality of the language and the political struggles made songs such as Silvio Rodriguez's dedication to Che Guevara, "Hasta Siempre, Comandante!," anthems of the Latin American Left. The halo of Che Guevara's figure helped the song cross the ocean and reach Europe, where it was covered, among other people, by Wolf Biermann. Sergio Ortega's "Venceremos" not only served as Salvador Allende's presidential campaign song but also, thanks in no small measure to the forced exile of Chilean *nueva canción* performers after the coup, was heard far beyond Chile. Not unlike the Soviet proletarian novel three or four decades earlier, *nueva trova* and *nueva canción* reached a pan–Latin American and even worldwide audience, thanks to the drama of Cuba's revolution and Chile's Popular Front, enthusiasms that endowed cultural products coming from those states with a measure of revolutionary prestige.[35]

Beyond regimes such as Czechoslovakia during the Prague Spring, Allende-era Chile, and Cuba in the first postrevolutionary decade, there were other ways in which transnational flows of guitar poetry were facilitated. There were a few festivals, such as the Chanson Folklore International, which took place every year between 1964 and 1969 in Burg Waldek, West Germany. Even though most of the performers and audiences were German speaking, rendering the "international" part of the title something of a misnomer, the festival did bring to German audiences foreign singer-songwriters such as the Americans Phil Ochs and Guy Carawan, the English performers Collin Wilkie and Shirley Hart, the Swedish duo Hai & Topsi, and the Pole Aleksander Kulisiewicz, among others.[36]

The case of Georges Brassens offers a different example of how guitar poetry sometimes crossed national and ideological-bloc boundaries. Testifying to Brassens's influence on Italian, German, and Soviet guitar poetry is the figure of François Villon, the seventeenth-century poet and outlaw, whom Brassens evoked in a number of his poems. The image of the freethinking rebel who ridiculed the powerful of his day in both poetry and life and got much fun out of it offered Brassens at the same time an attractive model and a useful genealogy for his own art and attitude to life. Villon, as presented by Brassens, was immensely appealing to other guitar poets. Indeed, in Wolf Biermann's "Ballad about the Poet François Villon," the medieval Frenchman appears not as a historic (and long dead) figure but rather as the lyrical I's "older brother and roommate," who lives the life of a house spirit, showing up to sing, drink red wine, or play some prank whenever there is a good friend and "maybe three pretty women" around. In the poem, Villon eventually breaks out of the privacy and atemporality of the room, encountering paradigmatic fixtures from East Germany's political order: first the boring *ND* (*Neues Deutschland,* the official party newspaper) and then the Berlin Wall, where border police try to shoot him down as he dances along the barbed wire.[37]

Bulat Okudzhava's "Prayer to François Villon" deploys the Frenchman's name for an entirely different purpose. As Okudzhava himself relates, the poem, which has little to do with Villon stylistically or thematically, was initially entitled "Prayer." When told that it could not be published under such an overtly religious title, Okudzhava simply added "to François Villon" to the title, thereby ostensibly removing the poem from the realm of present-day politics.[38] Thus the mention of François Villon allowed Okudzhava to play a prank on the authorities. Finally, Brassens's and respectively Villon's presence was greatest in Italy. Some of the lyrics of Fabrizio De Andre's third album, the 1966 *Tutto morimmo a stento* (We All Died Agonizingly) represent rather loose translations of Brassens's own poems dedicated to Villon's poetry.[39]

Guitar Poetry and the Musical Industries

Though Brassens reached a variety of audiences in different countries—largely in the form of LPs produced by recording companies—his was one of the few cases of a relatively symbiotic relationship between guitar poetry and the musical industries. Usually record companies, or rather their executives, shared politicians' wariness of guitar poetry's political engagement. Alternatively, they caved in to political or commercial pressures to stay away from politics or to depoliticize music through song selection, album cover design, or other means. The story of Pete Seeger is once again illustrative: well before the House Un-American Activities Committee hearing and government-initiated persecution, his name, along with those of a number of other folksingers, appeared on the pages of the *Red Channels* publication. Organized by professional anticommunists and covertly sponsored by the CIA, the booklet carried no juridical power. Nevertheless, those whose names were listed in it became political untouchables as far as impresarios and recording companies were concerned. Under the financial pressure of an ever-dwindling number of venues and the psychological strain of losing their audience, the Weavers, Seeger's band, collapsed.[40]

Indeed, while a whole transnational network of publishing houses and magazines carried leftist literature internationally throughout the twentieth century, the Left lacked a significant presence in the Western musical industry. In the rare cases when a recording company did undertake the international distribution of guitar poetry, the musical product that made it across borders was politically sanitized. When, for example, via the recordings of RCA and Arena Productions, Violeta Parra's songs reached U.S. listeners, they were in the form of enjoyable tunes shorn of political context. The song selection and marketing of her discs left little of the social engagement of a woman who had initiated the tradition of performers championing social justice and agitating for Chile's Unidad Popular coalition. Nor can one tell from these records that Violeta Parra was to Chilean *nueva canción* what Pete Seeger was to the U.S. folk revival of the 1960s: a doyenne, who brought folklore to the movement (through both her ethnographic work and her own modernization of those musics), who helped nurture young talents (not the least of which were those of her own family), and who colored *nueva canción* with her politics.[41]

The suspicion with which the music industry treated guitar poetry was mutual. Like most artists, performers of the genre sought as broad an audience as possible, as well as cultural recognition and remuneration, the road to which passed through the music industries. Their relationship with that industry was usually characterized by a certain ambivalence, however: a position between an all-out boycott and full embrace of the musical market. Indeed, it is this suspicion that kept guitar poetry from reaching the broadest possible audience, if also allowing it to retain its political thrust. Again, Woody Guthrie and Pete Seeger offer instructive examples of artists who gave up on lucrative contracts and labels when these would involve too great a compromise. In fact, it was an argument about whether the Weavers would do cigarette commercials at a time when they had no other source of income that ultimately resulted in Pete Seeger's departure ("Why couldn't it be for yogurt?" Seeger reportedly muttered. "At least I like yogurt!") and the group's collapse.[42]

Guitar Poetry and Rock

Guitar poets often insisted on maintaining the syncretic (musical, performative, poetic) nature of their performance and were unwilling to let their music assert its primacy.

Indeed, it was often guitar poets, and audiences themselves, who policed the border between their genre and professional music, considering its crossing tantamount to selling out. The most famous instance of such "crossing," Bob Dylan's first public performance with an electric guitar at the 1965 Newport Festival, incurred Pete Seeger's displeasure to the point where the otherwise serene Seeger shouted at the audio technicians: "If I had an ax, I'd chop the microphone cable right now." Subsequently explaining his reaction, he clarified his understanding of the border: "The issue was not that Dylan had performed with electric instruments—Howlin' Wolf had done that the day before, there were no prohibitions against it—but that no one could hear the words to Dylan's song.... [I] was sure that Dylan wanted the audience to hear the words—else why sing the song—and that the people in charge of the microphones were sabotaging him."[43] Seeger's explanation suggests one way of defining the often intangible boundary between guitar poetry and rock 'n' roll. The musical richness of the rock 'n' roll performance often leaves the lyrics unintelligible. Sometimes they are quite sparse to begin with. The primacy of the musical over the textual limits rock 'n' roll performers' capacity to control the political message of their songs and to construct a consciously political community in the way guitar poetry was able to do.[44]

Unlike the ascendant rock 'n' roll, guitar poetry communicated to its audiences with highly audible lyrics that were central to the whole performance. Across the different national guitar poetry traditions, there was an extensive practice of prefacing each song with a commentary. Especially popular among the "topical song" subgenre, this kind of preface offered an exegesis of the political references and of the implications of the song. Some of these commentaries, such as Phil Ochs's gleeful "I think Billy Graham should be castrated," were politically partisan to a degree that made record companies reluctant to include them.[45]

This is not to say, of course, that rock was apolitical. On the contrary, its capacity to construct oppositional publics was almost legendary, as the whole line of East European films in which rebellion begins with a rock concert testifies. The Czechoslovak Human Rights Movement, Charter 77, originated in 1977 as an effort to defend a rock band—The Plastic People of the Universe—from state persecution in 1977.[46] Rock music's relationship with its audience and political work was different from guitar poetry's, however. While rock famously mobilized its audiences for confrontation (Mark Mattern's first function), its deliberative capacities (Mattern's second function)—which are partly predicated on the political analysis offered in the lyrics—could not compare with those of guitar poetry.

The comparison with rock music also brings into relief guitar poetry's relatively poor transnational mobility. If, in the case of guitar poetry, there are many national instantiations of it but no supranational name for the genre, the English word for *rock* is used worldwide. In Eastern Europe, Latin America, and elsewhere, rock is perceived as distinctly Anglo-American in origin.[47] Even if a local band puts their own lyrics to their own music, the very act of choosing certain instruments and performance styles for their musical expression indexes the West. The work of musical recording companies also helps explain the ease with which rock crossed national boundaries in the First and parts of the Third World. The story of rock's spread throughout the Second World is more compli-cated, for there were no cultural industries to promote it; it was popular fascination with the West that generated significant demand for Western cultural forms "from below."[48]

Guitar poetry's gradual ceding of its cultural preeminence to rock, and its move toward cultural marginality, cannot be attributed solely to the repressive policies of the state or the work of the cultural industries. If *nueva canción* was repermitted in Chile a few years after the coup—in a relatively depoliticized form known as *nueva canta* (new song)—it returned without reassuming the place the cultural critic Alberto Moreno had optimistically predicted: "In any case, I have no doubt that on the day that Pinochet falls the New Song movement will flower once more, that Chileans will dance, and *nueva can-ción* will supply the music."[49] As the role of protest music was taken up by rock, Victor Jara gave way to los Prisoneros, a rock band. Such at least is Robert Neustadt's elegant reading of Gustavo Rodriguez's short story "El Clarevidente" (1996).[50] Rodriguez's story begins with the narrator's return to Chile after many years of exile during the dictatorship. His search for his own past is driven by memories of the woman he loved and with whom he listened to *nueva canción* and participated in Unidad Popular politics. When he does find her, he is taken aback by the ease with which she has shed her past and adapted to Pinochet's Chile. The musical tastes of her daughter (tellingly named Violeta, a suggestive reference to Vio-leta Parra), a heavy metal fan who despises *nueva canción*, come as another shock to him. Gradually, however, he realizes that Violeta finds in the music of Iron Maiden the kind of protest outlet that *nueva canción* once served for him. As this story suggests, rock music largely displaced guitar poetry as the preferred medium for political protest, but as usually happens with media, they helped shape the politics available to the publics.

Such was definitely the case in the USSR, where rock both expressed and shaped a new kind of protest culture (different from socialism with a human face) in the Brezhnev years. Jura, a friend of ethnomusicologist Martin Daughtry, eloquently describes his logic for abandoning guitar poetry in favor of the nascent Russian rock scene in the 1970s:

> Those who [in contrast to the rockers] kind of WEAKLY sang, in a maudlin fashion, their little songs to guitar [accompaniment] somehow this was not ANGRY enough, there was not enough ENERGY in it. Because I understood that armed with this type of song you can't destroy anything. But armed with THIS [rock music]—it's possible to find something to destroy. Over there [in avtorskaia pesnia], they don't scream. The singers [of these two genres] occupy two different positions. . . . Let's take Okudzhava as an example. What kind of internal solution can a person find, psychologically, when his society, is FUCKING him, for real—understand. He's hemmed in on all sides. When everything is SATURATED with ideology?[51]

Jura's sentiments and observations were widely shared by members of his generation on the other side of the Iron Curtain as well. Better than any scholarly account, they describe the affective forces at work in the loss of avant-garde audiences, such as Jura, and with it, the genre's move from a more central to a more peripheral position within different national cultures. While Vysotskii and Okudzhava's audiences grew numerically through the 1970s and the Grushin Festival gathered tens of thousands of fans on the Volga River for a few days, Soviet bardic song had lost its function as the leading genre laboratory within Soviet culture. It is telling that the preeminent guitar poets (Okudzhava, Vysotskii, Galich, as well as Aleksandr Gorodnitskii, Iulii Kim, Iurii Vizbor, and Novella Matveeva) had all made their artistic debut in a fairly narrow temporal window between mid-1950s and the late 1960s. By contrast, from the 1970s to the ending of the USSR in 1991, avant-garde youth audiences started flocking to informal rock concerts. Despite the occasional defections, such as Jura's, from one type of music to another (and the existence of a few hybrid performers such as Aleksandr Bashlachov, who have been variously classified as guitar poets or rock musicians), the audiences brought together by guitar poetry and rock music were very distinct.[52]

Such an observation could easily extend beyond the Soviet borders: of all the major national guitar poets listed in the beginning of this paper, only Jacek Kaczmarski reached prominence after the 1960s. Though shaped by very different sociopolitical and literary contexts, the evolution of guitar poetry outside the Soviet bloc reflected the same broad trends. In the United States, for example, the unity provided to singer-songwriters by the folk revival moment lasted only for a brief time and was certainly over by 1968. Because in the United States guitar poetry had functioned as "movement" music for the civil rights cause, "a singing movement par excellence," as Ron Eyerman and Andrew Jamison call it, the movement's decline in the late 1960s meant the shrinking of the audience for American folk music.[53] Phil Ochs could not survive the passage of the 1960s, falling victim to a mental illness and alcoholism and dying in relative obscurity in 1976. Pete Seeger, yet again left with a diminished audience, undertook new projects and causes such as the emerging ecological movement, which became a major addressee of his new songs. Another possible trajectory, illustrated by Bob Dylan, was to achieve a much broader audience by transitioning to rock, giving up on finger-pointing songs with concrete political references and on excessively lengthy compositions, which could not be neatly fitted into radio programs or otherwise reach a mass audience.[54]

Guitar poetry's subsequent move to the cultural periphery in the different national contexts should not belie its immense significance for the social movements of the 1960s. It was structured by those movements and in turn helped structure them by constructing musical publics coterminous with political ones. While other artistic forms—poetry, novel, theater, and film—also created publics that overlapped with the Left, only guitar poetry was coeval with the social movements of the 1960s. It thus best encoded what Raymond Williams called their "structure of feeling," his term for the social forces structuring people's affective lives in variable and transient, lived ways.[55] Indeed, this common structure of feeling—rather than ideology—best captures the ephemerality and context dependency of the democratic socialism of the 1960s and

allows us to complicate and question the scholarly narratives of transnational crossings that have gained increasing prominence in the study of the 1960s.[56] Studying
those structures as embedded in guitar poetry—in its performance, audiences, and
imaginary—offers a unique vantage point to the historian of the period.

Notes

I would like to thank the first readers of this paper, Michael Denning and Katerina Clark, for encouraging and clarifying my early thoughts. The feedback I received from the participants of the 2010 Fisher
Forum, and especially from my discussant, Donna Buchanan, has been invaluable. If there is any coher-
ence to this paper, it is due to the extremely generous comments of the forum's organizers: Anne Gorsuch and Diane Koenker.

1. Gerald Smith, *Song to Seven Strings: From Soviet Mass Song to Guitar Poetry* (Bloomington:
Indiana University Press, 1988).

2. As Donna Buchanan pointed out to me in conversation, the description of guitar poetry as
"global" or "international" is something of a misnomer. A more precise designation for the guitar poets
I bring up is *Euro-American,* for two reasons. First, the guitar was less rooted in most African and Asian
musical cultures. Second, the social movements in most Afro-Asian societies were of a very different,
anticolonial kind.

3. Most of the scholarly literature on U.S. guitar poetry comes in the form of individual singer-
songwriters' biographies: Pete Seeger, Woody Guthrie, Joan Baez. Sociologists Ron Eyerman and
Andrew Jamison have produced one of the few studies of U.S. singer-songwriter performance from the
1960s: *Music and Social Movements* (Cambridge: Cambridge University Press, 1998). The Italian song
movement has been a subject of a few collections, such as *Poesia Cantata 2: Die Italienischen Cantautori
zwischen Engagement und Kommerz* (Berlin: Max Niemeyer, 2002). The definitive study of German
guitar poetry is Katherine Goetsch's *Linke Liedermacher: Das politische Lied der sechziger und siebziger
Jahre in Deuschland* (Innsbruck: Lumbus, 2007). There are multiple such accounts of Latin American *nueva canción,* the most well-known of them being Osvaldo Rodriguez, *Nueva canción chilena:
Continuidad y reflejo* (Havana: Casa de las Américas, 1988). Soviet guitar poetry is probably the most
extensively studied with monographs such as Inna Sokolova's *Avtorskaia pesnia: Ot fol'klora k poezii*
(Moscow: Tsentr Vysotskogo, 2002).

4. Jürgen Habermas, *The Structural Transformation of the Public Sphere: An Inquiry into a Category of Bourgeois Society* (Cambridge, MA: MIT Press, 1989).

5. Charles Tindley's spiritual "I'll Overcome" had long been part of the repertoire of African
American churches when a version of it was used by striking black tobacco workers in North Carolina.
Zilphia Horton of the Highlander School taught the strikers' version to Pete Seeger, who liked to joke
that his "Harvard grammar" produced the final "We Shall Overcome." For the story of Seeger's role in
the popularization of the civil rights anthem, see David Dunaway, *How Can I Keep from Singing? The
Ballad of Pete Seeger* (New York: Villard Books, 2008), 275. For the lyrics of Biermann's "Wir sassen am
Feuer in Dunkeln," see Wolf Biermann, *Alle Lieder* (Cologne: Kiepenheuer und Witsch, 1991), 250. For
the lyrics of Okudzhava's "Soiuz druzei," see Bulat Okudzhava, *Chaepitie na Arbate* (Moscow: Moskva
Korona-Print, 1997), 226.

6. The poem was written in 1972, when the Soviet state partially lifted the emigration restrictions
for Jewish citizens. Persecuted and rendered unemployable for his political opposition, Galich himself
emigrated in 1974. Aleksandr Galich, "Pesnia iskhoda," in *Pesnia ob otchem dome* (Moscow: Lokid
Press, 2003), 358.

7. Mark Mattern, *Acting in Concert: Music, Community, and Political Action* (New Brunswick:
Rutgers University Press, 1998), 17–30.

8. See the chapter "Berlin—Music and Politics," in Albrecht Betz, *Hanns Eisler: Political Musician* (Cambridge: Cambridge University Press, 2006), 32–118.

9. Ibid., 119–64.

10. Il'ia Viniavkin, "Fenomen 'cantautore' v italianskoi kul'ture vtoroi poloviny dvadtsatogo veka i tvorchestvo Fabrizio de Andre" (PhD diss. abstract, Russian State University for the Humanities, 2006), 14.

11. Rina Benmayor, "La 'Nueva Trova': New Cuban Song," *Latin American Music Review* 2, no. 1 (Spring–Summer 1981): 14.

12. David Dunaway, "Charles Seeger and Carl Sands: The Composers' Collective Years," *Ethnomusicology* 24, no. 2 (May 1980): 159–68.

13. Nancy Morris, "Canto porque es necesario cantar: The New Song Movement in Chile, 1973–1983," *Latin American Research Review* 21, no. 1 (1986): 118.

14. Simon Keefe, "'La chanson c'est pour tout le monde': An Introduction to the Music of Georges Brassens," *Tempo* 212 (April 2000): 38–45.

15. Betz, *Hanns Eisler,* 148.

16. Dunaway, *How Can I Keep from Singing,* 123.

17. *Red Channels* was an anticommunist tract that listed 151 writers, musicians, actors, and entertainers as participants in a communist conspiracy in American media. Compiled by professional anticommunists with the FBI, it ruined many careers. *Red Channels: The Report of Communist Influence in Radio and Television* (New York: Counterattack, 1950).

18. Dunaway, *How Can I Keep from Singing,* 157.

19. Colin Netelbeck, "Music," in *The Cambridge Companion to Modern French Culture,* ed. Nicholas Hewitt (Cambridge: Cambridge University Press, 2003), 283.

20. Biermann, *Alle Lieder,* 204, 412.

21. Aleksandr Galich, "Predpolegaemyi tekst moei predpolegaemyi rechi . . . ," in *Pesnia ob otchem dome,* 381.

22. Aleksandr Galich, "Predpolegaemyi tekst moei predpolegaemyi rechi . . . ," Bard.ru., http://bard.ru/cgi-bin/mp3.cgi?id=113.15, music file, accessed 18 February 2012.

23. Andrei Krylov, "Russkie bardy v kontekste totalitarnoi sistemy," in *Poeziia i pesnia Vladimira Vysotskogo: Sbornik Statei,* ed. Sergei Sviridov (Kaliningrad: Izdatel'stvo Rossiiskogo Gosudarstvennogo Universiteta imeni Imanuila Kanta, 2006), 4–51.

24. For a brief biography of Galich, see the introduction to Gerald S. Smith's translation of his poetry, Alexander Galich, *Songs and Poems,* trans. and ed. Gerald S. Smith (Ann Arbor: University of Michigan Press, 1984).

25. Jiri Holy, *Writers under Siege: Czech Literature since 1945* (Eastbourne: Sussex Academic Press, 2010), 104–5.

26. Krylov, "Russkie bardy," 4–51.

27. Pete Seeger, *The Incomplete Folksinger* (New York: Simon and Schuster, 1972), 514–21.

28. Ibid., 373.

29. Ibid., 374. As Lewis Siegelbaum suggested to me in private correspondence, Seeger's observations reflect what he objectively saw, as well as his horizon of expectations about the audience.

30. Daniil Granin, "Mesiats naoborot," in *Sobranie sochinenii v vos'mi tomakh,* vol. 2 (St. Petersburg: Vita Nova, 2009), 369–469.

31. Anatoli Naiman, "Chastnaia tochka zreniia," *Evreiskoe slovo* 6 (19–25 February 2008): 6.

32. See the chapter "Die Jahre der Isolation (1965–1976)," in Jay Rossellini, *Wolf Biermann* (Munich: C. H. Beck, 1992), 47–84.

33. This attitude comes across very clearly in Aleksandra Vasilievna's novella *Moia Marusechka,* published in *Znamia* 4 (1999), http://magazines.russ.ru/znamia/1999/4/vasil.html: "We were visited by a delegation of German communists headed by Dean Reed. As he was singing "Da! Da! Da! Ja! Ja! Ja!,"

the secretaries were setting the table in the director's office: a glass of cocoa, a bowl of ice cream, and crackers covered with powdered sugar."

34. Aleksandr Rozenbaum, "Shestisotyi mers—eto kleimo," *Petersburg-Express*, 12 January 2000. In the interview, Rozenbaum goes on to praise Pinochet, who had impressed him very positively during a meeting.

35. Jan Fairley, "La nueva canción latinoamericana," *Bulletin of Latin American Research* 3, no. 2 (1984): 107–15.

36. The list is compiled on the basis of the tables of contents of the ten-disc set *Die Burg Waldek Festivals, 1964–1969: Chansons Folklore International*, Bear Family Records, B0015UGN3M, 2008, compact disc.

37. Biermann, *Alle Lieder*, 119–24.

38. V. P. Prishchepa, "Poteri i priobreteniia," in *Rossiiskogo Otechestva poet: E.A. Evtushenko: 1965–1995 g.*, ed. L. N. Makarova (Abakan: Khakassian State University, 1996), 344.

39. Fabrizio De Andre, *Tuti morimmo a stento*, Sony B001QBC3RU, 2009, compact disc.

40. Dunaway, *How Can I Keep from Singing*, 177–89.

41. Alberto Moreno, "Violeta Parra and la nueva canción chilena," *Studies in Latin American Popular Culture* 5 (1986): 122.

42. Dunaway, *How Can I Keep from Singing*, 238.

43. Alec Wilkinson, *The Protest Singer* (New York: Knopf, 2009), 13.

44. Such is the best explanation for another famous episode in American rock music history, in which Bruce Springsteen's socially critical song "Born in the U.S.A." was co-opted by Ronald Reagan's 1984 reelection campaign as a paragon of uplifting musical patriotism. The lyrics were clearly antiwar; they protested the social decline and callous treatment faced by returning Vietnam vets. The Reagan campaign, however, either had failed to hear and understand Springsteen's lyrics or had thought them secondary. The Republican endorsement provoked Springsteen's subsequent rejection and clarification. Springsteen's responses did not stop the Chrysler Company from offering him $12 million for the use of the song in a car commercial, an offer Springsteen declined.

45. Phil Ochs, *The Stable* (bootleg recording of a concert at East Lansing, MI, 26 May 1973), http:// rapidshare.com/files/236697644/Ochs_Stable.rar, music file (accessed 14 March 2012).

46. Michael Kilburn, "Antipoliticheskaia politika i antiesteticheskaia estetika," trans. T. Vorontsova, *Novoe literaturnoe obozrenie* 91 (2008): 266–305.

47. See Timothy Brown's account of the valences of rock in East Germany in his "1968 East and West: Divided Germany as a Case Study in Transnational History," *American Historical Review* 144, no. 1 (February 2009): 86–88.

48. For the authoritative account on Soviet rock, see Artemy Troitsky, *Back in the USSR* (Boston: Faber and Faber, 1988).

49. Moreno, "Violeta Parra," 108–26.

50. Robert Neustadt, "Music as Memory and Torture: Sounds of Repression and Protest in Chile and Argentina," *Chasqui* 3, no. 1 (2004): 128–38.

51. Martin Doughtry, "Ethics, Emotion, Metaphor, and Dialogue among Contemporary Russian Bards" (PhD diss., University of California Los Angeles, 2006), 246.

52. This point came out in the concluding Conference Roundtable, "Vladimir Vysotskii: Vzgliad s 21-go veka" (Moscow, 23 March 2003).

53. Eyerman and Jamison, *Music and Social Movements*, 103.

54. Ibid., 125.

55. Raymond Williams, *Marxism and Literature* (Oxford: Oxford University Press, 1977), 75–141.

56. On the transnational perspective of the 1960s, see the relevant chapters of Gerd Rainer Herd and Padraic Kenney, eds., *Transnational Moments of Change: Europe 1945, 1968, 1989*, (Lanham, MD: Rowman and Littlefield, 2004).

6 Songs from the Wood, Love from the Fields

The Soviet Tourist Song Movement

Christian Noack

Before pop and rock took hold of North America's and Europe's youth, a remarkable "folk revival" seized many countries in the developed world. As Rossen Djagalov writes elsewhere in this volume, in the early and mid-1960s, singer-songwriters in the United States, England, Germany, France, and Italy were performing songs they authored with simple guitar accompaniment. More often than not these singer-songwriters identified with the aims of the contemporary civil rights movement in the States (or incidentally with revolutionary and leftist governments in South America); they expressed a younger generation's growing dissatisfaction with the dull and often hypocritical participation of their parents in a conservative postwar order. Many songs featured critical comments on contemporary society, while they borrowed musically from simple patterns of national or international folk traditions. Songs of the American or Irish folkies, French *bardes*, or German *Liedermacher* were simple and catchy enough to be learned and performed by amateurs; the international folk scene was as much about singing and playing guitar as it was about listening to music and lyrics.

The closest Soviet equivalent to this global folk revival was "guitar" or "bard" poetry that emerged during the Khrushchev Thaw and gained enormous popularity during the 1960s. Whereas their Western counterparts occasionally faced politically motivated boycotts by radio stations or attempted censorship by record companies, Soviet bards were deprived of almost any media outlet. They had to stage their concerts in the kitchens of communal flats, in the courtyards of tenement blocks, or, most importantly, outdoors. Indeed, as I will try to show in this chapter, singing and songwriting in the Soviet Union were closely tied to habits of travel and tourism. While Western lyrics frequently alluded in an allegorical sense to being out and about—the myth of "the road"—in the Soviet Union the folk revival was intimately tied to the actual practice of travel and tourism. People gathered in the countryside to camp, eat, and drink in a natural and romantic environment. Joint singing through a shared canon of songs was the highlight of these outings. Tourism and singing songs became inseparable, the guitar becoming a potent symbol for Soviet tourism more broadly. Indeed, if especially in retrospect, "gitourism" has become a trademark for the Soviet 1960s as a whole.[1] This decade saw rising incomes, shorter work hours, growing mobility through better transportation infrastructure, and, under Brezhnev, a "deal" that conceded less state interference into private lives as long as political loyalty to the system could be taken for granted. Tourism offered Soviet citizens a sphere that provided distance from the increasingly empty ritualism of state and party duties. And it presented ample opportunities for meaningful social interaction beyond the routines of dull everyday life, whether at the workplace or in the narrow confines of private or family life. As Petr Vail' and Aleksandr Genis described the phenomenon in their seminal essay on the Soviet sixties: "The collectives roaming the countryside sang: crews of sailors or airliners, expeditions of prospectors [geologicheskie partii], rope teams of mountaineers, tourist groups . . ."[2]

My chapter starts with a review of a few authoritative attempts at a definition of the genre of "tourist," "amateur," and "author's" songs.[3] For the historian of Soviet society and culture, the differences ascribed by philologists are less important, however, than the striking similarities in the social practices that developed at the intersection between touring and singing. Hence my chapter does not provide an in-depth philological analysis of works of well-known authors or their amateurish epigones. I focus instead on what was at times called a *song movement*, namely the particular forms of sociability that developed in the Soviet context and the subsequent efforts at an institutionalization, initially under the roof of Soviet tourist organizations.

Huge outdoor rallies including open-air concerts with thousands of listeners quickly constituted the highlights of the season for many Soviet tourists. Increasingly, too, amateurs of the tourist song strove to stage concerts in urban cultural spaces. It is the history of institutionalization and urbanization of the tourist song movement that is most interesting. Did the move from outdoors to indoors change the character of the tourist song movement, and if so, in which ways? What compromises were required with Soviet institutions or officials in order to produce concerts and festivals? Almost by necessity, the growing popularity of outdoor concerts and the emergence of urban clubs rendered this form of grassroots culture increasingly visible. As I will show, organizing these forms of sociability became a matter of contest between several political and administrative bodies in the Soviet Union. Whether this entailed a clear-cut development from "alternative" outdoor festivals to "domesticated" concerts in designated cultural spaces will also be discussed.

Socializing with the devotees of the same kind of music (and even more, loathing those who preferred other music) was an essential part of the global folk revival.

While interactive playing and singing may have been less important in the West, where media and technical reproduction of music were more broadly available, much of the folk revival in the West was obviously about informal sociability too. Was the Soviet tourist song movement part of a global phenomenon in popular culture, then? In the conclusion of my chapter I will discuss why, some striking similarities notwithstanding, I consider the tourist song movement in the USSR a specifically Soviet phenomenon.

Finally a word about sources: this chapter owes its existence to the central role that tourism and the tourist song play in the living memories of the last Soviet generation. The fans of both Soviet bard poetry and spontaneous tourism run extensive websites that publish songs, lyrics, memories, and pictures. This activity is an indicator of the importance of the phenomenon in individual and collective memory, even as these memories may well be selective and contestable. Thanks to the gradual institutionalization of what was initially a grassroots movement in tourist and song clubs (a process that I describe below), there is abundant archival documentation available online, including, for example, the minutes of meetings between members of different tourist and song clubs during the late Soviet period. Given the scarcity of material on everyday history, these websites constitute an important repository for the historian of Soviet popular culture.

The Tourist Song

What then, in the Soviet Union, was a tourist song *(turistskaia pesnia)*? For the 1993 *Entsiklopediia turista* the tourist song emerged as a genre in the early 1950s. For urban tourists, exposure to nature provided a variety of "new impressions, unforeseen situations, and manifestations of the human character that fostered creativity." This allegedly made them express their feelings in songs. Interestingly, the entry does not attempt to define the tourist song in terms of content: namely, as a song about touring or traveling. On the contrary, the authors claim that tourists in the early years would have favored popular war songs and that the tourist song as a musical genre differed little from other "amateur songs" *(samodeiatel'nye pesni)*, being "melodious, cheering, and prevailingly at a slow pace."[4]

Other sources define the tourist song by its contents. L. I. Levin, in the lexicon *Estrada Rossii*, prefers the term hiking song *(pesnia stranstviia)*, arguing that it was "sometimes inaccurately called the tourist song." He also makes a connection between the hiking/tourist song and the "author's song" *(avtorskaia pesnia)*, usually described in Western sources as "bard" or "guitar poetry." According to Levin, the hiking song was the mainstay of song poetry produced during the Khrushchev years, the golden years of the author's song. For Levin this genre of songs was characterized by the central themes *(obrazy-mifologemy)* of "friend/friendship" and "the road," with the road symbolizing the path of life (including both ordeals and hopes), paths to oneself, and paths into the unknown. Levin concedes the existence of a broad variety of subgenres,

"from philosophical and witty lyrics to jests [and] from simple campfire lyrics to fragile romantic song fantasies."[5]

Although the encyclopedia and the lexicon approach tourist music differently,
both see the tourist song in terms of a larger context. Not entirely surprisingly, the
tourist's encyclopedia tends to treat song as an integral part of the tourist experience,
while the lexicon leans toward an identification of the tourist song with the larger phenomenon of the author's song. The latter view was endorsed by the encyclopedia, which
claims that "during the sixties and seventies author's songs, so called bard songs, very
popular at the time, spread into the milieu of tourism."[6]

A final source by I. A. Sokolova, this one a history of the famous Soviet bard
Vladimir Vysotskii, regards *author's song* as a generic term composed of subgenres
like the student song, the tourist song, the mountaineer song, and the geologist song.
Her extensive discussion of the phenomenon notes a shift in the use of the terms *amateur song* and *author's song*, with the former, she argues, being widely used during
the 1960s and the latter emerging in the second half of this decade but becoming predominant only during the 1970s and 1980s. For Sokolova, this transformation reflects
an increasing claim to respectability by the authors of song poetry. We will return
to this problem in the context of the development and increasing institutionalization of the tourist/amateur/author's song. For the time being it is more important
to note that Sokolova also treats the author's song as a broad social practice: "In the
beginning, when it developed in the second half of the 1950s, the author's song (not
yet known by this term then) did not have any oppositional character. It developed
as a leisure pursuit, it was an expression of young people's creativity. . . . The popular
[demokratichnaia] and accessible form of the song offered the best opportunities for
self-realization, and it was absolutely free."[7] Levin in the lexicon also deals with the
author's song as social practice in its own right when he writes that the "essence of
the author's song is anything but the writer's claim to authorship, melody, or interpretation."[8] According to Levin, it is a communication of the author's way of life and
his worldview through the medium of the song under the conditions of a face-to-face
encounter. The song becomes a medium for the lyrics—lyrics that Richard Stites has
summed up as "characterized by simplicity, honesty and directness unfamiliar to
official Soviet culture."[9] On the other hand, the lexicon places the "author's song" in
a specific communicative situation usually different from that of the concert. Levin
makes this point to distinguish the author's song from other forms of musical public
culture, especially *estrada*, and he devotes considerable space to alternative venues
of its performance, the company of friends *(druzheskie kompanii)* that might vary in
size, for example, or a festival that has larger numbers of visitors but that nonetheless
retains an informal atmosphere: "Ideally an audience that surpasses a critical mass
would consist of a number of 'companies of friends' that would acknowledge their
spiritual unity and their affiliation to a particular social group, referred to as 'us.'"[10]
Levin, like the authors of the encyclopedia, argues that the author's song emerged in

the 1950s. For him this phenomenon is closely linked with the intellectual rehabilitation of the individual in Khrushchev's Thaw, which resulted in the spread of the *kompaniia,* particularly among urban academic youth. "This period saw an upsurge in self-organized [samodeiatel'nyi] tourism and alpinism, which owed its popularity to the same quest for individual personal development. . . . Here, far from urban noise, far from the usual hassle and from responsibilities, under sometimes extreme conditions it emerged whenever the individual or the group was stable and living up to self-determined ideals. . . . And the ideal form of expression of the new group identity was the author's song, emphasizing its emotional dominant—confidence—through intonation."[11] This passage is very similar to the initially quoted narrative of the emergence of the tourist song as presented by the *Entsiklopediia turista.* More importantly it reestablishes the whole phenomenon of the author's song as social practice, and as one that has very much in common with tourist habits. I turn next to look at the particular forms of connection between tourism and song.

Post-Stalinist Escapism? Touring and Singing in the Soviet Context

The emergence of tourist/amateur's/author's songs predated World War II, yet most sources agree that they gained enormous popularity during the 1950s and particularly during Khrushchev's Thaw. Some authors describe a decline after 1968, the year of the suppression of the Prague Spring, whereas others maintain that the song movement survived, changing for better or worse during the 1970s and 1980s. Obituaries emerged with the demise of the USSR, as did news about a resurrection in the nineties and noughties.[12]

Whether 1968 was an important watershed in the song movement will be discussed in the final section of this chapter. Two important questions of interpretation must be answered first: How and why did simple habits like meeting and singing to guitar accompaniment become almost instantly a mass phenomenon in the post-Stalinist USSR? Why did the adherents of these leisurely pursuits also eventually strive for institutionalization, possibly with the premature end of the Soviet sixties in 1968? In other words, why did they seek to create clubs and organize regular rallies, meetings, or festivals? Finally, what does the enormous amount of primary and secondary source material (on the Internet) documenting the past and present of a movement, including heated debates on the role of "amateur song clubs," tell us about the popular nature of this phenomenon? In this part of the chapter I sketch an outline of a history of what became a "movement."

Vladimir Novikov, one of the protagonists of the tourist song movement in Kiev, looked back at the beginning of the movement in an article published in 1997.[13] From his point of view, Soviet tourism had a clear-cut social profile—98 percent of the tourists "were in some way or the other members of the intelligentsia." This may be a slight exaggeration, yet recent research has indeed confirmed that the lion's share of Soviet tourists and mountaineers, before Stalin and after, came from an academic background.[14] Not only were Khrushchev's regime and that of the early Brezhnev period characterized by increasingly growing cultural freedom, but educational policies also enlarged the social basis of the group: the absolute number of students doubled between 1950 and 1960 and again between 1960 and 1970. If 6 percent of the Soviet population held a higher education degree in 1959, the share rose to 11.5 percent in 1970. Within this group, sometimes termed "new middle classes," engineers and technical specialists *(inzhenerno-tekhnicheskie rabotniki)* formed the largest cohort. Educational opportunities were a privilege of the urban population: four times more urban than rural dwellers received university degrees in the 1970s. In the same period, the USSR experienced a second wave of urbanization; by 1961, every second Soviet citizen was a city dweller.[15] In other words: Soviet citizens became more educated and urban, and the number of *potential* tourists grew. Indeed, we find the numbers of practitioners organized in tourist clubs and sections of Soviet administration and enterprises increasing accordingly.[16]

The term *tourist* requires a degree of annotation here, as "tourism" in the Soviet context could connote two different variants of travel, both of them touring holidays. The first were organized tours by operators affiliated with the trade unions. These operators would transport tourists by train, bus, and later airplanes to famous sights at different destinations. The Soviet tourists to Czechoslovakia discussed in Rachel Applebaum's chapter traveled almost exclusively under such trade union auspices. Tourism could also mean active travel—hiking, canoeing, cycling—involving physical exercise, usually self-organized under the aegis of so-called tourist cells or sections in enterprises. This variety of tourism was also labeled independent, *samodeiatel'nyi turizm.* Both forms had uneasily coexisted since the 1930s, when the quest to develop a particular Soviet and proletarian form of tourism, distinct from what was practiced in the capitalist world, unleashed an institutional competition. In fact, neither the advocates of organized forms of social tourism nor those preferring autonomous trailblazing could oust their competitors. It deserves mentioning, however, that the latter position left a deep imprint in the official discourse on "true" Soviet tourism.[17]

The *samodeiatel'nyi* tourist regarded tourism as a physical exercise, as an examination of his or her own fitness and the group's spirit and cohesion. The rough and existentialist character of the grassroots variety, and its masculinist associations, help explain tourism's massive attraction for a postwar generation of students and young academics. Novikov, for example, maintained that after the Second World War young academics faced an unattainable role model in the shape of the war veteran, the *frontovik.* As a result, "Under the banner 'There is room for heroic deeds' [est' mesto podvigu] the younger generation, freedom-loving, sallied out to conquer the romantic great beyond [romanticheskie dali]."[18] Obviously, the disciples of this philosophy were the same as the singing tourists identified by the encyclopedia or the lexicon. Beyond this, the term *samodeiatel'nyi* provides another, certainly not accidental link between these tourists and a particular form of institutionalization of the movement, the "amateur song clubs" (*klub samodeiatel'noi pesni*), to which I will return in the following section.

As we have already seen, in historical narratives about the author's song, nature plays an important, almost active role. Vladimir Sapuntsov, a veteran of the author's song movement in Moscow, described the role of nature in a 1986 interview as follows:

> Basically you could sing to the guitar in your apartment, on a bench, and even . . . in the driveway. Yet amateur singers organize their rallies in the forest. Who would need all that additional hassle: backpacks, suburban trains, miles on foot? . . . I think you have to take a closer look: creating songs cannot be separated from being in the open country—that's inspiring. . . . When singing our favorite songs we want to relax, enjoy fresh air, listen to the rustle of the pine trees, accompanied by the crackles from the campfire—and there's a dozen or so campfires . . . We sing the songs of Okudzhava, Vizbor, Gorodnitskii, Nikitin, Kim, Berkovskii, Egorov, Kliachkin, Matveeva, Sukhanov, and other bard-poets, and obviously there will be new songs and new authors. . . . After the concert, all sing in their bivouacs, or "walk by the fires" as we call it of old . . . People at best sleep two or three hours on a rally, there is just no time as you want to hear and write down more.[19]

Sapuntsov's memories point to two important aspects at the intersection of tourism and artistic creativity. On the one hand, the singer-songwriter needs calm, natural surroundings to be inspired, to transcend the limits of his mundane and exhaustive urban existence. Sapuntsov enshrines a romantic concept of creativity here that was shared by many of his contemporaries. It almost became the trademark of the Soviet generation of the sixties. As Vail' and Genis write: "The traditional romantic conflict emerged transformed: in fact, it was not the lonely hero who faced a conservative public, but on the contrary a romanticized collective that struggled and convinced the occasional individualist. Public convention did not allow for not being romantic."[20]

On the other hand, engaging in grassroots tourism was fun and offered ample opportunity to regularly meet kindred spirits and exchange songs. M. Pasternak, a Moscow-based journalist, tourist, and later co-founder of an amateur song club, asserted in 1987: "I became acquainted with the author's song at school, when we did tourist trips. Then I found mountaineering attractive. In a bivouac I heard the songs of Okudzhava and Vizbor for the first time and took notes."[21] While well-known bard poetry played an important role in the development of the tourist song movement, many of the songs were instead simple by-products of tourist activities that reflected common experiences of a small peer group and possessed little significance for others. Some of them were rooted in the tradition of the *chastushki* folklore; others mimicked the style of bard poetry. Yet it is common wisdom in contemporary sources that some favorite tunes were shared by tourists all over the Soviet Union. More precisely, it was these songs that played an important role in linking the many small face-to-face *kompanii* or grassroots rope teams into a larger community of Soviet tourists.[22]

Vladimir Novikov maintained that many of the popular songs sung by the tourist in the 1950s dated back to the 1930s or the war. Among the songs and authors frequently credited we find "Nas utro vstrechaet prokhladnyi"; songs co-written by G. Lepskii and P. Kogan, like "Brigantina" and "Globus"; and Lepskii's "Kak iz dal'nego pokh-oda shel boets—sluga naroda," basically a war poem by Navrochatov. Other popular genres were underworld songs from Odessa *(blatnye odesskie pesni)* and, later, camp songs that were spreading after the rehabilitation of former Gulag prisoners during the 1950s. There were some similarities in the lyrics, as Soviet bards and singer-songwriters across the globe shared a common literary heritage from late medieval vagabond songs to nineteenth-century romanticism, but there is very little indication that the musical roots discussed in Rossen Djagalov's paper informed the harmonies or the melodies of Soviet guitar poetry. Music popular elsewhere during the late 1920s and 1930s either would not have reached a Soviet audience because of the relative seclusion of the country or would have been absorbed by officially sponsored genres like the "mass song" and thus would have constituted the very opposite of what guitar poetry or authors songs strove to achieve. In that sense, I would agree with Djagalov that guitar poetry, and with it tourist songs, developed largely in isolation from international trends in contemporary popular culture.[23]

Whatever the origin of the songs, it is interesting to reflect on their dissemination. Some of them, and probably the most successful ones, might have been spread through the media. In the late 1950s and the 1960s cinema played a significant role; indeed, travel and tourism became a very popular subject for Soviet filmmakers.[24] Printed media seems to have played a less important role, for a number of reasons. First, tourist songs, like guitar poetry, were not recognized as a legitimate form of literature, and only a minority of the bards were accepted members of the writers' union. This had, on the one hand, the advantage that bard poetry remained a "subcensorship" issue, simply not taken seriously by the watchdogs of the regime.[25] On the other hand, it meant that the usual printing outlets were inaccessible. Some songbooks were published with modest print runs, but basically the transmission of songs was a question of individual note taking and processing. This certainly helped the appeal of the songs as a non-state-sponsored form of creativity.

Songs most often spread informally. Novikov remembers that in the autumn of 1961, when two graduates of the Kiev Polytechnical Institute, Tamara Mishchenko and Viacheslav Lizunov, returned to their hometown, a company of friends met in their flat to listen (via the novelty of a tape recorder) to recordings of Okudzhava, Vizbor, and many other songwriters. Novikov's recollection elucidates the vast significance of the taping and copying of performances, known as *magnitizdat.* Similarly, tourists returning from their trips would bring new songs that fellow tourists from Sverdlovsk, Novosibirsk, Moscow, or "Piter" had taught them. Already in the winter of 1962, Lizunov and Mishchenko had edited a handwritten *samizdat* collection of tourist songs, made with the help of a friend in a few copies on carbon paper. "This was the first Kiev song collection, a naive, romantic and witty one," Novikov recalls.[26] The prospect of creating networks was an important incentive to engage in tourism, as the *samodeiatel'nye turisty* were indeed organizing all kinds of rallies and meetings to exchange other "deficit" items, like maps or information on new itineraries *(marshruty)* that they had acquired. The relationship between tourism and songs was made explicit, and was facilitated, when the illustrated monthly *Turist*, from 1966 onwards, printed the lyrics of one or two songs in every issue.

Learning new songs on hikes, and reproducing them, was an important part of the experience shared by tourists and singer-songwriters, even if this did not necessarily mean that engagement in grassroots tourism was all about canonizing songs. Yet the more popular ones clearly served as blueprints for amateur writers when, according to Novikov, "after the Twentieth Party Congress people started to sing their own songs: different kinds of songs, good ones and horrible ones. In student accommodations they sang about student life, in the forests at the campfires about tourism, and in the kitchens of the communal flats about themselves, about love, friends, and the times they were living in. They composed and sang to the piano, the accordion, or the guitar; the latter was something of a rarity then."[27] The quote illustrates, first, that while the author's song's emergence was closely linked to tourism, it was not practiced exclusively in the great outdoors. Indeed, dormitories or kitchens emerged as stages for joint singing during the Thaw. Second, three instruments for accompaniment are mentioned. While the piano was certainly not a practical instrument to carry on a hike, Novikov mentions the accordion and the guitar, suggesting that at the time it was not yet the default instrument it would quickly become.

As mentioned above, guitars were almost indispensable as an instrument that would accompany almost everything from the odd hiking song to shrewd bard poetry. Yet beyond this, the guitar became an almost omnipresent symbol in representations of Soviet tourism during the 1960s. Analyzing the visual imagery of the illustrated monthly *Turist*, I found the number of tourists posing with guitars in all possible walks of life simply stunning.[28] Against the backdrop of the importance of the guitar for the contemporary folk revivals in the West, or earlier tourist movements like the turn-of-the-century German *Wandervögel*, this is not entirely unexpected. Still, the role of the guitar is much less self-explanatory in the Soviet context. And as the Novikov quote above suggests, the guitar was not the only instrument that was used in the early days. Certainly, a guitar is much easier to carry along than a grand piano. But it is not easily stuffed into a rucksack, and there are number of other instruments like small melodeons that might have accompanied a song. Yet the guitar is arguably the simplest instrument to learn, and hardly any author's song required a mastery of more than three chords.[29]

Beyond questions of practicability, the rise of the guitar as a symbol is a story in its own right. Its Russian variant typically favored seven strings. In the wake of Stalin's cultural revolution, the guitar was condemned as a petit bourgeois instrument and associated with musical genres like gypsy romances, allegedly the preferred music of debauched NEP-era entrepreneurs, or NEP-men. The real proletarian played the accordion.[30] This prejudice had dire practical consequences; guitars ceased to be produced in the Soviet Union. Small manufacturers turned to more acceptable folk instruments like the balalaika. Only two or three luthiers continued to build instruments, and they switched to the classical six-string guitar, which had gained respectability because of the USSR's involvement in the Spanish Civil War. Andrés Segovia, for example, came to play concerts in the Soviet Union as a cultural ambassador for the Spanish republicans.[31]

The choice of the guitar could therefore be interpreted as a conscious countermotion against the pompous mass song culture propagated *inter alia* by Stalinist cinema. Indeed, some of the first bards used classical Russian-seven string instruments, and some of the songs and arrangements were clearly linked to nineteenth- and early twentieth-century traditions. Bard poetry and guitar poetry soon became synonyms. The guitar helped to emphasize a cultural break both with high culture and with the immediate Soviet past of the orchestrated mass song or orchestrated *estrada;* it witnessed a triumphant renaissance in Soviet popular culture from the late 1950s onwards.

The challenge was to obtain one.[32] This was not the least of reasons for song lovers to go networking. Joining a song club or traveling to a festival provided the opportunity to get one's hands on a fingerboard or to take guitar lessons, even if one did not possess a guitar. Beyond that, clubs and particularly festivals provided important marketplaces for obtaining equipment, and particularly guitars. Not only did the famous Grushin Festival, discussed in more detail in the following section, feature a guitar-shaped stage (which was copied by many minor festivals), but the winners of the competition would be awarded with guitars: a concert guitar for those who took first place in the contest for ensembles, a simple guitar for those who won the individual performers' competitions.[33]

The choice of the guitar thus set the followers of author's songs apart from other genres, whether they were traveling or not. Practically speaking, tourists and amateur singer-songwriters also shared a number of material needs, starting with the acquisition of hiking gear and tents (to be rented at the tourist clubs and cells), the provision of canned food (likewise purchased from the tourist clubs and cells), and the organization of meetings or exchanges with other *kompanii* beyond the local club. The latter was provided for by so-called "tourist rallies" *(slety turistskie),* which were organized on district and regional levels by the tourist clubs and cells.[34] Singing took place in all kinds of surroundings, but particularly the weekend hike to the countryside became a very common way of socializing. Songs were not limited to travel experiences, yet the theme of "the road" dominated.

Tellingly, the term defining the new leisure habit emerging in the post-Stalinist USSR vacillated between emphasizing the amateurish qualities of songwriting— *samodeiatel'nye pesni*—and the closeness to tourism in subject and practice—*turistskie pesni*. As described above, tourism in its grassroots variant was ideally suited to express the worldviews and interests of the postwar academic generation. The societal changes following de-Stalinization allowed for more tourism in terms of availability of free time, particularly for students and scholars. There was also more tolerance for private and semiprivate experiences. While the *kompaniia* of friends was in no way limited to the weekend outing, the *pokhod*, or hiking tour, added romanticism, something slightly more difficult to generate in the kitchen of a communal apartment. And if grassroots tourism was taken seriously, it could potentially put the group spirit to the litmus test.[35]

From Clearings to Clubs

Though much singing and touring coincided in the early days, during the 1960s and in particular the 1970s there was a parting of ways between the tourists who kept singing and song amateurs who were more interested in singing than in hiking. The following section traces the institutionalization of tourist meetings, *slety*, and the secession of a song club movement.

Tourist rallies were meetings in which active tourists from different parts of the Soviet Union competed in tourist skills like orienteering, setting up camps, or building a fire. The first tourist rallies in Kiev, for example, took place in the municipal park in 1954; student teams from the town's various higher education institutions furnished the participants. According to Vladimir Novikov, these rallies soon incorporated tourist song competitions into their programs. By contrast, separate musical events like public song festivals were slow to develop. Between 1964 and 1972 only four were organized, three by Kiev's tourist club and one in a Kiev university.[36]

Even if the tourist songs were merely incidental to the rallies, it was just a small step to the organization of festivals. Tourist rallies or *slety* needed a level of infrastructure, in the Soviet context usually provided by an organizational committee put in place by one or several tourist clubs or cells. A larger interregional meeting, for example, would require the selection of a site and the securing of a provisional right of use. Beyond that, if these places were located outside settled areas (as they usually were), the committees' tasks would comprise the provision of food and potentially the setting up of a fragmentary infrastructure.[37] The competitive character and the networking function of these rallies could be easily transformed into a tourist song competition, and this is exactly the prehistory of some of the most important regional or unionwide festivals, such as the one in Novosibirsk, that came into being during the 1960s.[38] A case in point is the famous Grushin Festival in Kuibyshev (Samara), which was held for the first time in 1968.[39]

The festival was named after Valerii Grushin, a student at the local Aviation Institute and a member of the municipal tourist club. Grushin had tragically died the year before while trying to save drowning fellow tourists. He was likewise known as a member of a small amateur group called the Beavers (*Bobry*) that performed tourist songs. According to its founders, the festival was dedicated to "publicizing the best tourist songs, selecting the best performers, and creating new tourist songs mirroring traits of genuine Soviet character." Already the first festival offered "a broad exchange of songs, lyrics, and recordings" besides the performances and the competition. The whole venue was largely improvised. "The stage consisted of a small spot on a slope, surrounded by a compact mass of people, windbreakers, rugs, sleeping bags, and anoraks [telogreki]; it was illuminated by campfires." Members of the jury were dispersed among the crowd. If this description anticipates Woodstock to a degree, so did the weather: the chairman of the jury, Boris Keil'man from Kuibyshev's Council for Tourism, announced the names of the winners "amid howling wind, lashing rain, and the sound of 'Globus,' the tourists' hymn."[40]

This first festival counted some six hundred visitors, and its resemblance to other tourist enterprises was underlined by the fact that it retained some athletic competitions. In its early days the Grushin Festival usually opened after a relay race starting in Kuibyshev's main square and finishing on the festival grounds on the banks of the Volga. The festival was extremely successful, the number of visitors more than doubling from year to year. In 1970, four thousand visitors from twelve cities were reported, a number that grew to twenty thousand visitors from forty-eight cities in 1975. A peak was reached in 1979, when a stunning one hundred thousand amateurs attended the festival. The festival was suspended between 1980 and 1986, but it saw new record numbers of participants in the late 1980s and late 1990s, again exceeding one hundred thousand visitors annually. Renowned bards like Aleksandr Gorodnitskii and Iurii Vizbor chaired the jury. At the same time the festival staged concerts by the country's most famous singers and songwriters. The big names among the laureates were Iurii Vizbor, Aleksandr Dol'skii, and Vladimir Lantsberg, all known to be practicing tourists and very popular bards.[41]

The sheer size of the festival exceeded the financial and human resources of the local tourist club. Therefore the organizers looked for powerful partners and found them in the regional tourist council (*oblastnoi sovet po turizmu*), the regional committee of the Komsomol, the regional tourist club "Zhiguli," and the tourist section of Kuibyshev's Polytechnical Institute.[42] This set of sponsors was remarkable not just for the inclusion of the Komsomol, so closely tied to party and ideology, but likewise for the participation of the tourist councils, which in contrast to the clubs and sections represented the much despised "organized" and "patronizing" variant of Soviet tourism.

As a lifestyle event not dissimilar from contemporary big rock festivals in the West, the Grushinka became the biggest venue in the history of the Soviet song movement and a model for many smaller events across the country. Regardless of their official sponsorship, festivals like this carried the ethos of the 1960s into the 1970s and 1980s and remained the most important hubs for the exchange of songs, lyrics, and recordings. As Vladimir Ogin, a tourist and singer-songwriter from Kazakhstan, put it:

There was a hunger for information; I knew a dozen of Vizbor's songs from a record that went "from hand to hand" for three years. I was convinced that Iurii Iosifovich must have new songs. But how would you be able to listen to them? . . . Only at festivals. . . . It was fashionable in those days [during the late 1970s] to walk around with a cassette recorder that was tied to your waist with a piece of string, and you would use a microphone attached to a long fishing rod to record everything happening on stage.[43]

In many respects the history of the Grushin Festival exemplifies what occurred locally throughout the Soviet Union, in some cases beginning much earlier and proceeding on a much smaller scale. Not entirely happy with seeing the song competitions just as an annex to tourist rallies, many of the song amateurs in the tourist clubs carved out their own niches in these institutions and initially organized divisions or sections especially devoted to tourist song concerts and competitions within existing clubs and sections.

In Sverdlovsk, for example, the municipal tourist club featured a section for tourist songs beginning in the early 1960s. The club counted among its members Aleksandr Dol'skii, who eventually became one of the Soviet Union's most famous bards.[44] In Leningrad the prehistory of the first song club started in a small café called Vostok that opened in 1961. It attracted a *kompaniia* of tourists and mountaineers. Monday meetings turned into little music sessions, with a preference for tourist songs. Vera Bordiuk, a member of the staff, began to promote public performances in 1963. The café was soon too small to accommodate the growing audience, and from 1964 onwards concerts were held in the House of Culture of the food industry workers. Among the early performers was Evgenii Kliachkin, another famous bard. When in 1965 the first large competitions were organized under the auspices of the local Komsomol, two famous song poets, Aleksandr Gorodnitskii and Iurii Kukin, allegedly made their first appearances on stage. What was now the club Vostok launched a regular evening concert series organized in the Kirov Culture Palace. This concert series would comprise a total of 213 performances over twenty-eight years.[45] Going mainstream and crossing the borders of official culture and its culture palace temples as the Leningraders did might well have been conceived by many contemporaries as a co-optation of subculture by the party's youth organization.

More typically, however, the early song clubs and sections would continue to organize tourist-style rallies in the countryside, referred to sometimes as festivals and sometimes as *slety*.[46] The members would prepare for the reception of incoming individuals and groups from other clubs and sections and would prepare performances individually or in small ensembles. Other important activities comprised, as already noted, the collection of songs, lyrics, and recordings and the compilation of songbooks.[47]

The relationship between organized tourists and organized singers proved to be precarious at times, however. Vladimir Lantsberg is said to have described the situation in the tourist club Piligrim prior to his arrival as follows: "[There was] a propensity for tourism, with the logical outcome . . . that the guys started to judge people on the basis of categories like: can you stuff ten kilograms more than anybody else into your backpack, are you more or less physically fit, do you have something to say or not, can you use the ax better than anybody else?"[48] Other reasons for the growing alienation between practitioners of tourist song and tourist structures might have been the proclivity for overregulation from above, which resulted in the growing passivity of members. In the case of Krasnodar's section of the tourist song, the responsible regional council for tourism regarded the organized singers and songwriters as a resource that they could send to its tourist bases and camps as entertainers. The notion of singers as government-sponsored entertainers certainly contradicted the idea of concerts or festivals as meeting places for people of kindred spirit. As a result, the section stopped promoting regular concerts and had trouble regularly organizing an annual regional competition in Krasnodar's theaters or concert halls. Beyond that, financial support from the council for tourism, six hundred rubles, materialized so late in 1975 that the regional festival was about to be cancelled. After it had been held, the organizers admitted that the communication with other clubs (in order to invite performers) had been sloppy. Most of the evening's scenario had been improvised, as well as the opening and closing ceremonies.[49] Therefore, the festival probably neither satisfied the council's interest in public representation of its activities nor pleased the crowd of tourist song devotees.

The report on other club activities during the same year, 1975, is no more encouraging. The song section failed to publish a songbook, as twelve out of thirty songs were allegedly "not up to artistic standards." Many planned concerts had to be cancelled, since the few active members were overstretched and occupied either with the preparation of the regional festival in Krasnodar or with preparations for performing at the Grushin Festival in Kuibyshev. The quality of the song section's collection of recordings was too poor to be exchanged with other clubs. Finally the section reported problems in obtaining a microphone (which obviously had to be bought "for cash," i.e., on the black market), and it turned out to be impossible to buy a guitar.[50] Again, this offers ample evidence that song sections possessed little appeal to the practitioners of the tourist song movement.

When song amateurs were looking for more professionalism and institutional backup, there were several ways for the Komsomol to become involved with amateur song clubs. This could be the case either if the scope of activities increased, as in the case of the Grushin Festival or the Leningrad club Vostok, or if clubs or sections performed poorly, as in Krasnodar. More often than not the party's youth organization was very welcome, for it lent some degree of respectability to the song amateurs' activities and could help provide access to cultural institutions, since the Komsomol was a much more serious Soviet organization than the less prestigious tourist bodies. For the protagonists of the song movement this choice came quite naturally, as the singing tourists belonged to a variety of other theatrical and musical amateur clubs that the

Komsomol already patronized in Soviet academic and cultural institutions. Clubs like those of the "merry and inventive" (*klub veselikh and nakodchivykh,* KVN) provided a stage for improvised performances in front of a small audience of peers. The limited public outreach of such student or amateur performers explains why the Komsomol was happy enough to encourage and endorse these "cultural activities" and to grant a degree of freedom and autonomy to these groups.[51]

While tourism, particularly the grassroots variant of *samodeiatel'nost',* offered opportunities to escape party tutelage and the social paternalism of Soviet mass organizations without trespassing the limits of what was ideologically acceptable, the active turn toward the Komsomol by song clubs seemed to indicate a change of priorities. Indeed, from the mid-1960s onwards amateur singers and songwriters seemed to prefer collaboration with the Komsomol or municipal authorities, or both, to any dependence on the tourism bureaucracy. Some tourist activities continued to play a role in the new song clubs, but it was the music that was more central now.[52] More often than not, emerging clubs were now designated as "amateur song clubs" (*klub samodeiatel'noi pesni,* KSP) and were run under the auspices of the Komsomol's municipal or academic branches. Clubs like "Poisk" in Vladivostok or the municipal club in Sverdlovsk, both founded in the mid-1970s, are examples of this trend. Vladivostok's Poisk was founded by some students from the geological faculty in the local Polytechnical Institute in October 1977. The statutes of the club were endorsed by the relevant Komsomol and students' union branches. It was not the first KSP in Vladivostok, and during its early days it seems to have been patronized by an existing KSP that resided in the House of Scientists. The president of the latter was a local Komsomol official, Boris Mezdrich.

Club life began in the following year, 1978, with the organization of a first festival. Club members also started to tour to other festivals and tourist rallies, covering virtually the whole geographical space of the USSR from Kamchatka to Tashkent to Moscow. The club was lucky enough to receive a whole floor in one of Vladivostok's historical buildings, centrally located but in dire need of restoration. These restoration works were undertaken by the club members themselves. The club comprised several sections, one responsible for organizational work, one for staging concerts, and another a technical section that would manage both the club's collection of recordings and its collection of "literature and information," including the club's library. Beyond that, the club maintained a small museum, a workshop, a photographic laboratory, and a treasury.[53]

One cannot help but note a tendency toward routinization in the 1970s and 1980s following on 1960s improvisation and experimentalism. The libraries and audio archives run by these clubs attained a particularly significant level of professionalism. Such archives were objects of deserved pride for the clubs, a good deal of whose activities aimed at the regular exchange of documents and recordings. Once a month the municipal KSP in Sverdlovsk, for example, offered its collection of recordings to a broader public, while members had permanent access and could borrow tapes. At the same time the club was eager to limit the numbers of "downloads," to use the contemporary term, for two practical reasons. First, they sought to minimize the wear on tapes and machines. Second, they wished to curtail financial exploitation of their amateur collection. Such collections were in all likelihood valuable enough to be copied for illegal commercial distribution, and the club had to react to signals it obviously received from the authorities, as sources mention. In addition to this activity, the Sverdlovsk club organized the usual local festival once a year plus fifteen to twenty performances for singer-songwriters from other parts of the Soviet Union. Its members traveled to three or four festivals annually. Rallies in the surroundings of Sverdlovsk were a regular feature of club life; performances during these weekend enterprises were less structured and competitive.[54]

Judging from materials these clubs provided for interregional meetings in the early 1980s, there was some continuity in the activities between the tourist clubs and sections and the amateur song clubs; the KSP, however, displayed a much more organized club life. Importantly, they distinguished between members and nonmembers, that is, occasional visitors to their concerts.[55] This does not necessarily testify for the musical professionalism of a club, though. Poisk in Vladivostok, for example, united devoted amateurs. Among the members were allegedly "neither songwriters, nor good ensembles or good singers." The club's members sought to compensate for these perceived flaws by "paying particular attention to the interaction with the audience during concerts."[56]

Yielding to or Playing with the Komsomol?

The transition from outdoor singing under the auspices of tourist organizations to more specialized song clubs under the auspices of the Komsomol began at the end of the 1960s and accelerated during the 1970s. Moscow provides an interesting case for this transition in the late 1960s. In the Soviet capital a group led by a charismatic tourist, Galina Zakharova, set up a club in 1965–66, securing one of the rare locations not too far from the center via the patronage of Moscow's council for tourism. At the same time, a competing group (Zakharova had earlier refused admission to some of its members) lobbied for support from the Komsomol. Aiming to use the full political weight of this organization, the lobbyists drew up their club statutes in close collaboration with the Komsomol and established themselves in Moscow's Sokol'niki neighborhood around 1967. At the same time, they allegedly sent their "agents" to the meetings of the other group to throw a spanner in its activities, which testifies to a degree of competition among the followers.[57]

While personal conflicts may have paved the way for collaboration with the Komsomol in the Moscow case, this was certainly neither the only nor the main reason:

> We perfectly understood why it was necessary to organize under the auspices of the Komsomol. It is very obvious how this organization [the Komsomol] works. They prefer to watch, wait, and see what happens in town, and then interfere and accuse

someone of ideological neglect and the like. But in this case we did not just want to be partners; we wanted to become a branch of the Moscow Komsomol. In other words, we wanted to be in direct subordination to the Komsomol in order to sort out all kinds of difficulties internally, to have all kinds of recommendations issued in a benevolent way. Instead of some sort of penalties we aspired to achieve some positive solutions.[58]

Oleg Chumachenko's retrospective 1982 account about his group's collaboration with the Komsomol implies a voluntary submission of the singers and songwriters to a degree of ideological control in exchange for the freedom to associate. Levin's initially cited entry in the *Estrada Rossii* lexicon provides a somewhat blunter judgment, for he sees the creation of the "amateur song clubs" as an attempt by the authorities to subvert the author's song movement: "Besides prohibition the authorities fell back on a strategy to take hold of [the author's song] from within through the creation of so-called KSPs [amateur song clubs]."[59]

Indeed, the growing role of the Komsomol has repeatedly been interpreted as an attempt to domesticate the movement, particularly as the movement coincided chronologically with important turning points in Soviet history: the early years of Brezhnev's reign were characterized by a narrowing of intellectual freedom. With the Prague Spring the regime's watchdogs grew even more suspicious, which led to an ideological freeze in the USSR after the suppression of the Czechoslovak movement. A majority of sources draw a clear line between a first stage of development, dated from the late 1950s to 1968, and a second one from 1968 to either the early or the mid-1980s.[60]

A number of scholars retrospectively reviewing the development of the genre suggest that this had serious repercussions for the social functioning of the song movement and consequently affected the contents of the songs and their presentation. Levin argues that

apathy, a cynical attitude, or even social schizophrenia replaced social optimism. Particularly among the intelligentsia, a person's identity was split into a public one, one that was supposed to follow the norms of society, and a private one, reserved for domestic purposes. . . . Consequently the role of subculture grew out of proportion; a subculture enriched with valuable substance acquired a function earlier unknown as the attainable island of spiritual freedom. . . . Freedom had been the very nature of the author's song, and it became an important and most democratic part and form of this culture.

Levin goes on to characterize the impact this had on the development of lyrics and the style of performance: "The bards that had come of age during the first period continued to develop their lyrical styles. But these were no longer the bright lyrics of the recent past. Very distinctly they were now evoking nostalgia for the past, bitterness about the losses and the betrayals, and an aspiration to preserve one's ideals, one's circle of close friends."[61] There is no space here to measure the accuracy of this thesis through a philological analysis of song lyrics. We can, however, consider the degree to which the emergence of the KSP and the involvement of Komsomol organizations can be seen as an attempt by the regime to tame the singer-songwriter movement during the 1970s and 1980s.

Reviewing the development of the Sokol'niki club in Moscow, Oleg Chumachenko discusses changing attitudes within the party and state apparatuses after the Prague Spring. Whereas before 1968 a kind of benevolent ignorance had prevailed and permitted an existence below the radar of censorship for the amateur or author's song movement, the official attitude was now becoming increasing negative: "Nobody wanted to play with the ugly duckling, one that might behave God knows how."[62] When the club tried to organize an open-air rally in the Moscow region in autumn 1968, the Komsomol, through its academic branches, contacted active amateurs and club members, openly threatening them with expulsion from the youth organization and relegation from the universities if they participated.

The rally took place all the same; it was precisely the attraction of such events with up to two thousand participants that caused problems with the security apparatus. In 1973, according to Chumachenko, the city administration held a special conference that instructed the Komsomol as well as student unions to exert more effective control over the KSPs. As a result, the organizers of the 1973 autumn rally were called to account. However, at the same time other amateurs organized a very successful festival in town, "Lefortovo—'73." They had secured the support of a number of high-ranking academics, and this obviously influenced the course of events. Lefortovo went unhampered, and Moscow's Komsomol leadership returned to a more benevolent stance. According to Chumachenko, the youth organization decided to play an active role in the creation of amateur clubs and strove to "appropriate" the movement.[63]

Indeed, the observation by Komsomol watchdogs all too obviously influenced the setup of many KSPs, beginning with their statutes. Whether voluntary or enforced, these statutes often stipulated that the members should be "taking an active stance and participating in the building of communism"; they stressed the educational role of the movement.[64] Commissions were put in place within the clubs meant to guarantee a degree of control over the repertoire, particularly during festivals. Singers and songs could be rejected if they were "lacking artistic qualities," as in the case of the never-realized Krasnodar songbook. Contemporary documents, like the scenario written for the regional festival in Krasnodar in 1975, increasingly constructed dichotomies of "us" and "them": " [Tourist] songs have found their audience, they are beloved and needed, they are sung. . . . But unfortunately, only a few hundred people know about that, while in the city the guitar continues to be played as a symbol of vulgarity and immorality."[65] In this case, it remains relatively unclear who the "other" might have been. Were political lyricists targeted or perhaps an emerging rock scene? Whoever may have been meant, however, the engagement of the Komsomol does not seem to have resulted in a unilateral victory of a new "establishment" over a 1960s Soviet "counterculture." Compromises were sought and found, as in the case of rallies organized by the Moscow

KSP. A central stage was reserved for performances of singers and songs that had been approved prior to the festival by the organizers, while there was a lesser degree of control over what happened on smaller side stages.[66]

This could backfire if a "gentlemen's agreement" to stay away from political themes, as Chumachenko described it, was ignored. In 1981, for example, some performers mimicked a Polish TV news show on stage. While *Pravda* bravely ignored the provocation in an article on the rally, the local party bosses fumed and demanded stricter controls.[67] Events like these are emblematic of the second Soviet "ice age" at the time of Chumachenko's 1982 report. Between 1980 and 1986 the Grushin Festival was called off, a decision retrospectively described either as a direct ban or, less despairingly, as a withdrawal of Komsomol subsidies. Obviously, the organization of interregional festivals was made conditional on the consent of central party and Komsomol officials. Indeed, some festivals were called off between 1980 and 1982, while other local rallies continued to be organized unhampered.[68] For the same reasons all efforts to create a nationwide "Union of Amateur Song Clubs" failed during the second half of the 1970s.[69]

Nonetheless, many adherents of the contemporary bard song movement reviewed the role of the Komsomol less negatively in hindsight. They criticized instead the increasing professionalism of the festivals. A tourist from Ufa complained that a number of well-known singer-songwriters started to ignore even big festivals like the "Grushinka" in case they were not offered the royalties they expected.[70] Others lamented the loss of spontaneity and creativity: "Dear festival functionaries! Do not exclude the works of masses of amateurs from the programs of the rallies—the jokes, welcomes, teahouses, sing-alongs [obshchie pesnopeniia], early morning jests, bonfires and dancing at night. Provide themes to the rallies to stimulate creativity. In the end of the day we are amateurs, not professionals, give us a chance. Do not try to imitate the high standards of concerts. That would be futile anyway. Do not turn the KSP rallies into expensive but weak author's song open-air concerts."[71]

Engagement or Entertainment?

Some, in what I would consider a reductionist view, might describe the emergence of amateur song clubs in the second half of the 1960s and the 1970s as a domestication of what earlier had been a vivid, alternative, if not subversive, music genre. Such a judgment would be based on an analysis of guitar poetry and its lyrics. The year 1968 would be seen as an important watershed, with some of the poets becoming dissidents or even being forced into exile and others simply losing their public relevance. As this story goes, rock 'n' roll replaced guitar poetry as the musical expression of dissent during the 1970s.[72]

If we look at the beginnings of what became a song movement during the Thaw, it is clear, however, that the writing and performing of songs more often than not stopped short of making political statements. Overtly political lyrics, as in the case of Aleksandr Galich, certainly owed their public life to a cultural liberalization that was gradually rescinded in the second half of the 1960s. Yet if we concentrate less on authorship and more on performance—that is, on the fact that a handful or so song poets created hundreds and thousands of imitators happily crowding forests and clearings around the industrial cities of the USSR from that time onwards—the song movement emerges as a social phenomenon that reflected social and cultural changes but hardly ever tested the limits of the permissible.

Both the habits of touring and of singing and songwriting were part of the first Soviet postwar generation's quest to find different styles of life and expression, and as such they were political. At the same time, these practices were hardly actively suppressed; at the very most they simply ceased to be sponsored by Soviet institutions. The emerging generation of the Soviet *shestidesiatniki* was urbanized and better educated, and they had to cope with a Stalinist mythology that depicted the generation of their parents as builders of socialism and front soldiers defending the fatherland. De-Stalinization and ongoing modernization required other, more civilian models of self-identification. Generational conflict was a commonality across the Iron Curtain, a common element in the sixties folk culture of both East and West. The constituent parts and the selective approach to national and international musical folklore, on the contrary, were dictated by national and political circumstances in each individual case. These circumstances naturally differed less between Western European countries and the United States than between those countries and the Soviet Union. Soviet authors or amateur singers were surely not immune to outside influences. By and large, however, the lyrics, the music, and especially the forms of sociability that the song movement developed were primarily Russian and Soviet, and part of this distinctiveness was its close link with the tourist movement.

From their American exile during the 1980s, Petr Vail' and Aleksandr Genis tried to deconstruct the spirit of the Soviet sixties. They focused on sociability, romanticism, an active interest in literature and poetry, and a cult of the road and traveling.[73] Participation in the tourist song movement did not require much more than acceptance of these values and offered ample and inexpensive opportunities to live them. Yet to the extent that tourist rallies and song festivals drew crowds they required more professionalism, and this resulted in a clear tendency toward institutionalization. Like the *samodeiatel'nye* tourists, the friends of the amateur songs tended to become more organized during the 1960s, either within tourist clubs or sections or in separate amateur song clubs. This rendered the movement more visible and made its perception by the regime as a threat more likely, particularly after 1968. Ironically, the song amateurs' quest for official sponsorship and tutelage rendered a paternalistic attitude on the part of the Komsomol, for example, easier.

As we have seen, there was a significant overlap in the motives for organization and networking between tourists and singer-songwriters, particularly the communication with other like-minded grassroots groups across the Soviet Union. Tourist rallies formed a model for what would develop into singer-songwriter festivals. Soviet councils for tourism represented an obvious source of support; their means were limited, though. The bigger festivals became and the more frequently concerts were organized, the more necessary municipal authorities and the Komsomol became as potential partners. The number of amateur song clubs detached from tourist structures grew significantly during the 1960s and particularly during the 1970s. On the one hand, this collaboration with municipal authorities or the party's youth organization exposed the singer-songwriters and their audiences almost inevitably to more control by ideological watchdogs of the system, particularly after the crushing of the Prague Spring (even though, as some of the examples have shown, there were opportunities to work around this control). But it should not be overlooked that growing professionalism became a problem in its own right. This happened to several contemporary folk movements in the West too. As in the famous case of Bob Dylan (following his Newport gig), singer-songwriters in the West who defected to rock music, signed contracts with major labels, or started to write music for commercials were perceived as traitors and consequently despised by hard-core fans. To be sure, Soviet singers and songwriters were hardly ever in a position to be "spoiled" by the state-run musical industry of the Soviet Union. Recording played an important role in the USSR, but it was important for the audience rather than the artist. In that sense, the established term *magnitizdat* is somewhat misleading. While reel-to-reel and later cassette recorders allowed performers to record and publish songs outside state-controlled media outlets, the process of copying went quickly beyond the artists' control, similar to contemporary downloading from the Internet. Indeed, the emerging song clubs and sections, whether tourist or not, engaged first and foremost in an exchange of recordings, even if they were not intended for passive consumption but for playing and singing along. Against this backdrop I doubt that the emergence of rock 'n' roll tapes, whether of Soviet or Western origin, constituted a direct challenge for the song movement. Rock 'n' roll was much more about listening to music and adopting poses or lifestyles, even if the early history of Soviet rock showed quite a degree of crossover between autochthonous song traditions and jazz or rock influence from abroad.

The song movement, then, changed over time, reacting to challenges from without and within. The organization of the amateur song clubs, the archival craze, the passion for recordings, and the growing size of some festivals threatened one of the song movement's main attractions: its performative character. The creation of informal sociability among kindred spirits had been at the very core. Shared identity was established through familiarity with the same songs; singing and playing them reinforced this companionship. Where cool and calculating professionalism reduced the role of communal performance, the songs formerly shared and "owned" by all potentially turned into collectors' items for dedicated fans.

My argument, in other words, is that professionalism, no less than the control of the Komsomol, endangered the popularity of the tourist song as a form of leisured sociability. While the processes of professionalization and institutionalization may have marginalized or radicalized some of the singer-songwriters and forced them into a countercultural role, the Komsomol's involvement should not been seen as only a clamp-down on a genre of literature and music that had gone unnoticed by censorship. On the contrary, some amateurs actively sought the involvement of the youth organization. To muster political (and cultural) acceptability and to create extended opportunities, they accepted the closer monitoring. As in the case of one of the Moscow KSPs, collaboration could be a conscious decision, an attempt to negotiate with the authorities.[74] In other words, the Komsomol played an important role in the creation of many amateur clubs at the same time as it enforced a degree of self-censorship.

In conclusion, while it is safe to say that the tourist song movement emerged during the Thaw and reached its climax during the 1960s, 21 August 1968 was not "the day the music died." Rather, this was the year the Grushin Festival started, doubling its audience from year to year until the late 1970s. Did the "last Soviet generation," those who followed the *shestidesiatniki*, adhere to the practices of their parents and join them, say, for the annual pilgrimage to the Grushinka? As my own conclusions are based on sources produced by members of amateur song clubs rather than those produced by singers and songwriters who remained unorganized or continued to work within the institutional framework of tourism, it is difficult to judge how far growing institutionalization edged out less documented grassroots practices. Judging from the continued popularity of tourism, it did not. Future research on the growing corpus of memorial literature, a genre of sources with its own intricacies, will suggest more answers. Judging by the liveliness of the debates on the Web and the mushrooming of song clubs wherever Russian speakers live today, there can be little doubt that the author's song movement experienced a triumphant revival among the first post-Soviet generation.

Notes

1. As this suggests, "There was even a particular term for it, like 'guitourism' *(giturizm)*: guitarist plus tourism." E. Dmitrakova, "Subkul'tura klubov samodeiatel'noi pesni," http://bards.ru/press/press_show.php?id=304&show=topic&topic=7&page=14 (accessed May 13, 2010).

2. Petr Vail' and Aleksandr Genis, *60-e: Mir sovetskogo cheloveka* (1988; repr., Moscow: Novoe literaturnoe obozrenie, 1998), 127.

3. See I. A. Sokolova, "Avtorskaia pesnia: Opredelenie i terminy," in *Mir Vysotskogo: Issledovaniia i materialy* (Moscow: GKTsM V. S. Vysotskogo, 2000), www.bards.ru, http://bards.ru/press/press_show.php?id=1892&show=topic&topic=8&page=14 (accessed 13 May 2010).

4. "Pesnia turistskaia," in *Entsiklopediia turista*, ed. E. I. Tamm (Moscow: Bol'shaia Rossiiskaia entsiklopediia, 1993), 90.

5. L. I. Levin, "Avtorskaia pesnia," in *Estrada Rossii: Dvadtsatyi vek. Leksikon* (Moscow: Rosspen, 2000), 11.

6. "Pesnia turistskaia," in Tamm, *Entsiklopediia turista*, 91.

7. Sokolova, "Avtorskaia pesnia."

8. Levin, "Avtorskaia pesnia," 9.

9. Richard Stites, *Russian Popular Culture: Entertainment and Society since 1900* (Cambridge: Cambridge University Press, 1992), 134–35. See also L. N. D'iakova, "Avtorskaia pesniia kak kommunikativnyi zhanr," *Vestnik Voronezhskoi GPU [Seriia: Filologiia, Zhurnalistika]* 1 (2007), http://bards. ru/press/press_show.php?id=1703&show=topic&topic=8&page=1.

10. Levin, "Avtorskaia pesnia," 9. On the *kompaniia*, see Juliane Fürst, "Friends in Private, Friends in Public: The Phenomenon of the *Kompaniia* among Soviet Youth in the 1950s and 1960s," in *Private Spheres of Soviet Russia*, ed. Lewis H. Siegelbaum (New York: Palgrave Macmillan, 2006), 229–49. See also Djagalov's discussion of "intimate yet public spheres" in his chapter.

11. Levin, "Avtorskaia pesnia," 10.

12. See also the discussion of the decline in Djagalov's chapter.

13. Vladimir Novikov, "Belyi list kievskoi avtorskoi pesni," *Graffiti* (Kiev) 2, no. 8, and 3, no. 9 (1997), http://bards.ru/press/press_show.php?id=993&show=topic&topic=9&page=1. See also Oleg Chumachenko, "Istoriia + teoriia," ca. 1982, from the archive of the KSP Poisk (Vladivostok), http://bards.ru/press/press_show.php?id=909&show=topic&topic=7&page=5 (accessed 26 May 2010); "Diskussiia kluba samodeiatel'noi pesni 'Poisk' g. Vladivostok," 16 November 1982, from the archive of the KSP Poisk, Vladivostok, http://bards.ru/press/press_show.php?id=335&show=topic&topic=7&page=14.

14. Diane P. Koenker, "The Proletarian Tourist in the 1930s: Between Mass Excursion and Mass Escape," in *Turizm: The Russian and East European Tourist under Capitalism and Socialism*, ed. Anne E. Gorsuch and Diane P. Koenker (Ithaca: Cornell University Press, 2006), 119–40; Eva Maurer, "Alpinizm as Mass Sport and Elite Recreation: Soviet Mountaineering Camps under Stalin," in Gorsuch and Koenker, *Turizm*, 141–62.

15. A comprehensive overview is provided by Manfred Hildermeier, *Geschichte der Sowjetunion, 1917–1991: Entstehung und Niedergang des ersten sozialistischen Staates* (Munich: Beck, 1998), 899–907, 924–31, and *Handbuch zur Geschichte Russlands*, vol. 5, pt. 2, *1945–1991: Vom Ende des Zweiten Weltkriegs bis zum Zusammenbruch der Sowjetunion*, ed. Stefan Plaggenborg (Stuttgart: Hiersemann, 2003), 623–57.

16. Cf. entries "Planovoi turizm" and "Samodeiatel'nyi turizm," in Tamm, *Entsiklopediia turista*, 10–11; Grigorii Usyskin, *Ocherki istorii Rossiiskogo turizma* (Moscow: Gerda, 2000), 159–86.

17. Christian Noack, "Building Tourism in One Country? The Sovietization of Vacationing, 1917–41," in *Touring beyond the Nation: A Transnational Approach to European Tourism History*, ed. Eric G. Zuelov (Farnham: Ashgate, 2011), 171–95.

18. Novikov, "Belyi list kievskoi avtorskoi pesni." Cf. the remarks on male role models in Catriona Kelly, *Refining Russia: Advice Literature, Political Culture, and Gender from Catherine the Great to Yeltsin* (New York: Oxford University Press, 2001), 351; and Mark Edele, "Strange Young Men in Stalin's Moscow: The Birth and Life of the Stiliagi, 1945–1953," *Jahrbücher für Geschichte Osteuropas* 50, no. 1 (2002): 37–61.

19. Vladimir Sapuntsov, interview, 1986, in M. Pasternak, "Pogovorim o KSP," *Moskovskii komsomolets*, 4 April 1986, http://bards.ru/press/press_show.php?id=297&show=topic&topic=7&page=10. See also A. V. Ukladova, "Nash klub avtorskoi pesni," n.d., http://bards.ru/press/press_show.php?id=414&show=topic&topic=7&page=7 (accessed 13 May 2010).

20. Vail' and Genis, *60-e*, 127. See also Stites, *Russian Popular Culture*, 145.

21. M. Pasternak, "Pogovorim o KSP," *Moskovskii komsomolets*, January 1987, http://bards.ru/press/press_show.php?id=298&show=topic&topic=7&page=10.

22. Sergei Selitskii, "AP i KSP—eto odno i to zhe? Ili gruppovshchina . . . ," *Kinomir*, no. 1 (6 June 2002), http://bards.ru/press/press_show.php?id=1775&show=topic&topic=7&page=1.

23. For the "mass song," see Karsten Brüggemann, *Von Krieg zu Krieg, von Sieg zu Sieg: Motive des sowjetischen Mythos im Massenlied der 1930er Jahre. Einführung, Texte, Übersetzung* (Hamburg: Kovač, 2001); Matthias Stadelmann, *Isaak Dunaevskij, Sänger des Volke: Eine Karriere unter Stalin* (Cologne: Böhlau, 2003).

24. According to Vladimir Ogai, a tourist from Kazakhstan, he came to learn about Vysotskii in the early 1970s through films and than started to participate in tourist rallies to hear more songs and eventually compose his own. Vladimir Ogai, interview, in Veta Nozhkina, "Chtoby zhit' kilometrami," *Avtorskaia pesnia v Kazakhstane*, www.akbard.kz/content/view/382/1/ (accessed 16 March 2012). *Vertical (Vertikal'*, 1967), a film about mountaineers, had featured Vysotskii as an actor, and the soundtrack comprised some of his songs. Vysotskii played a geologist the same year in Kira Muratova's *Brief Encounters (Korotkie vstrechi)*. Other bards like Vizbor wrote music for soundtracks as well, with *July Rain (Iiulskii dozhd'*, 1966) featuring the bard himself in a main role. Vizbor famously also played Bormann in the television classic *Seventeen Moments of Spring (Semnadtsat' mgnovenii vesny*, 1973) and minor roles in other films that featured tourism and travel, like *Moscow Travel (V Moskve proezdom*, 1971) and the elegiac *The Belorussian Station (Belorusskii vokzal*, 1973). The latter featured Okudzhava's songs. See David C. Gillespie, "The Sounds of Music: Songs and Soundtracks in Soviet Film," *Slavic Review* 62, no. 3 (2003): 473–90. Travel and vacation sites had become popular topics or settings for Soviet films in the early 1960s, with film comedies like *Three Plus Two (Tri plius dva*, 1963) after a Sergei Mikhalkov play, or *Welcome, or No Unauthorized Admission (Dobro pozhalovat', ili Postoronnym vkhod vospreshen*, 1964), a film that represented a pioneer camp as a mirror image of contemporary Soviet adult life. *Goodbye, Boys (Do svidaniia, mal'chiki)* of the same year juxtaposes lazy summer holidays with the imminent draft of young male adults into the army. Tourism and travel remained popular topics well into the eighties, with box office hits like *Sport Lottery 1982 (Sportloto-82*, 1982) and *Station for Two (Vokzal na dvoikh*, 1982), which portrayed trains and stations as spaces for extramarital relationships.

25. Sokolova, "Avtorskaia pesnia," uses the term *nepodtsenzurnaia forma poezii*.

26. Novikov, "Belyi list kievskoi avtorskoi pesni."

27. Ibid.

28. Christian Noack, "A Farewell to the New Man? The Male Tourist in Late Soviet Media," Unpublished paper, VII ICCEES World Conference, Berlin, 25–30 July 2005.

29. T. V. Cherednichenko, "'Gromkoe' i 'tikhoe' v massovom soznanie. Razmyshliaia o klassikakh-bardakh," *Sovetskaia muzyka*, no. 11 (1991), http://bards.ru/press/press_show.php?id=1779&show=topic&topic=8&page=4.

30. Brüggemann, *Von Krieg zu Krieg*, 26–27.

31. Dmitrii Malodetov, "Chtoby derevo zvuchalo . . . ," n.d., interview with luthier Nikolai Gusev, www.guitar-club.ru/3guitars/Gusev.htm (accessed 13 May 2010).

32. Novikov, "Belyi list kievskoi avtorskoi pesni."

33. B. Shabanov, "Imeni Valeriia Grushina," *Polet* (Kuibyshev), 7 October 1968, NaGrushe.ru http://nagrushe.ru/grushinskiy/papers/72-1grushinskii.html. See also the section "KSP, ansambli i pesnopeniia," in the collection of memories of participants entitled *Muzhskoi khor MIFI: K 50-letiiu so dnia osnovaniia. Sbornik statei i vospominanii* (Moscow: Inzhener, 2007), particularly Boris Anufriev's "Zaria KSP," 252–63 and Valerii Lapshinskii's "Zametki khorista-kspshnika: 20 minut u mikrofona," 269–73, and "Pochemu khoristy liubili slety KSP?," 273–75.

34. Dolzhenko's history of Soviet tourism describes the emergence of the rallies as a postwar phenomenon. Gennadii P. Dolzhenko, *Istoriia turizma v dorevoliutsionnoi Rossii i SSSR* (Rostov-na-Donu: Izdatel'stvo Rostovskogo Universiteta, 1988), 139–40.

35. Selitskii, "AP i KSP."

36. Novikov, "Belyi list kievskoi avtorskoi pesni." However, many universities regularly held student song competitions, which have likewise been recognized by veterans of the song movement as important role models for song club activities. See Igor Karimov, *"Istoriia Moskovskogo KSP": Nenauchnyi spravochnik* (Moscow: Samizdat, 2006), 1–2.

37. "Slet turistskii," in Tamm, *Entsiklopediia turista*, 109.

38. Karimov, *"Istoriia Moskovskogo KSP,"* 2.

39. According to Ogai, "They conducted festivals in Kuibyshev (today Samara) from 1969 [*sic*] onwards; initially they were developing as tourist ventures, only later did they become song festivals." Quoted in Nozhkina, "Chtoby zhit' kilometrami."

40. Shabanov, "Imeni Valeriia Grushina."

41. "Vserossiiskii festival' avtorskoi pesni imeni Valeriia Grushina," *Wikipedia*, http://ru.wikipedia.org (accessed 13 May 2010). The latest number given in the entry is for 2000, with two hundred thousand visitors.

42. "Iz istorii organizatsii festivalia avtorskoi pesni im. V. Grushina," n.d., *Vserossiiskii festival' avtorskoi pesni imeni Valeriia Grushina*, http://grushin.samara.ru/contents/20/245 (accessed 13 May 2010; no longer accessible); blog posting by "Gromov" referring to Anatolii Makeev's article, "Nekotorye detali istorii Grushinki," *NaGrushe.ru*, 3 February 2012, www.nagrushe.ru/grushinskiy/papers/319-unknown-grushinka.html.

43. Nozhkina, "Chtoby zhit' kilometrami."

44. T. Brusnitsina, "Opyt raboty sverdlovskogo gorodskogo KSP," Materialy dni samostoiatel'noi pesni v g. Vladivostok, 1983, http://bards.ru/press/press_show.php?id=446&show=topic&topic=7&page=9.

45. "Istoriia sozdanii i deiatel'nosti kluba 'Vostok,'" n.d., http://ksp-vostok.spb.ru/history.par (accessed 28 May 2010); Dmitrakova, "Subkul'tura klubov samodeiatel'noi pesni."

46. Pasternak, "Pogovorim o KSP" [1986]; Dmitrakova, "Subkul'tura klubov samodeiatel'noi pesni."

47. Chumachenko, "Istoriia + teoriia"; Pasternak, "Pogovorim o KSP" [1987]; A. Gusev, "Organizatsiia i rabota KSP. Rabota ispolnitelia nad pesnei: Rabota nad klubnoi programmoi. Nekotorye vyvody po seminaru 'Dni samostoiatel'no pesni—83,'" n.d., from the archive of the KSP Poisk, http://bards.ru/press/press_show.php?id=456&show=topic&topic=7&page=9 (accessed 13 May 2010).

48. "Diskussiia kluba."

49. Krasnodar tourist song section, 1975 documents, in Gosudarstvennyi arkhiv Krasnodarskogo kraia (GAKK), f. R 1624, op. 2, d. 72, ll. 28–31 (meeting of 10 June 1975).

50. Ibid., ll. 13–14 (report on 1975 activities).

51. Bella Ostromukhova, "Le Dégel et les troupes amateur: Changements politiques et activités artistiques des étudiants, 1953–1970," *Cahiers du monde russe* 47, no. 1–2 (2006): 303–25.

52. "The sacred tourist traditions are inviolable in the KSP," as the Moscow-based journalist Pasternak put it. Pasternak, "Pogovorim o KSP" [1986]; Selitskii, "AP i KSP."

53. This "archival craze" is an obvious reason for availability of rich documentation on websites like bard.ru. Cf. Sergei Rybalka, "Opyt raboty KSP 'Poisk' Dal'nevostochnogo Ordena Krasnogo Znameni Politekhnicheskogo Instituta im. V. V. Kuibysheva (g. Vladivostok)," 1983, from the archives of the KSP "Poisk" in Vladivostok, http://bards.ru/press/press_show.php?id=458&show=topic&topic=7&page=9 (accessed 13 May, 2010).

54. Brusnitsina, "Opyt raboty sverdlovskogo gorodskogo KSP."

55. Dmitrakova, "Subkul'tura klubov samodeiatel'noi pesni"; Brusnitsina, "Opyt raboty sverdlovskogo gorodskogo KSP."

56. Rybalka, "Opyt raboty KSP 'Poisk.'"

57. Chumachenko, "Istoriia + teoriia"; Compare Pasternak, "Pogovorim o KSP" [1987], and Anufriev and Lapshinskii, "KSP, ansambli i pesnopeniia," 250–51.

58. Chumachenko, "Istoriia + teoriia."

59. Levin, "Avtorskaia pesnia," 12.

60. S. P. Rasputina, "Sotsial'naia motivatsiia sovetskogo bardovskogo dvizheniia. Filiosofsko-sotsiologicheskii aspekt," in *Mir Vysotskogo: Issledovaniia i materialy*, vol. 3, part 2 (Moscow: GKTsM V. Vysotskogo, 1999), 375–79; Chumachenko, "Istoriia + teoriia"; for slightly differing chronologies, see Novikov, "Belyi list kievskoi avtorskoi pesni"; "Pesnia turistskaia," in Tamm, *Entsiklopediia turista*, 91; and Djagalov's chapter in this volume.

61. Levin, "Avtorskaia pesnia," 11. Cf. Sokolova's discussion of singer-songwriters' quest for "respectability" in "Avtorskaia pesnia."

62. Chumachenko, "Istoriia + teoriia."

63. Ibid.

64. Rybalka, "Opyt raboty KSP 'Poisk.'"

65. Krasnodar tourist song section, 1975 documents, GAKK, f. R 1624, op. 2, d. 72, ll. 6–7.

66. Chumachenko, "Istoriia + teoriia."

67. Ibid.

68. Ibid.; Makeev, "Nekotorye detali istorii Grushinki"; Anufriev and Lapshinskii, "KSP, ansambli i pesnopeniia," 264–65.

69. Mikhail Kordonskii, "Istoriia grabel' ot KSP do ChGK, ili tridtsat' let spustia," n.d., http://bards.ru/press/press_show.php?id=1357&show=topic&topic=7&page=5 (accessed 26 May 2010). Karimov, as quoted in Anufriev and Lapshinskii, "KSP, ansambli i pesnopeniia," 251, claims that at least a federation of clubs from Moscow, Leningrad, and Novosibirsk was created at a meeting in Petushki in 1967, with Sergei Chesnokov elected president. On Chesnokov, see also "Chesnokov, Sergei Valerianovich, 1943–,"www.bards.ru/person.php?id=3242 (accessed February 28, 2011).

70. Makeev, "Nekotorye detali istorii Grushinki."

71. Selitskii, "AP i KSP."

72. See the O'Doughtry quote in Djagalov's chapter in this book.

73. Vail' and Genis, *60-e*, passim.

74. Ways of "employing" the Komsomol and paying lip service to the required rituals during the 1970s and 1980s have been extensively documented and discussed by Alexei Yurchak, *Everything Was Forever, Until It Was No More: The Last Soviet Generation* (Princeton: Princeton University Press, 2006).

7 Look Left, Drive Right

Internationalisms at the 1968
World Youth Festival

Nick Rutter

WHEN FREE GERMAN Youth (FDJ) leader Günther Jahn addressed his delegation to the Ninth World Youth Festival just prior to departure on 19 July 1968, he urged them to speak with confidence—to "say the complicated *simply*, not the simple *complicatedly.*" To ensure that his seven hundred listeners understood, Jahn seasoned his speech with a touch of communist humor. West Germany's capitalists were "political eunuchs" who "know exactly how it's done, but just can't do it anymore." Capitalism's struggle to command the scientific-technical revolution was comparable to "the devil shearing a pig—a lot of squealing but little wool." And while "the enemy expects us to sit naked on his ideological hedgehog, we'll lather it up and shave it clean" before sitting. When asked how East German delegates should behave toward Romanians and Yugoslavs, the thirty-eight-year-old youth leader began with a joke from recent Warsaw Pact meetings in Dresden: How does Nicolae Ceausescu determine Romania's foreign policy? He "looks left, drives right."[1]

Jahn was well aware that the political reality of 1968 was more complex than the jokes implied. "Many an unfamiliar and refined counterargument will come [your way]," he warned, adding, "The adversary knows something about pretty packaging for ugly intentions." By advocating socialism in simple terms, the seven hundred FDJ delegates—60 percent men, another 60 percent over age twenty-four—would burn through the rhetorical fog that had settled over the socialist world. Wherever counterarguments came from, "whether from right or left, from front or back, argued openly or covertly, the essential issue we have to bring to the discussion is that the future of Germany, Europe, and the world belongs to socialism." Which socialism Jahn meant he did not say. Simplicity evidently did not require it.[2]

Young East Europeans were no strangers to political discussion in the 1960s.[3] Nor were discussion seminars new to the World Youth Festival, a Soviet-sponsored event that had already met eight times since 1945. But by the time Jahn gave his speech in late July, three circumstances ensured that debate would proceed in a sharper key in Sofia than before. First, a greater geographic and ideological variety of youth organizations would participate. Second, the student rebellions and Czechoslovak about-face for which 1968 is famous had come too quickly, threatening to scuttle the festival's effort to revive socialist solidarity. Third, the festival's Komsomol sponsors had planned to give political discussions special prominence in Sofia.[4]

By midsummer 1968, the rubric of "socialism" stretched from Mao's antibureaucratic "revolution in the revolution" and Che's *foco* militarism on the left to Alexander Dubček's "human face" all the way, arguably, to Willy Brandt's "new *Ostpolitik*" on the right. Though the "world communist movement" was a narrower, more precise designation, its ideological range was nearly as wide. Curiously, however, this is not the narrative we know best. Historians of the 1960s have long privileged centripetal "generational conflicts" over the centrifugal tugs of national doctrines and cultures. "National borders mean less than generational frontiers nowadays," a student told the London *Times* in June 1968; and for over two decades, historians have written accordingly. "The youth" of 1968, by this reasoning, was a collective noun, oriented against the state, the parents, the Cold War, but not against itself.[5] The following chapter does not dispute that an "*eros* effect," to borrow Herbert Marcuse's term, inspired students from different continents to join a perceived world revolution. Instead, it counters the prevailing tendency "to universalize . . . the subjectivity of these movements" and to portray the "internationalist sensibilities" of 1968 as ones that rivaled or even supplanted national identities.[6]

Existing scholarship is intentionally vague on what said "internationalist sensibilities" amounted to, as it is on who espoused them.[7] To identify sixties youth too exactly, we fear, is to put them back in the boxes they sought to escape. The labels *global* and *internationalist*, however, perpetuate the same confusion that Günther Jahn's "socialism" did in July 1968. Are we to presume that the young Frenchman who shouted in Prague, "All of a sudden, youth is the new *Internationale!*" felt as close to internationalists from Kiev as he did to ones from Munich? Likewise, can we assume that internationalist identities necessarily weakened national ones? One way to answer these questions is to look at how "68ers" behaved in international gatherings—particularly ones held outside the West. Transnational studies of sixties youth weave Prague into their narratives for this reason. "Once Paris had calmed in June," notes Richard I. Jobs, "Prague became the new destination of choice for the young of Europe."[8] In the Czechoslovak capital, young westerners encountered Czechoslovak peers who were ready to talk "about everything," kiosks that sold reliable news, and, in contrast to the city they had come from, a police force that let them be. Prague, by this reading, proved youth internationalism a transcontinental rather than merely transoccidental phenomenon.

What Jobs and other scholars overlook are the tensions that emerged between Czechoslovak youth and their Western "68er" peers. It is true that by May, politics and culture in Dubček's ČSSR were already more liberal than Leninist. Once the student internationalists decamped from Paris, the city's "human face" grew even more diverse, making it even less representative of the Soviet bloc. Even so, many New Leftists were as uncomfortable in Czechoslovakia as their Soviet peers. In late March 1968, the face of West Germany's antiauthoritarian Socialist Student Union (SDS), Rudi Dutschke, traveled south from Berlin to attend a Charles University conference entitled "Save Man—Peace Is Possible." Having grown up in the GDR, Dutschke was sympathetic to young Czechoslovaks' "democratic socialist" spirit in a way that his comrades in West Berlin were not. Nevertheless, the counterrevolutionary cynicism that he encountered took him aback. "They did not understand his Marxism," Dutschke's American widow recalls, "for them Marxism meant oppression." The disappointment was mutual. When conversation turned to the chance of a Soviet invasion, the Czechoslovaks told their German guest: "It can be here tomorrow, even if you don't believe it, Rudi."[9] Dutschke did not believe it. The Prague magazine *Student* characterized the SDS leader as a collision of "German romanticism and revolutionary radicalism" and typified his strain of revolutionary socialism as a vain attempt to match "the productive capacities of America with the ascetic morality of the Chinese." If Dutschke's New Left were to resettle in Prague alongside the French contingent, *Student* concluded, the result would be "only tired surprise."[10]

To induce pan-European, "internationalist sensibilities" from the Prague Spring, then, is like inducing NATO foreign policy from de Gaulle's. In both cases, anomaly belies geography. This chapter reevaluates sixties internationalism in the light of a more global, and in my view more representative, 1968 event than those in Paris and Prague. It is true that many World Youth Festival delegations obeyed Communist Party leaders and thus included as many apparatchiks as artists or athletes. (This is one reason why men and thirty-somethings outnumbered women and twenty-somethings in Jahn's East German group.) The *beatniks* at Christian Noack's Grushin festivals thus stood little chance of taking part.[11] One could infer from this that discourse in Sofia was just as skewed as in Prague, if only in the opposite direction—more Leninist than liberal. But before dismissing the festival as a nonrepresentative event, we should bear in mind two things: first, its diversity; second, anthropologist Alexei Yurchak's warning against binary thinking. Sofia's festival participants came from more places and subscribed to more doctrines than the Prague Spring's. Few Africans, Asians, or, ironically, Eastern Europeans visited Prague in summer 1968. By contrast, the Ninth Festival brought 130-odd nationalities to Sofia under banners reading, "Solidarity, Peace, and Friendship." Did state delegate selection make solidarity easier? Were most delegates speaking for the party, not their national peers? Here Yurchak's critique is helpful. If we accept his point that regardless of what socialist citizens thought about their governments they took solace in those governments' ideals, then the assumption that because East European delegations were state made they were nonrepresentative is suspect.[12] *Internationalism,* after all, was as popular a word in East Berlin and Sofia in 1968 as it was in Prague and Paris.

Like Rachel Applebaum's account of Soviet tourists to Czechoslovakia, this chapter looks away from the North Atlantic, the traditional focus of 1968 historiography, toward a little-known encounter that put the "internationalist sensibilities" of the "global sixties" to the test.[13] To explain the poor results, I draw heavily on the words that festival delegates spoke. "Different languages of radicalism arose in different contexts that shared a common vocabulary," writes the historian of China Arif Dirlik.[14] Polish dissident Adam Michnik agrees, adding that while he and his Warsaw classmates "fought for freedom," "students in the West fought against capitalism"—a "principal difference" not to be overlooked.[15] Orthodox socialists like Günther Jahn faced the same semantic challenge. The "pretty packaging" by "ultraleftist" elements that Jahn flagged in his predeparture lecture to GDR delegates relied on distorted Marxist language. As we will see, the events in Sofia affirm all three statements—the historian's, the Polish dissident's, and the FDJ first secretary's. "Common vocabularies" at the festival constituted neither a common language nor a common purpose. That nearly all eighteen thousand delegates condemned American imperialism in Vietnam was no guarantee of solidarity. What mattered in Sofia was not whether they condemned it, but how: In one voice or many? Simply or complicatedly?

The Festival's Global Sixties

For the World Youth Festival, the "global sixties" began in earnest in 1957 and ended a decade later. Seventeen months after condemning Stalin in February 1956, and nine after laying siege to Budapest, Nikita Khrushchev welcomed thirty-four thousand foreigners to Moscow to celebrate peace. The result was a public relations triumph. Journalists and delegates from nonindustrial states marveled at all the construction cranes. Western delegates remarked on the gregariousness of a population they expected to hide in the shadows. Moscow's vitality reflected not only citizens' sense that the bad times were past but also Khrushchev's blithe view of the times to come.[16] Security was so loose at the 1957 festival that Poles derided Russians; West Germans filmed how socialism's "other half" lived; and Soviet newspapers printed shots of *komsomolki* (female Young Communist League members) kissing Frenchmen—all testament to the USSR's renewed confidence in "proletarian internationalism."[17]

By March 1959, two years after the Moscow Festival, Komsomol-appointed organizers were in Vienna, planning the first festival beyond the bloc.[18] Three years later, the International Preparatory Committee (IPC) proceeded north to another "neutral" capital, Helsinki, followed by two failed attempts in Africa—in Algiers (1965), then Accra (1966). The festival's "global sixties" (1957–66) thus stood in stark contrast to the event's inaugural decade (1947–56), when it met in a different Warsaw Pact capital every two years and performed "peace and friendship" before a largely communist audience.

Though festival slogans changed little over its first two decades, the shift westward obliged planners to distinguish proactive, proletarian internationalism from the passive, liberal variety favored in Austria and Finland.[19] In Vienna, antifestival propaganda made the job easier than it might have been by convincing African delegates that Vienna's press boycott came per Washington's command.[20] In Helsinki in midsummer 1962, delegates reacted similarly on opening day, this time to young Finns throwing rocks at festival buses. The riots inspired twenty-nine-year-old Soviet delegate Evgenii Evtushenko to read a sixty-line poem aloud on Soviet television. Back home the star poet "had learned about fascism from books and films"; now in Helsinki he saw its "drooling, unkempt and sweat-faced ruffians . . . alive, in full play."[21] In Vienna, the "antifestival" newspapers, bus trips to the Iron Curtain, and Ella Fitzgerald concerts cosponsored by the CIA were no match for the fact that delegates from poorer countries had by and large traveled to Vienna for free, per communist generosity. In Helsinki, organizers' inability to cordon off a central Eighth Festival campus from the rest of town diminished the event's communal spirit considerably. That the antifestival propaganda of 1962 was subtler and more refined than in 1959, directed by a canny twenty-eight-year-old journalist named Gloria Steinem, only made matters worse.[22]

At the Western festivals, tension between good and bad internationalism—the proletarian versus the liberal varieties—compromised the slogan "for peace and friendship," as well as its ethos of free exchange. In Vienna, East European delegates who were not on stage spent their days on a thin Danube peninsula, guarded by watchmen from the Austrian Communist Party.[23] When Chinese performances ended, the largest socialist country in the world disappeared without a trace, unavailable to discuss the Great Leap Forward. In Helsinki in 1962, one year after the Berlin Wall's construction, FDJ choir members yanked a fellow singer out of the back seat of a taxicab, out of her refugee-fiancé's arms, and impounded her in the East German hotel in Helsinki's harbor: the *Völkerfreundschaft* (Peoples' Friendship) ocean liner. While West German news media touted thirty-seven East German escapes from the Eighth Festival, internal Stasi (GDR State Security) records tallied only nine. Considering the time that FDJ and Stasi officials had spent vetting prospective delegates, the difference was inconsequential; a loss of any personnel to the West was an even greater loss of face.[24] At a parade for nuclear disarmament on the penultimate day of the Helsinki event in 1962, World Youth Festival spokesman Jean Garcias finally buckled under the stress. He tore signs reading "Stop the Tests in East and West" out of Icelandic delegates' hands and ripped them into shreds on the pavement—in full view of the world press. A day earlier, Soviet science had dropped a forty-ton hydrogen bomb on Siberia.[25]

Especially troubling to Soviet observers in Helsinki in 1962 was the growing sense among African and Asian delegates there that the festival was a Cold War in miniature—an ideological debate irrelevant to their concerns. The forty-four Sri Lankans who left Helsinki prematurely told reporters that they had "looked forward to a real, fruitful exchange of varying opinions," only "to become embroiled in the Cold War."[26] It was partly to placate these critics that the IPC chose in 1964 to hold the Ninth Festival in Algiers. Of the twenty-four African colonies that declared independence between January 1960 and December 1963, Algeria, under the leadership of self-proclaimed "Islamic socialist" Ahmed Ben Bella, was Moscow's brightest prospect. By March 1965, however, four months from the opening ceremony, Ben Bella's government had alienated the IPC's largely white, East European staff to the point that "friendship" was weak, if not lost altogether. The head of Algeria's youth front assured the head of Vienna's anticommunist International Union of Socialist Youth (IUSY) that he would "give the festival a new orientation"—away from stale doctrines and immune to "*obstructive measures by anybody*," Moscow as well as Washington.[27]

Then, on 19 June 1965, a month from opening day, Ben Bella's top general arrested him. Whatever relief the IPC might have felt when news of the coup came was short-lived.[28] Six months before the Ninth Festival's second grand opening in Accra, another putsch—this time against Ghana's Pan-Africanist president, Kwame Nkrumah—precipitated an existential crisis at the IPC headquarters in Budapest. "Very shaken," but adamant that Helsinki would not be the festival's final showing, the one-hundred-person committee took a new, pragmatic course. Planners would henceforth value reliable sites over exotic ones; they would listen more closely to the KGB;[29] they would keep a closer eye on containing costs; and they would shift their sights from south to east. Cuba's threat to boycott the next festival unless it happened in one of the capitals "where USA-imperialism is currently under the most active combat, that is, in Hanoi or Havana," was ineffective. At a late January 1967 meeting in a Vienna labor union hall, the honor went to the only Warsaw Pact capital yet to host.[30]

The selection of Sofia signaled a shift from the festival's quixotic "global sixties" to a safer, more familiar alternative. The jeers heard in Vienna and Helsinki would turn to jubilation in Sofia. The Finnish police who in Evtushenko's words "ought to have hammered [the hoodlums] flat" would give way to a more vigilant and versatile force—one as comfortable in plainclothes as in uniform.[31] The defensive posture in Sofia would also enable collective, progressive action. In Africa the festival's purpose had been to reassert the USSR as role model to all nonindustrial, newly sovereign states—a title Mao's China had claimed for itself since the start of the decade. In Sofia the aim was similar, but the means had changed. Instead of out-scrambling China into Africa, the new strategy hinged on restoring Soviet-led solidarity, a principle the Chinese had spent their "global sixties" undermining.[32] All that was missing was an agent of reintegration. By mid-1967, thanks in part to Lyndon Johnson's stubbornness, in part to Soviet military aid to Southeast Asia, the agent was identified.[33] "The IX Festival should be a militant [boevoi], politically charged meeting," the Komsomol told Sofia in February 1968, at which the dominant theme would be "the solidarity of world youth with the people and youth of Vietnam."[34] Festival staples like juried athletic and artistic competitions would remain. But the emphasis in Sofia would fall on political discussion. In July 1968, the *World Student News*, one of the festival's primary mouthpieces, announced that the upcoming celebration would "differ from other Festivals by being highly political in nature," distinguished by "a larger number of political events in the form of seminars, forums, conferences."[35] And herein lay the crux of the new, defensive stance: by cheering Vietnamese guerrillas at every turn, the 1968 festival would distinguish *true* socialism, defined by solidarity, from the false, schismatic kind advanced by Mao and Castro. In Sofia, a slight to the festival or its sponsors would be a slight to Vietnam.

In hindsight, the plan to revive socialist solidarity by talking politics in early August 1968 seems myopic. Two weeks after the Sofia Festival's end, it took five hundred thousand Warsaw Pact troops to silence the Prague Spring. Considered on its own terms in its own time, however, the tactic made sense. In February 1968, when the Komsomol sent its directives to Sofia, "cultural revolution" was not yet a global slogan; Dubček was little known outside the ČSSR; and the Western New Left, in the Komsomol's words, was an emblem of "high political activity, a mass shift toward the left, and great interest in the theory and praxis of socialism" on the part of Western youth.[36] Finally and crucially, neither the Chinese nor the Cubans would be in Sofia to spoil the fete.

By July, youth officials across the bloc had cold feet. Bulgarian bureaucrats confided in the Western press that they "would have gladly postponed the entire undertaking had this been possible."[37] But after two cancellations in as many years, a third was untenable. To rewrite the program and replace seminars with more trips to the beach, meanwhile, would rile the Western leftists whom Moscow hoped to impress. The remaining option was familiar, and therefore easy to arrange. Unable to stem political discussion, the festival hosts would control it.

Orthodox Internationalism

How to talk to strangers was a question that had preoccupied festival hosts throughout the "global sixties." In 1957, in a 140-page *Bloknot agitatora k festivaliu* (Festival Agitator's Handbook), Soviet propagandists instructed readers to think of the event as an "exchange of opinions" founded on "respect for the convictions of each person."[38] In Vienna and Helsinki, by contrast, the anticommunist press had advocated silence. The day before the opening in 1959, a Vienna tabloid announced that delegates "will not be received with cheers," but "not with stones either."[39] This time, the city on the Danube would turn back its eastern invaders by way of sheer indifference.

Bulgaria's prefestival domestic propaganda bore a closer resemblance to Vienna's than to Moscow's. In four hundred radio "lectures" delivered over the course of the spring, and in newspaper characterizations of festival delegates as "fighters," "forces," and "fronts," state news media framed the event as a battle.[40] That Bulgarian media discouraged idle chatter between young Sofians and eighteen thousand foreigners is not surprising. Since March 1968, media across the bloc had blamed student disobedience in Warsaw, Belgrade, and Prague on Western influences. By 1968, the Black Sea coast was said to attract 2,500,000 foreigners per year—most, but certainly not all, from East Europe.[41] As hotels sprang up, the incidence of sexual liaisons between young Bulgarians and "Germans, Czechs, Poles, Swedes, Frenchmen, all sorts" increased as well.[42] Sofia, though far from the coastal resorts, had its own foreign accents. Rock records circulated widely enough that the capital's

Theater Academy set a musical to *Sgt. Pepper's Lonely Hearts Club Band* in fall 1967—all without a word of protest from the state.[43] That same October, Bulgarian First Secretary Todor Zhivkov delivered a scathing critique of the Dimitrov-Komsomol (DK), calling it a "dry and fossilized organization" in need of "radical reform."[44] On the eve of the Ninth Festival, however, Zhivkov's reforms remained on paper; the organization was unchanged. Cynicism among Sofia university students was almost as pronounced as among their peers in Prague. Foreign students noticed and responded much as Rudi Dutschke had done at Charles University that spring. Historian Maria Todorova recalls Latin American classmates at Sofia University asking her, "What's wrong with your generation? You are not revolutionaries."[45]

In 1968, Zhivkov's government thus struggled with a task only slightly less contradictory than the one assigned to festival planners in Vienna and Helsinki. His government was to hold a "militant" political festival centered on discussion (per Moscow's orders), all the while shielding young Bulgarians from foreign ideas. The Bulgarian solution divided Sofia's population in two. The broad masses were to exchange no more than pleasantries with their guests. Pupils at an English-language high school were told to "be nice, be polite, use your language in order to be helpful, but don't get involved in any political discussions."[46] The youth daily *Narodna Mladezh* (People's Youth) added that "hospitality does not require servile reflex *[sic]* and needless smiles." And days before the festival's start, Zhivkov's chief festival planner (and 1989 successor) Petr Mladenov announced that according to fresh intelligence, "several dozen" CIA-recruited neo-Nazis planned to sabotage the festivities.[47] For the most part, the instructions and scare tactics worked. "We looked, we had the feeling it was great fun," but "were [not] very much involved," recalls one Sofian.[48] Some residents managed to bring delegates home for shots of *rakia* or even to debate socialist theory and praxis.[49] But those who talked publicly faced swift consequences. Peter Broderick, an American student hired by the *Times*, the *New York Times*, and the *Economist* to cover the event, recalls chatting with a few young female translators in the Festival Press Center one morning, only to find them fired the next afternoon.[50]

If the first half of Bulgaria's strategy hinged on silencing Sofia's masses, the second set about training a vanguard to talk. Of approximately eight million Bulgarians, only 250 gained authorization to participate in festival seminars and forums.[51] Beginning in April 1968, these "spokespeople" trained intensively, tutored by experts and "eminent public figures"—a euphemism, perhaps, for the KDS (Bulgaria's KGB). Philosophers drafted position papers on "what future awaits mankind?"; economists on "the non-aligned countries and planning"; and participants in interdisciplinary "forums" prepared for broader topics like "the individual and the state."[52] Though the preparatory debate club's existence is no great surprise, the international planning apparatus to which it belonged is quite remarkable. Beginning in early summer, communist delegation leaders like Jahn sent the IPC a list of proposed remarks, from which the international committee fashioned a detailed, multinational outline for each seminar, complete with talking points and delegations assigned to address them. A forum on "youth and students in the fight for maintaining the world peace," for example, was to proceed like a choose-your-own-adventure book down one of three assigned paths after a Vietnamese delegate spoke.[53] The genius here was that all paths led to the same conclusion.

Noncommunist festival participants had complained about the artificiality of World Youth Festival seminars for many years, particularly their predrafted speaker lists and boring, pro forma speeches.[54] In Sofia it was no different. Communists spoke for as long as forty-five minutes, one after the other, interrupted by only "a few objections from West European students."[55] A thorough search for Yurchak's "deterritorialized discourses" in these speeches might find idiosyncrasies in how Mongolians or Poles defined "peace" or "friendship."[56] But outright departures from party-approved words and meanings did not happen. At the Komsomol meetings that Yurchak describes in *Everything Was Forever, Until It Was No More,* members derived satisfaction from pledging loyalty to the party, not because they liked it, but because the recitations reinforced a sense of unity. At seminars in Sofia, a similar logic applied. When West Europeans objected to a seminar's format, communists faulted not so much the "pretty packaging" of what was said as the sundering of solidarity. Thus, when the chairman of Rudi Dutschke's SDS, K. D. Wolff, accused a Bulgarian of speaking out of turn, the latter likened Wolff to a man "who once, thirty years ago, said that a lie told thirty times becomes true." The allusion, translated via headset to the audience, was not lost on Wolff, who immediately "storm[ed]" the podium, demanding the right to respond. Before he could, two plainclothes men had broken Wolff's glasses with a punch to the nose, then dragged the "short, somewhat rotund young man with a conceited mouth" out into the corridor.[57] The ejection triggered "loud applause" from a majority in the hall and outraged the rest. When one irate West German ordered the Bulgarian to share the name of the liar he had alluded to, and the man replied, "Josef Goebbels," noncommunists erupted, with a young Yugoslav woman demanding an apology. To East Europeans, Wolff's interruption of the ritualized seminar was criminal. To their critics, the inverse was true. It was not the disruption of solidarity or even the punch to Wolff's nose that had spoiled the seminar. It was the allusion to Goebbels—the words, not the deeds.

By Yurchak's reasoning, the westerners took the DK representative's words much too seriously. Rather than reading the allusion for what it was—a glib, "performative," party-line statement—they read it as a sincere, "constative" statement.[58] But the international nature of festival forums spoils this interpretation. May Day parades and Komsomol meetings derived their power from order. So long as everyone marched in line and sang in unison, the spectacle worked; society was united. But at international seminars this level of stricture would squander the discussions' credibility. Here discussants could step out of line without invalidating the enterprise, IPC discussion outlines notwithstanding. Thus, when a Czech stood up at one seminar and said, "If socialism means the elimination of exploitation of people by people, . . . then the free development of creative capacities must be enabled," no one shouted him down, and discussion continued unobstructed.[59] Where Wolff's infraction differed was that instead of merely reinterpreting a term, as the Czechoslovak had reinterpreted *socialism,* the New Leftist took aim at the seminar's legitimacy.

After his expulsion and the sharp words that followed, the Bulgarian speaker did his best to resume speaking as if nothing had happened. As he did, the lecture hall doors opened to let West German, Yugoslav, Czechoslovak, British, Dutch, Italian, Belgian, and Scandinavian delegates out.[60]

While some communist news media cast Wolff as a CIA saboteur, Bulgaria's *Narodna Mladezh* attributed his outburst to simple disorientation. Given Wolff's repeated provocations, "the reader might conclude that we are dealing with an accomplished West German member of the [Chinese] Red Guards, one armed with the invincible ideas of the Chairman, which among other things cure baldness, deaf-and-dumb people, and assist . . . the world revolution," the paper mocked. No need to be afraid, it assured; Wolff was just "a very confused man."[61] To right the confusion, the world communist movement had to restore its internationalist sensibilities.

Radical Internationalism

As Günther Jahn's thoughts on "pretty packaging" demonstrated at the start of our chapter, communists were not naive about the challenges they might face in Sofia. But neither were they pessimistic. One reason for confidence, as noted above, was Vietnam. Another was the fact that communists controlled National Festival Committees around the world, whose job it was to select delegates. In July, the French committee had barred several leaders of the May student uprising in Paris from the French delegation. Although French communist daily *l'Humanité* called the decision "a deliberate provocation," the blacklist had its desired effect. Police intercepted one French New Leftist at the Bulgarian border. In Sofia proper, IPC officials refused to grant two others festival passes.[62] To the Paris *communards'* astonishment, the event that spared Vietnam's and Palestine's freedom fighters no privilege gave the Sorbonne's no quarter.[63]

Parisians were not the only New Leftists to suffer discrimination in Sofia. Greek communists managed to silence representatives of the progressive, antijunta Lambrakis Youth.[64] The IPC told delegates from Iran's student union to march behind four "official" Iranians on opening day. Convinced that the unnamed men were émigrés enrolled at Soviet bloc universities, the students chose to carry their union's flag alongside Wolff and the West German SDS. They got as far as downtown, where six Bulgarians jumped from the crowd, seized the flag, and disappeared.[65] Ostensibly, Wolff's SDS deserved the same treatment. On 1 July 1968, Wolff had told the U.S. weekly *Reader's Digest* that the SDS intended not only "to give revisionists a bad time" in Sofia but "to blow [the festival] up." He had told communist members of the West German delegation that on account of China's and Cuba's absence it was the SDS's job to "represent their political line" in Sofia and that he agreed with Castro's demand that the Sofia Festival's motto include "revolutionary struggle" alongside "for peace, friendship and solidarity." Finally, the twenty-five-year-old Frankfurt law student made no secret of his plan to hold a sit-in outside the U.S. embassy in Sofia.[66]

Despite all this, the Bulgarian response to Wolff's planned sit-in was notably mild. Zhivkov's Foreign Ministry made one "low-pitch request" to the U.S. embassy to please move all its cars from the street into a state-owned garage.[67] For their part, West German communists did their best to dissuade Wolff, pointing out that departures from the program would only hinder solidarity and benefit the USA. Finally, hours after advertising the sit-in by unfurling a fifteen-foot banner in front of the seventy-thousand-person crowd at the opening ceremony, the SDS chairman awoke to a knock on his dorm-room door. Petr Mladenov, Bulgaria's chief festival organizer, spent the next half hour imploring Wolff to call the action off. A graduate of Moscow's Institute for International Relations, Mladenov appealed to internationalism in English, asking Wolff, "We are comrades, aren't we?" When that did not work he turned to barter: if Wolff canceled the sit-in, he could join the speakers' list at tomorrow night's fifty-thousand-person Vietnam solidarity rally. Wolff again refused.[68]

The next day, in front of a Bulgarian-built barricade outside the U.S. embassy, neither West German communists nor a block of smiling, singing "spontaneous Bulgarian workers" could wrestle Wolff away from his forty-odd fellow protesters. After escaping down a side street, an all-male, largely West German group of students climbed the shoulder-high wall of Georgi Dimitrov's mausoleum to address a growing crowd. "Folklore, athletics, and colorful tinsel," Wolff shouted, did not constitute a political event. Nor did the seizure of Mao portraits and Iranian flags connote democracy. As an Iranian delegate translated the ad-lib speech into Russian, the response was a mix of hisses and cheers. When a middle-aged Bulgarian standing close to the wall asked for the interpreter's name, Wolff relayed the question to the crowd, and "a slight surge forward," plus chants of "Police! Police!" suggested things might turn violent. And moments later they did. "A column of about 250 rugged-looking young Bulgarians, dog-trotting and with arms linked, singing communist songs, plowed into the crowd from behind." As nearly a thousand bodies scrambled forward, "trying to get out of the path of the oncoming juggernaut, another column of Bulgarians rammed into [it] from the front."[69]

Played up by the Western press and down by the bloc's, the antiauthoritarian "antifestival" in Sofia was a genuine insurgency. On a single afternoon, a Wolff-led teach-in happened on a dormitory lawn, participants in which then crashed a rally against the Greek junta and next visited the Chinese embassy, all aiming to give the "revisionists a bad time."[70] The insurgency, however, was not as simple as it seemed. "It isn't our intention to divide the festival," explained one West German New Leftist at a six-hour, closed-door conversation with Komsomol and FDJ counterparts. "But we couldn't let all that supposed '*druzhba*' [friendship] close our eyes to the fact that there are different opinions in the socialist camp," and that "the path to a unified socialist camp can only lead via discussions."[71] Another Wolff sympathizer stated the problem more succinctly. "Here at the festival they're always trying to cut our discussion short with the imploring words 'unity, unity, unity,'" he told the press. "But we want to discuss what the term *unity* means."[72]

If a defining characteristic of the New Left was its "discussion fever," Petr Mladenov and Günther Jahn considered the fever a waste of breath.[73] In preparation for an "ultraleftist" challenge in Sofia, communist planners had imagined seminars as engineers do construction sites: spaces to be filled on time, by plan. Though rigged speakers' lists were nothing new to veteran festival-goers, planners in 1968 seem to have made solidarity a prerequisite for discussion to a degree that predecessors in Moscow (1957), Vienna (1959), and Helsinki (1962) had not. We might attribute this revival of totalitarian control to the familiar narrative of Stalinism's revival after Khrushchev's fall. But the ideological battles of the "global sixties" provide a more convincing explanation. Soviet efforts to assuage the Chinese via public and private channels had failed. As the bitter exchange between *Pravda* and *Renmin Ribao* (People's Daily) in 1963 made clear, fruitful debate was especially hard when the words themselves were in question.[74] In Sofia, the new challenge to intersocialist solidarity, this time from the Western New Left, functioned similarly. To Wolff, solidarity was not the prerequisite to good discussion; it was the product. Internationalism was not a static pledge but a momentary condition.

Fortunately for Mladenov and Jahn, the great majority of delegates agreed with their hosts, not with Wolff. Still, contempt for the saboteurs from Frankfurt was a far cry from the "orthodox" internationalism endorsed by the festival's sponsors. Among the rest of the eighteen thousand delegates in Sofia in early August 1968, our final section suggests, diplomats outnumbered partisans.

Diplomatic Internationalism

On the second night of the festival, toward the end of the massive Vietnam solidarity rally that Wolff chose not to address, a U.S. diplomat noted a curious similarity: "As the rear echelons of delegations gradually disintegrated into small groups, the Vietnamese and Czechs emerged as the most active behind-the-scenes delegations." Though handicapped by language, the Vietnamese "aggressively" exchanged pins and badges with the international crowd. The Czechoslovaks "made use of numerous attractive girl members to seek out members of other delegations" before "explaining to small groups, including Bulgarian delegates, that the Czech youth supports the democratization program of their present leadership."[75] The similarity did not end on opening night. "In their personal demeanor," noted one Western report, the Vietnamese "seemed entirely nonmilitant" and "as a rule, humble."[76] In the *Economist*, Peter Broderick commented that the Czechoslovaks carried themselves in a similar manner, distinguished by "good humor and patience." The objective in Sofia, one Czech had told him, was to "act diplomatically" and "not let ourselves be provoked."[77]

That young Czechoslovaks and Vietnamese spoke a similar language in Sofia—friendly, humble, above all diplomatic—is striking in light of the contrary roles the festival assigned them. The IPC arranged no fewer than forty separate events in honor of the Vietnam War on the festival's first full day alone, highlighted by a reception at the "Vietnam Solidarity Center," where delegates could buy medals "made from downed US aircraft."[78] For the Czechoslovaks, on the other hand, trouble began at the border. Bulgarian guards turned back thirty-one festival card-carrying Bohemians who had hiked all the way from Pilsen, citing their "bedraggled appearance," and said the same after the hikers had showered and changed in a nearby village.[79] The following day, border guards emptied a Czechoslovakian truck of several thousand leaflets, including Prague's response to the Warsaw Pact's 15 July ultimatum.[80] The following morning, Czechoslovak delegates awoke to find missing the stage they had assembled in a park outside their Sofia dorm, on which ČSSR dancers, singers, and actors were scheduled to perform that afternoon. Witnesses said they saw uniformed men do the job, but Sofia's police blamed hooligans.[81]

The chicanery against the Czechoslovaks occurred just as an "extremely nervous" Leonid Brezhnev reiterated the Warsaw Pact's warning to Dubček inside a train car on the Slovak-Ukrainian border.[82] Dubček responded politely that the ČSSR would continue to chart its own course to socialism, and nine hundred kilometers to the south, Czechoslovak delegates told skeptical delegates the same. After a brash display at the opening ceremony, when a group of them had paused in front of Zhivkov's honor box and chanted in Russian, "Nasha demokratiia nashe delo!" (Our democracy's our business!), the five-hundred-person delegation reportedly received a series of telegrams from Prague, all underscoring the need to "emphasize loyalty to the alliance and continued progress toward socialism in the ČSSR."[83] Not all Czechoslovaks heeded the warnings. Some chanted "Rudi Dutschke," others exited the aforementioned seminar in solidarity with KD Wolff.[84] On the whole, though, the Czechoslovaks held themselves to a "very liberal" standard, recalls Wolff. "You have the right to speak," they told him. But they refused to support the statements themselves. To antiauthoritarians' frustration, the Czechoslovak delegates "would never enter into the questions of world revolution."[85]

Like the Czechoslovaks, the Vietnamese pursued contrary missions at the 1968 festival, one assertive, the other appeasing. The beleaguered, post-Tet government in Hanoi was thankful for the ten-day, all-expenses-paid spectacle on its behalf, and for the fourteen train cars of material aid (GDR motorbikes, Hungarian radios, et al.) that sailed from the Black Sea to Haiphong at the end of the event.[86] In return, Vietnamese delegates played the cause célèbre graciously. A female sniper waved to the seventy thousand people attending the opening ceremony as the PA system credited her with killing nineteen Americans in just twenty-one shots. A Soviet documentary film shows a South Vietnamese man in fatigues smiling and waving from a jeep as it creeps through a throng. And at a "friendship meeting" with the U.S. delegation, Vietnamese delegates exchanged "buttons, jewelry and articles of clothing" with tearful Americans, then clapped ecstatically when a young man in sideburns lit his draft card on fire.[87]

Hanoi had long been wary of placing both feet in any one socialist camp.[88] And while the Tet offensive signaled Hanoi's gravitation toward Moscow, away from Beijing, the North Vietnamese saw no sense in antagonizing anyone, least of all their longtime chief ally. When a South Vietnamese representative spoke at the Vietnam rally, he therefore made sure to thank not only the Soviets and Bulgarians but also the Chinese.[89] In three discussions with West German antiauthoritarians inside the Vietnam Solidarity Center, Vietnamese students "very much held themselves back, as they had throughout the festival, even as regards the allegation of fascism against K. D. Wolff." Ever-mindful of burning bridges, even to the radicals from Frankfurt, the students from Vietnam added "that they considered us [the West German radicals] good comrades-in-arms."[90]

Vietnam and Czechoslovakia were not the only delegations to speak softly in Sofia. Contrary to State Department predictions of acrimony from "Fidelistas . . . , and Maoists, not to mention autocentrists, polycentrists, and various stripes of nationalist-Communists such as the Romanians," and contrary to Petr Mladenov's warning about neo-Nazi "shock troops," Ceausescu's Romanians and Willy Brandt's West Germans were by and large polite and inconspicuous.[91] The result was too temperate. In February, the Komsomol had hoped to build a fire of anti-American anti-imperialism hot enough to soften national identities. By August, the anti-American spirit appeared to be hotter at the Democratic Party Convention in Chicago than it was at the World Youth Festival in Sofia.

On the festival's second-to-last afternoon, the IPC granted Wolff's SDS contingent permission to lead a seminar of its own. In a packed Sofia University lecture hall, West German New Leftists asked a largely communist audience to consider "strategy and tactics of the anti-imperialist struggle."[92] After a "deafening" quarrel over who should sit on the seminar's "panel," and after several plenary votes to resolve the dispute, the debate began with a eulogy to Chairman Mao. Next, a Bulgarian derided the *Little Red Book* as "a species of oriental despotism." Wolff replied that nothing in China compared to "terrorist Stalinism in some Soviet states." A Soviet responded by calling Wolff's ultraleftism rightism by another name.[93] At the climax of the six-hour discussion, a Venezuelan "with the *habitus* of an operetta dictator" skipped ahead of thirty-five registered speakers to deliver an hourlong, two-part polemic: one pro-Soviet, the other anti-Wolff. At one thirty in the morning, a Bulgarian stood up and declared the meeting finished. The microphones fell silent, the lights went out, and the liveliest discussion of the ten-day festival ended in indignation. On their way out of the hall, East Germans struck up the "Internationale"; Bulgarians "laughed up their sleeves"; and "reserved" Czechoslovaks, Yugoslavs, and Romanians expressed their sympathy to "very frustrated" West Germans.[94] The antiauthoritarian debate had died by decree.

To some observers, the failure to resurrect solidarity in Sofia was a consequence of youth hostility to state authority. To others, state intolerance for spontaneity was at fault. Youth versus state, however, is a "one-dimensionalized" narrative.[95] As Alexei Yurchak and Kristin Ross suggest, generational conflict explains national disharmony no better than class conflict once did.[96] And as the preceding pages have shown, it explains international disharmony equally poorly. In Sofia, the rift was not between old states and a youth international; it was between contrary understandings of words like *solidarity, global,* and *internationalism.* In place of a generation gap, this chapter faults a semantic one.

It also asserts the endurance of national identity at one of the twentieth-century's greatest enactments of "internationalist sensibilities," the World Youth Festival. Cross-border alliances, of course, occurred at the 1968 festival. The Komsomol praised East German, Polish, and Soviet delegations as the event's "antifascist center," and Günther Jahn reported that "per our initiative, youth secretaries . . . from the USSR, Bulgaria, Poland, Hungary, and the GDR meet daily to coordinate." In the antiauthoritarian camp, meanwhile, Wolff attracted a potpourri of 150 to 300 "Australians, Dutch, Austrian, Belgians, et al."[97] Read backward, however, these statements describe a different scenario. The "antifascist center" included just three out of fourteen socialist countries (three of which—Cuba, China, Albania—had not even bothered to attend); Jahn's "coordination" meetings began on the fourth day, by which time Wolff's insurrection was already world news; finally—and to my mind most importantly—Wolff's antinational "internationalists" attracted less than 2 percent of total delegates.

Historians have long acknowledged the 1960s as a dissonant decade. Only recently, however, have they tracked its dissonant notes across national borders. The shift from comparative to transnational history writing—from how students in different countries challenged similar structures in similar ways to how they influenced one another—has yielded new insights.[98] But this historiography remains anchored in the mid-Atlantic and fixed on conflicts between young and old rather than young and young. This chapter contributes to a growing literature on the communication breakdown that the world Left suffered over the course of the "global sixties." These works follow New Leftists eastward to meet with Slovak students in March 1968, where "the disappointment was radical and mutual"; they track Czech students to West Berlin, where they visited Rudi Dutschke in hospital (a right-wing gunman had nearly killed him shortly after his return from Prague), and where it seemed that "many among the German [SDS] were being politically radical just for the sake of being so"; they even accompany African leftists to Moscow, where racist violence prompted statements like "We would rather live without friends than accept this kind of friendship."[99] In each instance, guests and hosts hoped to kindle the same fire of solidarity that the Komsomol tried to build in Sofia in 1968. Cultures, prejudices, and in particular languages, however, got in the way. By August 1968, the "international communist language" that had resonated at earlier Stalinist festivals was broken, and for several years could not be put back together again.[100]

After returning to Frankfurt, Wolff boasted on West German radio: "We managed to politicize the whole festival—above and beyond just folklore and athletic events, [we] set a discussion in motion."[101] The Vietnamese returned home from Sofia with their bags full. The East Germans said the complicated so simply that they struck onlookers as "self-absorbed, arrogant," in all, "unbearably German." And the "virtual absence of direct contact [between foreign delegates and] the Bulgarians" suggested that Zhivkov's masses had done their part.[102] One could argue, on the basis of these outcomes, that festival planners, like Ceausescu, had negotiated a successful "look left, turn right" pivot in 1968: away from adventure, back to security, all in the name of internationalist solidarity. But to contemporaries, as to historians, Sofia's proclamations of internationalism rang hollow. Zhivkov's assurance to the press that "one language resounded at the Festival" is a telling example.[103] Unlike Vienna (1959) and Helsinki (1962), and unlike Algiers and Accra (1965–66), in Sofia in 1968, festival friends and enemies spoke the "same vocabulary" but meant different things. What had been a celebration of "sports, culture, politics," a Dutch festival veteran reported, was now "first and foremost politics." And what had been politics was now "words, words, words."[104]

Notes

1. Jahn defined the Romanians and Yugoslavs as "our friends" but told FDJ delegates to respond to their "questions and arguments" "factually but with conviction [sachlich aber bestimmt]." See "Lektion auf dem Vorbereitungslehrgang . . . ," and "In den Seminaren . . . ," in Foundation Archives of Parties and Mass Organizations of the GDR (hereafter SAPMO) Bundesarchiv Berlin-Lichterfelde (hereafter BAB), DY/24, vol. 8293, 1–33.

2. Ibid., 12–13.

3. William Taubman, *The View from Lenin Hills: Soviet Youth in Ferment* (New York: Coward-McCann, 1967).

4. Described by the Komsomol as "the most representative" festival since the event's founding in 1947, Sofia attracted five hundred youth organizations, including the first ever state-sponsored Western delegation from the Federal Republic of Germany. See Russian State Archive for Social-Political History—Youth Division (hereafter RGASPI-m), Spravochnaia 255, l. 185.

5. For a recent example, see Richard Ivan Jobs, "Youth Movements: Travel, Protest, and Europe in 1968," *American Historical Review* 114, no. 2 (2009): 379–80.

6. On Marcuse's "*eros* effect," see George Katsiaficas, *The Imagination of the New Left: A Global Analysis of 1968* (Boston: South End Press, 1987), 6–7. The first quotation is from that book, xiv; the second is from Jobs, "Youth Movements," 376. See also M. Klimke and J. Scharloch, eds., *1968 in Europe: A History of Protest and Activism, 1956–1977* (New York: Palgrave, 2008), 2.

7. Though Timothy Brown acknowledges this vagueness, his local/global binary also rests on a poorly defined notion of what united the latter half—the "global" sixties. See Timothy Brown, "'1968' East and West: Divided Germany as a Case Study in Transnational History," *American Historical Review* 114, no. 1 (2009): 69–96.

8. Jobs, "Youth Movements," 400.

9. Gretchen Dutschke, *Wir hatten ein barbarisches, schönes Leben: Rudi Dutschke* (Cologne: Kiepenheuer und Witsch, 1996), 193–94.

10. Paulina Bren, "1968 East and West: Visions of Political Change and Student Protest from across the Iron Curtain," in *Transnational Moments of Change: Europe 1945, 1968, 1989*, ed. Gerd-Rainer Horn and Padraic Kenney (Lanham, MD: Rowman and Littlefield, 2004), 124–25.

11. See Noack's chapter in the present volume. I stumbled upon the Grushin Festival myself while in Russia in 2008.

12. Alexei Yurchak, *Everything Was Forever, Until It Was No More: The Last Soviet Generation* (Princeton: Princeton University Press, 2005), 1–9.

13. See Applebaum's contribution to the present volume. On the prevailing view of a "global sixties" founded on youth solidarity, see Jobs, "Youth Movements," 387–88, 400–402; Martin Klimke, *The Other Alliance: Student Protest in West Germany and the United States in the Global Sixties* (Princeton: Princeton University Press, 2010), 5, 91–100; Jeremi Suri, *Power and Protest: The Global Revolution and the Rise of Detente* (Cambridge, MA: Harvard University Press, 2003), 194–206.

14. Arif Dirlik, "The Third World," in *1968: The World Transformed*, ed. Carole Fink, Phillipp Gassert, Detlef Junker, and Daniel S. Mattern (Cambridge: Cambridge University Press, 1998), 315.

15. "Von '68 nach '89: Jiri Dienstbier, Jiri Grusa, Lionel Jospin, Adam Michnik, Oskar Negt und Friedrich Schorlemmer im Gespräch," *Blätter für deutsche und internationale Politik* 8 (August 2008): 33.

16. Elena Zubkova, *Russia after the War: Hopes, Illusions, and Disappointments, 1945–1957*, trans. Hugh Ragsdale (Armonk, NY: M. E. Sharpe, 1998), 199–201. On Khrushchev's optimism, see Aleksandr Fursenko and Timothy Naftali, *Khrushchev's Cold War* (New York: Norton, 2006), 145.

17. On the Poles, see Secretary of TsK, LKSM (Komsomol) Belarus, G. Kriulin, et al., "Report on the Polish Delegation's Participation in the VI World Festival of Youth and Students," 4 September 1957, RGASPI-m, f. 3, op. 15, d. 195, ll. 170–71. On German filmmakers, see *Moskau-1957*, West German art-doc filmmaker Peter Schamoni's 1957 master's thesis short, filmed on cameras loaned from his Munich film

school (in author's possession). On kisses, see Kristin Roth-Ey, "'Loose Girls' on the Loose? Sex, Propaganda and the 1957 Youth Festival," in *Women in the Khrushchev Era*, ed. Melanie Ilic, Susan E. Reid, and Lynne Attwood (New York: Palgrave Macmillan, 2004), 76–95.

18. N. S. Diko, interview by author, Moscow, 20 October 2008.

19. Here I liken "positive" internationalism to the Soviet term, *positive neutrality*. On the creation of this neologism under Khrushchev, see Wolfgang Mueller, *A Good Example of Peaceful Coexistence? The Soviet Union, Austria, and Neutrality, 1955–1991* (Vienna: ÖAW, 2011), 39–76.

20. "Gespräch im Gesamteuropäischen Studienwerk e.V. in Vlotho am 30 Sep 1959," in BAK, B/136/3795, 4.

21. Evgenii A. Evtushenko, "Sniveling Fascists," trans. D. Rottenberg, www.leninist.biz/en/1969/FSP533/16-Snivelling.Fascism (accessed 2 April 2010); "Communists: The Uninvited Guests," *Time*, 10 August 1962.

22. Steinem served as the chief administrator of CIA-funded antifestival activities in Vienna (1959) as well as Helsinki (1962). See Hugh Wilford, *The Mighty Wurlitzer: How the CIA Played America* (Cambridge, MA: Harvard University Press, 2008), 141–48.

23. Stephan Friedberg, *Arbeitsgemeinschaft 'Sommerkurs': Abschlußbericht über die VII Weltfestspiele* (Vienna: PagoBuchdrückerei, 1959), 3.

24. For the West German count, see "37 Teilnehmer aus der Zone in Helsinki geflüchtet," *Die Welt*, 7 August 1962; for the Stasi count, see Report to W. Ulbricht, E. Honecker, et al., 23 August 1962, in Federal Commission for State Security Files—Berlin (BStU), MfS ZAIG 638, 7.

25. NATO Committee on Information and Cultural Relations (CICR), "Eighth World Youth Festival," 11 September 1962, Archive (Brussels), AC/52–WP(62)36, 4–5.

26. "Bericht über die VIII. Weltfestspiele . . . ," 31 August 1962, in BAK, B/153/1930, 234; W. Wiskari, "Ceylonese Quit Red Youth Fete," *New York Times*, 5 August 1962.

27. "Bericht über die Tätigkeit der Delegation des ZRs der FDJ in Algier," 5 April 1965, in SAPMO-BAB, DY/24/2437, 12–17, and in IUSY collection, folder 710, International Institute for Social History (IISH), Amsterdam.

28. FDJ Secretary Frank Bochow, who represented the FDJ on the IPC in 1965, says he felt no remorse on learning of Ben Bella's fall. Frank Bochow, interview by author, Berlin, 15 May 2009.

29. A. A. Lebedev, former Komsomol representative on the International Union of Students (IUS), interview by author, Moscow, 27 October 2008.

30. On the Vienna meeting, see "Beschluss der Vollsitzung des Politbüros [der KPD]," 29–30 August 1968, in SAPMO-BAB, BY/1/3884, 5; "Betr.: Entsendung einer Delegation des ZRs der FDJ zur Teilnahme a.d. Tagung d. [IVK] für die IX. Weltfestspiele," in SAPMO-BAB, DY/30/IV A 2/16, vol. 34, 2; untitled report from Bundespolizeidirektion Wien, Abt. 1, 27 January 1967, in Austrian State Archives (ÖStA), AdR, BMI, 23.193-17/67, 2.

31. Helsinki police deployed tear gas against the rioters "for the first and last time in the history of Finnish police," writes historian Jan Krekola, author of "Peace and Friendship or Freedom?" (unpublished conference paper, in author's possession), 9.

32. Lorenz Lüthi, *The Sino-Soviet Split* (Princeton: Princeton University Press, 2008).

33. Ilya V. Gaiduk, *The Soviet Union and the Vietnam War* (Chicago: Ivan R. Dee, 1996), ch. 11.

34. "Directives to Soviet Representatives on the Permanent Commission of the IPC (International Preparatory Committee) for the IX World Festival . . . ," RGASPI-m, f. 1, op. 67, d. 188, ll. 97–98.

35. D. Abuyuri, "The Busiest Young Man in Sofia," *World Student News* (Prague) 22, no. 7 (July 1968): 23.

36. KMO (Committee of Youth Organzations) to TsK VLKSM (Komsomol), "Information on Several Problems with International Preparation for the IX World Festival . . . ," 27 February 1968, RGASPI-m, f. 1, op. 67, d. 188, l. 92.

37. Norddeutscher Rundfunk (NDR), "Echo des Tages," 30 July 1968, BStU, HA XX 17242, 56.

38. K. Lutovinova, "Advice for the Agitator," in *Bloknot agitatora k festivaliu* (Moscow: Moskovskaia Pravda, 1957), 82.

39. "An die Jugend aus aller Welt!" *Kurier* (Vienna), 25 July 1959.

40. Karin Taylor, *Let's Twist Again: Youth and Leisure in Socialist Bulgaria* (Vienna: Lit Verlag, 2006), 54.

41. Frank Bochow, "Betr: Info über die Tagung des IVK," 7 December 1967, in SAPMO-BAB, DY/24/10283, 8.

42. Georgi Markov, *The Truth That Killed*, trans. L. Brisby (London: Weidenfeld and Nicholson, 1983), 87–98.

43. Maria Todorova, phone interview by author, 16 March 2010.

44. Michael Costello, "The Bulgarian Youth Discussion," 13 February 1968, 3, in Open Society Archives (hereafter OSA), www.osaarchivum.org/files/holdings/300/8/3/pdf/7-1-272.pdf; Radio Free Europe Research, Bulgaria, no. 48, 15 July 1968, 3.

45. Todorova, interview.

46. Karin Taylor, "Socialist Orchestration of Youth: The 1968 Sofia Youth Festival and Encounters on the Fringe," *Ethnologia Balkanica* 7 (2003): 51.

47. R. T., "The Ninth World Youth Festival: A Preview," Radio Free Europe Research, 16 July 1968, in OSA, 5, www.osaarchivum.org/files/holdings/300/8/3/text/7-1-188.shtml; *Deutscher Bundesjugendring Festival-Pressesonderdienst*, no. 3, 28 July 1968, in BAK, B/145/4003, 2–3.

48. Taylor, "Socialist Orchestration of Youth," 53.

49. Todorova, interview.

50. Peter Broderick, phone interview by author, 2 April 2010.

51. R. T., "Ninth World Youth Festival: A Preview," 9.

52. Taylor, "Socialist Orchestration of Youth," 49.

53. "Programm d. Teilnahme d. DDR-Delegation an Veranstaltungen . . . ," in SAPMO-BAB, DY/30/ IV A 2/16, vol. 35, 2.

54. For one example, see Erwin Bresslein, *Drushba! Freundschaft? Von der Kommunistischen Jugendinternationale zu den Weltjugendfestspielen* (Frankfurt: Fischer, 1973), 119–20.

55. G. D., "Bericht über die 9. Weltfestspiele in Sofia," in BAK, B/166/1303, 6–7, 15.

56. Yurchak, *Everything Was Forever*, 114–18.

57. Wouter Gortzak, "Socialistisch Incident in Sofia," *Allgemeen Handelsblad* (Amsterdam), 17 August 1968; "Information: Erneute Provokation des SDS-Vorsitzenden Wolff," 4 August 1968, in BStU, HA XX 10503, 189.

58. Yurchak, *Everything Was Forever*, 19–27.

59. G. D., "Bericht," 5.

60. The Bulgarian was not the first to compare West German student radicals to Nazis. In early June 1967, at an SDS congress in Hannover, the philosopher Jürgen Habermas accused the SDS of "left-fascism." My account of the "Individual and Society" forum draws on MfS, "Report on the . . . SDS Press Conference Held in the Reception Hall of Hotel 'Hemus,'" Sofia, 4 August 1968, BStU, HA XX 10412, 421–25; "Information: Erneute Provokation," 188; Gortzak, "Applaus en protest in Sofia," *Groene Amsterdamer*, 10 August 1968; Marianne Henkel Bericht, in BAK, B 166/1303, 15.

61. G. Gurkov, "Barrikada," *KP*, 1 August 1968; "An Embarrassing Affair," *Narodna Mladezh*, 6 August 1968, trans. in Airgram U.S. embassy Sofia to Dept. of State, 8 August 1968, in U.S. National Archives and Records Administration (hereafter NARA), 59/150/64/7/4, box 1514, folder CSM 14-2 (6/1/68).

62. CISNU (Iranian Student Union), "Erklärung der Konföderation iranischer Studenten hinsichtlich der Eröffnungsfeierlichkeiten des Festivals," Berlin, 2 August 1968, BStU, MfS HA XX 11412, 63–64.

63. For the full text of a protest flier signed by seven student unions at the Sofia festival in support of the Iranian Student Union (CISNU) on 30 July 1968, see BStU, HA XX 11412, 64; CISNU, "Erklärung," HA XX 11412, 63–64.

64. KMO to TsK VLKSM, "Information on Results of the IX World Festival . . . ," 20 August 1968, RGASPI-m, f. 1, op. 67, d. 207, l. 49; GDR Ministry for State Security (MfS) "Information on the SDS Press

Conference Held . . . in the Breakfast Room of Hotel 'Hemus,'" 31 July 1968, BStU, HA XX 10412, 324; G. D., "Bericht," 8.

65. CISNU, "Erklärung," BStU, HA XX 11412, 62–63.

66. The terms adopted by the IPC were *peace, friendship, solidarity*. Though the archives do not say why the IPC let the SDS in, three justifications are likely. First, SDS delegates had stood up for the Eighth Festival in Helsinki; second, the League provided West Germany's Festival Committee with crucial non-communist cover; third, like the New Left at large, the SDS was an ideological conglomerate, one in which a pro-Soviet minority had steadily gained influence since the late 1950s (West Germany's Supreme Court banned the Communist Party, the KPD, in 1956, only to permit the German Communist Party [DKP] to form in 1968, shortly after the Sofia Festival). That communists took a majority of SDS seats on the West German delegation was no accident; it was their job to keep Wolff's "ultra-Left" in check. On SDS relations with the Soviet bloc, see T. Fichter and S. Lönnendonker, *Kleine Geschichte des SDS* (West Berlin: Rotbuch, 1977); Hubertus Knabe, *Die unterwanderte Republik: Stasi im Westen* (Berlin: Propyläen, 1999), 182–260. For Wolff's statements, see airgram from Amconsul Frankfurt to DOS, 2 July 1968, in NARA, 59/150/64/7/4, box 1514, folder CSM 14 (1/1/67); Beschluss d. Vollsitzung d. Politbüros (KPD), 29–30 August 1968, in SAPMO-BAB, BY/1/3884, 5, and its addendum, 6.

67. Airgram from American consul Frankfurt to DOS, 2 July 1968, in NARA, 59/150/64/7/4, box 1514, folder CSM 14 (1/1/67).

68. K. D. Wolff, interview by author, Frankfurt, 7 February 2009.

69. Airgram Sofia to DOS, 1 August 1968, in NARA, 59/150/64/7/4, box 1514, (6/1/68); Helmut Herles, "Ein Getrümmel unter Linken," *Frankfurter Allgemeine Zeitung*, 31 July 1968.

70. The embassy turned the activists away, commenting that China was too busy conducting revolution to talk about it. GDR State Radio Committee, Information Division, "RIAS, Rundchau am Abend," 5 August 1968, BStU, HA XX 17242, 63.

71. G. D., "Bericht," 13–14.

72. "Elaboration on the Press Conference with KD Wolff on 4 August 1968 in 'Hermus,'" 5 August 1968, BStU, HA XX 10412, 425.

73. Nina Verheyen, "'Diskussionsfieber: Diskutieren als kommunikative Praxis in der westdeutschen Studentenbewegung," in *Ein Handbuch zur Kultur und Mediengeschichte*, ed. Martin Klimke and Joachim Scharloth (Stuttgart: Metzler, 2007), 209–22.

74. Lüthi, *Sino-Soviet Split*, 219–45.

75. Sofia to Secretary of State (Rusk), 30 July 1968, in NARA, 59/150/64/7/4, box 1514, folder CSM 14-2 (6/1/68), 3.

76. "Der Deutsche Bundesjugendring in Sofia: Vorläufiger Bericht," in BAK, B/145/4003, 8.

77. Broderick, "Communist Youth Displays Its Discontent," *Economist*, 13 August 1968.

78. Sofia to Secretary of State (Rusk), 15 July 1968, in NARA, 59/150/64/7/4, box 1514, folder CSM 14-2 (1/1/67), 2.

79. Bresslein, *Drushba! Freundschaft?*, 136.

80. Sofia to Rusk, 30 July 1968, in NARA, 59/150/64/7/4, box 1514, folder CSM 14-2 (6/1/68).

81. Deutscher Bundesjugend Ring (German Federal Youth Council), "Der DBJR in Sofia: Vorläufiger Bericht," n.d., in BAK, B/145/4003, 11.

82. Jaromir Navratil, *The Prague Spring 1968* (Budapest: Central European University Press, 1998), 302.

83. G. Jahn, Festival Report, 31 July 1968, in SAPMO-BAB, DY/30/IV A 2/16, vol. 36, 7.

84. Quinn Slobodian, *Foreign Front: Third World Politics in Sixties West Germany* (Durham: Duke University Press, 2012), 196.

85. Wolff interview.

86. "Hinweise zur Auswertung der IX. Weltfestspiele . . . ," in SAPMO-BAB, DY/30/IV A 2/16, vol. 36.

87. U.S. delegate Leslie Cagan, phone interview by author, May 2010; *A Time to Live!* (Sovexportfilm, 1969) includes extended footage of the meeting.

88. Qiang Zhai, *China and the Vietnam Wars, 1950–1975* (Chapel Hill: University of North Carolina Press, 2000), 176–80.

89. Radio Free Europe Research, Situation Report Bulgaria, no. 52, 30 July 1968, 1.

90. Henkel, "Bericht über die Reise der vds . . . ," in BAK, B/166/1303, 7–8.

91. Airgram from DOS to all U.S. diplomatic posts, 19 April 1968, in NARA, Folder: CSM 14-2 (1/1/68), 4.

92. Peter Broderick, "Sofia Youth Parley Ends in Dissension," *New York Times*, 7 August 1968.

93. Telegram from Sofia to DOS, 7 August 1968, in NARA, folder CSM 14-2 (6/1/68), 2; Gortzak, "Socialistisch Incident in Sofia."

94. G. D., "Bericht," 16; Gortzak, "Socialistisch Incident in Sofia."

95. Herbert Marcuse entitled his influential 1964 critique of Soviet socialism *One-Dimensional Man* (Boston: Beacon, 1964).

96. Kristin Ross gives a compelling critique of how pop culture and scholarship have confined the Paris events of May 1968 to "youth revolt," obscuring the challenge they posed to bedrocks of modernity like "the social division of labor." See Ross, *May '68 and Its Afterlives* (Chicago: University of Chicago Press, 2002).

97. KMO to TsK VLKSM, "Information on Results of the IX World Festival . . . ," 20 August 1968, RGASPI-m, f. 1, op. 67, d. 207, l. 47; Festival Reports, 31 July 1968 and 1 August 1968, in SAPMO-BAB, DY/30/IV A 2/16, vol. 36, 7 and 2 respectively.

98. In the former category are Katsiaficas, *Imagination of the New Left* and Suri, *Power and Protest.* In the latter are Klimke, *Other Alliance,* and Anne E. Gorsuch and Diane P. Koenker, eds., *Turizm: The Russian and East European Tourist under Capitalism and Socialism* (Ithaca: Cornell University Press, 2006).

99. Gerd Koenen, *Das rote Jahrzehnt: Unsere kleine deutsche Kulturrevolution, 1967–1977* (Köln: Kiepenheuer und Witsch, 2001), 218; Bren, "1968 East and West," 126; Julie Hessler, "The Death of an African: Race, Politics, and the Cold War," *Cahiers du monde russe* 47, nos. 1–2 (2006): 55. For a compelling account of East German prejudice directed at Africans, see Young-Sun Hong, "'The Benefits of Health Must Spread among All': International Solidarity, Health, and Race in the East German Encounter with the Third World," in *Socialist Modern: East German Everyday Culture and Politics,* ed. Katherine Pence and Paul Betts (Ann Arbor: University of Michigan Press, 2008), 183–210.

100. The language was restored, in part if not in whole, at the Tenth Festival in East Berlin, 1973. Quotation from Vincent Tortora, *Communist Close-Up: A Roving Reporter behind the Iron Curtain* (New York: Exposition Press, 1953), 24.

101. Westdeutscher Rundfunk (WDR) II, "SDS und VDS über ihre Aktivität bei den kommunistischen Weltjugendfestspielen," 8 August 1968, BAK, B/136/3797, Heft 1.

102. Gortzak, "Applaus en protest," 1.

103. R. T., Radio Free Europe Research, "The Ninth World Youth Festival: A Review," 23 August 1968, in OSA, 1.

104. Gortzak, "Applaus en protest," 1.

8 A Test of Friendship

Soviet-Czechoslovak Tourism and the Prague Spring

Rachel Applebaum

THE 1960S WAS an era of unprecedented transnational exchange. From Tokyo to Chicago, people watched the decade's defining moments of protest, revolution, and war play out in real time on their television sets. Fashion and rock music traveled from the streets of London to New York's galleries and nightclubs. Rebellious students in Paris and Milan mimicked the style—and sometimes the politics—of revolutionary leaders in Latin America and China.[1]

As the chapters in this volume reveal, the sixties was also a time of increased transnational exchange within the socialist world. In Havana, Cubans were introduced to material goods and culture from the USSR at the 1960 Soviet exhibition; in Sofia, activists from socialist countries around the world gathered at the Ninth World Youth Festival.[2] Paradoxically, such contacts, which were designed to increase solidarity in the bloc, instead revealed political, national, and cultural discord. This essay examines one aspect of this process of transnational contact and rupture: "friendship" between the USSR and Czechoslovakia, as seen through the lens of Soviet-Czechoslovak tourism during what was arguably the most important event of the socialist sixties, the 1968 Czechoslovak reform movement known as the Prague Spring.

Gerd-Rainer Horn and Padraic Kenney have recently argued that a transnational approach is especially suited to "the study of great events that simply cannot be captured within the narrative of one country."[3] Their call for transnational history has been reflected in several recent accounts of the Prague Spring, which detail its effects on international diplomacy.[4] Yet the story of how the reform movement changed relations between ordinary Soviet and Czechoslovak citizens has not been told. This chapter aims to begin to fill this lacuna.

Initially, the Soviet Union promoted "friendship" between its citizens and those of its satellite states as a means to maintain power in postwar Eastern Europe. The construction of socialism in the Eastern bloc countries, overseen jointly by the Soviet and Eastern European communist parties, was to provide the political basis for unity among the region's diverse peoples. On an everyday level, Soviet cultural exports, the study of the Russian language, and a variety of institutions and programs promoting cultural exchange, such as friendship societies, pen pal correspondences, and student exchanges, were to foster mutual understanding, or what the Soviets called *sblizhenie* (rapprochement) within the socialist camp. The idea of Soviet-Czechoslovak friendship was based on the theory that *sblizhenie* would occur as each country's citizens acquired knowledge of the other's history, language, and culture.

During the "revival of Soviet internationalism" that took place during the Thaw following Stalin's death in 1953, mass tourism became a key element in what I call the friendship project between Soviets and Czechoslovaks.[5] From the start, tourism was a medium through which ordinary Soviets and Czechoslovaks negotiated the power dynamics between their countries.[6] These dynamics—and with them Soviet-Czechoslovak tourism—became increasingly fraught in the mid-1960s, when the Czechoslovak government began to enact political and cultural reforms that challenged the authority of the USSR.

Soviet-Czechoslovak friendship as embodied by tourism was not just an instrumental project; it was also utopian. As such, it mirrored the broader spirit of the socialist sixties. Spurred by dramatic events like the Cuban Revolution and Iuri Gagarin's space flight, the era's utopianism can be seen in the ideals of the Soviet reform-minded intelligentsia known as the *shestidesiatniki*, as well as in such diverse phenomena as the grassroots origins of the tourist song movement in the Soviet Union and Soviet planners' attempts to introduce "rational consumption" as an alternative to Western consumerism.[7] It was even apparent at the 1961 Twenty-Second Party Congress, where Nikita Khrushchev announced that the USSR would achieve communism in twenty years.[8] Along these lines, Soviet and Czechoslovak officials imagined that tourism and other new forms of social contacts between their countries would result in "a new socialist type of international relations," in which an alliance between nations would be embodied by personal ties between citizens.[9] Tourists also repeated this fantasy. "I went to that country as a tourist, acquainted with it from books, the stories of comrades, newspapers, and magazine articles. I returned a sincere friend of that country, its people," a Muscovite wrote after returning from a trip to Czechoslovakia.[10]

I begin this chapter with a brief overview of Soviet tourism to Czechoslovakia in the years leading up to the Prague Spring, which provides a sense of how the events of 1968 changed the experience of Soviet tourists in Czechoslovakia. I then discuss Czechoslovak and Soviet attempts to reform tourism—and their countries' broader relations—in the mid-1960s. From there I describe the reactions of Soviet tourists to Czechoslovak culture in the mid-1960s. Finally I turn to tourism during the events of the Prague Spring itself, and the ensuing Soviet invasion and occupation of Czecho-slovakia, through the end of 1969, when the reformers had been overthrown and the Soviet government was becoming confident that "normalization" had been achieved.

Sources

This chapter's conclusions are based on two main sets of sources. The first is travel writing published in Soviet and Czechoslovak guidebooks, magazines, and journals. Such texts, with the exception of those published in Czechoslovakia in 1968 when cen-sorship was lifted (discussed later in this chapter), generally provide an official "script" prescribing appropriate behavior and interpretations for tourists. The second source set is trip reports filed by the leaders of Soviet tour groups with two of the organiza-tions responsible for organizing Soviet tourism to Czechoslovakia: the trade unions' tourism councils, and Sputnik, the Komsomol's travel agency. Unfortunately, because of the current inaccessibility of the archives from Čedok, the Czechoslovak state travel agency, this chapter is weighted toward the experiences of Soviet tourists in Czecho-slovakia. I have included information from a small number of reports by Soviet Kom-somol guides and translators from the summer of 1968 describing their experiences working with Czechoslovak tourist groups in the USSR, but these do not provide a large enough sample to make broader conclusions about the experience of Czechoslo-vaks in the Soviet Union.

The trip reports provide a range of information about Soviet tourism to Czecho-slovakia, including the sites tourists visited, the people they met, relations with their Czech guides, and, especially in reports from 1968 and 1969, the political situation they encountered. A limitation, however, is that trip leaders presumed to speak for the experiences of the entire group and that they often tended to be members of the Com-munist party or Komsomol. In some cases they even held positions in city or regional party branches. The groups they led, on the other hand, were often not members of the party.[11] This may account for some of the pro-Soviet political and cultural views expressed in the reports. In addition, like other people who wrote to the Soviet author-ities, trip leaders had to be cautious of the views they expressed. As Anne Gorsuch has noted from a broad analysis of Soviet trip reports in the 1950s and 1960s, "Each trip leader had to fulfill the multiple, and sometimes untenable roles of cultural guide, political leader, and informant."[12] As I have tried to show, there was a large variation in trip reports on Soviet tourism to Czechoslovakia, particularly in the postinvasion period, though after August 1968 the tourists themselves seem to have been of a higher political caliber than in previous years.[13]

An Empire of Liberation: Soviet Tourism to Czechoslovakia before the Prague Spring

A 1963 guidebook to Karlovy Vary, the historic spa town in Czechoslovakia, advised Soviet tourists, "A tour of the city-resort usually begins from the V. I. Lenin Square.

This square is located several hundred meters from the hotel 'Moscow.' In the center of the square is the hotel 'Central,' where in 1936 the writer Aleksei Nikolaevich Tolstoi and his wife lived."[14] As this excerpt indicates, Soviet tours to Czechoslovakia—and indeed the Eastern bloc as a whole—were designed to emphasize the familiar. Describing the Soviet domestic tourist experience, Anne Gorsuch has argued that "postwar tourism was decidedly not about forming 'new impressions' but about internalizing official ones." Quoting Linda Ellerbee, she describes such tourism as a "ritual of reassurance."[15] This description also fits the Soviet tours of Czechoslovakia designed by Intourist (the Soviet state foreign travel agency) and Čedok. In addition to the country's traditional landmarks and natural wonders, such as the Prague castle and the caves near Brno, tourists' itineraries highlighted sites with Russian/Soviet associations. Among these were Soviet war memorials and cemeteries, the museum of Lenin in Prague, the house where Maxim Gorky had lived in Mariánské Lázně, and the Karl Marx museum and monument to Peter I in Karlovy Vary. Soviet tourists were frequently billeted in hotels named after Soviet cities. For entertainment they attended dinners with Czechoslovak comrades in honor of significant occasions in Soviet life such as Khrushchev's seventieth birthday, or performances of Russian ballets.[16] These itineraries thus mirrored official goals for Soviet-Czechoslovak relations, and cultural and political differences were deemphasized. Instead, the tourists' attention was directed to the unifying power of socialism. The underlying assumption was that as socialism advanced in Czechoslovakia the country would become more like the USSR, thus ensuring mutual understanding.

At the end of World War II, Czechoslovakia arguably offered the most promising conditions for Soviet ambitions in Eastern Europe. The specter of the Western powers' betrayal of Czechoslovak sovereignty at Munich in 1938 led the country to seek postwar security with the Soviet Union. The USSR's popularity was further augmented by the Soviet army's role in liberating the country from the Nazis in the spring of 1945. In addition, widespread support within Czechoslovakia for socialism and enthusiasm for pan-Slavism aided relations. Yet despite these positive indicators, the question of Czechoslovak autonomy remained a thorn in Soviet-Czechoslovak relations. Following the schism between the Soviet Union and Yugoslavia in 1948, the Communist Party of Czechoslovakia (KSČ), under the slogan "The Soviet Union Is Our Model," sought to Sovietize most aspects of public life.

Tourism was supposed to symbolize a new reciprocity in Soviet-Czechoslovak relations in the post-Stalin period, but vestiges of Soviet domination nevertheless remained. Soviet travel literature about Czechoslovakia depicted the USSR as an empire of liberation for having freed Czechoslovaks from the "bourgeois exploitation" of the First Republic (1918–38) and, more significantly, from the Nazi occupation.[17] The gratitude and even adulation Soviet tourists expected from their Czechoslovak hosts feature prominently in their trip reports.[18] Czechoslovaks "see in Soviet youth above all the representation of a nation of liberators," a Sputnik group from the Crimea reported in 1965.[19] A tourist group from the Tula region, who visited Bratislava on a holiday commemorating the Soviet liberation in 1964, observed, "The whole city came to the hill to lay flowers at the monument to the liberators. We . . . could not hold back tears from emotion. At the hill there was even an improvised meeting with children, who presented us with albums and asked for autographs."[20]

Despite such harmonious accounts, Soviet tourism to Czechoslovakia also reflected tensions in Soviet-Czechoslovak power relations. A recurrent source of contestation between the countries was the inclusion of landmarks from Czechoslovakia's presocialist past in Soviet tourists' itineraries, particularly churches and castles. "The group was not as interested in the life of barons who lived two hundred to three hundred years ago, whom even many people in Czechoslovakia don't know much about, as they were in the contemporary life in this country: how people work, spend their leisure time, how workers study, what their interests are," a trip leader from Arkhangel'sk claimed.[21] Such complaints from Soviet tourists represent more than simply a confrontation between Soviet-style socialism and the remnants of Czechoslovakia's bourgeois past; they detail the ongoing struggle between Soviet and Czechoslovak nationalisms that lurked beneath rhetoric of international friendship. In the 1960s, as Czechoslovakia grew more independent from the Soviet Union, Soviet-Czechoslovak tourism increasingly became a battleground between competing national and collective forms of identity.

Tourism with a Human Face: Debates in the Mid-1960s

In the mid-1960s, tourism became a focal point in debates over the modernization of Soviet-Czechoslovak relations. In 1967, the popular Czechoslovak journal *Květy* (Flowers) published an interview between its editor, Jan Zelenka, and the Soviet ambassador to Czechoslovakia, Stepan Chervonenko, on relations between their countries. Zelenka argued that despite the long history of Soviet-Czechoslovak friendship, "a space for human relations" was still missing. Tourism was one of the areas he suggested where this new space might be created. Zelenka complained that tourism "between Čedok and Intourist is too overorganized [pereorganizovan]," "too confined by defined boundaries [slishkom szhat opredelenymi ramkami]. It is the type of tourism that predominates in the majority of . . . civilized, culturally developed countries. But tourism between our countries [should be] much more."[22]

Zelenka's remarks were echoed by citizens in both countries, who pointed to contradictions in the way rhetoric about transnational "friendship" translated into policies on tourism. For instance, Soviets and Czechoslovaks were encouraged to become friends through pen pal correspondence, yet until 1965, Soviet restrictions prevented its citizens from traveling to Czechoslovakia on private visits to nonfamily members, and vice versa. Pen pals thus could meet only by traveling with tourist groups.[23] Soviet citizens found such limitations humiliating. A trip leader from the Kalinin region, in his report back to the tourism councils, wrote:

> In the future, in order to develop friendly relations between our peoples, it would be expedient . . . to give the most morally stable and politically literate people the right to take trips around the country individually, so that the Soviet person could freely visit his Czech friend, and Czechs their Soviet friends. The existing limitations cause harm to the business [prinosit' vred delo] of strengthening friendship. . . . We were bombarded with questions: Why can the Germans, Americans, Brits freely travel to visit their Czech friends, and why can't our best, dearest friend—the Russian—travel to visit a Czech?[24]

Even after the Soviet Union signed an agreement to open up visaless travel with Bulgaria, Czechoslovakia, Poland, and East Germany in 1965—a policy designed to allow Soviet citizens to visit nonrelatives in these countries—a variety of bureaucratic obstacles remained in place. The inviting party had to issue his guest an invitation, which had to be reviewed, for trips to Czechoslovakia, by both the Soviet and Czechoslovak police. In addition (as the Czechoslovak embassy in Moscow complained), the Soviets did not advertise the terms of the new agreement in public, or even to Intourist and other tourism agencies. Soviet officials responded to the Czechoslovak government's complaints by saying they had no intention of broadly publicizing the rules for visaless travel. In frustration, the Czechoslovak embassy in Moscow concluded, "Tourism between the ČSSR and the USSR is an area of contact that does not completely correspond with the level of political, economic, and cultural ties between our countries."[25] These discussions reveal the limits of Soviet internationalism: the extent to which the Soviet Union still feared foreign influences in the 1960s—even from the very people who were supposed to be its friends.

Swinging Czechoslovakia

In the mid-1960s, Czechoslovakia underwent belated de-Stalinization, resulting in at least a partial "erosion of the Iron Curtain."[26] Prague, in particular, was transformed from yet another "gray" Eastern bloc city into the unofficial capital of cosmopolitan activity—and 1960s culture—in the region. Tourists from all over the world flocked to the country.[27] At the Prague castle, "All possible languages are heard," *Sotsialisticheskaia Chekhoslovakiia* (Socialist Czechoslovakia) bragged, "Russian, German, English, Italian, Spanish—even Esperanto and Japanese."[28] A *New York Times* article from May 1968 enthused, "Prague is a throbbing city. Something close to hand-to-hand combat is required to conquer a table at a restaurant after the evening's activities, and taxis are as elusive after dark as the strains of music in the night air."[29] The contrast between the fervent Czech capital and staid Soviet cities was readily apparent to Soviet observers. For some, including reformist members of the intelligentsia and the small "colony" of Soviet journalists and functionaries who lived in Prague, this difference was exciting. "Prague exuded inspiration," Sergei Iurskii, a Soviet actor who visited Czechoslovakia in the winter of 1968, remembered.[30] Artemy Troitsky, who spent his adolescence in Czechoslovakia, where his parents worked for the journal *Problemy mira i sotsializma* (Problems of Peace and Socialism), recalled:

In Prague everything was simple. There were several clubs in the centre of the city . . . and every week there were concerts by beat groups. The Matadors played like The Yardbirds, The Rebels played "west coast," Framus-5 played r'n'b and The Olympics sang in Czech in the Beatles' style. . . . My favourite book at the time was, of course, *The Catcher in the Rye* and for want of a hunter's cap I walked around Prague in a yellow chequered cotton cap with a long visor, eyeing all the stunning grown-up girls in mini-skirts, inhaling other people's tobacco smoke while standing in line for concert tickets, running "Crystal Ship" through my head over and over again.[31]

For many Soviet tourists, however, encounters with this heady atmosphere amounted to culture shock. Many of the new trends on display in Czechoslovakia fell outside the purview of what was officially acceptable in Soviet society. Soviet tourists frequently expressed anger and bewilderment when describing their exposure to these new phenomena, including nonrepresentational art, 1960s counterculture, and the sexual revolution. "During a visit to the picture gallery in the city of Bratislava we were told that they didn't have a building to display classical art," the trip leader of a group from Kemerovo reported. "A building, however, had been found for abstract 'art,' where for the most part naked women are 'drawn' in the strangest poses. Our mood was spoiled after seeing these 'masterpieces.'"[32] Similarly, a group from Belarus described their confusion upon encountering abstract art at the National Gallery in Prague: "The accompanying translator Ženja Kudritská and our guide tried their best to justify the abstract art paintings, to prove that abstract art has a great future. . . . Unfortunately almost no one in our group knew that in Czechoslovakia for a long time there has been a discussion going on in the press about socialist realism as an outmoded method of art, and that abstract art has many admirers in the ČSR. For all the members of the group that was unexpected."[33]

Such comments reveal Soviet tourists' discomfort upon realizing that they no longer represented a cultural vanguard in the eyes of their Czechoslovak hosts. On the contrary, they found themselves relegated to the role of provincial cousins in Czechoslovakia's swinging cities. Tourists from Sverdlovsk were shocked by the capital's hippies: "Groups of young men with messy hair down to their shoulders and barefoot girls roam the streets of Prague, evidently without any real occupation."[34] The leader of a Komsomol tour group appeared simultaneously attracted and repelled by pictures of "girls in miniskirts, and even a series of postcards of naked women and girls" for sale at city kiosks. He concluded, "We saw much that was good and wonderful in golden Prague, but that kind of thing and similar occurrences . . . left an unpleasant aftertaste of disappointment in the soul."[35]

Even more unsettling for Soviet tourists was the fact that many of their Čedok guides seemed to enjoy shocking them with political commentary that fell far outside the norms of Soviet-Czechoslovak relations. In Prague these guides were freelancers who led tourist excursions in their free time; they represented a cross section of Czechoslovak society, "students, housewives, pensioners, civil servants," as well as "young historians," who worked the tourist circuit as a form of professional training. In addition to extensive schooling in the history of the city's monuments, the guides were expected to be fluent in the languages of the tour groups they led.[36] Interestingly, probably because of the latter requirement, many of the guides for Soviet tour groups were Russian émigrés or their children.[37]

A group from Kyrgyzstan in 1965 complained that its guide's "ideological-political level does not fulfill the requirements for working with foreigners. It wasn't pleasant for us to hear praise for abstractionism, the standard of living in the FRG, and that in the [Soviet] Union, 'everything is done under pressure.'"[38] Two years later, a group from Iaroslavl' accused their guide, a student at an institute of higher education, of "disrespect to our country" because he "constantly tried to prove that we are incorrectly informed by our press about the state of affairs in the West, etc." The group suggested that guides for Soviet tourists should be more experienced and better "prepared politically."[39] Instead of potential friends, Soviet tourists increasingly viewed all Czechoslovaks as provocateurs. A Komsomol group complained: "In a series of instances several Czech citizens tried to turn completely neutral conversations into discussions of complex political problems, asking provocative questions, purposefully giving incorrect commentary [zavedomo oshibochno kommentirovali] on issues of Soviet domestic and foreign policy." Of their three Czech guides, they added, "Only Miroslav Adamec was sufficiently erudite and prepared for work with Soviet tourists; however, even he made attempts to tell anti-Soviet anecdotes and to sing forbidden songs."[40]

The Prague Spring

Alexander Dubček's promotion to first secretary of the KSČ in January 1968 marked the official beginning of the Prague Spring. In the following months, victims of the Stalinist terror in Czechoslovakia were rehabilitated, censorship was first relaxed and then lifted entirely, and a variety of political clubs were formed, leading to talk that the country might even embrace a multiparty system for the first time since 1948.[41] These changes had a deep impact on the experiences of both Czechoslovak tourists in the USSR and Soviet tourists in Czechoslovakia. Tourism came to highlight the very thing it had been intended to erase: political and cultural differences between the two countries. For Soviet tourists who had previously complained about the inclusion of too many churches and castles on their tours, the scenes they now witnessed appeared heretical. A group of schoolteachers observed May Day celebrations in Prague and declared themselves "shocked": "The city was poorly prepared for the holiday, the show was absolutely disorganized, there were no flowers. . . . A group of students from the medical faculty marched with slogans in support of Israel. Others marched with portraits of Masaryk. And no one stopped [them]. And when we asked why this was so, the answer was: we have democracy, everyone is allowed to express their own opinions."[42] A group from Sverdlovsk who visited Prague in July noted: "Meetings were going on in the central streets from morning until late in the evening. A collection of signatures was organized in support of the liquidation of the people's militia [narodnoi militsii]; moreover, [these petitions] were signed by tourists from the FRG, England, etc. Portraits of Masaryk [and] Beneš were displayed in kiosks and shop windows, but there were none of the leaders of the communist movement."[43] During the Prague Spring, even those sectors of Czechoslovak society committed to maintaining close ties with the Soviet Union began to openly question many of the traditional tenets of their country's relationship with the USSR. *Svět sovětů* (World of the Soviets), the official magazine of the Union of Czechoslovak-Soviet Friendship (SČSP), which had once extolled all aspects of life in the USSR, now published a series of articles reevaluating Czechoslovak-Soviet relations, in between spreads on fashion, film stars, and even photographs of topless women: "It is very alarming that after chanting slogans about eternal friendship over and over, how small in fact our intimate [důvěrná] knowledge of each other is: that is, factual and unsentimental knowledge, including various weaknesses and shortcomings. . . . Results, not words, must become the measure of our friendship."[44] The quest for "factual and unsentimental knowledge" found its way into Czechoslovak travel writing about the Soviet Union. The Prague Spring's travel writers sought to undermine the USSR's official, sanitized image, especially its role as the singular model for Czechoslovakia's political development, by exposing contradictions between Soviet propaganda and the reality of daily life in the USSR. They depicted the Soviet Union as a country of contrasts, caught between success and failure: the model urban planning of the New Arbat in Moscow versus the destruction of the city's historic neighborhoods; "stores with tiring lines from morning to night, from week to week, for everything," versus "modern means of transport"; "comfortable new cities" in Siberia versus the monotony of panel high-rises replacing traditional wooden villages. "It is . . . a land whose people make unbelievably perfect rockets and spaceships, transplant artificial organs, yet bungle the simplest skilled handicrafts," one article concluded.[45] The Soviet service industry's failings were highlighted; anecdotes about rude taxi drivers and salespeople belied the myth of the USSR as a land of "friends" and inspired unfavorable comparisons with Czechoslovakia.[46]

In this new approach, instead of emphasizing similarities between Soviet and Czechoslovak society, travel accounts argued that mutual understanding should be predicated on respect and tolerance for fundamental differences. In reevaluating relations with the Soviet Union, *Svět sovětů* wrote, "It will be necessary to emphasize more often that the Soviet Union is not Czechoslovakia, that we cannot apply our standards to it, that the mentality of the Soviet people is not the same as ours. . . . This is natural, logical, and could not be otherwise." This new attitude undermined a central aspect of the friendship project between the USSR and Czechoslovakia: the idea that socialism alone could provide the basis for *sblizhenie*. "We agree that we are all part of a shared socialist program and that we have definitely put an end to capitalism. But otherwise everyone is different [každý jinak]."[47] Such statements mark an important shift in the balance of power in Soviet-Czechoslovak relations. Czechoslovaks now saw their nation as supplanting the Soviet Union as the vanguard of the socialist world. These new political differences between Czechoslovakia and the USSR put a strain on tourism. Politics had, of course, always been central to tourism between the countries, but before the Prague Spring it had served as a unifying factor, as both sides were engaged in building the same type of socialism. Soviet tourists traveled to Czechoslovakia as ambassadors of socialism; Czechoslovak tourists went to the Soviet Union to see a vision of their own future. In 1968, however, the two countries' conceptions of socialism diverged. For Czechs, the ability to express political as well as cultural differences with the Soviet Union was liberating, even intoxicating. It represented a fundamental reversal in the balance of power. Iurskii, the Soviet actor who traveled to Prague in the winter of 1968, described this imbalance in an anecdote about being interviewed by Czech reporters. "These were strange interviews. The interviewers asked me little, instead they talked more, [they] breathlessly described their [country's] changes."[48]

For most Soviets, this reversal in the status quo was more disturbing; the revival of Czechoslovak autonomy represented an attack on Soviet hegemony. In Soviet accounts, previously friendly and deferential Czechs were transformed into arrogant, aggressive proponents of their country's new political path. "From the very first day of their arrival in our country, this group radically differed from all previous Czech groups I've worked with," a Komsomol interpreter reported. He claimed that the Czech tourists were disrespectful to the Soviet Union: they dismissed Siberia and Central Asia as impoverished and laughed at a brochure about class conflict they found on a train, claiming "capitalist exploitation no longer exists."[49] A Soviet guide for a group of Czechoslovak teenage pioneers and their leaders remarked, "According to the leaders of the group, none of the members had received special instructions before their trip to the Soviet Union, but every citizen of the ČSSR knew that the group was . . . 'asked to tell the truth about the events in Czechoslovakia.' It must be said that the leaders of the group continually fulfilled this request."[50] The situation was the same for Soviet tourists in Czechoslovakia. "During the [train] journeys from Čop-Prague, Prague-Brno, Brno-Oloumoc . . . several representatives of the Czechoslovak young intelligentsia and students tried to foist [naviazyvat'] political discussions on the tourists of our group, they tried to propagandize the political platform laid out in 'Two Thousand Words.'"[51]

Soviets' tendency to portray themselves as unwillingly drawn into political disagreements with heretical Czechs may have been an attempt to shield themselves from accusations by the authorities of showing sympathy with their Czechoslovak interlocutors. Czechs were eager to use Soviet tourists in particular as witnesses to refute claims in the Soviet press about counterrevolutionary activity in their country. One trip leader reported how a Prague TV correspondent had stopped him as his group visited the Prague castle in July 1968 and asked whether he had seen anything on his trip to corroborate "rumors abroad that things are not calm in our country." The guide answered in the negative. In his report back to the Komsomol shortly after the Soviet invasion of Czechoslovakia, however, he claimed, "Now I am very displeased with my answer. If this question had been asked when I read the announcement by the five communist parties [about the invasion] and had spent even two more weeks in the country, then the answer would have had to have been different."[52]

To avoid such potential faux pas, officials in the Soviet tourism industry tried to prepare Soviet tourists for encounters with their ever more troublesome Czechoslovak "friends." At least some Soviet tourist groups received lectures on the political situation in Czechoslovakia, including decisions issued by the Presidium and Central Committee of the KSČ and the contents of the Two Thousand Words Manifesto detailing support for the political reforms. One group even met with Soviet delegates returning from the World Youth Festival in Sofia (described by Nick Rutter in this volume), who reported on the "moods" of Czechoslovak youth.[53]

In Czech accounts, the dynamics of curiosity were reversed. Instead, *they* were the ones besieged by curious Soviets, who, deliberately kept in the dark by their media, were eager to learn the truth about events in Czechoslovakia. A Czech journalist recounted how his peaceful train journey from Moscow to Kiev was interrupted when the other passengers discovered where he was from. The Soviets rushed into his compartment, offering food and peppering him with questions about whether it was really true that censorship had been lifted in Czechoslovakia.[54] In his account, and others like it, the argument that ensued did not result in any revelations on either the Czech or Soviet side, but it did lead to a new version of mutual understanding between them—in effect, an agreement to disagree: "I freely confess that in the heat of the debate we said some sharp words to each other, which would in no way be allowed in diplomatic protocol. But it never for an instant ceased to be a lively and passionate dispute between friends, [one] that was discussed so passionately precisely because it was about the friendship and reciprocity that deepen knowledge and understanding."[55]

Difficult Journeys: Tourism after the Soviet Invasion

The night of 20 August 1968, a Komsomol tour group from Chita was in Karlovy Vary: "The town was clean and quiet; the well-designed shop window displays sparkled with cleanliness. In the evening twilight the lights burned at the hotels Volgograd and Moscow. In the cozy little square our Lenin stood on a short pedestal. . . . In the morning we woke up to the terrifying howl of the loudspeaker. In tones reaching a howl, radio station announcers reported . . . the occupation of Czechoslovakia by the Warsaw Pact forces." When the group ventured out of their hotel, they witnessed two men across the street chopping down a sign with a slogan by former Czechoslovak first secretary Klement Gottwald, "With the Soviet Union for eternity."[56] The report's jarring juxtaposition of the "clean and quiet," "cozy" Czechoslovakia before August 20 and the chaos the Soviet tourists awoke to the next morning serves as a useful metaphor for how the invasion transformed Soviet tourism to Czechoslovakia. What little remained of the ritual of reassurance came to a dramatic end. Soviet tourists were no longer welcomed as "liberators." Instead, they came to be treated by both Czechs and the Soviet government as representatives of an occupying regime.

With the invasion, Soviet tourists' entire experience in Czechoslovakia changed. Guides refused to take them to the sites traditionally included on their itineraries, such as the Lenin museum and landmarks associated with World War II or Soviet-Czechoslovak friendship. When a group from the Penza region passed the Soviet World War II tank monument in Prague, their Czech guide was pointedly silent, instead directing their attention to a nearby "modern vegetable store."[57] Other guides even replaced the traditional landmarks celebrating Soviet power with new ones designed to flaunt its oppression: the facade of the National Museum in Prague riddled with bullets from Soviet tank fire, the square named after Jan Palach, the Czech student who had burned himself to death to protest the invasion.[58]

Soviet tourists now faced a range of humiliations during their travels. Locals excoriated them as "fascists" or "Asians," or simply yelled at them to get out of the country.[59] A series of (empty) Soviet tour buses were vandalized.[60] Workers refused to meet them, they were denied service in shops, and they complained that while Western newspapers were widely available it was impossible to obtain the Soviet press.[61] Many of their Čedok guides made no attempt to conceal their antipathy toward the Soviet Union. In 1969 a group from Kalinin complained that at a ceremonial dinner sponsored by Čedok on the anniversary of the October Revolution they were mysteriously presented with calendars from 1968 and tourist brochures titled "Prague in August 1968." The Čedok guide for a group from Kirovanda region told them: "You should not make your conclusions from the speeches of those demagogues who have been telling you about the friendship and brotherhood of our peoples. All of that is idle talk. The feeling of friendship must be in the hearts of people, and we have absolutely none [of this left] after August 1968."[62] "The general opinion of the group about the trip is difficult to express in two words," a trip leader from Kuibyshev concluded. "Almost no one expressed regret about the trip, but the trip also brought little joy."[63]

Why did the Soviet government continue to promote tourism to Czechoslovakia at a time when even the secretary of the Central Committee for the Union of Czechoslovak-Soviet Friendship estimated that only 20 percent of the population "firmly support cooperation with the USSR"?[64] Soviet authorities did suspend Sputnik groups from traveling to Czechoslovakia immediately following the invasion, but they reinitiated them in mid-October 1968.[65] One answer is that exposing Soviet citizens to anti-Soviet attitudes and behaviors in Czechoslovakia probably helped augment support for the invasion within the USSR. While the sympathy of Soviet dissidents and some students and members of the intelligentsia for the Prague Spring is well known, there does not appear to have been much popular support for the Czechoslovak reforms within broader Soviet society.[66] Confrontations with angry Czechoslovaks could be used as further proof that the invasion had been necessary, underscoring Soviet propaganda that loyal Czechoslovakia had been taken over by "rightist forces" in the pocket of Western imperialists.[67] "The events that took place in Czechoslovakia once again reminded us that we must be vigilant, that the forces of imperialists and worldwide counterrevolution do not slumber and do everything to estrange the brother peoples of the socialist countries," a trip report from a group from Kaliningrad concluded.[68]

At the same time, Soviet officials saw tourism as a key element of their policy of "normalization": the attempt to return both internal Czechoslovak politics and Soviet-Czechoslovak relations to the pre-1968 status quo.[69] In the fall of 1968 and throughout 1969 Soviet tourists became ambassadors of normalization, called upon to defend Soviet actions to the Czechs and Slovaks they met on their travels.[70] For such tourists, the pleasures of travel now took a back seat to political duty. The composition of the tourist groups changed accordingly: they now included more "propagandists" and other party functionaries.[71] Ambassador Chervonenko argued that the quantity of Soviet tourists traveling to Czechoslovakia was less important than "the quality of their ideological and moral preparation." He urged Sputnik, in particular, to select tourists for these trips carefully. The ideal candidates were "politically prepared communists and Komsomol members who will be able to lead discussions [and] explain the policies of the KPSS and the Soviet government in relation to Czechoslovakia."[72] Special emphasis was also placed on sending groups of World War II veterans who had taken part in the liberation of Czechoslovakia in 1945 to meet with their Czechoslovak counterparts.[73]

What are we to make of the notion that Czechoslovaks angry about their country's occupation by Soviet forces would be assuaged by the presence of a supporting army of Soviet tourists? A similar idea was proposed by the Soviet Central Committee's Department of Agitation and Propaganda, suggesting Soviet-Czechoslovak relations could be improved by organizing sports or chess matches between the Soviet occupation forces and local youth, complete with exchanges of pins and other "souvenirs."[74] Such expressions of faith in the healing powers of transnational, interpersonal ties can also be found in Soviet tourists' trip reports from the postinvasion period. Noting that youth tended to be the most anti-Soviet segment of Czechoslovak society, they suggested sending more youth tourist groups to the country;[75] when workers refused to meet them, they proposed equipping future Soviet groups with Lenin pins that they could offer to any locals they met by chance.[76]

Do these proposals demonstrate cynicism, idealism, or simply lack of imagination regarding relations with Czechoslovakia? The answer seems to be all of the above. The stubborn clinging to the traditional rituals of Soviet-Czechoslovak friendship speaks to the cynicism at the root of Soviet policy to Czechoslovakia, where rhetoric about transnational friendship served to sugarcoat imperialist aims. But it also returns to the utopianism that continually coexisted with that cynicism and that reached its apex during the Prague Spring. This was the fantasy of *sblizhenie*: the idea that the better Soviets and Czechoslovaks came to know each other, the closer the two nations would become, and that personal ties between citizens could transcend national differences. It was an idea that remained powerful, at least on the Soviet side, even after the events of the Prague Spring.

Soviet tourists were mixed in their assessments of whether this strategy was successful. Several divided the Czechoslovak population into categories based on their support for the Soviet Union or lack thereof. One group, for instance, suggested three categories: those in their forties and fifties, who related well to Soviet tourists; twenty-five- to forty-year-olds, who were "reserved"; and youth (under twenty-five), who expressed negative attitudes toward the USSR.[77] War veterans were the most likely to show support for the Soviets. A group of Soviet tourists made up entirely of World War II veterans visited Slovakia in May 1969 and attended a memorial ceremony at the site of the battle of the Dukla Pass in Prešov, which they described in terms similar to the standard, pre-1968, liberation narratives: "The older generation begged [us] not to consider the events [of 1968] their fault [and said] that nonetheless friendship and brotherhood will be restored. During the delivering of souvenirs to the Slovak officers and expressions of thanks for preserving the memorials to the soldiers, some of the residents and officers of the Czechoslovak army cried."[78] Other groups were more equivocal. "A mood unfriendly to the Soviet people still reigns among some citizens of the ČSSR. . . . Healthy-minded people say that a lot of time is required in order to renew a normal position."[79] Still other groups gave more pessimistic accounts of their missions to convert Czechoslovaks to the path of normalization. One group reported that although they were all members of the regional or city branches of the Moscow Komsomol, they still felt underprepared when they encountered such statements as "[In World War II] your people bore the brunt of the victims—but that was done to strengthen the influence of the USSR . . . in the West," and "We want to find our own path, like in Yugoslavia." For discussions with Czechs to "have some kind of useful outcome," they suggested that future tourist groups be given handouts with typical questions and arguments that the Czechs might advance, along with possible answers and counterarguments from the Soviet perspective.[80] Another group simply concluded, "Contacts with the local population were of no consequence. We did not meet with any warm relations from the side of the Czechs and Slovaks."[81]

The Quest for Mutual Understanding

Many obituaries have been written for the Prague Spring. In his history of postwar Europe, Tony Judt writes that the Soviet invasion marked the moment when "the soul of communism had died" on the Continent.[82] Petr Vail' and Aleksandr Genis argue that it signified the end of the sixties era in the USSR.[83] Was the Soviet occupation of Czechoslovakia also the death knell for the dream of friendship of the peoples?

From the beginning there were always two sides to the friendship project between the USSR and Czechoslovakia: a political strategy to maintain Soviet power, and a utopian attempt to create a new, socialist form of foreign relations founded on transnational, personal connections. In terms of the first goal, despite the Soviets' show of military force in the invasion, "the events in Czechoslovakia" resulted in a significant erosion of Soviet power. As Nick Rutter's chapter on the 1968 World Youth festival shows, the Prague Spring was but one event in the 1960s that undermined solidarity in the socialist bloc. Scholars have also noted that the seeds of the Soviet Union's own collapse were planted during the Prague Spring; many of Gorbachev's reforms during perestroika were based on those initiated by Dubček twenty years before.[84]

But what of the second goal? As this chapter has shown, in the mid-1960s both Soviets and Czechoslovaks complained that their countries' relations, including in the realm of tourism, were overly formulaic and restrictive. The Prague Spring changed that, although ultimately not in the ways that either side had hoped. The volatile political situation in Czechoslovakia, combined with the suspension of censorship in the Czechoslovak press, did, however, result in a brief period of openness between Soviets and Czechoslovaks that was unprecedented and would not be repeated until at least 1989. For the first time Soviets and Czechoslovaks engaged in real conversations and arguments touching on such previously taboo subjects as freedom of the press, travel, and the advantages of socialism as compared to democracy.[85] These debates began during the Prague Spring itself with *Svět sovětu*'s travel articles about the USSR, the political arguments that ensued on Soviet tourists' trips to Czechoslovakia, and Czechoslovaks' travels to the Soviet Union. What is surprising is that they continued even after the invasion. A Czech guide's denunciation of a group from Kazakhstan as "occupiers" led to a spirited argument about the meaning of the term.[86] A group from Sverdlovsk stayed up until four in the morning arguing with their Czech guides about the invasion, Czechoslovak history, and the Vietnam War.[87] Later they met two students on a train, who volunteered to act as guides and show them around Prague. "The discussions ended in an uncompromised struggle,"[88] the group concluded. At the same time, the tourists and the students seem to have developed some affection for one another. "During our walks, when we noticed an anti-Soviet slogan on a wall, one of the guys turned his back to us. They were both embarrassed."[89] A Komsomol group traveling to Czechoslovakia in February 1969 concluded, after a chance meeting with some local youth, that "despite the fact that at times [our] arguments were very heated and critical, we were able to reach normal human relations with them; we met again, and with the guys from Prague we will to some degree even remain friends in the future. . . . This was all despite the fact that neither we nor they succeeded at changing the opinions of the other."[90] Such accounts hint that the crises of the Prague Spring and the invasion may have, briefly, created a version of the "space for human relations" that both Czechs and Soviets had begun advocating for in the mid-1960s. In this respect, the utopianism of the 1960s lingered on even after the political reforms of the Prague Spring had been reversed.

Notes

1. On the political and cultural movements of the 1960s as a global phenomenon, see *1968: The World Transformed*, ed. Carole Fink, Philipp Gassert, and Detlef Junker (Cambridge: Cambridge University Press, 1998); Mark Kurlansky, *1968: The Year That Rocked the World* (New York: Ballantine, 2004); Arthur Marwick, *The Sixties: Cultural Revolution in Britain, France, Italy, and the United States, c. 1958–1974* (Oxford: Oxford University Press, 1998); and Tony Judt, *Postwar: A History of Europe since 1945* (New York: Penguin Press, 2005), chs. 12 and 13.

2. See the chapters by João Gonçalves and Nick Rutter in this volume.

3. Gerd-Rainer Horn and Padraic Kenney, "Introduction: Approaches to the Transnational," in *Transnational Moments of Change: Europe 1945, 1968, 1989*, ed. Gerd-Rainer Horn and Padraic Kenney (Lanham, MD: Rowman and Littlefield, 2004), x.

4. See, for instance, *The Prague Spring and the Warsaw Pact Invasion of Czechoslovakia in 1968*, ed. Günter Bischof, Stefan Karner, and Peter Ruggenthaler (Lanham, MD: Lexington Books, 2010), and *Prazhskaia vesna i mezhdunarodnyi krizis 1968 goda: Stat'ii, issledovaniia, vospominaniia*, ed. M. G. Tomilina, S. Karner, and A. O. Chubarian (Moscow: MFD, 2010).

5. On Soviet internationalism in this period, see Eleonory Gilburd, "To See Paris and Die: Western Culture in the Soviet Union, 1950s and 1960s" (PhD diss., University of California, Berkeley, 2010), ch. 1, "Soviet Internationalism," 16–46. See also Eleonory Gilburd, "The Revival of Soviet Internationalism in the 1950s," in *The Thaw: Soviet Society and Culture in the 1950s and 1960s*, ed. Eleonory Gilburd and Denis Kozlov (Toronto: University of Toronto Press, forthcoming). On Soviet tourism to Eastern Europe, see Anne E. Gorsuch, "Time Travelers: Soviet Tourists to Eastern Europe," in *Turizm: The Russian and East European Tourist under Capitalism and Socialism*, ed. Anne E. Gorsuch and Diane P. Koenker (Ithaca: Cornell University Press, 2006), and Zbigniew Wojnowski, "Patriotism and the Soviet Empire: Ukraine Views the Socialist States of Eastern Europe, 1956–1985" (PhD diss., University College London, 2010), esp. ch. 2, "National Supremacy: Soviet Travels in Eastern Europe," 106–39.

6. In 1967, 38,923 Soviet tourists visited Czechoslovakia through the auspices of the state travel agency, Intourist, the trade unions, and Sputnik, the Komsomol's travel agency. Approximately the same number were expected to travel to Czechoslovakia in 1968, according to a 1966 agreement on tourism between the USSR and Czechoslovakia, yet because of the events this article examines, only 24,031 did. By November of 1969, instead of the planned 32,343, Intourist predicted the number of Soviet tourists visiting Czechoslovakia would be around 28,675. Data on Czechoslovak tourism to the USSR from November 1969 indicate that 42,346 people came in 1967 and 29,405 in 1968, while 25,410 were projected for 1969. See reports and other documents on agreements regarding the exchange of tourists between the USSR and Czechoslovakia, 1969, in Gosudarstvennyi arkhiv Rossiiskoi Federatsii (hereafter GARF), f. 9520, op. 2, d. 24, l. 30.

7. On romanticism as integral to the Soviet sixties, see Petr Vail' and Aleksandr Genis, *60-e: Mir sovetskogo cheloveka* (Moscow: Novoe literaturnoe obozrenie, 1996), and Vladislav Zubok, "Soviet Society in the 1960s," in Bischof, Karner, and Ruggenthaler, *Prague Spring*, 75–102. On the tourist song movement and Soviet planners' ideas of "rational consumption," see the chapters by Christian Noack and Susan Reid, respectively, in this volume.

8. Nikolai Barsukov, "The Rise to Power," in *Nikita Khrushchev*, ed. William Taubman, Sergei Khrushchev, and Abbott Gleason (New Haven: Yale University Press, 2000), 60.

9. "On the Creation of the Soviet-Czechoslovak Friendship Society," 1957, in GARF, f. 9576, op. 2, d. 53, l. 33.

10. Letters to the Union of Soviet Friendship Societies, 1957–58, in GARF, f. 9576, op. 4, d. 38, l. 5.

11. Trip leaders sometimes made references to separate meetings they held with the party members on their tours; for an example, see reports by group leaders on trips to Czechoslovakia, 1969, in GARF, f. 9520, op. 1, d. 1344, l. 60.

12. Anne E. Gorsuch, *All This Is Your World: Soviet Tourism at Home and Abroad after Stalin* (Oxford: Oxford University Press, 2011), 22.

13. Usually information in these reports on the composition of individual tour groups was limited to the city or region where the tourists came from and, in a few cases, their professions. Of the forty-three reports examined for this chapter, only two provide the tourists' professions. Anne Gorsuch reports that in the late 1950s and early 1960s the majority of Soviet tourists traveling to Eastern Europe were from the technical and creative intelligentsia: "academics, cultural workers, factory managers, party functionaries, housewives." See Gorsuch, "Time Travelers," 210. It seems unlikely that the composition of Soviet tourists groups to Czechoslovakia in 1968–69 had changed significantly, although groups after the invasion seem to have included more party members and functionaries than previously.

14. Aleksei Kraizinger, *Karlovy Vary: Putevoditel' dlia sovetskikh turistov po gorodu-kurortu* (Prague: Svět sovětů, 1963), 34.

15. Anne Gorsuch, "There's No Place Like Home: Soviet Tourism in Late Stalinism," *Slavic Review* 62,no. 4 (Winter 2003): 784–85.

16. Reports by leaders of tourist groups on trips to Czechoslovakia, 1964, in Rossiiskii gosudarstvennyi arkhiv sots'ialno-politicheskoi istorii, Molodezhnyi arkhiv (hereafter RGASPI), f. M-5, op. 97, d. 207, l. 150; reports by group leaders on trips to Czechoslovakia, 1962, in GARF, f. 9520, op. 1, d. 493, l. 28; reports by leaders of tourist groups to Czechoslovakia under the auspices of Intourist, vol. 1, 1964, in GARF, f. 9520, op. 1, d. 726, l. 24.

17. I would like to thank Michael Geyer for suggesting the term *empire of liberation*.

18. Reports by group leaders on trips to Czechoslovakia, 1963, in GARF, f. 9520, op. 1, d. 599, l. 48.

19. Reports by leaders of tourist groups about trips to Czechoslovakia, 1965, in RGASPI, f. M-5, op. 1, d. 326, l. 57.

20. Reports by leaders of tourist groups to Czechoslovakia under the auspices of Intourist, vol. 1, 1964, in GARF, f. 9520, op. 1, d. 726, l. 105.

21. Reports by group leaders on trips to Czechoslovakia, 1965, in GARF, f. 9520, op. 1, d. 891, l. 14.

22. *Květy*, October 1967, article translated into Russian, in "Material from the Soviet Embassy in Czechoslovakia on Issues Related to the Czechoslovak Press," in Arkhiv vneshnei politiki Rossiiskoi federatsii (hereafter AVP RF), f. 198, op. 49, r. 113, d. 10, l. 44.

23. For examples of SSOD's responses to Soviet citizens' requests to visit pen pals in Czechoslovakia, see correspondence between the Society for Soviet-Czechoslovak Friendship and individual citizens of the Soviet Socialist Republics, 1958, in GARF, f. 9520, op. 1, d. 32, l. 27 and 1. 136.

24. Reports by group leaders on trips to Czechoslovakia, 1965, in GARF, f. 9520, op. 1, d. 891, l. 62.

25. "The State of Tourism and Private Visits by Czechoslovak and Soviet Citizens after the signing of the Protocol on Visaless Contacts between the ČSSR and the USSR in 1965," in Archiv Ministerstva zahraničních věcí (hereafter AMZV), TO SSSR, Tajne, 1965–69, box 2, folder 6.

26. "Problems Related to the Struggle against the Infiltration and Influence of Anticommunist Ideology and Propaganda in the ČSSR," in Ústav Soudobé Dějiny (hereafter ÚSD), Sbírku dokumentů Komise vlády ČSFR pro analýzu událostí let 1967–1970, inv. 274, sign. DI/274 k. 7, l. 12.

27. In the first four months of 1968, tourism from the capitalist countries increased by 25 percent. Czechoslovak Ministry of Foreign Affairs to Kosygin, 15 May 1968, in AMZV, TO SSSR, Tajne, 1965–69, box 2, folder 6.

28. "Znakomtes," *Sotsialisticheskaia Chekhoslovakiia*, no. 12 (1967): 8.

29. "Cultural Life in Prague Is Thriving amid Change," *New York Times*, 28 May 1968.

30. S. A. Iurskoi, "Zapadnyi ekspress," excerpted in *Praga: Russkii vzgliad. Vek vosemnadtsati-vek dvadtsat' pervyi* (Moscow: VGBIL, 2003), 295, originally published as S. A. Iurskoi, *Igra v zhizn'* (Moscow: Vagarius, 2002).

31. Artemy Troitsky, *Back in the USSR: The True Story of Rock in Russia* (Boston: Faber and Faber, 1987), 29.

32. Reports by group leaders on trips to Czechoslovakia, 1966, in GARF, f. 9520, op. 1, d. 1007, l. 61.

33. Reports by leaders of tourist groups about trips to Czechoslovakia, 1965, in RGASPI, f. M-5, op. 1, d. 326, l. 73.

34. Reports by trip leaders to Czechoslovakia, 1968, in GARF, f. 9520, op. 1, d. 1238, l. 22.

35. Reports by leaders of tourist groups about trips to Czechoslovakia, part I, January–August 1968, in RGASPI, f. M-5, op. 2, d. 87, l. 186.

36. "Znakomtes," *Sotsialisticheskaia Chekhoslovakiia*, no. 12 (1967): 8.

37. See for instance, reports by group leaders on trips to Czechoslovakia, 1969, in GARF, f. 9520, op. 1, d. 1344, l. 64.

38. Reports by leaders of tourist groups about trips to Czechoslovakia, 1965, in RGASPI, f. M-5, op. 1, d. 326, l. 137.

39. Reports by trip leaders to Czechoslovakia, 1967, in GARF, f. 9520, op. 1, d. 1131, l. 2.

40. Reports by leaders of tourist groups about trips to Czechoslovakia, 1965, in RGASPI, f. M-5, op. 1, d. 326, l. 59.

41. Mark Kramer, "The Czechoslovak Crisis and the Brezhnev Doctrine," in Fink, Gassert, and Junker, *1968*, 122–23.

42. Reports by leaders of tourist groups about trips to Czechoslovakia, part I, January–August 1968, in RGASPI, f. M-5, op. 2, d. 87, l. 16.

43. Reports by trip leaders to Czechoslovakia, 1968, in GARF, f. 9520, op. 1, d. 1238, l. 22.

44. "Mluví se o nás," *Svět sovětů*, 12 March 1968, 13.

45. "O Sovětském svazu nově-ale jak?" *Svět sovětů*, 28 May 1968, 3–4.

46. "Kolik tváři má Moskva?" *Svět sovětů*, 4 June 1968, 3.

47. "O Sovětském svazu nově-ale jak?" 3.

48. Iurskii, "Zapadnyi ekspress," 295.

49. Reports by guide-interpreters on the arrival of groups from Czechoslovakia in the USSR, 1968, in RGASPI, f. M-5, op. 1, d. 628, ll. 140–41.

50. Reports by guide-interpreters on the arrival of groups from Czechoslovakia in the USSR, July–September 1968, in RGASPI, f. M-5, op. 1, d. 629, ll. 42–43.

51. Reports by leaders of tourist groups about trips to Czechoslovakia, part I, January–August 1968, in RGASPI, f. M-5, op. 2, d. 87, l. 54. The Two Thousand Words Manifesto, written by prominent members of Czechoslovak society, expressed support for the Prague Spring reforms. For the text, see *The Prague Spring 1968*, ed. Jaromír Navrátil (Budapest: Central European University Press, 1998), 177–81.

52. Reports by leaders of tourist groups about trips to Czechoslovakia, part I, January–August 1968, in RGASPI, f. M-5, op. 2, d. 87, l. 106.

53. Ibid., l. 183.

54. "Listy z ukrajinského deníku," *Svět sovětů*, 18 June 1968, 5.

55. Ibid.

56. Reports by leaders of tourist groups about trips to Czechoslovakia, part I, January–August 1968, in RGASPI, f. M-5, op. 2, d. 87, ll. 188–89.

57. Reports by group leaders on trips to Czechoslovakia, 1968, in GARF, f. 9520, op.1, d. 1237, l. 3.

58. Reports by leaders of Soviet tourist groups on trips to Czechoslovakia, vol. 1, 1969, in RGASPI, f. M-5, op. 2, d. 129, l. 91.

59. "Excerpt from the Protocol No. 61 9s of the Secretariat of the Central Committee" (material originally from Russian archives), in ÚSD, 5266 Z/S/120, l. 198.

60. Aide-mémoire from the Soviet Embassy in Prague to the Czechoslovak Ministry of Foreign Affairs, 31 July 1969, in AMZV, TO. SSSR Tajne, 1965–69, box 7, folder 3.

61. Reports by group leaders on trips to Czechoslovakia, 1969, in GARF, f. 9520, op. 1, d. 1344; reports by group leaders on trips to Czechoslovakia, 1968, in GARF, f. 9520, op. 1, d. 1237, l. 3.

62. Reports by group leaders on trips to Czechoslovakia, 1969, in GARF, f. 9520, op. 1, d. 1344, l. 121.

63. Reports by group leaders on trips to Czechoslovakia, 1968, in GARF, f. 9520, op. 1, d. 1237, l. 10.

64. "Tourism and the Activity of Intourist, 1969," in AV PRF, f. 198, op. 50, p. 120, d. 21, l. 38.

65. Ibid., l. 1.

66. On the reactions of the intelligentsia, see, in particular, Ludmilla Alexeyeva and Paul Goldberg, *The Thaw Generation: Coming of Age in the Post-Stalin Era* (Boston: Little, Brown, 1990), 209–11, and Zubok, "Soviet Society in the 1960s," 92–96. On reactions within broader Soviet society, see Amir Weiner, "Déjà Vu All Over Again: Prague Spring, Romanian Summer and Soviet Autumn on the Soviet Western Frontier," *Contemporary European History* 15, no. 2 (May 2006): 187–89, and *Russia's Sputnik Generation: Soviet Baby Boomers Talk About Their Lives*, ed. and trans. Donald J. Raleigh (Bloomington: Indiana University Press, 2006).

67. For an example, see "Document No. 114: *Pravda* Editorial Justifying the Invasion, August 22, 1968 (Excerpts)," repr. and trans. in Navrátil, *The Prague Spring 1968*, 457.

68. Reports by group leaders on trips to Czechoslovakia, vol. 2, 1969, in GARF, f. 9520, op. 1, d. 1345, l. 25.

69. The term *normalization* was used as early as June 1968 by the Central Committee of the Communist Party of the Soviet Union, in a report about providing assistance to the KSČ to "normalize the situation in the country." "On Acquainting the TsK KPSS with the Position in Czechoslovakia, 1968–69," in Rossiiskii gosudarstvennyi arkhiv noveishei istorii (hereafter RGANI), f. 5, op. 60, d. 1, l. 92. For uses of the term by Czechoslovak leaders following the invasion, see H. Gordon Skilling, *Czechoslovakia's Interrupted Revolution* (Princeton: Princeton University Press, 1976), 802. *Normalization* has also become a historiographical term used to denote the broader postinvasion period in Czechoslovakia, extending through the late 1980s. See Paulina Bren, "Mirror, Mirror on the Wall . . . Is the West the Fairest of Them All? Czechoslovak Normalization and Its (Dis) Contents," *Kritika* 9, no. 4 (Fall 2008): 804.

70. "Excerpt from the Protocol No. 61 9s of the Secretariat of the Central Committee" (material originally from the Russian archives), in ÚSD, 5266 Z/S/120.

71. See "Developing Friendly Contacts between Regions of the USSR and Regions of the ČSSR," in RGANI, f. 5, op. 61, d. 10, l. 50; and reports by group leaders on trips to Czechoslovakia, 1968, in GARF, f. 9520, op. 1, d. 1237, l. 2.

72. "Tourism and the Activity of Intourist, 1969," in AV PRF, f. 198, op. 50, p. 120, d. 21, l. 1.

73. Reports by group leaders on trips to Czechoslovakia, 1969, in GARF, f. 9520, op. 1, d. 1344, l. 3.

74. "On Agitation-Propaganda Work in Czechoslovakia," 1968, in RGANI, f. 5, op. 60, d. 37, ll. 28–30.

75. Reports by group leaders on trips to Czechoslovakia, 1969, in GARF, f. 9520, op. 1, d. 1344, l. 53.

76. Ibid., l. 15.

77. Ibid., l. 7

78. Ibid., l. 2.

79. Ibid., l. 88.

80. RGASPI, f. M-5, op. 2, d. 129, l. 52.

81. Reports by group leaders on trips to Czechoslovakia, 1968, in GARF, f. 9520, op. 1, d. 1237, l. 9.

82. Judt, *Postwar*, 447.

83. Vail' and Genis, *60-e*, 310.

84. See Robert English, *Russia and the Idea of the West: Gorbachev, Intellectuals and the End of the Cold War* (New York: Columbia University Press, 2000), ch. 3.

85. The role of tourism in promoting unprecedented openness within the Eastern bloc was not limited to Soviet-Czechoslovak relations. See an interesting article about arguments over the future

of communism in Czechoslovakia between locals in Prague and tourists from the GDR, "Tourists Debate Prague Citizens," *New York Times*, 29 July 1968, 3.

86. Reports by leaders of Soviet tourist groups on trips to Czechoslovakia, vol.1, 1969, in RGASPI, f. M-5, op. 2, d. 129, l. 103.

87. Ibid., l. 3.

88. Ibid.

89. Ibid., 5.

90. Ibid., l. 47.

POPULAR CULTURE AND MEDIA

9 Postmemory, Countermemory

Soviet Cinema of the 1960s

Lilya Kaganovsky

Iɴ 1979, ɪɴ what was to be Her last interview, Larisa Shepit'ko spoke of a "genetic memory" that had left a clear "trace" on her second feature film *Wings* (*Kryl'ia,* 1966). Referring to her first film, *Heat* (*Znoi,* 1963), Shepit'ko underscored the similarity between herself and the protagonist: "He was my contemporary," she said, "he was eighteen and I was twenty-one. We were people of the same generation—the generation of the early sixties." *Wings,* on the other hand, was a different story:

> We, my film colleagues and I . . . dared to pass judgment on the older generation, on
> our fathers, and this imposed on us a particular responsibility. We needed to prove
> that we had the right to judge them. . . . On screen, we began a conversation about
> the not-so-easy lives of the wartime generation after the Victory. It was no longer
> possible for me to become one with the heroine—I didn't have my own experiences
> to rely on. Instead, I worked from intuition, from a kind of intuitive genetic mem-
> ory. If there really was such a memory—the memory of what happened during the
> war to my father and my mother and what happened to them in the difficult years
> after the war—then this memory is etched into the film.[1]

I have opened my discussion of Soviet sixties cinema with this passage from Shepit'ko because it helps to formulate what I take to be one of the central themes of the films made during this decade: memory (specifically, traumatic memory, the memory of the war) and its relationship to the generation that came after, the generation that did not live through Stalinism or the Second World War but that nevertheless felt itself to be responsible for the events of the past. This form of remembering has been called "postmemory," and, as Marianne Hirsch and others have defined it, it describes the relationship of the second generation to powerful, often traumatic, experiences that preceded their births but that were nevertheless transmitted to them so deeply as to seem to constitute memories in their own right.[2] As Hirsch has formulated it, postmemory is distinguished from memory by generational distance and from history by deep personal connection: "Postmemory is a powerful and very particular form of memory precisely because its connection to its object or source is mediated not through recollection but through an imaginative investment and creation. This is not to say that memory itself is unmediated, but that it is more directly connected to the past. Postmemory characterizes the experience of those who grow up dominated by narratives that preceded their birth, whose own belated stories are evacuated by the stories of the previous generation shaped by traumatic events that can be neither understood nor recreated."[3] Emerging from the field of Holocaust studies, this term resonates with Soviet cinema of the 1960s, which, from the beginning of the Thaw to the onset of Stagnation, set itself up against or counter to the cinema of Stalinism, with its utopian musical comedies, its grand historical films, its vicious traitors, and its epic battles for the victory of the Soviet Union on domestic and foreign fronts. Instead of monumentalism and the "Grand Style," sixties cinema gives us daily routine and intimate, domestic lives. It shows us interiors of communal apartments, whose crowded private spaces tend to be always in the middle of renovation. It takes us to wide, empty city streets where protagonists stroll in a way more resembling the Baudelairian *flâneur* than the New Soviet Man. Its distinctive visual features are the flashback, the closeup, the pan, the long take, and the use of the fisheye lens—an ultra-wide-angle lens that provides a 180-degree sweep, keeps almost everything in focus at once, and visibly distorts the edges of the screen. On Soviet screens, the Thaw was reflected not only by new storylines, new protagonists, and a general turn away from the discourse of socialist realism but even, as Oksana Bulgakowa has shown, by new bodily norms. The new young actors copied the relaxed bodily gestures of Hollywood and European stars: the loose hips of Elvis Presley, the bare feet of Brigitte Bardot, James Dean's slouch. In Soviet sixties cinema, tense back muscles are relaxed to show the body as liberated; slouched postures become a sign of antiauthority and nonconformity; there is a "liberation of legs and hips," "a new impetuousness" as protagonists fly up and down stairs; a freedom of the youthful body. Even the traditional May Day parade in Marlen Khutsiev's *Lenin's Guard* looks messy compared to its thirties' cinematic prototype when everyone marched in lockstep.[4]

At the level of storytelling, sixties cinema was marked by narrative fragmentation that spoke to an inability to tell a coherent story. Petre Petrov notes the consistency with which "everything subject to the force of time, everything bearing the mark of transience," is "arrested," indeed, "frozen" in Thaw cinema: "Childhood, youth, Spring, flight, pursuit, are all detached from the continuums of beginnings and ends, starting points and destinations, to which they had belonged, and are given independence and substantiality of their own."[5] Birgit Beumers points out specifically the ways in which all the war films (from the Thaw and the later 1960s) are fragmented in relation to time and chronology. She writes, "The flashback in silent cinema had been used for dreams or visions; in the 1920s the past could appear in montage sequences to explain cause and event or to juxtapose; Socialist Realism made filmic narratives linear and chrono-logical," while the Thaw began to use the flashback "to explain action" and indulge in "psychological realism."[6] Sixties cinema relies heavily on the flashback to structure—or more vitally—to deconstruct chronology and linearity. Time no longer flows in one direction (always toward a clear utopian future) but is halted, frozen, rewound, frag-mented, and erased. The trauma at the heart of Soviet sixties cinema is the trauma of the disjuncture of time: the historical time of the past and the seemingly anchorless, futureless, present.

The chronological limits of the Thaw are usually marked by events in Soviet politi-cal history: the beginning of the Thaw is associated with the death of Stalin, and the end with Khrushchev's removal from office (1964) and the Eastern bloc's invasion of Czechoslovakia (1968). Thus, in a sense, the Soviet 1960s actually covers two historical periods—the end of the Thaw and the beginning of Stagnation—and the films of the decade articulate the transition from the one to the other. We might argue (as Vladi-mir Semerchuk does) that sixties cinema was born with Marlen Khutsiev's 1962 *Lenin's Guard (Zastava Il'icha)*, released in censored and reedited form as *I Am Twenty (Mne dvadtsat' let)* in 1965.[7] The change from the optimism of the Thaw to the pessimism of Stagnation happens in or around 1966, with the release of *Wings, July Rain, The Long Happy Life*, and *Andrei Rublev*, and in 1967, with the release of *The Story of Asya Kliachina, Who Loved But Did Not Marry, Brief Encounters, The Commissar, No Ford through the Fire*, and *Three Days of Victor Chernyshev*.[8] It was at this point that the censors, already nervous from a lack of clear ideological directives, banned a number of films—including *Wings, Brief Encounters*, and *The Commissar*—whose nonlinear, fragmented narratives appeared to distort both Soviet reality and its heroic past.

While the films of the early Thaw concerned themselves explicitly with represen-tations of the Second World War, the new generation of filmmakers that came into prominence in the mid- to late sixties addressed something that we might call, follow-ing Shepit'ko, genetic memory, or following Hirsch, postmemory: a working through of a trauma that was not their own, that "belonged" to the previous generation, but that nevertheless continued to haunt the present.[9] While Thaw cinema remembers the traumas of war, Soviet sixties cinema, on the surface, seems to be located entirely in the present. Its most representative films are not historical; rather, they depict daily life, seemingly caught up in the minutiae of everyday existence, its modernity and contemporaneity. Indeed, the films are so "unsaturated" by history that they project a kind of anomie—a feeling that the characters live lives unconnected to the outside world, to history, to the previous generation: "Yes, we are cut off, and the link with the outside world is broken," Lena's new friend Zhenya tells her on the phone in *July Rain*. Yet films that are most clearly associated with the decade—such as Khutsiev's *Lenin's*

Guard and *July Rain,* Shepit'ko's *Wings,* Askol'dov's *The Commissar,* and Muratova's *Brief Encounters* and, I would argue, *The Long Farewell*—are structured around the loss of something that can never be recovered or repaired. This loss is articulated each time as the loss of men: of fathers, husbands, and lovers, whom we see only in flashback or not at all. But it is also metaphorical: it speaks to the unbearable trauma of the loss of paternal authority, of masculinity as absence.[10]

Trauma works against closure; it does not allow for comprehension, and it interrupts or breaks down narrative. As Cathy Caruth has argued, "What causes trauma, then, is a shock that appears to work very much like a bodily threat but is in fact a break in the mind's experience of time."[11] We see this most clearly at work in Askol'dov's 1967 *The Commissar,* where a "flash forward" makes possible the sudden intrusion of World War II and the Holocaust into a narrative of the Russian Civil War. Set in the years 1918–20, the film's central action takes place in the town of Berdichev, where Klavdia Vavilova, a Red Army commissar, has been demobilized to give birth to her baby. During the childbirth scene, we see a series of flashbacks and images of Klavdia's lover, killed in battle. But while these flashbacks point to tragedy and loss, they do not in themselves constitute a radical break. They are easy to assimilate into the larger narrative of the war. The device of the flash forward, on the other hand, speaks to a completely different form of trauma: a rupture in time that can be neither covered over nor repaired. Hiding in the basement during an air raid, Klavdia watches the members of the Magazanik family dancing in the dark to keep from being afraid. Abruptly, the scene shifts and we see the Magazanik family and the other Jews of the town walking into an internment camp. Inside, the men and women wear striped pajamas we associate with German concentration camps, and all are marked with the Star of David. Suddenly we find ourselves, not in 1919, but in 1941. Yet, the Holocaust is not simply imagined here as the necessary outcome of the passivity of the Jews; nor is it something that will have been prevented by the victory of the Red Army and the formation of a new Soviet state. Rather, it marks a traumatic rupture, a memory that has not been successfully processed or assimilated, that has not been "worked through," but that disrupts linear time, causing narrative to break down.[12]

If we place Soviet sixties cinema in its more "global" context, we can see the ways in which it too participated in the cinematic renaissance of the postwar period, whose most famous schools were Italian neorealism and the French Nouvelle Vague (New Wave). These movements were the by-products of a destroyed and politically compromised film industry; and the films of the French New Wave, taking over where Italian neorealism had left off, launched a brand-new generation of young avant-garde filmmakers whose films looked radically different from the "tradition of quality" practiced by the French cinema of the previous decade. Neorealism, the Nouvelle Vague, and the Soviet "New Wave" share formal elements: a preference for episodic and unconnected narratives, an open story structure, location shooting, the use of nonprofessional or semiprofessional actors, anecdotal "slice-of-life" scenes, and an "elegantly restless camera" that suggests a disregard for conventional film-making but also a desire to get away from a kind of "logocentric" discourse—that is to say, a discourse in the service of a governing idea that occupies much of classic narrative cinema. As André Bazin once said, speaking about the Agnès Varda's first film, *La pointe courte*, "There is a total freedom to the style, which produces the impression, so rare in cinema, that we are in the presence of a work that obeys only the dreams and desires of its *auteur* with no other external obligations."[13]

In the sixties, Soviet cinema experienced a rebirth after the extreme film shortages of the immediate postwar period. As Alexander Prokhorov notes in *Springtime for Soviet Cinema*, by the late 1950s all the studios of the Soviet Union were releasing about a hundred films a year, and by the mid-1960s the production stabilized at an average annual output of 150 films. Mosfil'm, the major studio of the country, was completely rebuilt, and in the 1960s Russia had one of the highest attendance rates per capita at movie theaters in the world. During these years, "Only vodka outstripped cinema in generating revenues."[14] The older generation of filmmakers that made a significant impact on Thaw and sixties cinema included Mikhail Kolotozov, Grigorii Kozintsev, and Mikhail Romm. The All-Union State Cinema Institute (VGIK), the main Russian film school, played a major role in the production and development of new cinematic talent: its instructors in the 1960s included Sergei Gerasimov (who trained Kira Muratova) and Aleksandr Dovzhenko (who trained Larisa Shepit'ko). Mikhail Romm's workshop or "ministudio" within Mosfil'm (opened in the late 1950s but shut down in 1960) provided the infrastructure for new and experimental projects and made possible the careers of a new generation of filmmakers, including Andrei Konchalovskii, Gleb Panfilov, Larisa Shepit'ko, Vasilii Shukshin, and Andrei Tarkovskii. As Ian Christie put it, Romm launched the sixties' New Wave.[15]

While Soviet sixties cinema can easily be placed within a "global" context in terms of its style and even, to some degree, its preoccupations (with youth, with alienation, with the possibility of a countercinema to work against the rigid codes of the previous decades), we can also trace a series of concerns that mark it as a product of a particular Soviet history and of a particular Soviet generation. Starting with Khutsiev's 1962 *Lenin's Guard*, we see that the alienation common to both Italian neorealism and the French New Wave is here the product of a generational split, the gap between the parents that lived through the war and the children that were born after. The generation gap is by now a standard observation about the culture of the sixties—as Vitalii Troianovskii puts it in his study of the sixties, "The first thing you notice when you look at the screen heroes of the 1960 is their youth."[16] And in *July Rain*, Alik declares, picking up the guitar, "How *not* to sing in a country filled with youth?" (Kak ne zapet' v molodezhnoi strane?)

But if we return to Shepit'ko's observation with which this chapter started, we can see that this generational split, seemingly celebrated by sixties culture, came at some cost: while the new generation (both behind the camera and on the screen) took it upon itself to judge the previous one, their own experiences were profoundly marked by the traumas of their parents. Not able to identify with what their parents went through, the new generation nevertheless found themselves living through the aftereffects of the trauma, dominated, as Hirsch suggests, by narratives that preceded their birth, their own "belated" stories evacuated by the stories of the previous generation that were shaped by traumatic events that could be neither understood nor recreated. The alienation, isolation, and fragmentation at work in sixties cinema is produced by the traumatic rupture in "time" that creates an unbridgeable gap between the generations. We might note with some irony Nikita Khrushchev's attack on *Lenin's Guard* for precisely failing to reflect on how Soviet youth "continued the heroic traditions of earlier generations."[17]

Lenin's Guard is a story about three friends, Sergei, Kolia, and Slava, trying to find their proper place in Soviet society. It is important to note that Sergei, our main protagonist, is coming back not from war but from mandatory military service. The trauma of war is represented by the picture of Sergei's father hanging on the wall, the father's letters from the front, and the mother's silences. When Vera, Sergei's sister, finds ration cards in an old book, she cannot understand what they mean because their meaning is tied to events forever foreclosed. As the mother tells her story of losing the ration cards and going out to the countryside to dig for potatoes (and returning to Moscow alone in the dark, surrounded by Germans), Vera demands to know about herself: "Where was I?" she keeps asking. "You didn't exist yet," says the mother, and when pressed to know why not, she repeats, "You didn't exist yet."

A memorable point in the film is a dream sequence in which Sergei is reunited with his father, killed during the war. Khutsiev seamlessly connects the dream sequence to everyday reality: as Prokhorov notes, "The viewer hardly notices the transition from Sergei's being in his apartment awake to his crossing the border of reality and stepping into the world of the war years, where he meets his father as a man younger than the protagonist is in the film's present."[18] Sergei's dream of his father plays out a cliché of the father-son relationship: what Sergei wants from his father is advice on "how to live." But this dream of paternal authority, of the "subject presumed to know," is undermined by the father's age—the father is two years younger than Sergei and therefore cannot offer him any advice beyond the basic. "Just live," he says. His final words to Sergei, echoing the ghost of Hamlet, are "Remember me."

Lenin's Guard is about the difficulty, the near impossibility, of maturation because all the previous models are either missing or compromised: commenting on the film in 1965, the writer Efim Dorosh notes that even Anya's father is compromised by an immediate association with Stalinism: "As soon as he begins to speak . . . about the necessity of knowing how to live, one immediately imagines him as one of those

Figure 9.1. Generation gap: Sergei and Anya's father in *Lenin's Guard* (1965).

who, perhaps indirectly, perhaps in one cell only, created that which we now call the cult of personality."[19]

Sergei has no father to tell him how to live, Kolia is being asked to assume the old Stalinist role of informer, and Slava fails to be either a good husband or a good father because he hasn't yet given up on his boyish desires or his childhood friends. The film frequently returns to the playground at the base of the apartment buildings where the three friends live—the swing set, the seesaw, the merry-go-round—visually reinforcing the theme of childhood that the young men can't quite leave behind.

In sixties cinema, fragmentation at the formal level (on the visual and sound tracks) echoes the disconnection between characters, their distance from each other. For example, Khutsiev's *July Rain*, a quintessentially New Wave film, opens with a ten-minute tracking shot through the streets of Moscow that at first glance gives the impression of continuity (of both time and space). The wide-screen format and the fisheye lens take in everything at once, giving Moscow streets the curvature of the earth.[20] The striking visuals are accompanied by an equally distinctive sound track: the sound of a radio being periodically changed from one station to another. The sound is disjointed: it is, first of all, pointedly nondiegetic because it is mismatched in terms of exteriority/interiority—we are outside moving along Moscow streets, but the sound seems to come from an interior space, either a car or an apartment. This radio sound is a "voice-off," existing in a space somewhere beyond the frame, a place we cannot see. Second, the sound is pointedly fragmented: we hear snippets of classical music, jazz, French chanson, a soccer match, a broadcast for children, programs in English, Radio "Mayak" announcing the time, and the distortion from the changing radio dial. The international (if not to say cosmopolitan) nature of the radio programs means that even though we are at the very center of the Soviet Union—in Moscow, on Gorky Street—we are listening to a short-wave radio receiving broadcasts from beyond its borders. (Yet as Zhenya says later in the film, "We are cut off, and the link with the outside world is broken.")

But there is yet more fragmentation here, because the tracking shot itself is not actually continuous—this is not a single take—but interrupted by still images of Renaissance paintings (or, more accurately, posters of Renaissance art mass-produced at Lena's workplace). There is a comment here about art in the age of mechanical reproduction, about film as translation, reproduction, copying; but it is also about disjuncture and interruption. The camera seems at first merely observational as it moves along the streets capturing the crowds going about their normal daily lives, but as it moves closer, looking for its object, the people it is watching become disconcerted, staring back at the camera that is looking at them. Khutsiev is playing with cinema verité techniques, and the effect is to underscore the presence of the cinematic apparatus, to provoke the subjects the camera is trying to film, and to remind the viewer that we are spectators. (Which is to say, it is another form of disjuncture: rather than being captivated by the events unfolding before us on the screen, losing ourselves in the fiction, we are constantly being jolted out of our spectatorial complacency and forced to remember that we are watching a film.) As the camera "locates" its object, Lena, and begins to follow her down the street, we see her turning around and glancing over her shoulder, aware that she is being followed, watched, filmed, reproduced.

July Rain was compared to the work of Michelangelo Antonioni almost immediately after its premiere and, like the films of Antonioni, was accused by Soviet critics of "plotlessness" and "anemia."[21] The movie critic Rostislav Iurenev, writing for *Sovetskaia kul'tura* in August 1967, pointed to the film's "boring" characters, "most boring parties," and "the tedious picnic" scene as other points of resemblance between this film and the work of Antonioni—only in the case of the Italian director, the "anomie" and disconnectedness stemmed from postwar bourgeois alienation, which made no sense in the Soviet context.[22] It depicts the empty lives of a now thirty-something generation, and it is precisely in the atmosphere of anomie and disconnectedness that we see the effects of trauma and postmemory at work. Like the opening sequence, there seems to be nothing that binds people together, nothing that connects people to each other. After their chance meeting, Lena and Zhenya spend much of the film talking on the telephone, but in the end they too are

Figure 9.2. Anomie: Volodya and Lena in *July Rain* (1966).

unable to find real intimacy. The telephone is an excellent metaphor for the problem of "connection," emphasizing the illusion of proximity: the telephone is an apparatus that carries a disembodied voice across distances without ever bridging the gap it is meant to cover over. "Listen, Zhenya," Lena says, "Maybe you don't actually exist? Well, maybe you are not really there. Maybe there's just your voice?"

For many critics, Khutsiev's *July Rain* marks the end of the Thaw, with its hopes and utopian illusions of a new community that could be reforged after the crimes of Stalinism and the trauma of World War II. The camera acts as a distanced observer, detached from the characters and the mise-en-scène; the cameraman German Lavrov observes and follows the characters, but always at a distance, never identifying with anyone's point of view (as Prokhorov notes, this practice is more typical of the horror or detective genre than of melodrama).[23] Here we don't have the individual in the community but "more a faceless flow of bodies mirrored by the grayish flow of automobiles on the street; merging as self-loss."[24] Contemporary Soviet critics, on the other hand, saw in the film's closing sequence a renewed sense of community and relation, "three generations of Russians coming together. . . . The individual that cannot be mass-produced [Lichnost' ne poddaiushchaiasia massovomu tirazhu]."[25]

Indeed, as we watch Lena walking again through Moscow, she smiles softly to herself, finally freed from the "impersonal" relationship with Volodya. Exiting onto the street, she walks past preparations for a celebration, seeing fragments of images on giant canvases and people carrying huge letters that will presumably form a slogan commemorating the war. She then walks through a reunion of war veterans on Victory Day, May 9, in Sverdlov Square. On the one hand, this scene recalls Kalatozov's ending to *Cranes Are Flying*, and we can see that the link forged between Veronika and the nation in Kalatozov's film is unforged here. Lena does not become a part of this celebration but remains on the outside, a mere spectator. The sound we hear at first is appropriately upbeat: a folksy victory song (with a chorus of voices joining in for the refrain) as we see veterans of the Great Patriotic War reunite with their comrades and fellow soldiers. This scene belongs almost to a different film, and *July Rain* cannot sustain it for long. Suddenly, we are looking, no longer at veterans, but at young men and women, college students and high school students—the next generation. Cinematic time is slowed as we linger on individual faces, the shots at first nearly empty, with figures standing apart and looking in different directions, but progressively becoming more crowded. Lena has disappeared completely (just as in the opening sequence she emerged out of the crowd of people walking down the street, now she dissolves back into that crowd, the camera no longer interested in following her). Instead, the film ends on a medium closeup of a boy's face, looking back at the camera. We understand that there is an unbridgeable gap between generations, a historical rupture caused not simply by the war but by the way people are able to relate to it as a memory. The giant letters that will form a slogan celebrating the victory over the Germans are disassembled, their meaning forever postponed or deferred.

This deferral is partially caused by absence: over and over again sixties films center on missing or absent men—fathers, husbands, lovers. The dream of meeting again the missing father that we see played out in *Lenin's Guard* is just one instance of this, repeated in *July Rain,* where preparations for the father's homecoming are interrupted by news of his sudden death. Lena's friend Zhenya seems to be just a "voice" on the telephone, and her fiancé Volodya can be described only in the negative: "Doesn't drink, doesn't lie, doesn't chase after women." The lyrics to the song played at one of "boring" parties stresses the role playing that is masculinity, referring to being a man as a "job" or an "occupation": "Comrade Man, we envy your job!" (Tovarishch muzhchina, a vse zhe zamanchiva dolzhnost' tvoia). Like *Lenin's Guard*, there are no real "men" here yet; instead we have a generation that doesn't quite know how to grow up.

Again and again (in a manner recalling the compulsion to repeat), films from the sixties imagine masculinity as a series of traces. In *Lenin's Guard,* the father is a picture on the wall, a voice reading a letter from the front, a flashback. In *July Rain,* the trace is reduced to a telegram announcing the father's death. In Kira Muratova's *Brief Encounters* (1967), we see the central male character, Maksim, only as a memory. The film has three timelines, two of which are given in flashback (the story of Valentina and Maksim; the story of Nadia and Maksim) and one of which is set in the present (the story of Valentina and Nadia). As Jane Taubman notes, there are sixteen flashbacks in all, arranged out of chronological order and only barely motivated by events in the present.[26] Valentina and Nadia are both in love with Maksim, and the film is built around the anticipation of his homecoming, which is forever postponed. The flashbacks give us his story in bits and pieces, and always from the female point of view—Maksim appears always in someone else's memory, conscious of being looked at, examined, analyzed.[27] At several points throughout the film he asks the women to stop looking at him: in his first meeting with Nadia, he claims that he cannot play because Nadia is looking at him too intensely (a line he repeats again in a different flashback), and he suggests to Valentina that if she truly loved him, she would look at him with her eyes "half-closed," with "blind eyes."

In the present time line, Maksim is merely a trace: he is the missing addressee of Valentina's nighttime monologues; a guitar left hanging on the wall; a voice barely heard over the phone; a tape recording on a reel-to-reel player; an empty place setting at a table set for two. As I. Izvolova observes in regard to the cassette player, "Once again, in place of the real arrival of her beloved, Valentina Ivanovna receives another indirect proof of his existence in the form of a tape recording."[28] Like his voice, Maksim's absence haunts the film. While the story told in *Brief Encounters* is the story of two women, at its center is the missing piece: the lost object that cannot be reclaimed through the work of memory.

Though there is nothing obviously traumatic about *this* memory, it nevertheless reveals the structure of absence at work in the Soviet films of the sixties. As film historian Andrei Plakhov noted, after seeing Muratova's 1989 *Aesthenic Syndrome,* "Now it has finally become clear what Muratova had in mind (it seems the censors were among the first to understand this) in her early films, when she filled them full of female languor and agitation. The capricious, high-strung emotions came not from loneliness, from the absence of a concrete man . . . , but from the suspicion that 'man' in general no longer exists in the world, that he has become a myth, like Vysotsky's hero from *Brief Encounters,* like Vysotsky himself."[29] If we consider Muratova's film alongside Larisa Shepit'ko's *Wings,* for example, we can see that a similar mechanism is at work, but its impact now is clearly traumatic: in *Wings* we are given (at first seemingly unmotivated) shots of a sky as seen from the cockpit of an airplane, a vision of an endless and forever receding horizon. The visions are at first disorienting, not only because we don't yet have a context into which we can fit them (we don't yet know that Nadezhda, our main character, used to be a pilot and that she still dreams of flight), but also because of the canted angle of the shot: the airplane from which we "see" is turned at a forty-five-degree angle in relation to the line of the horizon, reorienting our vision. The shots of the sky are finally contextualized by two flashback sequences, making it clear that their visual breakthrough is a manifestation of a traumatic memory. As Nadezhda walks in the rain holding before her a handful of berries, she remembers the "time before"—her convalescence during the war, Mitya, a fellow pilot and object of her affection, her return to combat, and his death. It is important to note that in the flashback that breaks through the narrative we see Mitya *as Nadezhda once saw him:* the shot is from her point of view, her look firmly aligned with the camera.

Just as in *Brief Encounters,* this is not an "unmediated memory" but a memory filtered through the subjectivity of the female protagonist. While Nadezhda herself remains invisible offscreen, we hear her voice addressing Mitya. Moreover, this memory sequence is not continuous but is further disrupted by the device of the freeze-frame: the flashback is not seamless, and its construction is made visible through the halting of time as shots are frozen on the screen and the magic of cinema as "moving" pictures is disrupted. This happens with the happy memory of Mitya himself, with the camera freezing on a closeup of his face, as well as with the memory of his death. As Nadezhda flies over the crash site, the sight of Mitya's burning plane is captured like a snapshot, immobilized in time. Once again, we are looking for the "missing piece"—the masculine subject—that seems to exist only in the past, only as a memory of the female protagonist. Flying combat next to him and then in circles around him as his plane begins to smoke and lose altitude, Nadezhda watches helplessly as Mitya's plane crashes to the ground. The final shot of this flashback is again given to us as a point-of-view shot, from the cockpit of Nadezhda's plane as she flies over the burning airplane, while people on the ground run toward the crash site. Like Maksim, Mitya here is the *"objet a,"* the object cause of desire, the film's missing piece.[30]

Picking up on all of these themes, however, is Muratova's 1971 *The Long Farewell,* which again centers its narrative on a missing paternal figure—Zhenya's ex-husband and Sasha's father, an archaeologist away somewhere in Novosibirsk. Again we are given the father as a series of traces: as handwriting, as a speaker on the other end of a telephone line (whose voice we cannot hear), as a box of photographs. The photographs—or rather, slides—are particularly interesting because the mechanism of their presentation speaks both to the theme of absent fathers and to cinema's relationship to memory. In two separate scenes we watch characters project slides onto the double doors of the apartment: first, Sasha looking at drawings of horses, possibly from his father's archaeological digs; then, Zhenya looking at photographs of Sasha and his father. The transparency of the images is emphasized by the fact that we can still see the frame of the double doors behind them. Both times, the door opens and another character walks in, opening up a hole in the projected image and providing a stark contrast between the image and physical reality. The projected slides are a metaphor for memory, and their transparency and impermanence (the last batch of slides catches on fire) speak to the profound sense of loss at work in this film. At the end, Sasha decides to stay with his mother, and the dream of being reunited with the father is forever foreclosed.

In *Death 24x a Second,* Laura Mulvey argues that at the point of registration cinema, like photography, participates in the inscription of reality in an unprecedented way: "something must leave, or have left, a mark or trace of its physical presence" in order for an image ("always specific and unique, although endlessly reproducible") to be made. This image, however, remains unprocessed—it cannot be understood—until it is organized and placed alongside other images that give it meaning. For Mulvey, cinema is defined as the registration of an image onto a surface, as the "mark of light." And it gains meaning only in retrospect: not at the moment of registration

Figure 9.3. Projection: Sasha and his father in *The Long Farewell* (1971).

but at the moment of assembly and projection. As Mulvey puts it, there is a parallel here with Freud's concept of "deferred action" *(Nachtraglichkeit),* the way the unconscious preserves a specific experience, while its traumatic effect might be realized only by another, later event. This "storage function" of cinema may be compared to "the memory left in the unconscious by an incident lost to consciousness," writes Mulvey. "Both have the attributes of the indexical sign, the mark of trauma or the mark of light, and both need to be deciphered retrospectively across delayed time."[31]

Photographs, suggests Hirsch, locate themselves precisely in the space of contradiction between the myth of the ideal family and the lived reality of family life: "Since looking operates through projection and since the photographic image is the positive development of a negative, the plenitude that constitutes the fulfillment of desire, photographs can more easily show us what we wish our family to be, and therefore, what, most frequently, it is not."[32] In suggesting the term *postmemory,* Hirsch insists that it is a powerful and very particular form of memory precisely because its connection to its object or source is mediated not through recollection but through an imaginative investment and creation: "Photographs in their enduring 'umbilical' connection to life are precisely the medium connecting first- and second-generation remembrance, memory and postmemory. They are the leftovers, the fragmentary sources and building blocks, shot through with holes, of the work of postmemory. They affirm the past's existence and, in their flat two-dimensionality, they signal its unbridgeable distance."[33] "Not only is the Photograph never, in essence, a memory," writes Roland Barthes, "but it actually blocks memory, quickly becoming counter-memory."[34]

The "genetic memories" etched into the films of the sixties belong to a prior generation—they are at once part of and not part of the filmmakers themselves, they speak through them about the trauma that came before. Deciphered retrospectively across delayed time, they show us the impossibility of the two generations coming together in understanding. In Soviet sixties cinema, the series of flashbacks, the freeze-frames, the traces of voices left on tape recorders or heard over phone lines act as "symptoms" making legible the work of trauma. Soviet sixties cinema can only stage the reunion with the father or husband or lover as an imaginary act, a wish fulfillment, a projection. Their fragmented narratives can no longer tell a straightforward story because the building blocks of those stories are shot through with holes. So instead they give us a perpetual present, a youth that will never grow old, and a long farewell to what can never be brought back.

Notes

1. E. G. Klimov, ed., *Larisa: Vospominaniia, vystupleniia, interv'iu, kinostsenarii, stat'i* (Moscow: Iskusstvo, 1987), 181.

2. For detailed discussion of postmemory as it relates to the Holocaust, see Marianne Hirsch, "The Generation of Postmemory," *Poetics Today* 29, no. 1 (Spring 2008): 103–28, and *Family Frames: Photography, Narrative, and Postmemory* (Cambridge, MA: Harvard University Press, 1997); Mieke Bal, Jonathan Crewe, and Leo Spitzer, eds., *Acts of Memory: Cultural Recall in the Present* (Hanover, NH: University Press of New England, 1998).

3. Hirsch, *Family Frames*, 22.

4. Oksana Bulgakowa, *Fabrika zhestov* (Moscow: NLO, 2005); Oksana Bulgakowa, dir., *The Factory of Gestures: Body Language in Film* (PPMedia and Stanford Humanities Lab, 2008), DVD, 160 minutes.

5. Petre Petrov, "The Freeze of Historicity in Thaw Cinema," *KinoKultura* 8 (April 2005), www.kinokultura.com/articles/apr05-petrov.html.

6. Birgit Beumers, *A History of Russian Cinema* (Oxford: Berg, 2009), 128.

7. Vladimir Semerchuk, "Smena vekh: Na iskhode ottepeli," in *Kinematograf ottepeli: Kniga vtoraia*, ed. Valerii Fomin (Moscow: Materik, 2002), 155.

8. *Kryl'ia* (Larisa Shepit'ko, 1966); *Iiul'skii dozhd'* (Marlen Khutsiev, 1966); *Dolgaia schastlivaia zhizn'* (Gennadii Shpalikov, 1966); *Andrei Rublev* (Andrei Tarkovskii, 1966); *Istoriia Asi Kliachinoi, kotoraia liubila, da ne vyshla zamuzh* (Andrei Konchalovskii, 1967); *Korotkie vstrechi* (Kira Muratova, 1967); *Komissar* (Aleksandr Askol'dov, 1967); *V ogne broda net* (Gleb Panfilov, 1968); *Tri dnia Viktora Chernysheva* (Mark Osep'ian, 1968).

9. Thaw-era classics about the Second World War include Mikhail Kalatozov's *The Cranes Are Flying* (*Letiat zhuravli*, 1957) and Grigorii Chukhrai's *Ballad of a Soldier* (*Ballada o soldate*, 1959) but also Lev Kulidzhanov and Iakov Segel's *The House I Live In* (*Dom, v kotorom ia zhivu*, 1957), Mikhail Romm's *Nine Days of One Year* (*Deviat' dnei odnogo goda*, 1961), and Andrei Tarkovskii's *Ivan's Childhood* (*Ivanovo detstvo*, 1962).

10. In *Cinepaternity*, Helena Goscilo and Yana Hashamova refer to the epidemic of "fatherless-ness" in Post-Soviet film and in post-Soviet culture as a "metaphysics of absence," tracing it back to the catastrophic loss of male lives in World War II. See Helena Goscilo and Yana Hashamova, eds., *Cinepaternity: Fathers and Sons in Soviet and Post-Soviet Film* (Bloomington: Indiana University Press, 2010), 1–25.

11. Cathy Caruth, *Unclaimed Experience: Trauma, Narrative, and History* (Baltimore: Johns Hopkins University Press, 1996), 61.

12. The film was based on one of Vasilii Grossman's first short stories, "In the Town of Berdi-chev" (V gorode Berdicheve, 1934) that did not, of course, contain such a flash forward: in the story, Klavdia imagines walking through the village holding her baby, as a way of getting back across the front lines. When Nazi Germany invaded the Soviet Union in 1941, Grossman's mother was trapped in Berdichev by the invading German Army and was eventually murdered together with twenty thousand to thirty thousand other Jews who had not evacuated. The device of the flash forward reproduces this traumatic history as a memory of the future.

13. Quoted in Richard John Neupert, *A History of the French New Wave Cinema* (Madison: University of Wisconsin Press, 2007), 60–61.

14. Alexander Prokhorov, "The Unknown New Wave: Soviet Cinema of the 1960s," in *Spring-time for Soviet Cinema: Re/Viewing the 1960s*, ed. Alexander Prokhorov (Pittsburgh: Russian Film Symposium, 2001), 8. See also Beumers, *History of Russian Cinema*, 112–45.

15. Ian Christie, "Back in the USSR," *Film Comment* 36, no. 6 (November/December 2000): 39–43. For overviews of 1960s cinema, see Valerii Fomin, ed., *Kinematograf ottepeli: Dokumenty i svidetel'stva* (Moscow: Materik, 1998); Josephine Woll, *Real Images: Soviet Cinema and the Thaw* (London: I. B. Tauris, 2000); Prokhorov, *Springtime for Soviet Cinema*. The 1962 volume *Molodye rezhissery sovetskogo kino* includes essays by Neia Zorkaia on Tengiz Abuladze and Maia Turovs-kaia on Marlen Khutsiev; *Molodye rezhissery sovetskogo kino: Sbornik statei*, ed. Ariadna Sokol'skaia (Leningrad: Iskusstvo, 1962). In 1965, the leading Soviet film journal *Iskusstvo kino* published an overview of twenty-six new directors, including Otar Ioseliani, Elem Klimov, Andrei Konchalovskii, Kira and Aleksandr Muratov, and Larisa Shepit'ko. See "Nachalo (predstavliaem molodykh rezhis-serov)," *Iskusstvo kino*, no. 6 (1965): 27–49.

16. Vitalii Troianovskii, "Novye liudi shestidesiatykh godov," in Fomin, *Kinematograf ottepeli: Kniga vtoraia*, 6.

17. Woll, *Real Images*, 147.

18. Prokhorov, "Unknown New Wave," 15.

19. Efim Dorosh in "Mne 20 let: Obsuzhdenie fil'ma," *Iskusstvo kino* no. 4 (1965): 27–46.

20. Originally developed for use in meteorology to study cloud formation and called "whole-sky lenses," fisheye lenses quickly became popular in general photography for their unique, distorted appearance. They are often used by photographers shooting broad landscapes to suggest the curve of the earth. In fisheye lenses, the visual angle is close to or more than 180 degrees in at least one direction.

21. See the public discussion of the film in March 1967, cited in Lev Anninskii, *Shestidesiatniki i my* (Moscow: Kinotsentr, 1991), 142.

22. I am grateful to Susan Larsen for sharing with me her excellent reading of *July Rain*.

23. Woll, *Real Images*, 222; Prokhorov, "Unknown New Wave," 17.

24. Prokhorov, "Unknown New Wave," 17.

25. E. Sidorov, "Mne 30 let," *Iunost'* 9 (1967): 87–88.

26. Jane A. Taubman, *Kira Muratova* (London: I. B. Tauris, 2005), 15.

27. Susan Larsen, "Korotkie vstrechi / Brief Encounters," in *The Cinema of Russia and the For-mer Soviet Union*, ed. Birgit Beumers (London: Wallflower, 2007), 124–25.

28. I. Izvolova, "Zvuk lopnuvshchei struny," *Iskusstvo kino* 10 (1968): 113.

29. Andrei Plakhov, "Kinematograf v podpol'e," *Strana i mir* 1 (1991): 156, quoted in Taubman, *Kira Muratova*, 12.

30. For my full discussion of these two films, see Lilya Kaganovsky, "Ways of Seeing: On Kira Muratova's *Brief Encounters* and Larisa Shepit'ko's *Wings*," *Russian Review* 71, no. 3 (Fall 2012): 482–99.

31. Laura Mulvey, *Death 24x a Second: Stillness and the Moving Image* (London: Reakton Books, 2006), 8–9.

32. Hirsch, *Family Frames*, 8.

33. Ibid., 22–23.

34. Roland Barthes, *Camera Lucida: Reflections on Photography* (New York: Hill and Wang, 1981), 91.

10 The Politics of Privatization

Television Entertainment
and the Yugoslav Sixties

Sabina Mihelj

ONE OF THE key dilemmas in scholarly debates about the sixties concerns the relationship between political contestation and culture. Were the struggles of the sixties primarily political, or should we rather see them, as Arthur Marwick suggests, as part and parcel of a "cultural revolution" whose impact went well beyond the realm of politics?[1] As the editors of a recent themed issue dedicated to the international 1968 put it: Did cultural change "merely [provide] the background for the political upheavals of the Sixties," or did it define "the very essence of this contentious period"?[2] Rather than opt for an account that gives greater prominence to either one or the other, this chapter approaches the sixties as a period during which the nature of politics itself, along with its link to culture, underwent a profound transformation. Both east and west of the Iron Curtain, long-established fault lines of political struggle, tied to the alternative visions of modernity espoused by communism, liberalism, and fascism, gave way to issues of living standards and social welfare, as well as to dilemmas of family relations, racial segregation, and youth culture—all issues traditionally on the margins of political debate, or considered parts of the private sphere and culture rather than politics proper. The venues and forms of political communication changed as well. As political contestation shifted to the realm of the private and the everyday, political struggle was increasingly waged through objects, symbols, and genres of popular culture and everyday life.

Nothing perhaps illustrates this shift better than the iconic "kitchen debate" between Richard Nixon and Nikita Khrushchev at the American National Exhibition in Moscow in 1959. During a series of impromptu exchanges that took place at various locations at the exhibition, the topic of conversation moved from the space and arms race to the question of which country was better equipped to provide its citizens with a high standard of living, thereby symbolically marking the shift in political priorities from the public to the private domain. "Would it not be better," asked Nixon, "to compete in the relative merits of washing machines than in the strength of rockets?"[3] Khrushchev took up the challenge. The seven-year economic plan adopted in 1959 promised to improve the provision of consumer goods and raise the living standards of Soviet citizens, and thanks to the mass housing campaign launched a few years earlier, thirty-eight million Soviet families moved into new apartments between 1953 and 1970.[4] Similar developments were under way elsewhere in the region: from Moscow and Warsaw to East Berlin and Budapest, growing numbers of socialist families experienced the sixties through the acquisition of their own private apartment, or even a family house.[5] The supply of consumer goods and private services improved as well—most obviously in Yugoslavia, but also in East Germany, Poland, and Hungary.[6] Across the socialist East, Stalin's death also opened doors for more conciliatory economic policies and informal workplace bargaining that contributed to improved working conditions as well as higher wages.[7] Slowly but surely, average livelihoods were getting better, and it was becoming abundantly clear that both the domestic legitimacy and the international prestige of the socialist project, just like those of its capitalist rival, hinged increasingly on the quality of everyday life.

Both east and west of the Iron Curtain, this expansion of politically relevant issues went hand in hand with the broadening of political participation. By challenging established political priorities and becoming more closely linked to the personal and the everyday, politics became attractive to a number of constituencies that would otherwise shun public debate: women, ethnic and racial minorities, youth, and the working classes. These constituencies, in turn, helped diversify the languages and arenas of public contestation and invested political meaning in forms of expression ranging from music tastes and sexual preferences to fashion choices and television entertainment. To be sure, the forms and extent of political contestation in the socialist East were significantly more subdued and circumscribed than those in the capitalist West and had to reckon with a state apparatus that was far more willing to resort to censorship and brute force. Nonetheless, the new possibilities spurred by post-Stalinist reforms did give rise to a considerably more relaxed political environment and thereby enabled the socialist East to join in the transnational upheavals of the sixties.

As this chapter seeks to demonstrate, television came to play a central role in these developments, acting as an important conduit of the privatization of politics and of the parallel growth of political participation. Both in the socialist East and in liberal democracies of the West, the 1960s were a decade of rapid expansion of television infrastructure and spectacular growth in the number of television receivers. At the start of the decade the United States and Britain were well ahead of any competition,

Table 10.1. ČSSR Diffusion of Television by Number of Inhabitants per TV Set

	UK	France	FRG	Ireland	Portugal	GDR	CSSR	USSR	Bulgaria	SFRY
1960	4.9	23.9	12.0		193.2	16.8	17.1	44.1	1577	612
1965	4.0	7.4	5.1	9.7	48.8	5.3	6.6	14.4	44.5	34.3
1970	3.4	4.6	3.6	6.8	22.3	3.8	4.6	6.9	8.2	12
1975	3.0	3.5	3.4	5.6	12.8	3.2	4.0	4.6	5.8	7.7

Calculations based on the total number of television licenses (or equivalent) and population estimates based on nearest census figures. Sources: Brian R. Mitchell, *International Historical Statistics: Europe, 1750-2005*, 6th edition (Basingstoke: Palgrave Macmillan, 2007) and Boris Alekseevich Miasoedov, *Strana chitaet, slushaet, smotrit: statisticheskiĭ obzor* (Moscow: Finansy i statistika, 1982).

but over the coming years countries on both sides of the Iron Curtain saw their television audiences increase at remarkable rates (table 10.1).

The mere expansion of broadcasting technology was of course not the only factor that made television so central to the privatization of politics and the expansion of political participation in the sixties. More decisive were its audiovisual character and the social uses of television that became prevalent in this period, above all the institutionalization of television viewing as a private and mass activity. Unlike radio, television had the ability to incorporate a much wider range of cultural forms and genres, including visual ones, and therefore had the means to make public affairs appealing to a considerably wider range of audiences. At the same time, the growth of private television ownership meant that experiences previously available only to the few were now accessible in the privacy of one's home—a fact that made the consumption and interpretation of political, cultural, and moral messages far less predictable and transparent, and considerably more open to individual whims.

The precise cultural and political implications of these changes are not easy to pin down. It is tempting to suggest—as many contemporary commentators in the West did—that the arrival of television actually prompted a decline, rather than growth, of public engagement. Already in the early postwar years, American sociologists Paul Lazarsfeld and Robert Merton suggested that the mass media instigated a passive, purely cognitive relationship to political reality and led citizens to mistake "knowing about problems of the day for doing something about them."[8] A few decades later, Michael Robertson likewise suggested a link between television and the weakening of public engagement but provided a different explanation: in his view, the negative coverage of the political process prompted cynical attitudes, and it was those that ultimately led to an estrangement from politics.[9] Even in recent years, the decline in civic engagement is often blamed on television, its privatizing effect on leisure time, its infatuation with apolitical entertainment, and its tendency to instigate pessimism and low levels of civic trust.[10]

Recent research on socialist television adopts a similar line of argument. In Kristin Roth-Ey's view, the adoption of domestic rather than collective television viewing gave rise to a cultural experience that was fundamentally different from the one envisaged by Soviet cultural ideals and dealt a deadly blow to the capacity of Soviet culture to act as a mobilizational tool. By the time the Soviet Union started falling apart in the late 1980s, its mass culture, with television at its core, had lost its ability to inspire and mobilize and had instead turned into a conduit of "experiences and ways of being in the world unconnected to broader political projects of any kind."[11] Paulina Bren's analysis of communist culture in post-1968 Czechoslovakia offers a broadly similar conclusion, though the focus here is not on the privatized nature of television viewing as such but on the specific cultural narratives spun by the little screen, particularly those embedded in the most popular television serials. These serials, argues Bren, acted as key vehicles of officially endorsed privatized citizenship and its preferred forms of family and work life, leisure practices, and intimate relationships, and they had a profoundly depoliticizing effect on Czechoslovak society after 1968.[12]

While such interpretations certainly elucidate important aspects of the privatization of politics in the socialist East and its links with television, the insight they offer is only partial. There are two main reasons for this. First, for all the similarities with the West, we should keep in mind that the scope, practices, and meanings of private life in the East were significantly different. The myriad forms of surveillance and the intricate networks of unofficial informants, though not without their own limits, clearly made socialist privacy far more circumspect and open to state control.[13] In purely material terms, socialist family dwellings were generally smaller than Western homes and, thanks to the preference for multistory apartment blocks, more standardized and more exposed to the prying gaze of neighbors and authorities.[14] Also, at the level of official attitudes and policies, support for privatization did not entail a retreat of the state from private affairs. In the Soviet Union, for instance, the provision of single-family apartments may have turned the need for privacy into a legitimate element of socialist life, but it also stirred up concerns over the decline of public life and was paralleled by state-led efforts to incite greater political participation.[15] In short, in the socialist context, privacy was and remained a profoundly public matter. It is feasible to expect that socialist television policies followed a similar logic—accepting the legitimacy of private television viewing but at the same time envisaging television as a mobilizer that would bind the private spaces of family homes to the common, public realm.

Second, the nature and consequences of socialist privatization and television culture were changing with time and context. By the 1970s, television was a well-established, nearly ubiquitous element of everyday life in the socialist East. Broadcasters had become accustomed to a diversity of tastes, stratified by age, gender, ethnicity, and class, and had developed program and genre solutions to respond to them—either by accepting the rifts between different publics as insurmountable or by bridging them using polysemic programs such as *Semnadtsat' mgnovenii vesny* (Seventeen Moments of Spring, 1973), discussed by Stephen Lovell in his chapter. This was also a time when communist authorities started taking television seriously not only as a technological challenge but as a communicative device with wide-ranging political and cultural repercussions. Political control over television increased, and communist elites became much more involved in decisions over content. In this context, television was far more likely to encourage depoliticization and a retreat into privacy. In the 1960s, by contrast, the challenge of mass, private television viewing was a new thing, one that neither broadcasters nor politicians had yet learned to master. Aided by the relaxed political climate following the Thaw and the popular fascination with the new medium, private television viewing had the potential to turn into a profoundly political experience.

To demonstrate these points, the remainder of this chapter examines the rise of television and the transformation of politics in socialist Yugoslavia. As shown through the investigation of archival documents and popular television serials, the privatization of politics and the proliferation of television sets in Yugoslav homes did not automatically go hand in hand with depoliticization. Rather than prompting a retreat into privacy, these changes initially encouraged greater popular participation in public affairs.

Yugoslav Television between Entertainment and Political Mobilization

News of television's imminent arrival to Yugoslav homes in the latter half of the 1950s was greeted with a familiar mixture of apprehension and enthusiasm. On the one hand, the prospect of mass television viewing inspired utopian projections of a better, more educated, refined, and politically engaged society. On the other, it provoked fears of social isolation, physical and mental passivity, and cultural mediocrity.[16] According to a literary scholar, for instance, television simply did not deserve to be considered as part of culture.[17] By the mid-1960s, those concerned about the corrupting effects of television on Yugoslav society could find much to worry about. Already the earliest audience studies confirmed that viewers were treating television as a source of entertainment rather than education or political engagement. According to a survey conducted in 1963 in the Yugoslav republic of Serbia, programs combining music, humor, and other forms of entertainment were achieving the highest viewing figures and together with transmissions of football matches regularly rivaled the popularity of prime-time news programs.[18] A study conducted among Croatian viewers in 1965 reached a compatible conclusion: 51.3 percent of those included in the survey described television as a means of relaxation and entertainment, and only 20.3 percent said they used it primarily as a means of information gathering.[19]

While members of the political and intellectual elites often reacted to this situation with disdain and fear, television professionals and the technical intelligentsia, eager to promote the development of the medium, were quick to suggest that the problem perhaps lay not so much in popular preferences for entertainment as such but rather in the quality of entertainment on offer. A report prepared in 1964 by the Yugoslav Radio-Television, discussed by the highest political bodies at the federal level, made it clear that entertainment was an integral segment of television programming. In the sphere of culture and art, stated the report, television had the task of "providing cultural relaxation and entertainment to the greatest possible number of viewers, without at the same time neglecting the works of special artistic value."[20] The yearbook of Yugoslav Radio-Television defined the aims of Yugoslav broadcasting in a similar way. Yugoslav television was expected to provide programs that were attractive to "all social strata" and "offered entertainment and relaxation" but also contained "an educational or moral message."[21] The solution was thus to be sought, not in treating entertainment as a necessary evil, but in finding ways to accommodate both the popular and the refined and in seeking to ensure a high level of political enlightenment, moral education, and entertainment among the population as a whole.

Another factor that encouraged such attempts to embrace entertainment and use it as a conduit of educational and moral messages was the official endorsement of popular participation in political affairs. As policy documents from the 1960s made clear, Yugoslav media were expected to function not only as means of top-down transmission of information but as a "political forum" designed to give voice to public opinion and help solve the pressing tasks of Yugoslav society. The "current stage of development," argued a programmatic document adopted in 1965, required the working people of Yugoslavia "to use the mass media to express their views regarding their own social life and further development," as well as to engage in the "struggle of opinions" and constructive criticism aimed at improving current conditions.[22] General cultural policies followed a similar tune. A document setting out the principles of cultural development, issued by the Association of Cultural Organizations in the Republic of Slovenia, could not be clearer: "The further development of culture is increasingly dependent on the mobilization of a wide number of citizens. Only mass cultural activity and large-scale cultural education of the working people [can provide] the basis of cultural development, new relationships, and a socialist ethics."[23]

Yugoslav television professionals were quick to exploit the opportunities opened by new political principles and emphasized the immense powers of television and their beneficial impact on Yugoslav society. In a lecture delivered in 1964 to the Educational-Cultural Council of the Croatian Assembly, the director of Radio-Television Zagreb argued that recent political reforms enabled radio and television to "fully realize their potential" and "allow the society to even more directly influence the work of self-managing organs."[24] The already mentioned report prepared by the Yugoslav Radio-Television in 1964 provides another case in point. Here Yugoslav television is praised for contributing to the "modernization of political work," for bringing the work of political bodies closer to millions of people, and for turning into a true "political forum."[25]

During the 1960s, humor was often at the center of efforts to bring television to bear on the political development of the country. There are several reasons for this. First, humor was perceived as a cultural form that had the potential to address contemporary realities in a critical as well as an entertaining manner. A number of studies conducted in the 1960s by the research unit of Television Belgrade—one of the main venues for radio and television research in Yugoslavia at the time—focused on "engaged humor" and on the ability of humorous programs to unmask the mechanisms of contemporary social problems.[26] Second, programs containing humor were immensely popular with audiences. According to a representative poll conducted in Serbia in May 1967, as many as 68.2 percent of viewers wanted television programs to contain more "humorous-satirical programs"—by far the most sought-after genre—while only 6.3 percent opted for more information and 10.8 for more educational programs.[27] Third, humorous programs were a well-established ingredient of Yugoslav radio production at the time, and television could draw on a pool of existing creative expertise—not a minor factor in times when both funding and experience were in short supply.

The remainder of the chapter examines two humorous TV series and uses them as a starting point to investigate the link between television, the privatization of politics, and popular participation in socialist Yugoslavia: *Spavajte mirno* (Sleep Peacefully), produced by TV Belgrade in Serbia in 1968, and *Naše malo misto* (Our Small Town), produced by TV Zagreb in Croatia in 1970 and 1971.

Self-Management and the Contradictions of the Yugoslav Sixties: *Sleep Peacefully*, Protest, and Containment

The airing of *Sleep Peacefully* in the spring of 1968 came after a prolonged period of unusually frank and vibrant public debate and wide-ranging reforms. The economic roots of these upheavals are well known. The early 1960s brought a decline in labor productivity and per capita real wages as well as a slowdown of economic growth. The ensuing reassessment of existing economic models gave rise to economic reforms that reduced administrative control over several areas of economic life, including the banking system, prices, and foreign trade, and fostered a shift from investment to consumption.[28] Despite much hyperbole surrounding the reforms, however, implementation was sluggish and benefits were slow to materialize. Rates of economic growth continued to decline, real wages were at best stagnant, and unemployment remained high[29]—a problem compounded by the coming of age of the postwar baby boom generations, which significantly increased the pressure on the labor market. To make things worse, income disparities were increasing as well,[30] and so was the frequency of workers' strikes; by 1969, the number of registered strikes, most common among industrial workers and miners, grew to two thousand.[31]

In and of themselves, not all of these problems were new—unemployment, for instance, had been rising throughout the 1950s, despite high rates of economic growth.[32] Yet in contrast to the 1950s, the underlying weaknesses of the Yugoslav economic system now grew in magnitude and were more openly discussed in public. While the initial stirrings of discontent, such as the early strikes among miners in Slovenia in the late 1950s, received little media coverage, the situation in the 1960s was different.[33] Public discussion of economic reform, living standards, unemployment, and social inequalities became more frequent and open.[34] The brewing dissatisfaction was not only surfacing in obscure intellectual and professional magazines; it was palpably present also in the mainstream press and on television screens. In 1965, TV Belgrade launched a series of talk shows entitled *Aktuelni razgovori* (Current Debates), aimed at addressing the most pressing social problems and involving contributors ranging from factory workers to some of the highest representatives in the Yugoslav economy and politics.[35] Television entertainment—including comic TV series such as *Sleep Peacefully*—turned political as well and helped translate the rather abstract terms of public debate into a language that was appealing to the wider population.

This explosion of public engagement cannot be reduced to economic reasons alone; it was also actively encouraged by the communist authorities themselves and was aided by political reforms that sought to reduce the role of the party and the state and to encourage popular participation in political affairs.[36] Central to these reforms was the notion of "direct self-management"—an idealistic vision of a society in which all public affairs are run directly by workers rather than by the party or by the state, and in which all property, including factories, is "socially owned." Originally devised in the aftermath of Yugoslavia's expulsion from the Cominform in 1948, the ideal of self-management provided a key pillar of Yugoslav political identity and served as a marker of Yugoslav specificity and superiority vis-à-vis the Soviet Union as well as vis-à-vis the capitalist West. By means of self-management, went the argument, Yugoslav society would steer away from the dangers of excessive bureaucratization that allegedly plagued the Soviet Union, as well as from the corrupting effects of unbridled economic liberalism supposedly rife in the West, and would thereby move toward a more advanced stage of socialism.[37] The political and economic reforms of the 1960s were presented as groundbreaking changes devised to make way for such developments.

With hindsight, such promises sound misleading; despite the reforms, Yugoslav politics and economy remained far from the self-management ideal. Yet as the debates sparked by *Sleep Peacefully* suggest, the discourse of self-management nevertheless commanded considerable influence over Yugoslav citizens and played an important role in the changing topography of sixties politics. On the one hand, the ideal of self-management suggested that the good life was now truly within reach and in fact dependent on one's own involvement in the managing of Yugoslav society. This not only encouraged the airing of critical opinions and popular dissatisfaction but also instigated the broadening of political participation. But the ideal of a self-managing society also served to obscure the real mechanisms of power. If the true road to socialism lay in avoiding the extremes of excessive bureaucratization and wild market liberalization, and in transferring power from the state and the party to the self-managing workers, then the ones to blame for any setbacks were neither the members of the League of Communists nor the state officials, but the self-managers themselves—or, indeed, the society as a whole, which was not yet mature enough to sustain a full-fledged system of self-management. This logic locked the dynamics of reforms into a frustrating circle, simultaneously encouraging popular dissent while also deflecting attention from the real causes of Yugoslav problems and thereby preventing the articulation of true alternatives and solutions.

The debates surrounding *Sleep Peacefully* demonstrate how this logic worked in practice. In line with the notion of self-management and the requirement to bridge the chasm between the mass and the elite, producers of television entertainment were encouraged to engage with the pressing issues of the day and find ways to use popular formats to raise critical awareness. *Sleep Peacefully* represented one of the most acclaimed—as well as most controversial—attempts to use humor as a means of critical consciousness-raising. The series comprised eight episodes, all addressing major "social problems," including unemployment, income disparities, social solidarity, and corruption. Each of these issues was introduced through the personal experiences of a fictional character with a tellingly oxymoronic name Srečko Napast—"Lucky Menace."[38]

In the opening episode the jobless and penniless Lucky is caught stealing caviar from a local self-service market and ends up facing a trial at the "court of self-managers." The plot of the series is organized around the trial, which probes the rights and wrongs of Lucky's individual deeds and raises questions about the collective responsibility of the society as a whole. The central character is unmistakably critical of the current state of socialism and openly states that being jobless and hungry in socialism "is a disgrace." He also suggests that his theft was effectively a rebellious act prompted by social inequalities—caviar, he argues, is regularly eaten by those at the top of the socialist hierarchy, yet he has never been invited to take his share. After the last episode, viewers themselves were asked to vote for who was to blame for Lucky's misery and were offered two possible culprits: the main character himself and "the self-managers."

The series struck a sensitive chord with the audiences. Television Belgrade was inundated by thousands of letters and phone calls, the overwhelming majority of which congratulated the authors for articulating what everyone felt yet nobody allegedly dared to speak about. As one of the many letters stated, "This program is our reality—although bitter and coarse, it represents our reality."[39] Quite unsurprisingly, the series prompted unease among communist authorities, and the various pressures that ensued eventually pushed the writer-director of the series Radivoje-Lola Đukić to accept premature retirement in 1970.[40]

However, a closer analysis of viewers' letters received by TV Belgrade suggests that popular discontent rarely amounted to a rejection of the ideal of self-management as such. To be sure, part of the reason lies in the nature of the question posed, which offered only two possible culprits for Lucky's misfortunes: the main character himself and "the self-managers." Nonetheless, the results are strikingly consistent and cannot stem from the manipulative question alone. Out of the 954 viewers' letters analyzed by TV Belgrade's researchers, the vast majority (92.8 percent) refused to lay the blame on the central character.[41] Instead, the viewers most often accused "the self-managers" (35.6 percent) and "company managers" (24.6 percent) and occasionally "the society" (6.2

percent) and "the collective" (6.2 percent), while only a minority believed that the system of self-management as a whole (3.8 percent) or the highest state and party representatives (1.5 percent) were to blame.[42] Judging from these responses, the viewers saw the problem not so much in the system of self-management itself as in its incomplete implementation and various "deformations," including bad legislation, lack of education, acts of unscrupulous individuals who were taking advantage of the system, and so on.[43] Rather than providing an insurmountable challenge to established ideals of socialist Yugoslavism, such answers remained firmly within the frame of dominant political discourse.

The tendency to ascribe blame to the "deformations" of the existing system, rather than to the system itself, was also the approach adopted by Yugoslav authorities when facing student protests in the summer of 1968. In his televised appeal, Tito sided with the protesters, expressed agreement with their criticisms of Yugoslav reality, and asked them for help with making Yugoslav society better.[44] The majority of students embraced the offer; in 1968 alone, the proportion of League of Communists members below twenty-five years of age almost doubled.[45] According to John Lampe, Tito decided to co-opt the students to prevent them from joining forces with disgruntled workers, but "overall, the experience helped convince Tito, Kardelj, and many of the communist leaders that enlightened public opinion would support putting socialism, however ill-defined, ahead of the market mechanism in Yugoslav self-management."[46] It is feasible to suggest that the *Sleep Peacefully* series, despite encouraging popular dissatisfaction and provoking disquiet among the authorities, helped prepare the grounds for these developments. In sum, the combined effects of political reforms and the ability of sixties television to translate abstract public debates into entertaining personal stories did encourage greater popular involvement with public affairs, yet also contained the seeds of its containment.

Enter the Yugoslav Seventies: *Our Small Town* and the Comforts of Late Socialism

Like the airing of *Sleep Peacefully* in 1968, the broadcasting of *Our Small Town* in 1970–71 came at a time when public debate and popular discontent were reaching a boiling point. In the years that separated the two series, however, the realm of political contestation grew even wider, this time to make room for the rise of constituent Yugoslav nations—Serbs, Croats, Slovenians, Macedonians, Montenegrins, and Bosnians—as increasingly decisive players in the political life of the country. Over the course of the sixties, the combination of political and economic reforms and a more open climate facilitated the consolidation of key nation-building institutions below the federal level. In the realm of culture, policies aimed at creating an integrated Yugoslav culture were abandoned in favor of divergent history and literary teaching in each of the republics.[47] The Yugoslav media system was undergoing similar changes: republican media, including television broadcasters such as TV Zagreb and TV Belgrade, turned into protonational outlets, targeted first at local national audiences and only then at the wider Yugoslav imagined community.[48] Just like the participants of the World Youth Festival in Nick Rutter's contribution to this volume, and the Soviet tourists and their Czechoslovak hosts in Rachel Applebaum's chapter, the key actors of the Yugoslav sixties were using a common vocabulary but increasingly speaking in different tongues. Before long these developments prompted a revival of nationalist antagonisms and regional economic rivalries.[49]

These changes coincided with a mounting sense of insecurity and frustration. Successive reforms appeared to have little immediate effect on the standard of living. Unemployment and living costs continued to rise, and growing numbers of Yugoslavs were leaving the country in search of employment in the West. By 1971, an estimated 860,000 Yugoslavs—the vast majority, 38.4 percent, from Croatia—worked abroad.[50] In the increasingly messy struggle for power, nationalism provided a convenient shorthand for explaining the roots of Yugoslavia's problems, as well as for envisioning possible solutions to the crisis.[51] As a result, tensions between the proponents and opponents of economic and political liberalization became intertwined with national antagonisms. Economic liberalization and political decentralization were associated with the aspirations of Slovenians and Croats, while central economic planning and decision making was seen as the option preferred by Serbs. Outbursts of nationalist fervor became particularly acute in Croatia, where they ultimately precipitated a wave of mass protests that erupted across the republic in autumn 1971, with students again as a key constituency.[52] This escalation sounded a death knell for proponents of the nationalist cause and supporters of economic liberalization alike, first in Croatia and then elsewhere in the federation. The threat posed by nationalist tensions prompted the aging Yugoslav president Tito to intervene and turn the course of Yugoslavia's development back toward the core principles of Marxism-Leninism. By the end of 1972, many of the leaders of political and economic reforms that had marked the 1960s had disappeared from the public stage. The Yugoslav sixties had ended.

The TV series *Our Small Town* offers a perfect vantage point for a discussion of the role of television in these changes and the continuities and discontinuities between the Yugoslav sixties and seventies. The series is set in a picturesque small town on the Adriatic coast, in the Croatian region of Dalmatia, and follows the life of local inhabitants from 1936 to 1970. Every episode is introduced by a narrator—the town postman—who usually provides the moral of the story, followed by the episode itself. The two central characters are the town's doctor, Luigi, who studied medicine in Padua and is an avid reader of Dante but also has a weak spot for younger, sexually attractive women, and his middle-aged, utterly patient and forgiving sweetheart Bepina, whose only goal in life seems to be to please her partner and eventually marry him. Other prominent characters include their friends and acquaintances, in particular the owner of the local hotel and his wife, members of the local Communist League branch, the local barber and priest, and others. The episodes are tied together primarily by the ups and downs of Luigi and Bepina's relationship and the everyday worries and humorous incidents involving their friends and acquaintances. Broader social issues are not entirely absent but mostly function as an inconsequential backdrop for central developments to do with personal relationships, leisure activities, and shopping trips to Trieste.

The series is rather remarkable for the marginal role of blue-collar workers and peasants, who otherwise played a central role in Yugoslav television entertainment at the time. The key characters of *Our Small Town* are employed in the service industry and hold rather independent or even managing positions. Although they are regularly depicted in work-related situations, work does not really seem to feature prominently in their lives—at least not as something they are particularly invested in or worried about. These are evidently not characters akin to the unfortunate Lucky Menace from *Sleep Peacefully;* their jobs are secure and their lives are comfortable and slow-paced. This slow-paced life is, in fact, one of the overriding motifs of the series and is often explicitly defended as the best possible way of life. The following excerpts, taken from the postman's introduction to the eighth episode of the series, provide a case in point:

> My gosh! What else will they come up with?! Look at what petty complaints they have about my story—that it is developing too slowly, that it has a weak plot. . . . Go to hell! When was it ever the case that things were happening quickly around here, in our small town?! Whoever wanted a quick life went to America, or today, to Germany! . . .
>
> You see, we were never particularly fond of fast life and efficient work in our small town. To hell with work! What benefit does one have from work? Our motto is: The less we work, the better we live! And if we do work, then we work slowly, and we live slowly.

The way of life described by the postman is obviously miles away from the mass civic engagement envisaged by the ideal of self-management. Yet at the same time it is also neither explicitly anti-Yugoslav nor unambiguously pro-Western. Quite to the contrary; the slow-paced life of "our small town" is set against what is presented as the Western way of life, characterized by speed and efficiency, as well as a lack of pleasure and joy. Neither could it be said that *Our Small Town* posed an insurmountable challenge to existing political and economic arrangements, or to the legitimacy of communist rule. Despite its mildly mocking portrayals of communist officials, and regardless of its insistence on ideals of life that were somewhat at odds with official values, *Our Small Town* could easily be read as a defense and even celebration of the socialist Yugoslav way of life, with all its deficiencies.

The arrival of World War II during the fourth episode, for instance, sees all the central characters joining the struggle on the side of communist partisans, with Doctor Luigi taking care of wounded partisans. Above all, the insistence on "our" way of life and its superiority vis-à-vis the life in the West was sending a clear message that the way out of the quagmire of reform did not lie in embracing Western models: insofar as Yugoslav socialism was capable of tolerating the idiosyncrasies of Yugoslav regions and nations, and insofar as it was able to offer the comfort of a leisurely life, complete with a measure of consumer goods, travel abroad, and a summer holiday on the Adriatic coast, it seemed preferable to the drudgery of long working hours and hectic life in the capitalist West. The fact that the cozy socialist paradise could not be available to all did not seem to matter. As the town's postman suggested, labor migration to the West could be written off as a matter of choice rather than necessity, an opportunity open to those who might be bored with the slow pace of Yugoslav life.

For some segments of the communist elites in 1971, the glorification of consumerism and leisure and the lack of respect for communist authorities may have been too much to stomach, but the developments in the following years attest that it did not fall on deaf ears. Notwithstanding all the purges that swept through the federation in 1972, many of the changes brought by the sixties were there to stay. The new constitution, enacted in 1974, inaugurated a further decentralization of the country and an additional strengthening of republics-cum-nation-states. As far as the economy is concerned, the emphasis on heavy industry was abandoned in favor of a more consumer-friendly regime. While the underlying economic weaknesses remained unchanged, Western loans and remittances sent by Yugoslav citizens working abroad helped keep the country afloat throughout the decade.

In the realm of television culture, the production of entertainment continued to flourish but was far more closely supervised by the authorities. Radio-television centers were requested to prepare their yearly work plans well in advance and to submit them to the scrutiny of a wide range of political committees that assessed their compatibility with official policy goals. Humor abandoned the public domain and retreated into the privacy of socialist homes—a tendency already visible in *Our Small Town* and most clearly exemplified in TV Belgrade's blockbuster *Pozorište u kući* (Theater in the House, 1973–84). The other trajectory of retreat was tied to the revival of Yugoslav myths, above all the myth of the common struggle against fascism during World War II. Many of the most popular series broadcast in the 1970s, including TV Belgrade's *Otpisani* (The Outcasts, 1974) and TV Zagreb's *Kapelski kresovi* (The Bonfires of Kapela, 1975), center on the heroic actions of Yugoslav civilians engaged in fighting the fascist enemy. In sum, the expansion of politics had run its course—after a decade of growing political engagement, the private and the public started parting ways. The seventies had begun.

One may be tempted to suggest that the particular patterns of socialist privatization and television culture traced in this chapter are unique to Yugoslavia. There is certainly much that sets the Yugoslav version of socialism apart from its siblings elsewhere in Eastern Europe, and it is feasible to argue that the Yugoslav media and political reformers enjoyed a greater level of freedom than their counterparts in the Soviet bloc. Nonetheless, there is enough evidence to suggest that these were differences in degree rather than in kind and that similar patterns of growing public participation in the sixties, followed by increased political control and retreat into privacy in the seventies, appeared elsewhere in the socialist East. During the 1960s, encouraged by the new possibilities spurred by post-Stalinist reform, socialist television across the region became considerably more open to critical debate. Newly introduced television programs tackled explosive issues such as unemployment, corruption, social inequalities, and freedom of speech. Czechoslovak television offered its viewers televised confrontations between political prisoners of the Stalinist era and their prosecutors and scenes of Soviet troops descending on Prague in

August 1968,[53] while the Hungarian current affairs program *Forum* featured party leaders and representatives of various ministries answering questions posed live over telephone.[54] In the Soviet Union, a local station in Kuibyshev produced a program in which the journalist confronted the members of the City Executive Committee with probing questions from the public, while a similar program broadcast in Soviet Estonia featured government ministers answering questions from viewers.[55]

In contrast, the 1970s were marked by a tightening of political control over television, as well as by a more explicit, top-down appropriation of popular entertainment as a tool of political communication. At the Socialist Unity Party (SED) conference in 1971, a figure no less prominent than Erich Honecker described East German television as boring and called on broadcasters to provide their audiences with more entertainment.[56] In postinvasion Czechoslovakia, television professionals were urged to invest more heavily in light entertainment in an effort to win the hearts and minds of the masses and prevent them from turning their antennas to television signals from Austria and West Germany.[57] In the Soviet Union, the ability to spend a relaxing evening in front of the TV set came to be viewed as a right—as reflected in the statement, "The Soviet person has the right to relax in front of the television after a day's work," attributed to none other than Leonid Brezhnev.[58] As a result, television professionals across the socialist East were becoming increasingly adept at entertaining their viewers, but they did so in ways that steered clear of controversial public issues. Much like the most widely watched TV serials of the Yugoslav seventies, the most popular Czechoslovak serials of the decade frequently depicted the dramas of private, everyday life in the socialist present.[59] The Yugoslav serials depicting the common struggle against fascism during World War II also had their counterparts elsewhere in the socialist East, such as the already mentioned Soviet spy thriller *Seventeen Moments of Spring* (1973).

We should of course be wary of exaggerating the contrast between the socialist sixties and the socialist seventies. As the Yugoslav case suggests, the official endorsement of popular participation that marked the sixties had its clear limits and effectively ended up containing and pacifying popular dissatisfaction. Likewise, it would be misleading to see the seventies as an unambiguously stagnant or conservative decade. At least some of the political constituencies that came to the fore in the sixties—the constituent nations of socialist federations, youth, and to a lesser extent ethnic minorities and women—continued to gain visibility, if not formal recognition.[60] In the Soviet Union, the seventies may have been a time of political stagnation and of a retreat from the public sector, but they were also a time of consumer revolution,[61] and thus a period when the fantasy of a modern Soviet consumer, embedded in the domestic appliances of the sixties discussed by Susan Reid in her chapter, turned into a lived reality for growing numbers of Soviet citizens.

On the little screen, even the otherwise apolitical forms of entertainment, centered on depictions of private life and mythologized recollections of World War II, sometimes left room for subtle criticism and irony, or at the very least allowed for a range of individual interpretations. In Yugoslavia, the comic twists and turns of everyday life depicted in *Theater in the House* (1973–84) and *Vruć vetar* (Hot Wind, 1980) occasionally poked fun at the seamy underbelly of Yugoslav affluence, including unemployment and reliance on mass labor migration to the West. Likewise, the Soviet variety show *The Pub of 13 Chairs* regularly included stand-up comedy stints parodying the shortcomings of Soviet society, such as the scarcity of consumer goods and the mismatch between political visions and everyday life.[62] Such forms of ridicule were a far cry from the more openly politicized forms of humor in the sixties. Nonetheless, they serve as a reminder that even during the 1970s socialist popular culture was not ideologically uniform and that self-congratulatory, mythologized portrayals of socialist reality could coexist with more ambiguous messages. Only by attending to such contradictory tendencies, discontinuities as well as continuities, can we fully appreciate the nature and consequences of sixties politics and culture for the socialist East.

Notes

1. Arthur Marwick, *The Sixties: Cultural Revolution in Britain, France, Italy and the United States, c. 1958–c. 1974* (Oxford: Oxford University Press, 1998).

2. "The International 1968, Part I: Introduction," *American Historical Review* 114, no. 1 (February 2009): 43.

3. Richard Nixon, "The Kitchen Debate," in Richard M. Nixon, *The Challenges We Face: Edited and Compiled from the Speeches and Papers of Richard M. Nixon* (New York: McGraw-Hill, 1960), 224. See also Richard Nixon and Nikita Khrushchev, "The Kitchen Debate," July 24, 1959, transcript at *Teaching American History, Document Library*, http://teachingamericanhistory.org/library/index.asp?document=176.

4. Steven E. Harris, "'I Know All the Secrets of My Neighbours': The Quest for Privacy in the Era of the Separate Apartment," in *Borders of Socialism: Private Spheres of Soviet Russia*, ed. Lewis H. Siegelbaum (Basingstoke: Palgrave Macmillan, 2006), 171.

5. For East Germany, see Paul Betts, "Building Socialism at Home: The Case of East German Interiors," in *Socialist Modern: East German Everyday Culture and Politics*, ed. Katherine Pence and Paul Betts (Ann Arbor: University of Michigan Press, 2008), 71–95; for Poland, David Crowley, "Warsaw Interiors: The Public Life of Private Spaces, 1945–1965," in *Socialist Spaces: Sites of Everyday Life in the Eastern Bloc*, ed. David Crowley and Susan E. Reid (Oxford: Berg, 2002), 181–206; for Hungary, Virag Molnar, "In Search of the Ideal Socialist Home in Post-Stalinist Hungary: Prefabricated Mass Housing or Do-It-Yourself Family Home?" *Journal of Design History* 23, no. 1 (2010): 61–81.

6. On the growth of consumerism in East Germany, see Mark Landsman, *Dictatorship and Demand: The Politics of Consumerism in East Germany* (Cambridge, MA: Harvard University Press, 2005); for Yugoslavia, Patrick H. Patterson, *Bought and Sold: Living and Losing the Good Life in Socialist Yugoslavia* (Ithaca: Cornell University Press, 2011); for a general regional overview, see Ivan T. Berend, *Central and Eastern Europe, 1944–1993: Detour from the Periphery to the Periphery* (Cambridge: Cambridge University Press, 1996), 153–221.

7. Mark Pittaway, *Eastern Europe, 1939–2000* (London: Hodder Arnold, 2004), 68–69, 75, 78.

8. Paul F. Lazarsfeld and Robert K. Merton, "Mass Communication, Popular Taste and Organized Social Action" [1948], repr. in *Media Studies: A Reader*, ed. Paul Marris and Sue Thornham (New York: New York University Press, 2001), 23.

9. Michael J. Robinson, "Public Affairs Television and the Growth of Political Malaise: The Case of 'The Selling of the Pentagon,'" *American Political Science Review* 70, no. 2 (1976): 409–32.

10. Robert Putnam, *Bowling Alone: The Collapse and Revival of American Community* (New York: Simon and Schuster, 2000), 216–46.

11. Kristin Roth-Ey, *Moscow Prime Time: How the Soviet Union Built a Media Empire and Lost the Cultural Cold War* (Ithaca: Cornell University Press, 2011), 24.

12. Paulina Bren, *The Greengrocer and His TV: The Culture of Communism after the 1968 Prague Spring* (Ithaca: Cornell University Press, 2010).

13. See, e.g., Paul Betts, *Within Walls: Private Life in the German Democratic Republic* (Oxford: Oxford University Press, 2010), 21–50.

14. See, e.g., Harris, "I Know All the Secrets"; Crowley, "Warsaw Interiors."

15. Susan Reid, "The Meaning of Home: 'The Only Bit of the World You Can Have to Yourself,'" in Siegelbaum, *Borders of Socialism*, 147.

16. Stojan M. Zalar, "Posebno (čeprav obširno) poročilo iz New Yorka: Vse o ameriški televiziji," *Tedenska Tribuna*, 23 August 1956, quoted in Boris Grabnar, "Slovenska televizija v zrcalu publicistike, kritike in znanstvenih raziskav," *Bilten službe za študij programa RTV Ljubljana* 32, no. 2 (1972): 10, in Arhiv Slovenije (Archives of the Republic of Slovenia, hereafter ARS), 1215 Radiotelevizija Slovenija (Radiotelevision Slovenia, hereafter RTS), box 163.

17. Janko Kos, "Slovenska kultura in socialni sloji," *Sodobnost* 1 (1969): 1011–2, quoted in Grabnar, "Slovenska televizija v zrcalu publicistike," 19–20.

18. Jugoslovenski institut za novinarstvo, "Dokumentacija uz teze o mestu, ulozi i zadacima štampe, radija i televizije o daljem razvoju društveno-ekonomskih odnosa," 1965, 8, in Arhiv Jugoslavije—Archives of Yugoslavia (hereafter AY), f. 142, Socijalistički savez radnog naroda Jugoslavije (Socialist Alliance of the Working People of Yugoslavia, hereafter SAWPY), box 207.

19. Nikola Vončina, *Najgledanije emisije, 1964–1971: Prilozi za povijest radija i televizije u Hrvatskoj V* (Zagreb: Hrvatska Radiotelevizija, 2003), 152.

20. Jugoslovenska radio-televizija, "Stanje i problemi razvitka televizije u Jugoslaviji," Belgrade, 1964, 26, in AY, 130 Savezno izvršno veće (Federal Executive Council, hereafter FEC), box 566-942.

21. *Godišnjak Jugoslovenske radiotelevizije 1966* (Belgrade: Jugoslovenska radiotelevizije, 1967), 170.

22. Jugoslovenski institut za novinarstvo, "Dokumentacija uz teze o mestu."

23. "Teze o nekaterih problemih perspektivnega razvoja kulture v obdobju 1964–1970," 1964, in ARS, 1589 Centralni Komite Zveze Komunistov Slovenije, box III-145.

24. Ivo Bojanić, "Radio i televizija u SRH: Danas i sutra," *Naš studio: List kolektiva Radiotelevizije*, no. 2 (October 1964): 5.

25. Jugoslovenska radio-televizija, "Stanje i problemi," 4–5.

26. See, e.g., Centar Radiotelevizije Srbije za istraživanje javnog mnenja, programa i auditorijuma (Radio-Television of Serbia, Center for Public Opinion, Program and Audience Research, hereafter RTS-CPOPAR), "Anketa o humorističkim emisijama," Report 47, 1961, RTS-CPOPAR, "Angažovani humor u emisijama Radio Beograda," Report 252, 1967; RTS-CPOPAR, "Izvodi iz analize humorističko-satiričkog programa Televizije Beograd, emitovanog u prvom polugodištu 1968: Godine," Report 301, 1968.

27. RTS-CPOPAR, "Mišljenja i stavovi gledalaca o televizijskom programu," Report 218, 1967, 5.

28. Dennison Rusinow, *The Yugoslav Experiment, 1948–1974* (London: C. Hurst, 1977), 172–79.

29. For unemployment data, see Susan L. Woodward, *Socialist Unemployment: The Political Economy of Yugoslavia* (Princeton: Princeton University Press, 1995), 193.

30. For data on industrial wage differentials, see Howard M. Wachtel, "Workers' Management and Interindustry Wage Differentials in Yugoslavia," *Journal of Political Economy* 80, no. 3 (1972): pt. 1, 540–60.

31. Nebojša Popov, *Društveni sukobi, izazov sociologiji: "Beogradski jun" 1968* (Belgrade: Službeni glasnik, 2008), 163.

32. Woodward, *Socialist Unemployment*, 193.

33. On the lack of early coverage, see Popov, *Društveni sukobi*, 164.

34. Examples can be found in U.S. Information Agency (hereafter USIA), "Living Conditions in Yugoslavia," R-82-64, 1964, 7–10, in National Archives and Records Administration (hereafter NARA), Record Group (hereafter RG) 306, USIA Series P142 Research Reports, 1960–99, box 20.

35. Over the five years of its existence, the producers of the program processed 11,770 letters and more than 20,000 telephone calls posing questions for the program. RTS-CPOPAR, "Pet godina 'Aktuelnih razgovora,'" Report 371, 1.

36. Rusinow, *Yugoslav Experiment*, 148–52, 197–202.

37. Ibid., 47–58.

38. RTS-CPOPAR, "Analiza pisma gledalaca upućenih serijskoj emisiji 'Spavaje mirno' + pisma gledalaca upućenih serijskoj emisiji 'Spavaje mirno'—izvodi," Report 354, 1969, Part I, 1.

39. Ibid., Part II, 2.

40. As suggested by Đukić himself in a recent recollection of events. See Mirjana Gumbovski, "Veselje za narod," *Večernji list on-line*, 21 August 2008, http://82.103.130.111/dodatni_sadrzaj/clanci.119.html:279233-Veselje-za-narod.

41. RTS-CPOPAR, "Analiza pisma gledalaca," Report 354, Part I, 9.

42. Ibid., Part I, 11.

43. Ibid., Part II, 10.

44. Rusinow, *Yugoslav Experiment*, 236–37.

45. Ibid., 239.

46. John Lampe, *Yugoslavia as History: Twice There Was a Country*, 2nd ed. (Cambridge: Cambridge University Press, 2000), 302.

47. Andrew B. Wachtel, *Making a Nation, Breaking a Nation: Literature and Cultural Politics in Yugoslavia* (Stanford: Stanford University Press, 1998), 173–97.

48. Gertrude Joch Robinson, *Tito's Maverick Media: The Politics of Mass Communications in Yugoslavia* (Urbana: University of Illinois Press, 1977), 16–25.

49. Lampe, *Yugoslavia as History*, 304–9.

50. Ibid., 13.

51. Rusinow, *Yugoslav Experiment*, 266–73.

52. Ibid., 291–307.

53. Bren, *Greengrocer*, 20–29. See also Airgram from the American Embassy Prague to Department of State, "Television Panel Grapples with Tough Topics," 3 March 1968, in NARA, RG 59, General Records of the Department of State, 1763–2002, Central Foreign Policy Files, 1966–1969, box 409, folder TV, 1/1/67.

54. Burton Paulu, *Radio and Television Broadcasting in Eastern Europe* (Minneapolis: University of Minnesota Press, 1974), 374.

55. Ibid., 128.

56. Rüdiger Steinmetz and Reinhold Viehoff, "The Program History of Genres of Entertainment on GDR Television," *Historical Journal of Film, Radio and Television* 24, no. 3 (2004): 320.

57. Bren, *Greengrocer*, 121–22.

58. Roth-Ey, *Moscow Prime Time*, 201.

59. Bren, *Greengrocer*.

60. Tony Judt, *Postwar: A History of Europe since 1945* (London: Penguin, 2005), 484–503.

61. Natalya Chernyshova, "Consumer Revolution? Society and Economy in the Soviet 1970s," paper presented at the Association for Slavic, East European and Eurasian Studies conference, Los Angeles, 18–21 November 2010.

62. Paulu, *Radio and Television*, 177.

11 Playing Catch-Up

Soviet Media and Soccer Hooliganism, 1965–75

Robert Edelman

DURING THE FALL of 1945, in the afterglow of Allied victory, the Dinamo Moscow soccer team traveled to Great Britain for a goodwill tour.[1] Dinamo, the newly crowned Soviet champion, funded and run by the People's Commissariat for Internal Affairs (NKVD), was to play the Welsh lower-division side, Cardiff City, the Scottish power Glasgow Rangers, and the famed London clubs Arsenal and Chelsea.[2] Both the USSR's leaders and its ordinary citizens had long wondered how their teams would do against the world's best. From the outset, diplomatic and political isolation had made the regime and its citizens intensely curious about the outside world and equally concerned about how that outside world perceived them. Between the wars the Soviet press had continually reported on the leagues of capitalist nations, while the library at the Stalin Institute of Physical Culture collected hundreds of training manuals and histories of the game. The USSR's teams could not compete against the West, but Soviet professionals and fans were far from ignorant of football under capitalism.

Moscow clubs had played Czechoslovakian professionals in 1934 and 1935 and had done well, but a 1937 tour of the USSR by a team of Basque stars drawn from the powerful Spanish league turned out to be a humiliation.[3] Now Dinamo, strengthened by four players from other teams, was to take on the very founders of football. Between the wars, the British had disdained international competitions, convinced in their increasingly shabby isolation that teams from the Continent were inferior. Yet the war had not been kind to the British. Formal league schedules had been suspended, and teams from the powerful English league were in disarray.[4] By contrast,

Dinamo Moscow, using the authority of the police, had kept their playing staff intact far away from the front. They had taken part in a number of local competitions and had toured throughout the rear. Their players were healthy and in peak condition. Still, Great Britain was the homeland of soccer, and Soviet sports officials, along with their counterparts in the Central Committee, were far from certain of victory.

There was little buildup of the tour in the press. Three other Soviet clubs were sent on simultaneous trips to play weaker foes in Eastern Europe in order to mitigate the risk to always fragile prestige. The expected victories of the other Soviet sides could, if needed, vitiate the sting of possible defeat in Britain. As things turned out, the party leadership had little to fear. British fans were intensely interested in the visitors from a wartime ally for whom they felt deep gratitude. Tens of thousands overflowed Chelsea's Stamford Bridge ground for the first match. Sitting on the stadium roof and packing the field to inches from the sidelines, they watched Dinamo produce a thrilling brand of soccer, dominating play and gaining a 3-3 draw. Chelsea fans carried their guests off the field, and the British press lavishly praised the play of the "the mysterious Russians." Little else could have more powerfully demonstrated the benefits of sporting diplomacy to Stalin, who was otherwise completely uninterested in matters athletic.[5]

The party leadership had taken another risk that paid off handsomely. Live broadcasts by the era's great sports announcer, Vadim Siniavskii, were beamed back to the entire USSR. Fans worshipped at the shrines of their radios and rejoiced in the belief that their "school" of football was the equal of the mighty "English." Immediately after the Chelsea match, Soviet press coverage of the rest of the Dinamo tour became extensive and positive.[6] Fans now learned more about life in the United Kingdom. The team's social and cultural program was discussed in detail. The result was a vicarious form of soccer tourism. It all felt quite normal, one might say civilized—the sort of thing other citizens of the world enjoyed. With victory in war and on the playing field, the USSR ended its international isolation.[7] Having sacrificed so mightily, millions of ordinary Soviet citizens now dreamed of a new world of peace and harmony as well as greater creature comforts, more personal freedoms, and more contacts with foreigners. The Dinamo tour, with ecstatic Brits embracing their guests, seemed to promise them just that.[8]

Each year's number of international matches became a clear marker of Soviet relations with the outside world. Soccer, with its mass appeal, offered a special but seemingly safe portal through which ordinary Soviets could imagine the world beyond the Soviet Union. The televising of international soccer matches back to the USSR began in 1965. Every fortnight when Soviet teams were still in the competitions, two or three games would be shown on Wednesday nights from far-off places to which a limited number of Soviet fans now could hope to travel. The result was a kind of "football tourism" that broke down Soviet citizens' sense of isolation and opened up new possibilities about which they could now dream. Football tourism provided vivid images of Western style and culture for Soviet citizens increasingly eager to consider themselves part of a global consuming public. This was not without problems, however. Soviet television picked up local feeds and could not control the images seen by its own audiences. As we will see, televised scenes of fans in capitalist countries, behaving excitedly and often badly, influenced the actions of Soviet citizens who watched these contests in the millions.[9]

This transnational connection intersected with a growing fragmentation within the state and between state and society that coalesced in the decade beginning in the mid-1960s. The culture of football spectatorship, with its varied local loyalties and intense emotions, provided multiple signs of the erosion of the old state-society duality that may, in fact, have never really explained historical realities. This chapter will explore the evolution of these consequences by tracing the development of international soccer matches played by Soviet clubs, a development that exposed millions of Soviet football fans to cultural changes around the world, including the long hair and bad manners that began to characterize international soccer in the 1960s. I pay special attention to a key match in 1972, when Soviet viewers were exposed to an unprecedented display of spontaneous violence at the conclusion of a televised match between Glasgow Rangers and Dinamo Moscow. The match spurred a new culture of soccer hooliganism inside the Soviet Union, a culture that shared a growing obsession with "deficit" Western goods and cultural symbols like clothing and rock 'n' roll.

To Play or Not to Play

International football had always provided clues to the USSR's relationship with the outside world. During 1946 and 1947 these contests were frequent, but with the onset of the Cold War in 1948 they ceased to be part of the Soviet sporting calendar. The national team, which had not played since 1937, was revived for the 1952 Helsinki Olympic Games (the Soviets' first). In contrast to the conquest of Britain, they suffered ignominious defeat in the quarterfinal at the hands of Tito's renegade Yugoslavs. Immediately the doors to the outside world were again shut, but within months of Stalin's death Soviet clubs once more were traveling to play outside the country and welcoming sides from both Eastern and Western Europe. The national team was reassembled in 1954, and the next year Moscow fans welcomed the newly crowned world champions from West Germany.[10] The Soviet victory in this match accompanied a rapprochement in relations with the defeated enemy and the return of the last German POWs.[11] A year later, the USSR got its revenge against the no longer hated Yugoslavs, defeating them in the final of the 1956 Olympic soccer tournament, a lesser competition because of the formal amateurism of Eastern bloc players. In 1958, the *sbornaia* (national team) went to its first World Cup, where they lost in the quarterfinals to the host Swedes. The famed Thaw of the early Khrushchev era had its soccer equivalent. Cultural diplomacy, particularly sporting diplomacy, became a significant part of the Cold War rivalry, and in order to be a player in this arena one had to play.

During the fifties, Soviet clubs took on some of the best teams in Europe, but throughout the Continent the organization of these games was haphazard and ad hoc. Soviet football officials were careful to schedule these matches in August and November. Because the Soviet league ran from spring to fall while most European leagues ran from fall to spring, it was advantageous for Soviet clubs to play foreign teams at times when their opponents were just rounding into form. Aided by these artificial advantages, such world-class sides as Spartak, Dinamo, and Torpedo produced a strong if deceiving record. In the soccer world, these exhibitions are called "friendlies." In the USSR they were described as "comradely" *(tovarishcheskii),* but party and sports officials, along with the press, treated them as "serious examinations" of the nation's *futbol.* These successes seemed to correlate with growing Soviet power and international prestige in the early years of the Cold War.[12] Yet the coaches, players, and fans (not to mention journalists in private) knew their teams were not playing the world's best on level playing fields.

In 1955, the recently formed Union of European Football Associations (UEFA) inaugurated the Champions Cup competition to determine the entire continent's best team. The anarchy of international club play was now replaced by a structured and fair competition, which was won for the first five years by Real Madrid. The Communist Party of the Soviet Union wanted no part of a competition dominated by the favorite club of the Spanish dictator Francisco Franco, nor can it be said that Franco had been willing to allow players from any Eastern bloc nation entry into Spain.[13] Only in 1961, when Portugal's Benfica finally broke Real's streak, did Soviet leaders even begin to discuss the possibility of participation. That same year witnessed the beginning of a second international competition, this for national cup winners. Ten years later a trophy for well-placed runners-up (the UEFA Cup) was added to the international calendar. These tournaments were designed to give structure, meaning, and monetary value to contests between the best clubs from all the nations of Europe. They were knockout tournaments for large monetary prizes. Teams played home and away matches, the winner to be determined by the total number of goals. UEFA's idea proved highly successful competitively and economically, and over the last decades of the twentieth century the cups grew in size, commercial visibility, media transmissions, and revenue.[14]

Soviet party leaders and sporting officials were especially wary of the new competitions. The advantage they had gained from selective scheduling was now lost. One could no longer carefully choose one's opponents. Instead, matchups were determined by purportedly blind and fair draws. In addition, Soviet clubs were hurt by their league's summer schedule. The Eurocups were divided into fall and spring sessions. Things would usually go quite well for Soviet clubs in the fall. They were in peak form, while their opponents had just begun their seasons. Then the winter break would come. Cup play resumed before the next Soviet season began. Having gone months without serious competition, few of the USSR's clubs made it past what came to be called the "March Barrier." Only Dinamo Kiev (1975 and 1986) and Dinamo Tbilisi (1981) succeeded in claiming the less prestigious Cup Winners' Cup. The USSR's greatest triumph in club football came in 1975, when Dinamo Kiev defeated the powerful European champions, Bayern Munich, in what was called the Super Cup. Everything else on the club level produced frustration and feelings of inferiority.

Starting in 1965, when the USSR at last took part, the Eurocups had a significant cultural impact on the nation's teams, their supporters, and television viewers more generally. When Soviet clubs played foreign opponents in away matches, the contests were usually televised live back to all or parts of the Union.[15] The matches were preceded by press discussions of the upcoming opponent's history, stadium, and present level of play. Soviet citizens were transfixed, especially when they could view one of the great temples of the game, be it White Hart Lane in London, the San Siro in Milan, Hampden Park in Glasgow, the Bernabeu in Madrid, or the Nou Camp in Barcelona.[16] The veteran Soviet-era journalist Nikolai Dolgopolov, who wrote for *Komsomol'skaia pravda* (Komsomol Truth) and *Trud* (Labor), recalls never missing a cup match. "We saw," he said, "things we never had seen before in our lives." These included foreign teams wearing the latest and most stylish gear from such sporting goods giants as Adidas. Advertising boards along the sidelines, intended for capitalist audiences, hawked goods and services no Soviet could hope to buy legally. Dolgopolov claimed to be "not interested" in the antics of foreign fans, with their songs, chants, fireworks, and bad behavior. He preferred to concentrate on the game itself, but clearly he and others could not ignore what was going on in the stands.[17]

The television showed what Soviet officials preferred to ignore, namely that the rest of the world was changing. The sixties rebellion of youth affected the young men who played for the Continent's best clubs. They wore their hair long and refused to tuck in their shirts. They felt free to challenge openly the authority of referees and coaches. Accordingly, not all the lessons Soviet fans took from these experiences were positive. The midsixties also witnessed the first wave of something altogether different from the rebellious but largely nonviolent youth culture. Soccer hooliganism, most notably in Great Britain, had come to scar the game. Over the course of the previous century and a half, disorder at football matches was common both outside and inside the USSR, but the new hooliganism in the United Kingdom was different. It was organized, and much of the violent action took place outside the stadium. Young working-class males, many of them unemployed or underemployed, were only the most conspicuous elements of a movement that also attracted sons of the middle class.[18]

Yet such behavior was not restricted to capitalist nations. In the fall of 1967, during the flowering of the Prague Spring, Torpedo Moscow traveled to Trnava to play

Spartak Trnava in the second round of the Cup Winners' Cup. The match was televised back to the USSR. Long-standing anti-Soviet sentiment inside the Eastern bloc had grown especially intense with the rise of Alexander Dubček's "socialism with a human face." Even before the 1968 invasion, Czechoslovakian fans had treated visiting Soviet teams with hatred and contempt. They booed, whistled, cursed, and threw objects at the "fraternal" players. Led by their great star Eduard Strel'tsov, Torpedo thoroughly dominated their hosts. Soon the local fans invaded the field and attacked several Torpedo players, including Strel'tsov.[19]

Disorder had also been part of Soviet soccer matches. Yet such moments were exceptional. When riots occurred, they were usually touched off by dubious refereeing, and the unruliness was largely confined to the stadium grounds.[20] Most of these disorders went unreported, but accounts of the Spartak-Dinamo Kiev match in Moscow on 18 April 1970 mentioned the ejection of large numbers of drunken fans. Massive quantities of vodka bottles and hand weapons were confiscated during a Spartak-Torpedo game soon thereafter. It is impossible to discern if fans of other clubs behaved in similar ways, since the press seemed to focus on Spartak supporters.[21] Yet it is highly unlikely that such behaviors were limited to one club. Given what we know of historic Russian drinking habits and the well-publicized actions of soccer fans worldwide, such phenomena were surely widespread. They became a significant concern in the press starting in 1970.

The Moment of Consequences

Soviet fan behavior reached a turning point in 1972. As with so many other forms of popular culture, football hooliganism emerged later than it did in the West. The Cup Winners' Cup final was held in the Catalan metropolis of Barcelona. Dinamo Moscow was to take on Glasgow Rangers, their foes in 1945. This was the first time a Soviet club had made it to one of the Eurocup finals, and there was no question that such an event would be shown live, even if the game took place in a nation still ruled by Franco. During the sixties, Rangers (the Protestant club) had come to play second fiddle to their local archrivals Celtic (the Catholic club). Now they had unexpectedly defeated the great Bayern Munich in the semifinal.[22] Dinamo, only rounding into form early in the Soviet season, had beaten the East German club, Dinamo Berlin.[23] The giant Nou Camp Stadium, then undergoing remodeling, was filled with sixty thousand "lovers of football." Thirty thousand of them were Glaswegians. Only four hundred Soviets made the trip. Many of these supporters were surely trustworthy members of the KGB, eager to cheer on their "colleagues."

For decades, Rangers fans (indeed all Glasgow fans) had earned a well-deserved reputation for uproarious and often dangerous behavior. The love of the city's two religious communities for their teams and their long-standing hatred for each other had become deeply felt parts of fan identities. Given the harsh historic economic realities of Scotland's largest city, these tensions often led to violence. The deadliest match panic in British history had taken place at Rangers' Ibrox Park.[24] Describing the events of 1972, the *Times* reported: "The Scots arrived [in Barcelona] in 90 charter flights, buses and private cars. . . . Spaniards watched in bewilderment as groups of them marched down the avenidas. Many were in kilts and wore scarves in their team's colors. They crowded bars in the old city and took over every available hotel room."[25] Once in the Nou Camp on match day, the Rangers' red, white, and blue army spilled onto the field and produced clamorous cheering and chanting even before the kickoff. Viewing the BBC video of the match does not, however, give the impression that this activity was particularly malevolent.[26] From the game's first moments, Glasgow supporters were enjoying one enormous and exciting sporting holiday. In the great tradition of the British stadium, they were on their feet and in constant motion throughout the entire match. "All sorts of scenes," said the unnamed BBC announcer, "are going on in the terraces."[27]

Under their coach and former star Konstantin Beskov, Dinamo Moscow had been an attacking side. Yet in their first big European final they chose instead to take a more cautious defensive approach.[28] Despite a decent first ten minutes, Beskov's strategy proved a colossal failure. Rangers gained the initiative in the twenty-third minute, when Colin Stein seamlessly brought down a looping thirty-meter pass on the dead run and blasted it into the upper corner. Stein would later say, "My abiding memory of the game is scoring my goal. . . . I turned around and there was a red, white and blue tidal wave coming at me. There were about 30,000 Rangers fans in the Nou Camp that night and most of them seemed to be on the park each time we scored." The BBC's man asked prophetically, "Where are the Spanish police? One shudders to think what will happen if they win."[29] Later press accounts described truncheon-wielding Spanish police intervening to get the Rangers fans back in the stands. Rangers would go on to score just before and just after halftime. After each goal, their supporters were back on the pitch, intimidating, poking, and taunting Dinamo players. Beskov's plan was in tatters.

In response the Dinamo boss went back to what his team did best—attack. In the fifty-seventh minute, Beskov brought on the speedy forward Vladimir Eshtrekov, who scored three minutes later. At this point the tide turned, and Dinamo, whose players were far fitter than their often chubby opponents, begin to press forward for the next half hour. By this point the neutrals in the stands had shifted their support to Dinamo. Rangers fans grew uncomfortable and nervous. Their joy turned to a noisy anxiety. In the eighty-sixth minute Aleksandr Makhovikov scored to bring Dinamo back to 2-3. The Rangers players tired while their fans chewed on their scarves and demanded the referee blow his whistle to end the game. Two minutes later, the whistle was indeed blown, but it was for a foul on Rangers. Their fans incorrectly thought the game had ended and flooded forward onto the field in mad celebration.

Happy long-haired youths were to be seen everywhere in a scene that looked more like Woodstock than a typical soccer riot. The British video of the match reveals a crowd that is joyous and relieved—a football carnival. Later Soviet accounts described them as drunken, belligerent, and ugly, seeking to put pressure on the Dinamo players and intervene in the match to stop the Dinamo storm and preserve their heroes' victory. UEFA's subsequent investigation determined this invasion to be "a misunderstanding" that had "no decisive influence on the game."[30] It took roughly five minutes to restore order with what appears to have been minimal police force. Play resumed, but by this time Dinamo had come unstrung and the less fit Rangers players had recovered their wind. The intervention had worked. Beskov would later say his players had lost the rhythm of an attack that might well have led to a third and tying goal.

After two minutes, the final whistle did sound and the fans were back on the field. An estimated four thousand Scottish supporters were trying to touch their heroes and tear up pieces of the newly historic turf. In the face of the flood of largely young and largely male Scottish humanity, the announcer initially remarked, "The players will be suffocating. . . . The police have no chance." The episode soon turned ugly. The police, it turned out, had more than a chance. Several hundred of Franco's "finest," wielding truncheons and batons, appeared in order to clear the field for the ritual awards ceremony. Rangers fans resisted, and a pitched battle ensued.[31] Dinamo would claim that several of their players were attacked by bottle-wielding Scots. Those still in the stands rained down more bottles, cushions, and seats. Others came onto the field to reinforce their countrymen. None of this can be seen on the available footage, which ends before the rioting turned ugly. Yet the next day's *Guardian* described the "shameful behavior" in some detail. There were numerous arrests. An estimated one hundred fans and police were injured. Several Rangers supporters lay unconscious on the grass, and a number of policemen were bloodied.[32] The Soviet delegation claimed that Dinamo's Joseph Sabo and Eshtrekov had been struck by broken bottles. UEFA had historically done Soviet sides few favors. Their report claimed that there was no proof of any such attacks, incredibly noting, "No bottles were to be found on the pitch." Nevertheless, the United Kingdom's leading liberal daily noted: "Three years ago Rangers were warned by the European authorities about the penalties which their supporters' behavior could bring about after similar riots at Newcastle. Now this culmination of three days of bad behavior in and around Barcelona may yet lose them the cup." A protest immediately came from Dinamo demanding a replay.[33] Telegrams, telexes, and letters soon followed from the Soviet Football Federation. There was precedent for such a step, which UEFA had indeed taken after fan violence had interrupted a 1968 cup match between Inter Milan and Borussia Moenchengladbach.

A detailed, measured, and well-sourced game account appeared in the 26 May issue of *Sovetskii sport*. Drawing extensively from the Spanish and international press, the unnamed author(s) described the Scottish invasion of Barcelona in the days before the match and confirmed the version of events offered by the *Guardian*. The great Dinamo goalie Lev Iashin, just recently retired, was quoted from a United Press dispatch. "We might have been successful if the spectators had not run onto the field. This crowd consisted of drunk people who were out of control." Citing UEFA rules in detail, *Sovetskii sport* went on to call for a replay. The text of the Soviet Football Federation's formal protest to the UEFA office in Bern was printed in full.[34] Since the Spanish referee (unlike the one in the previous case) had managed to get the match to reach the full ninety minutes, the Soviet protest was denied. Thirty years later the scandal still evoked bitter memories. Dinamo's official club history published in 2000 described the Glaswegians wrecking cafés and cars throughout the city.[35] There were more injuries and more arrests. After an investigation, UEFA banned Rangers from European competition for two years, later reduced to one.[36]

Watching in Moscow, groups of young Spartak fans thought this kind of behavior a great way to exert influence on the outcome of a match. Chanting and cheering was one thing, but this final act of mass unruliness seemed inspired, even empowering, and certainly great fun. They also took in the fact that the team hurt by the Scots' actions was Spartak's historic and bitter rival. Sixteen at the time, the future historian and youthful Spartak fan Yuri Slezkine recalls being "excited" by the actions of the Rangers fans. He especially remembers their "long hair."[37] Even the Rangers players wore their hair at Beatle length. The seemingly contradictory combination of youth rebellion and soccer hooliganism was compelling. Racing onto the field and interrupting a match at a crucial juncture seemed to young Soviets to be much a more concrete and powerful act than politely cheering on one's favorites. Spartak's fortunes on the field had dipped in recent seasons, and this seemingly new form of action appeared to be a far more direct way of helping their favorites.[38]

This was not the unanimous reaction of Soviet fans. Vladimir Titorenko, today the editor of the Russian sports daily *Sportekspress*, was thirteen at the time. A supporter of TsSKA (the army club), he was moved to tears of frustration by the actions of the Rangers supporters. Growing up in the sheltered environment of a closed city outside Moscow, Titorenko, unlike Slezkine, was not part of the capital's more bodacious fan culture. The younger Titorenko's reaction was likely more typical of Soviet fans.[39] Much the same could be said of Soviet soccer's most accomplished historian, Aksel' Vartanian, who watched the match as a mature adult living in Tbilisi and reacted with much disapproval. Dolgopolov, a lifelong Dinamo Moscow fan, could only read about the match, as he was on assignment in Iran, but he recalls being "shocked and disappointed." Today, when Russians are asked about the early Eurocups, the 1972 final is virtually the only game all can recall with even a measure of clarity.[40]

Nevertheless, numerous Soviet young people, alienated in varying degrees and occupying various social stations, were positively impressed by the spectacle on the field of the Nou Camp. The next spring at the beginning of the 1973 season, about forty young men gathered at the east end of Lenin Stadium. They had joined twenty thousand others for the first game of the Moscow schedule as Spartak took on Ararat of Erevan. They were wearing red and white striped scarves and waving Spartak banners. These items had not been purchased at the Spartak team store. No such store existed at the time. Instead, the paraphernalia was homemade. These new kinds of supporters called themselves *fanaty,* best translated into current parlance as "ultras." As the USSR had opened up to the rest of the world, future Soviet hooligans were able to study the "English model" through TV and the press, both of which reported on the phenomenon in the most negative of tones.[41] Yet it should be noted that the range of popular reactions to the 1972 final involved what can only be called a conflation of a seemingly benign sixties youth culture with the violence and nihilism of soccer hooliganism. Both were from the West, and both emerged in the middle of the decade, but the two were quite different in spirit and social composition.

Over time, forty grew to hundreds and then thousands who stood in one or another unpopulated section of the vast Lenin Stadium. The *fanaty* chanted, sang, cheered, and gave grief to visiting teams and referees alike. Suffice to say, not all of these loudly delivered fan discourses were fully cultured. At this early moment, these young supporters did not seem to be especially drunk or violent. However, their sheer exuberance and spontaneity attracted the attention of both the police (who also read the press) and the volunteer militias *(druzhiny)* who were charged with maintaining not only order but calm in the stands. Neither set of guardians of order proved capable of distinguishing between high-spirited raucousness and authentically dangerous violence. Rough treatment in turn pushed many of these exuberant fans into less benign activities.

The supporters of other clubs came to adopt similar behaviors, and before long the media were filled with even more complaints about young men (and women) who used sport as an excuse for acting badly. Accounts of drunken and misbehaving fans at domestic matches continued to appear in the sporting press. Even fans who simply screamed too loudly *(krikuny)* or carried on too enthusiastically became targets of criticism. Over time, pictures of confiscated vodka bottles and nonlethal weapons became a journalistic staple.[42] By the mid- to late seventies Soviet hooliganism had moved outside the stadium. As John Bushnell has shown, young fans of Moscow's various clubs formed fluid street gangs who came to cover walls with football graffiti and battle with each other for what they defined as urban turf.[43] They terrorized metro riders and destroyed property in ways that clearly challenged social norms. Although their actions were transgressive in a context that did not appreciate transgression, they were not explicitly political in any traditional sense.[44] The Spartak hooligan groups were the largest and best organized. Dinamo Moscow and TsSKA, whose gangs formed in response to Spartak, were collectively smaller. Fan loyalty alone marked one group from the other. Most, but not all, were young, working-class males who were not always satisfied with beating up each other. Nearby innocents were also fair game. None of the various Moscow clubs was associated with a particular region or neighborhood, as was so common in a place like Britain, where footballing identities were closely tied to geography and class.

In the United Kingdom, this new wave of fan violence had started during the 1960s.[45] Soccer hooliganism in the USSR was instead a part of the socialist seventies. This kind of cultural time lag has been common throughout Russian history. Russians have absorbed foreign practices in ambiguous and often contradictory ways. It cannot be said, therefore, that the fan violence associated with global soccer fit comfortably into the larger youth rebellion of the sixties.[46] Smashing property and heads ran counter to the mantras of "Peace, Love, and Happiness." The televising of the Eurocups started in 1965, but, as noted, the social and cultural consequences of these sporting events were not fully manifested until somewhat later.[47] Both the Cold War consensus in the West and the Soviet Thaw had begun to unravel. Meanwhile the stresses of continuing Soviet urbanization combined with balky economic development led young men to behave badly. In hooliganism, as in so many other areas of politics and culture, the USSR was playing catch-up.

Not by Futbol Alone

Middle-aged and older Soviet citizens came to look with bewilderment at the strangely dressed and coiffed young people who were consciously choosing to act in an "uncultured" manner. Needless to say, foreign soccer players and their fans were far from the only sources of the contagion. The student movements and youth rebellions of the sixties were global phenomena that could not be walled off at the USSR's borders. Starting in the fifties, rock had been seeping through the many cracks in the information system. By 1970, self-contained *beatgruppy* could be found in virtually every institution throughout the vast nation. In my own experience, nearly every department at Moscow State University sponsored one or more such groups. Indeed, these bands had to have sponsors. If not, they would be engaging in "small business." The old x-ray plates of pirated 45s and 78s were replaced by a flood of long-playing *plastinki* that had been inundating the country through foreign tourists, students, and diplomats. Soviet tourists who had traveled to East and West Europe in greater numbers also brought back records.[48]

Soccer players from the best Soviet clubs were regularly abroad, and virtually all of them speculated in hard currency in order to obtain a wide range of foreign items. LPs were near the top of the list. While players from most teams surely tasted the fruits of their journeys including the new music, the young men of Spartak were especially active consumers and purveyors of everything from the Beatles and Hendrix to the Stones and beyond. The club had a tradition of jazz lovers, from Nikita Simonian and Sergei Sal'nikov in the late forties through Iuri Sevidov and Galimzian Khusainov during the late sixties.[49] Many of their fans among the stars of *estrada* also knew a great deal about hipper Western music.[50] Such early seventies Spartak mainstays as Evgenii Lovchev and Gennadii Logofet made the transition to rock. Lovchev, who sported a modest Paul McCartney haircut, often appeared in public wearing clothes that could not have been purchased in any Moscow store.[51] Logofet recalls that on their foreign travels Spartak players had less supervision than those of Dinamo or TsSKA. Many, like Logofet, spoke some English and had opportunities to shop and perhaps take in concerts on their own.[52] Still, it would be an exaggeration to say that soccer dominated the broader Soviet consumption of Western popular culture. The football world was but one of many subcultures experiencing the wave of Western influence then washing over the USSR.

By the early seventies, the demeaning and dispiriting struggle for *defitsitnye* items had become more intense as *blatnye* relations sucked up a growing segment of the Soviet economy.[53] Millions of Soviet citizens came into contact with gray and black markets, and this corruption inevitably extended to soccer. Here the game did not simply reflect the stagnation at the top. The old state and society duality no longer explained the course of Soviet history. Trends in the highest political structures no longer had a direct impact on the circumscribed and specialized sectors of a swiftly changing society. State and society no longer moved in lockstep. Each was now dancing a different dance, and in the sixties dancing partners no longer touched. Instead of reflecting developments at the political apex, soccer now provided observers of Soviet life with a way to comprehend deeper and broader social change.

The corrupt practices of the soccer world during the early seventies were no more or less destabilizing than those of music, film, and a hundred other activities (from car repair to mushroom hunting) that millions of Soviet citizens engaged in more or less on their own. Young football "ultras" did not cause the breakup of the Soviet Union. They had no clear political program, and they did not make independent demands upon the crumbling state structures. Rather than change the system, they simply tried to avoid it as best they could. To the many disaffected subcultures of this period, one can add television-watching "couch *kartoshki*" and flag-waving *fanaty*. All were seeking, for better or worse, to create identities of their own while eschewing those offered by the party-state. The regime may have organized and presented soccer and other sporting spectacles, but the audiences consumed those spectacles in their own ways. In the process they created contested meanings that, like so much else during the Soviet period, had unintended consequences.

Watching at Home

The experience of watching any soccer match on Soviet television, not just the European cups, changed fan culture for viewers of all ages. The highly masculinized and rowdy world of the stadium was not always carried over to watching at home in the relatively new and private space of the Soviet apartment. Live broadcasts of any sort were minefields of unintended consequences. The first such program was a soccer game in 1949. In television's infancy, its forms, contents, and purposes were the subject of worldwide discussion. In the West, politicians, artists, and intellectuals thought TV had enormous potential to educate. Soviet politicians, artists, and intellectuals were no less excited and uncertain about the paths the new medium might take.[54]

What was supposed to inspire workers to exercise could also expose the uninitiated to the disorderly behavior of players and fans. The combination of sport's essential unpredictability and the uncertainties of live telecasts came to pose special dangers for a party-state that prized control over the often unruly masses.[55] Regardless of the sport, badly behaving players or incompetent, perhaps dishonest referees could have a dangerous impact on those in the stands and, with them, those watching at home. It was feared young people would make heroes of "hooligan" players.[56] One TV critic even chastised the directors of televised hockey games for rewarding those guilty of on-ice misdeeds by focusing on such rule breakers sitting in the penalty box.[57]

There were other dangers. After decades of so many falsehoods, the telecast of a live sporting event amounted to an island of authenticity that could not easily be manipulated. If viewers could see what actually happened, commentators could only spin the events that had been shown on the screen. The factuality of what may have just transpired could not be so easily explained away. As such, televised sport in the USSR, despite the many well-documented pathologies of Soviet media, retained a certain core of honesty throughout its entire history. In general, most Soviet sport was presented in the Victorian spirit of "rational recreation," with the goal of educating intelligent viewers who would choose to exercise in order to emulate their high-performance heroes. Yet football and hockey players could behave violently, undermining their assigned duty as role models. These kinds of incidents created problems for announcers and directors, who could not easily ignore such bad examples for Soviet youth.[58] While sport could and did play a positive instrumental role, it was also an arena of pathologies that were harder for commentators to explain.

Here I must temporarily abandon my stance as professional historian and replace it with that of participant-observer. Much of what I have related here is based on my own viewing of Soviet television from 1970 up to the collapse. In 1975, I went so far as to buy a small TV, which I smuggled into the dorm at Moscow State University. While nightly viewing improved my Russian and gave me an instant topic of conversation with all manner of Soviet males, I more often watched in friends' homes in Moscow, Leningrad, Kiev, Tbilisi, Vilnius, and Erevan. I cannot say I saw any broadly generalizable behaviors. In some places we watched quietly and politely, drinking at roughly the normal level for a Soviet evening. In most such cases, women were present. Football watching was, nevertheless, a heavily masculinized activity, and my experiences in these homosocial environments usually involved more drinking, leading to a loosening of tongues. Russian is an incredibly rich language with bizarre and convoluted curses. The worst epithets were reserved for poorly performing players on the favorite team of my particular host of the day or evening. A few of the cleaner terms were *pederast, alkogolik,* and *gomoseksualist.* The onomatopoetic *v zhopu* does not require translation. Referees were, of course, not exempt. Bad work provoked the cry of "Sudia na mylo!" which, according to the twisted syntax of this particular idiom, meant "Turn the referee into soap." This too was more likely to be heard in the stands than in a living room. Announcers also came in for colorful criticism, published and unpublished.[59] For myself, I can't remember which was more difficult, keeping up with the vodka consumption or making sense of the rich flood of profanity.[60]

Recent, more systematic research on football watching has been carried out by the German scholar Manfred Zeller, who engaged in archival work (mainly fan mail) and conducted interviews with former Soviet citizens. In a recent article that focuses on Kiev in the sixties, he suggests ways that television, a consumer item that virtually everyone had, changed the experience and meanings of watching soccer. By the 1960s the game was broadcast all over the vastness of the USSR. "The extension of television's broadcasting range created translocal and transnational modes of consumption and identification that helped citizens integrate themselves into a Soviet order that they imagined and negotiated by themselves through semi-public [activities]."[61] This "integration" could simultaneously have a centrifugal impact when it came to questions of nationality. Citizens from many non-Russian republics came to identify with Dinamo Kiev's relatively recent and highly power-ful challenge to the Russian center. In 1961, they became the first provincial side to take the Soviet championship, a feat they would repeat on numerous occasions thereafter.

Additionally, as TV became the primary source for watching football, it was carried out in the porous privacy of the newly constructed Soviet apartment—porous because walls were thin, rooms were small, and bugging devices were easily installed. The stadium was also a place where the public and private could collide and mix, but this may have been even more true of the apartment. Watching football, according to Zeller, was "private and public at the same time," in other words a liminal space, and what sort of human activity could be a better fit to occupy such a space than sport, one of the most liminal human activities of all?[62] It occupies public spaces (the stadium), semipublic spaces (the street, courtyard and bar), and theoretically private spaces (the apartment). Zeller describes 1960s Kievan viewing experiences that were relatively orderly, cultured, and rational. He attributes this to the varying degrees of a female presence at the time of viewing. To this one might add the low-key, unemotional tone of most Soviet announcers. All this tracks with my own highly unscientific experience. The authorities were often perplexed by what they had wrought in making apartments so broadly available, but the contradictions of privacy and individualism appeared to have outweighed the dangers to public order posed by the rampant and potentially dangerous masculinity of the stadium.

Which Sixties?

Stuart Hall argued that audiences for the products of mass culture industries responded in a variety of ways. The very liminality of sport as a form of popular culture would seem to be a guarantee of such variety. Following Gramsci, Hall suggested that under capitalism those differing responses divided the audience and generated consent for the authority of dominant social groups.[63] Something quite different took place when Soviet audiences began watching their clubs playing in European stadiums. In this case, the variety of responses undermined the authority of a regime that, at least initially, offered only one way of understanding the spectacles it was presenting to the masses.

What emerged during the sixties (and early seventies) was an ongoing negotiation between an internally divided state and a changing and ever more various and complex society. In the process, the very borders between the two players in this old two-sided game were eroded if not obliterated. All sorts of middle layers emerged both within the regime and among the public. In 1945, the party had taken the risk of broadcasting the tour of Great Britain. Twenty years later they took another risk in televising the Eurocups. This step was yet another response to the wishes of an increasingly curious sporting audience, in other words a demand from below. At no time in Soviet history did the authorities shield the citizens from the events and practices of football under capitalism. Soviet media had paid continuous attention to sport outside the borders. Put most simply, the menu of soccer attractions made available by the regime to the nation's fans evolved continually throughout Soviet history. The sport authorities needed to provide compelling sporting attractions, and the Eurocups were especially compelling, not to mention profitable.

Yet as we have seen, live television of spontaneous and unpredictable sporting events was tricky. Soviet audiences could witness things the authorities did not wish them to see. They could derive their own meanings of what they had seen. They could discuss these events among themselves. Throughout the sixties and early seventies these various discourses expanded and interpenetrated. Television intensified them, yet could not by itself control the sense the multiple Soviet publics made of them. Unfortunately for historians' purposes, these discourses are difficult to recover. In the truest sense of the term, they are hidden transcripts that everyone knew about but hardly anyone wrote about. Interviews and memoirs, with their problems of retrospectivity, are all we have.

In the process of watching their teams take on Europe's best, Soviet fans developed fractured loyalties. Supporters of Dinamo Kiev would more often than not root for the opponents of Spartak and vice versa. Fans of Dinamo Tbilisi took pleasure in the travails of Ararat Erevan. As Zeller noted, national tensions could be exacerbated. Provincial towns could confront the power of the center. The sorts of solidarities among Soviet clubs in international competition that the regime would have desired were often but not always undermined. In his massive history of Moscow, Timothy Colton describes a decline in the capital's authority that began in the sixties.[64] This process was reflected in the emergence of scores of provincial teams, all of which clamored for a place in the soccer sun.

Soccer hooliganism, a sign of tensions between young and old learned from the British masters, introduced yet another social tension that did not emerge fully until the early seventies. Long hair and bad manners were yet another sign of the withering away of the Soviet state's authority. All of these tensions emerged full-blown in the last Soviet decades, but they had their roots in the seemingly optimistic socialist sixties. At the 1966 World Cup, the USSR achieved its best result, making the semifinal. It was the first World Cup televised back to the nation. Even the English fans, with the unwashed kept out of the stadiums, were on their good behavior. The future seemed bright, but as things turned out the rest was all downhill.

Notes

I will be employing a trans-Atlantic nomenclature in this essay, calling the game here in question both soccer and football.

1. The Soviets were invited by the English Football Association, despite their not belonging to the international soccer federation (FIFA).

2. Aksel' Vartanian, *Sto let Rossiiskomu futbolu* (Moscow: Gregory Page, 1995), 95; Mikhail Iakushin, *Vechnaia taina futbola* (Moscow: Fizkul'tura i sport, 1988), 87–96; I. S. Dobronravov, *Na bessrochnoi sluzhbe futbolu* (Moscow: Luch-1, 2000), 136–38.

3. Eduard Nisenboim, *Spartak offitsial'naia istoriia: 1922-2002* (Moscow: Medea, 2002), 51–55.

4. David Goldblatt, *The Ball Is Round: A Global History of Football* (London: Viking, 2006), 329.

5. Robert Edelman, *Serious Fun: A History of Spectator Sports in the USSR* (New York: Oxford University Press, 1993), 87–91.

6. Robert Edelman, *Spartak Moscow: A History of the People's Team in the Workers' State* (Ithaca: Cornell University Press, 2009), 147.

7. *Futbol nashego detstva*, TV program, Gosteleradio, 1984.

8. Elena Zubkova, *Russia after the War: Hopes, Illusions and Disappointments* (Armonk, NY: M. E. Sharpe, 1998), 22; Vera Dunham, *In Stalin's Time: Middle-Class Values in Soviet Fiction* (Cambridge: Cambridge University Press, 1976), 17; Eric Duskin, *Stalinist Reconstruction and the Confirmation of a New Elite* (New York: Palgrave, 2001), 2; Sheila Fitzpatrick, "Post-War Soviet Society: The Return to Normalcy," in *The Impact of World War II on the Soviet Union*, ed. Susan Linz (Totowa, NJ: Rowman and Allanheld, 1985).

9. Aksel' Vartanian, phone interview by author, Moscow, 23 September 2010; "Novoe litso 'Olympiakosa,'" *Sovetskii sport* (hereafter *SS*), 15 September 1971; "Iozef Venslosh i ego komanda," *SS*, 15 September 1971; "Debiut za 'Spartakom,'" *SS*, 16 September 1971; "Khoziaeva-neudachniki," *SS*, 23 September 1971; "Do zavtra na stadione 'Dinamo,'" *SS*, 29 September 1971; "Miach kruglyi, pole zelenoe" and "Poka pobedy s sukhim schetom," *SS*, 30 September 1971; "Piat' zarubezhnykh sopernikov," *SS*, 10 October 1971; "Gotovy k liuboi pogode," *SS*, 29 October 1971; "'Inter' razgromlen, 'Inter' protestuet," *SS*, 22 October 1971; "Dinamovtsy v chetvert' finale," *SS*, 14 November 1971; "Distsiplinirovannye chempiony," *SS*, 15 September 1972; "Ratsionalisty iz Madrida," *SS*, 25 October 1972; "Evropeiskii ekzamen," *SS*, 7 March 1972; "Kak eto bylo v Belgrade," *SS*, 12 March 1972.

10. Erik Eggers and M. Kneifl, "'Wir sind die Eisenbrecher v Adenauer gewessen': Das Fussball-Landerspiel Sowjetunion vs. BRD am August 21, 1955 in Moskau im Kontext der bundesdeutschen Aussenpolitik," *SportZeiten*, 6 January 2006, 111–42.

11. Vartanian, *Sto let rossiiskomu futbolu*, 116.

12. "Soviet Teams Enter the International Arena," *Letopis' sporta*, TV program, Rossiya 2, 2009.

13. Keir Radnedge, *50 Years of the Champions League and European Cup* (London: Carlton Books, 2005), 48–65.

14. Goldblatt, *Ball Is Round*, 681–773.

15. Games not involving Soviet clubs, including the final, were not shown until the eighties.

16. For the first season of such play, see, "Ia videl Torpedo," *SS*, 25 September 1966; "Chto vy znaete o 'Belgrade,'" *SS*, 27 September 1966; "'Spartak' i 'Belgrad' kubkovye boitsy," *SS*, 28 September 1966; "Itog—po dvum vstrecham," *SS*, 30 September 1966; "Bol'shoi futbol'nyi den'," *SS*, 30 September 1966; "Milanskii dialog," *SS*, 2 November 1966; "Bol'shoi futbol'nyi den'," *SS*, 2 December 1966; "'Rapid'-'Spartak,'" *SS*, 8 December 1966; "Dva gola Mazzioli," *SS*, 10 December 1966.

17. Nikolai Dolgopolov, phone interview by author, Moscow, 1 December 2010.

18. The pioneering research on British soccer hooliganism was done by John Williams, Eric Dunning, and Patrick Murphy, *Hooligans Abroad: The Behaviour and Control of English Fans in Continental Europe* (London: Routledge, 1984) and *The Roots of Football Hooliganism: An Historical and Sociological Study* (London: Routledge, 1988). See also Gary Armstrong, *Football Hooliganism: Knowing the Score* (Oxford: Berg, 1998). For a sensationalized but intelligent memoir of the hooligan experience, see Bill Buford, *Among the Thugs* (New York: Norton, 1992).

19. Vartanian, interview; Mikhail Prozumenshikov, *Bol'shoi sport i bol'shaia politika* (Moscow: ROSSPEN, 2004), 296–344.

20. Aksel' Vartanian, "Draki pri sotsializme," *Sportekspress futbol*, no. 27 (1999): 32–35.

21. Nisenboim, *Spartak offitsial'naia istoriia*, 233.

22. Radnedge, *50 Years*, 70–71.

23. "Pervyi shag sdelan," *SS*, 7 April 1972.

24. Bill Murray, *The Old Firm: Sectarianism, Sport and Society in Scotland* (Edinburgh: John Donald, 1984), 183–84.

25. "Rangers Increase Their Status in Europe," *Times*, 5 May 1972, 24.

26. Personal copy. The DVD comes from the BBC feed. The version I viewed was produced, distributed, and probably edited by Glasgow Rangers Football Club.

27. Ibid.

28. Radnedge, *50 Years*, 224–25.

29. DVD, BBC feed.

30. Union of European Football Associations (hereafter UEFA) Records Management, RM00006117.

31. Murray, *Old Firm*, 179. The confrontation with the Spanish police is not preserved on the DVD of the match produced by Glasgow Rangers Football Club.

32. "Rangers Win but Dynamo Claim Replay," *Guardian*, 25 May 1972, 35. Bizarrely, the account offered by the *Times* mentioned the limited field invasions after the goals but said nothing about the battle royal after the match.

33. UEFA Records Management, RM00006117; "Protest," SS, 26/5/72.

34. *SS*, 26 May 1972. The match would have ended too late in Moscow time to have made the deadline for the 25 May issue.

35. Dobronravov, *Na bessrochnoi sluzhbe futbolu*, 225.

36. UEFA Records Management, RM00006122.

37. Yuri Slezkine, electronic communication to author.

38. Unofficial program *Klub bolel'shchikov Spartaka*, "Kogda khodiat legendy," Spartak-Rotor, Moscow, 24 September 1990.

39. Vladimir Titorenko, phone interview by author, Moscow, 24 September 2010.

40. Vartanian, interview; Dolgopolov, interview.

41. *Klub bolel'shchikov Spartaka*.

42. *Izvestiia*, 7 August 1960; "Bol'shoi futbol'nyi den'," SS, 4 August 1970; "Bol'shoi futbol'nyi den'," SS, 5 August 1970; "Bol'shoi futbol'nyi den'," SS 27 August 1970.

43. John Bushnell, *Moscow Graffiti: Language and Subculture* (London: Unwin and Hyman, 1990), 30–40.

44. Ibid., 30–40.

45. Williams, Dunning, and Murphy, *Hooligans Abroad*.

46. Alexei Yurchak, *Everything Was Forever, Until It Was No More: The Last Soviet Generation* (Princeton: Princeton University Press, 2006).

47. Moshe Lewin, *The Soviet Century* (New York: Verso, 2005), 317–33.

48. Artemy Troitsky, *Back in the USSR: The True Story of Rock in Russia* (New York: Omnibus, 1987); Richard Stites, *Russian Popular Culture: Entertainment and Society since 1900* (Cambridge: Cambridge University Press, 1992), 192–201.

49. Aleksandr Soskin, *Sergei Sal'nikov* (Moscow: Knizhnyi klub, 2004), 8–9; Nikita Simonian, *Futbol, tol'ko li igra?* (Moscow: Izdatel'sko-Torgovyi Dom Grand, 1998); Nisenboim, *Spartak offitsial'naia istoriia*, 97.

50. Nikita Simonian, interview by author, Moscow, 20 January 2002.

51. Igor Goranskii, *Evgenii Lovchev* (Moscow: Knizhnyi klub, 2002); Evgenii Lovchev, interview by author, Moscow, 15 September 2003.

52. Gennadi Logofet, interview by author, Moscow, 5 September 2000.

53. Alena Ledeneva, *Russia's Economy of Favours: Blat, Networking and Informal Exchange* (Cambridge: Cambridge University Press, 1998).

54. Christine Evans, "From Truth to Time: Soviet Television, 1957–1985" (PhD diss., University of California, Berkeley, 2010), 18–51.

55. G. Elenskii, "Sport na stol'ko zrelishche," *Zhurnalist*, no. 3 (1969): 25.

56. Lev Filatov, "Futbol'nye protivorechiia," *Zhurnalist*, no. 4 (1972): 26–27.

57. Elenskii, "Sport na stol'ko zrelishche," 25.

58. Ibid., 24–26.

59. B. Batanov, "Esli by ia byl kommentatorom," *Zhurnalist,* no. 7 (1976): 78–79.

60. Robert Edelman, "Sport on Soviet Television," in *Sport and the Transformation of Modern Europe: States, Media and Markets, 1950–2010,* ed. Alan Tomlinson, Christopher Young, and Richard Holt (London: Routledge, 2011), 100–12.

61. Manfred Zeller, "'Our Own Internationale,' 1966: Dynamo Kiev Fans between Local Identity and Transnational Imagination," *Kritika* 12, no. 1 (Winter 2011): 57.

62. Manfred Zeller, "Soccer and the Living Room: Sport Reception and Private Life in the Late Soviet Union," paper presented at the annual convention of the American Association for the Advancement of Slavic Studies, Boston, 12 November 2009.

63. Stuart Hall, "Notes on Deconstructing the Popular," in *People's History and Socialist Theory,* ed. Raphael Samuel (London: Routledge and Kegan Paul, 1981), 232. See also Antonio Gramsci, *Selections from the Prison Notebooks* (New York: International Publishers, 1971), 417.

64. Timothy Colton, *Moscow: Governing the Socialist Metropolis* (Cambridge, MA: Harvard University Press, 1995), 434.

12 Listening to *los Beatles*

Being Young in 1960s Cuba

Anne Luke

THE PICTURE OF a socialist 1960s cannot be complete without exploration of the small Caribbean island that bucked the regional trends and chose to follow a political model from the other side of the world rather than the one on offer on its doorstep. Beyond a Cold War political appraisal of a bipolar world lies a story where a fluidity of exchange is in evidence, where transnational cultural flows meld with national cultural distinctiveness to create a new texture of the everyday in Cuba. In cases where imported cultural motifs have an impact, they reemerge, "Cubanized," as new hybrid cultural expressions. These reflect the effervescence of a 1960s culture that allowed for the fluidity of meanings and that could thereby cross national boundaries and be transformed.

The rehabilitation of the Beatles in Cuba in 2000, when Fidel Castro unveiled a sculpture of John Lennon seated on a bench in a park in Havana, led to a resituating of 1960s youth culture on the island. The term *los Beatles* is now used in Cuba to represent the imported music—accessible but of ambiguous official standing—of Cuban youth cultures in the 1960s. This article will plot the coordinates of some of these youth cultures in Havana in that decade, including the culture of the young poets of the El Puente group, the growing popularity of foreign music, the emergence of new styles and public spaces, and finally the importance of a new Cuban music, *nueva trova*. The texture of 1960s life can most readily be found by examining Havana's public spaces, and quite literally to plot these coordinates is to go on a journey of just a few blocks around the public spaces of the Vedado zone of the city.

This is not a story of the state determining one course of action and anti-state actors another. To suggest that young people listening to new music or wearing new styles were acting in deliberately counterrevolutionary or dissident ways would be to miss the very nature of Cuban popular culture in the sixties and its development. This article instead sees youth popular cultural engagement in the city as existing on a continuum from definable subcultural groupings at one end to engagement with popular general cultural trends at the other. Anne Gorsuch identifies a similar phenomenon, particularly with reference to dance and dress, among Soviet youth in the 1920s, where there was an "extreme and self-conscious example of bohemian subculture [the young aristocrats]" but where "elements of bohemian visual and behavioral vocabulary trickled down through other layers of society and were adopted in less-radical forms by working-class, student and even communist youth."[1] I contend that rather than being only overtly antiestablishment or risky, Havana youth culture of the first decade of the Revolution merged external motifs with internal movements. The experience of young people in Cuba shows a search for identity that was vibrant and experimental and that reflected the newfound confidence of an empowered generation within and beyond Cuban shores.

The Sixties and the Cuban Case

How useful are the sixties as a unit of analysis in the Cuban case? Arthur Marwick, for whom the sixties run from 1959 to 1974, confesses that his consideration of the period may be most relevant to a study of the West;[2] but in admitting to his Western-centric position, he opens the door for research into the sixties from alternative perspectives that allow a broader transnational and/or global position. Youth is a relevant unit of analysis, as it does seem to experience transnational influences with particular intensity. Eric Hobsbawm argues that the 1960s saw the emergence of a global youth culture resulting from improved technology, travel, and media, which together resulted in young people experiencing fashion, sex, drugs, and rock music as an international phenomenon.[3]

The Cuban case elucidates the value of examining the local and the global in tandem. On the island, the 1960s have become a popular unit of analysis for several reasons. First, the Cuban Revolution became part of the global sixties as the revolution, and in particular the hero-martyr figure of Che Guevara, captured the imagination of youth movements across the globe. Second, the sixties *(los sesenta)*, in Cuban historiography, have a natural beginning (the victory of the 26 July Movement on 1 January 1959) and end (the failure of the attempted ten-million-ton sugar harvest of 1970). Finally, the sixties are mythologized within contemporary Cuban culture, particularly since the withdrawal of Fidel Castro from frontline politics. Exploring what is underneath this myth is part of the purpose of this research. Antoni Kapcia has explored the importance of myth in Cuban national identity *(cubanía)* at length, centering on history as a "myth-system" with a focus on national liberation and radical nationalism.[4] The mythologization of the 1960s, I would argue, can be seen as the next logical sequence in this myth-system. Geographically, it is impossible not to see Cuba as an historical anomaly, leading Kapcia to ask, "Does Cuba fit in yet or is it still exceptional?"[5] Yet the global sixties existed in a form in Cuba that is still perceived as contested territory, particularly with reference to youth. For example, in John Kirk and Leonardo Padura Fuentes's 2001 interviews with Cuban cultural producers, the musician Leo Brower was alone in referring to the controversial stance, in the 1960s, of the dual youth culture forms of expression of wearing long hair and listening to the Beatles.[6] This version of the global youth culture experienced in Cuba in the field of popular culture was a "Cubanized" version. What at first glance appears Western, and at second glance appears Cuban, can, on continued reflection, be understood as a fascinating hybrid of the local and the global.

Becoming Youth

The uncertainties of life in the early years of the Cuban Revolution are clearly demonstrated elsewhere in this volume by João Gonçalves, who points to the island's "conflicted transition to socialism" as debates raged over which political model would best suit Cuba's ideology of nationalism and progress. From the initial euphoria of January 1959, an emerging political discourse developed that, once forged in those key early years of the Revolution, became remarkably stable. Youth was central to this discourse. The majority of young people played some part in the construction of the Revolution, whether as literacy teachers, leaders and members of cultural groups (aficionados), militia members and members of the Association of Young Rebels (AJR), or, later, members of the Union of Young Communists (UJC). It is through the latter youth organizations that the official voice of Cuban youth can be heard.[7] The unstable history of these organizations as they attempted to fulfill the tasks set out for them and as they moved from mass organizations to a single highly selective one, led to one of the key lines of conflict in the 1960s for young people and featured UJC-prompted moral panics raging over what the UJC perceived as dissolute Western displays of youth culture. The force of the ideology of "Work, Study, the Rifle" (the slogan of the UJC) played a strong role in directing the youth organization.

The key role given to young people in Cuba and the increasingly hagiographic treatment of youth as a group emerged from the ethos of the new leadership of Cuba, which took its inspiration from traditional notions of nationhood: it was a revolution led by a group of young rebels who were associated by the Cuban public not with the corrupt political practices of the past but with the heroic guerrilla struggle in the mountains to the east of the island in the second half of the 1950s. The rebels of the Sierra Maestra guerrilla struggle of the 1950s, including Fidel and

Raúl Castro and Che Guevara, identified with youth. They represented the renaissance of the Cuban nation and saw the heroic young fighters of the wars of independence as their forefathers. They espoused and promoted an idealized vision of youth linked to historical heroes and martyrs and characterized by a belief in the innate purity and enthusiasm of youth coupled with an existence increasingly, as new generations grew to maturity, untainted by the bourgeois past. Fidel Castro, in an important speech to a youth congress in 1962, articulated this idealized view of youth: "Believing in the young means seeing not just their enthusiasm but also their ability, not just energy but also responsibility, not just youth but also purity, heroism, character, determination, love for the nation and belief in it, love for the Revolution and faith in it, confidence in themselves, a profound belief that youth can achieve things, that it has ability, a profound conviction that great responsibilities can be placed on young shoulders."[8] This is typical of much of the dominant 1960s discussion of youth found in leadership speeches and texts, which, in tandem with the creation of new youth organizations, elevated youth to a position of prominence.[9]

This hagiography of youth over the course of the 1960s in Cuba was complemented by youth taking center stage elsewhere in the world. In January 1967, *Time* magazine nominated the "Young Generation" as its Man of the Year, a development that reached the pages of Cuban magazine *Bohemia*, a Cuban lifestyle magazine: "Greater than its numbers, says *Time* magazine, is the impact that [the young generation] has on every area of contemporary life, from politics to pop art, from fashion to finance, from civil rights to civil disobedience. It is the generation that stands up to the old folk like LBJ."[10] The consciousness within Cuba of the importance of youth was complemented by an awareness of the influence of the Cuban Revolution on the increasingly important and high-profile external youth movements. Pride in the Revolution and the leadership role of Cuba helped form a confident body of young people on the island, and Cuba took credit for radicalizing young people outside Cuba.[11] This influence was perhaps exaggerated, but there were certainly strong links between Cuba and leftist movements in Europe and the USA.[12] The iconolatry associated with the image of Che Guevara, particularly after his death in 1967, as used by student protesters externally, gave rise to an excitement in Cuba over the emergence of an external, politicized and to some extent anticapitalist (or at least antiestablishment) group. Cuba may have been an island blockaded economically by its large neighbor, but it was by no means isolated. People were busy with the tasks of building the Revolution, but the feeling among young people of being part of something larger was reflected in the cross-fertilization between Cuba and the outside. Both on and off the island, youth began to occupy center stage.

Havana Youth in the 1960s: Public Spaces, Music, and Style

Public Spaces

The celebratory mood in January 1959, as Fidel Castro and his group of rebels victoriously entered Havana while Fulgencio Batista fled the country, symbolized a reclamation by the Cuban people of their own streets. The sociocultural landscape of Havana in the 1960s changed radically from the city of the 1950s. The exodus of over half a million Cubans between 1960 and 1974 had the subsidiary effect in Havana of moving poorer families into vacated housing in previously middle-class areas, so the ethnic and class distribution of the city changed.[13] The zone in Havana that had been deemed most exclusive and most dominated by American interests was Vedado, which, along with its neighboring borough Miramar, had been home to twenty elite American social clubs.[14] Yet Vedado also had a more seedy side. It had been the center of the *bonche* (violent gang) activity of the 1950s, much of which had taken place in the zone around the university.[15] The district's hotels and nightclubs had been associated with North American gangster activity as well as prostitution and gambling. Over the course of the 1960s, the Vedado zone of Havana, within which were located La Rampa (one of the streets in Vedado formerly known for prostitution), the newly built Pabellón Cuba, the Colina (university steps), the newly built Coppelia ice cream parlor, and a stretch of the "Malecón" (seawall), was co-opted by young people as the public space of the newly empowered generation. It is no accident that an examination of youth in 1960s Havana always leads us to Vedado: students, musicians, poets, and subcultures all coexisted in this risky but also revolutionary semipublic space.

El Puente, Ginsberg, and the Enfermitos

In the early years of the Revolution, the pioneers of the emerging youth culture were the young poets and intellectuals of the El Puente group, who sought to assert their revolutionary and generational identity and who also engaged with cultural imports in the fields of both high and popular culture. This group, named after the independent publishing house that disseminated their work, and under the leadership of poet José Mario Rodríguez, emerged in 1960. El Puente is hard to categorize; poet Gerardo Fulleda León argues that "we weren't exactly a literary movement . . . rather a group of young people who needed to express ourselves through literature."[16] On the other hand, Josefina Suárez (also one of the group but not published) argues, "I think that we did consider ourselves a literary group, for some people even a literary 'generation,' but our attitude was not exclusive."[17] The reality is probably somewhere in between the two positions. They identified themselves as a group through personal links, friendships, and common aims. They had a public space in which they met, the Gato Tuerto bar in Vedado, where they listened to *feeling* music, a style of U.S.-influenced music popular in the 1950s. They also spent evenings and nights of songs, poems, and conversation sitting outside on the Malecón.[18] They incorporated significant numbers of black writers, which Fulleda argues was "something never seen either before or since in the history of Cuban literature."[19] Members of the group were, in 1962, aged between seventeen and twenty-six. Artistically the group never had the time to mature or consolidate its literary identity, but it did emerge as a youth culture incorporating identification with poetry, music—from feeling to "whatever Beatles we could get hold of"—and extravagant forms of dress. The group also participated in rallies and organized the Brigada Hermanos Saíz, a cultural organization for young amateur artists. Most were students at the University of Havana.[20]

This type of group was the very essence of what made the Cuban sixties, insofar as it identified with and worked for the Revolution but also tested the limits of the Revolution and was part of the process of defining exactly what the Revolution was. It was culturally permeable (in terms of both high culture and popular culture) and aware of outside music and literature. As in the Soviet Union, where there was an "ambiguity in the judgment of foreign influences in music, art and culture [that] opened up a space of interpretation of what concrete foreign cultural forms might mean in different contexts," the Cuban sixties saw mixed attitudes to outside trends, which allowed considerable latitude to new cultural interpretations within Cuba.[21]

The El Puente group was dissolved in 1965, accused of "a number of aesthetic (transcendentalism), moral (homosexualism), and, primarily, political (being unreliable as revolutionaries) sins."[22] El Puente then remained unreported in Cuban accounts of the cultural history of the Revolution until highlighted in a 2005 issue of *Gaceta de Cuba*. This silence over El Puente included a silence about the links between these young poets and the visit to Havana of U.S. poet and counterculture guru Allen Ginsberg.[23] Ginsberg was invited to Havana as a judge in the Casa de las Américas annual book competition, and during this time he spent considerable time in the company of several members of the El Puente group, including José Mario.[24] There was some excitement over Ginsberg's visit, which José Mario, writing from exile in Paris in 1969, described as a "happening," but his visit became controversial and ended in Ginsberg's deportation from Cuba.[25] The controversy centered on Ginsberg's homosexuality, his promarijuana stance, and his criticism of the treatment of the *enfermitos*.

The *enfermitos* were a small youth subculture based in Vedado, in particular La Rampa, and connected to the arts scene.[26] They listened to European or North American music, danced the twist, wore flamboyant (even effeminate) fashions, and drank alcohol. They were frowned upon particularly by the Union of Young Communists. In an article in the UJC publication *Mella*, the *enfermitos* were criticized as attempting to be *neoyorquino* or *europeo*, that is, uncritically adopting an imported ideology that had nothing to do with—or was even dangerous to—Cuba: "Their ramblings range from the idiotic to the counterrevolutionary, such as the view that 'there is no freedom if a group has no means of expression or vehicle through which to show its idea of the world,' they stretch the concept of 'sick.'"[27] The article insisted that there was no risk from this group, which was called "a meager minority"; that La Rampa was the property of all Cubans, not merely this small group; and that young people could "clean up" from the inside out to rid themselves of this small element.[28] The extremism of the UJC may be evident here, however, as the *enfermitos* were not demonized to such an extent elsewhere: in the university students' magazine *Alma Mater* the *enfermitos* were later treated somewhat more mildly. They were compared to the Teddy Boys in the United Kingdom and the beatniks in the USA insofar as the use of fashion defined their membership in a certain group. They were described as "an alienated group, a million miles away from the construction of socialism."[29] To an extent this was true: the group was a hangover from 1950s U.S.-dominated Havana, and most Cubans were too busy with the task of building the Revolution to have time for this borderline culture. They were, however, only at one extreme of the continuum of youth culture. The "softer" version consisted of the many young people who enjoyed cultural imports and new forms of dress but did so nonostentatiously and nonexclusively. Much the same pattern can be seen in the Soviet Union, and there are clear parallels here between the *enfermitos* and the Soviet *stiliagi* subculture discussed by Alexei Yurchak. Yurchak describes a Soviet "tendency to critique extreme manifestations of 'bourgeois' influences while tolerating or overlooking more common and less conspicuous tendencies among wider groups of youth." Like the *enfermitos,* the *stiliagi* were portrayed in the Soviet press as "a small and insignificant group of deviationists, bourgeois sympathizers, and uneducated loafers," while those young people who were interested in similar (Western) cultural forms among broader cultural interests were not criticized and might even themselves be critical of the *stiliagi*.[30]

Ginsberg learned of the plight of the *enfermitos* from the young poets of El Puente and openly criticized their treatment, as well as the Cuban treatment of homosexuals.[31] Part of the conflict between Ginsberg and the Cuban authorities was based on differing views of what constituted "revolution." Ginsberg understood revolution to mean (in part) the acceptance of homosexuality and the legalization of marijuana. He took those views to Cuba expecting, according to his biographer Barry Miles, to experience a sympathetic viewpoint but instead discovering that the Cuban vision of revolution—schools, hospitals, and literacy—had nothing to do with his vision.[32] Certainly, it is impossible to separate Ginsberg's visit from issues of homosexuality, which, even more than his attitude to marijuana, explain his eventual discrediting. Institutionalized homophobia was deep-seated in 1960s Cuba. The public display of homosexuality was abhorred,[33] and those young poets who spent time with Ginsberg fell under suspicion, were subjected to arrest, and sometimes, as in the case of José Mario (a homosexual himself), were sent to one of the Military Units to Aid Production (UMAPs)—forced labor camps that existed in Cuba from 1965 to 1967.[34]

El Puente was certainly not a counterrevolutionary group. It was a cluster of young revolutionary artists and their associates dealing with the new atmosphere of a socialist revolution in Cuba and exploring the meaning of revolution to young Cubans. They were tainted by association with certain trends—such as public displays of homosexuality and the externally influenced youth culture of the *enfermitos*—that were coming to be considered counterrevolutionary by some in the UJC. All these trends existed and overlapped in 1960s Cuba and were on the continuum of youth culture from the unacceptable to the tolerated to the encouraged, with many young people moving backwards and forwards along this line.

Coppelia, Style, and the Music Scene

The closure of the El Puente publishing house, in part due to the association between the group and (overt) homosexuality, Allen Ginsberg, and public displays of affiliation with "Western" culture, did not stamp out the evolving Havana youth culture. By the later 1960s, youth culture in Havana had solidified around music and fashion and had found expression in the public spaces of Vedado, in particular the Coppelia ice cream parlor. The importance of Coppelia is paramount to the geography of Havana youth culture—it was a revolutionary initiative, built in the sixties, representing leisure, well-being, and production under the new regime; it was a public space but not as contested as the street, available to all in the heart of the Vedado area.

Coppelia became the site of the *Batalla de Virginidad*, a reaction to the liberalization in sexual relations that Cuba was experiencing.[35] The miniskirt for women and long hair for young men, so popular among young people, were seen by some observers as representative of this sexual revolution, with older people even attempting to cut the hair of young men and to pull skirts down to protect the modesty of young women. The miniskirt, perhaps the most noticeable development in female fashion imported into Cuba, received a varied welcome. A light-hearted view of this phenomenon is evident in Ñico's 1968 cartoon revealing a generational angst over the new fashion: in the cartoon two women wear miniskirts, one of them saying to her tailor, "Whatever anyone says, I am not moving without wearing a miniskirt"; the other looks surprised as a (male) car driver says to her, "Why do you bother wearing anything at all?"; and an old woman looks over the scenes, saying, "What a disgrace! It was different in my day." At the bottom of the cartoon runs the line, "Do you have young taste? Well, use it then!"[36] The cartoon implies that if young women choose to wear a miniskirt they must expect the consequent *piropo* (flirtatious or cheeky remark from a man). While there was female empowerment in the Cuban 1960s, there was no clearly definable feminist movement, so there is no Cuban feminist critique of the miniskirt. Western fashion, like the long hair of young men, produced a generational angst rather than a political one, and if anything the dominant discourse in this country with its deeply rooted machismo tended to savor any development that was pleasing to the male gaze.

Through the use of Western style, the young people who hung out in Coppelia were a definable youth culture distinguishable from other generations in how they expressed themselves. The resemblance to the U.S. counterculture is, however, slightly misleading. They were not a mirror image of that counterculture, and in some ways their behavior was more reminiscent of a subculture in their use of *bricolage* to give new meanings to public life.[37] For example, the cane-cutting boots that were provided free to young people doing voluntary work in the country became a fashion item when the volunteers returned to the city. This reconceptualization of meanings represented a type of liberation, particularly for young women, where involvement in voluntary work removed them from the traditional role ascribed to them and permitted them greater freedom in public life. The young woman wearing no makeup, volunteering as a militia member or cane cutter, spending time away from her family at a young age, found a new identity outside traditional femininity with its *casa/calle* (public/private) divide.

Here in Vedado this young generation of men and women found one of the keys to their youth culture—music—and new music found its audience. Music dominated young people's leisure time in the Cuban 1960s, with three forms prevailing: protest song, rock music, and *nueva trova*.[38] Protest song *(canción protesta)* was a powerful musical discipline to which Cuba had a proud history of contributing. In July 1967 a festival of protest song (Primer Encuentro de Canción Protesta) was held in Varadero and Havana, which led to the establishment of the Center for Protest Music in 1968.[39] One cartoon in *Bohemia* at the time illustrated Cubans' pride in being a musical vanguard. Entitled "La canción protesta," cartoonist Ñico showed a Cuban holding a guitar, singing "Guantanamera," "Si yo tuviera un martillo" (Pete Seeger's "If I Had a Hammer"), and "Sí, somos americanos" (by Chilean protest singer Rolando Alarcón).[40] The central position of the Cuban bearded revolutionary in the cartoon reflects the leadership role that Cuba felt it held within the protest song movement. The transmission of protest music across national boundaries was imperfect: in his contribution to this volume, Rossen Djagalov mentions that *nueva trova* singers did not meet with Pete Seeger when Seeger visited Havana in 1971. Additionally, Bob Dylan's defection to rock music in 1965 led some in Cuba to feel that the protest song movement was in crisis.[41] Having said that, the clear flows between countries (implying, with the inclusion of Seeger in the cartoon discussed, a translation of the lyrics as well as the music) contributes to a sense of global reach in the field of protest music in the 1960s.

Rock music was accessible to Cuban young people in the 1960s through radio broadcasts, live performances, and informal record exchanges. On occasion, the reception of rock music was seen as problematic or controversial, a stance for which the UJC was particularly but not exclusively responsible. Such a position is equivalent to (and highly reminiscent of) that of the "Bolshevik moralists" to whom Anne Gorsuch refers in the case of the early Soviet state. As in the case of Komsomol members, the focus on asceticism and discipline evokes clear parallels.[42] The musical controversy came to the surface in 1967 when the United States' policy to broadcast rock music to Cuba for the purposes of subverting Cuban youth led to the withdrawal of rock music broadcasts from Cuba's official media.[43] Yet rock music and the Beatles in particular seemed to strike a chord with young people,[44] a trend that can also be seen at that time in the Soviet Union, where, according to Artemy Troitsky, "the Beatle's happy, harmonious vocal choir proved to be just the voice for which our confused generation was waiting."[45] The Cuban academic Dénia García Ronda remembers this as the *Batalla con los Beatles*.[46] In this battle the lines of conflict were drawn between those young people who loved rock music and continued to listen to the music of the Beatles and those young people who held the view that it was a harmful bourgeois indulgence and associated it with subcultures such as the *enfermitos*. The second line of conflict was generational, and in Cuba, as in Eastern Europe, and indeed globally, rock music "pitted the younger generation against the older generation."[47]

Despite the politico-cultural battle and the removal of rock music from the official airwaves, young people continued to listen to the Beatles and other external music. Cuban musicologist Clara Díaz explains how this was possible: "There was a secret record exchange between young people announced through an alternative hit parade of groups and solo artists whose music was not officially in circulation."[48] Furthermore, despite the difficulty of obtaining Beatles and Rolling Stones originals, recordings of their songs by Spanish or Latin American groups were readily available.[49] The transmission of song is discussed in Christian Noack's chapter in this volume, in which he explores how Soviet tourist songs proliferated through the tape-recording of performances. In the Cuban case, the song became the traveler, received sometimes in its direct form and at other times through the mediated environments of performance and translation.

It was the act of listening, rather than the meaning of the lyrics of the songs, that made consumption of external music significant. Indeed, young people in Cuba would sing along to Beatles songs without necessarily knowing the meaning of the lyrics.[50] Kenneth Leech's contention that "the ideas expressed through pop songs may . . . be potentially and actually subversive of the established order" and thereby central to understanding youth culture does not apply in this case.[51] The Cuban case rather has parallels with the USSR, where Yurchak describes the creation of the "imaginary West," with symbols of the West becoming "empty husks, from which the original literal meanings were drained."[52] The songs took on a new cultural meaning quite apart from any impact of the lyrics. Because the recordings were considered almost clandestine, they gave Cuban young people a means to express themselves by distinguishing those people who listened to Western music from those who did not.

The second half of the 1960s witnessed the emergence of a new genre of Cuban music known as *nueva trova,* the final coordinate in our picture of Havana youth culture at the time. *Nueva trova* helped feed the desire of young people for music that was live as well as recorded. Certainly, the radio was popular, with cartoonist Aristide terming the phenomenon "Radiomania."[53] Furthermore, television was an important medium for the dissemination of the new Cuban music. It was the live domain, however, that gave the impetus to this new musical form. This was in part because guitar music lends itself to the spontaneity of live performance, as Noack and Djagalov have argued elsewhere in this volume. Added to that, a Cuban tradition of live music in various forms produced a high proportion of both professional and amateur musical performers, relative to the population, in both classical and folk traditions.[54] *Nueva trova* (literally "new *trova*") was in name a descendant of the rich seam of musical tradition *(trova)* running through Cuban history. In a musical sense, though, *nueva trova* emerged through a combination of protest music and rock. *Nueva trova* was a form of guitar poetry, which, as Djagalov argues in this volume, acquired a "liminal, semiofficial status." It enjoyed a broad appeal among young people in part because it brought together, through its two key protagonists of the late 1960s, diverse fan bases. Silvio Rodríguez attracted white urban Cubans who were fans of external music, and Pablo Milanés attracted black Cubans favoring national music.[55]

Despite this rich heritage and broad appeal, *nueva trova* did not have a straightforward birth. The dissemination of *nueva trova* music began through spontaneous nightly gatherings at the Coppelia ice cream parlor. *Nueva trova* entered the broader public domain in June 1967, when the cultural supplement of the national daily paper *Juventud rebelde, El caimán barbudo,* organized an event at the Museo Nacional de Bellas Artes that, along with poetry readings, included a performance from the twenty-year-old Silvio Rodríguez.[56] Rodríguez began to appear regularly on the television show *Mientras tanto* in 1967, which showcased his songs and turned him into a celebrity, fulfilling, for Cuba's young men and women, the desire for a new kind of revolutionary hero. In early 1968, Silvio Rodríguez was described in the Cuban magazine *Bohemia* as "the *star* of a youth that is devoted to carrying out great social undertakings."[57] Not only a musician, Silvio Rodríguez had been a member of the Association of Young Rebels. He had participated in the literacy campaign and the *aficionados* movement, and, by 1967, he had carried out his national service (SMO). Like many of the El Puente writers, he participated in the Revolution, and young people and cultural critics alike saw him as an example of the new generation of revolutionary cultural producers.

Yet at the very moment that Silvio's popularity was reaching new heights, he encountered difficulties. Rodríguez found himself at the center of a row over what was acceptable and revolutionary and what was not. The difficulties emerged from Rodríguez's open admiration of external music, a position that struck a chord with the many young people of Havana: he declared, on air, his indebtedness to the music of the Beatles. Immediately, in April 1968, "conservative tendencies" in the Instituto Cubano de Radiodifusión (ICR, the Cuban Broadcasting Institute) withdrew *Mientras tanto* from broadcast.[58] Silvio Rodríguez then spent five months on a fishing boat named Playa Girón, during which time he wrote a wealth of songs.[59] One of these, "Debo partirme en dos" (I've Got to Cut Myself in Two), reflected on the removal of the show from Cuban television:

> Some say turn this way, and others, turn that,
> But all I want is to speak, to sing.
> And if because of that they stop the show—my show—so be it.[60]

This 1969 lyric demonstrates the difficulty the young singer-songwriters encountered as they struggled to play music that they considered to be firmly revolutionary. In the late 1960s the protagonists of *nueva trova* were a new generation, created from within the Revolution, who, according to Cuban musicologist Clara Díaz, "constituted a vanguard that confronted conservative ideas in that era";[61] in other words, they were, rather than a countervanguard, an alter-vanguard. According to Robin Moore, they "considered themselves as patriotic and rebellious at the same time, ready to defend Cuba despite the fact that it might not always give them reason to feel proud."[62] Rodríguez's lyrics contained an alter-discourse that was not contrary to the dominant discourse of youth but that challenged dominant notions of *vanguardia*, the idea that young people should be a revolutionary vanguard in the way understood by, for example, the UJC, and redefined what constituted a good young revolutionary. This stance as alter-vanguard led to an uneasy relationship with certain cultural bureaucrats such as those at the ICR and also led to problems for the black musician Pablo Milanés, who, for reasons that still remain unclear, was arrested and sent to a UMAP in 1966.[63] Yet despite these difficulties, *nueva trova* remained popular because it reflected a confident Cuba and represented national identity more accurately than the would-be purveyors of moral panic—a Cuba that was confident enough in its own identity to be unafraid that external influences would drown out national culture.

The 1960s were experienced by many in Cuba as a renaissance of the Cuban nation, newly liberated from external political and economic forces. The sense of liberation and the search for a new revolutionary identity led to new patterns of everyday life. Young people, in Havana in particular, were at the forefront of this new search for identity. They were essential to the building of the Revolution, both participating in and triggering revolutionary initiatives. They were heralded as the guardians of the future of the Cuban nation and were endowed with an unprecedented importance. At the same time, young people were at the forefront of the development of a new popular culture. Havana youth in the 1960s had access to public spaces in which to express themselves, and it was here that the new culture developed. This culture, focusing on music, fashion, and leisure time, was a fusion of Cuban forces, both new and traditional, with external cultural motifs. This hybridity proved controversial at times, and some young people encountered difficulties due to the variety of ways in which new youth cultures were received.

The diversity of the socialist 1960s was reflected in the excitement, controversy, and uncertainty witnessed in the socialist world in that decade. The utopian dream of communism under the gleaming Caribbean sun met with unexpected clashes, via inter- and intragenerational conflict and political upheaval and via an exploration of the means by which to unite this new revolution with new cultural forms emanating from both within and outside the island. The difficulties and controversies, though, are only one side of the story. A fuller picture shows the effervescence of a new era and the excitement of a young generation that was building a revolution while listening to *los Beatles*.

Notes

1. Anne E. Gorsuch, *Youth in Revolutionary Russia: Enthusiasts, Bohemians, Delinquents* (Bloomington: Indiana University Press, 2000), 120.

2. Arthur Marwick, *The Sixties: Cultural Revolution in Britain, France, Italy and the United States, c. 1958–c. 1974* (Oxford: Oxford University Press, 1998), 16.

3. Eric Hobsbawm, *Age of Extremes: The Short Twentieth Century, 1914–1991* (London: Abacus, 1995), 33. The literature on 1960s youth in the West is vast. For a cross-national overview of the links between cultural and political youth movements, see David Caute, *Sixty-Eight: The Year of the Barricades* (London: Paladin, 1988), and Marwick, *Sixties*. For examples of writing on youth through personal memoir, see Todd Gitlin, *The Sixties: Years of Hope, Days of Rage* (New York: Bantam, 1987); Andrew Sinclair, *In Love and Anger: A View of the 'Sixties* (London: Sinclair-Stevenson, 1994); and Tariq Ali, *Street Fighting Years: An Autobiography of the Sixties* (London: Collins, 1987). From the mass of writing on the counterculture, I select Theodore Roszak, *The Making of a Counter Culture* (London: Faber and Faber, 1968); Kenneth Leech, *Youthquake: The Growth of a Counter-Culture through Two Decades* (London: Sheldon Press, 1973); and Jonathon Green, *All Dressed Up: The Sixties and the Counterculture* (London: Pimlico, 1999). For a class analysis of sixties youth, including a critique of the hippie movement, see Graham Murdock and Robin Mccron, "Youth and Class: The Career of a Confusion," in *Working Class Youth Culture*, ed. Geoff Mungham and Geoff Pearson (London: Routledge, 1976), 10–26.

4. Antoni Kapcia, *Cuba: Island of Dreams* (Oxford: Berg, 2000), 171.

5. Antoni Kapcia, "Does Cuba Fit Yet or Is It Still 'Exceptional'?" *Journal of Latin American Studies* 40, no. 4 (2008): 627–50.

6. John Kirk and Leonardo Padura Fuentes, *Culture and the Cuban Revolution: Conversations in Havana* (Gainesville: University Press of Florida, 2001), 100, 102.

7. The history of Cuban youth organizations was not straightforward. Initially the Socialist Youth (Juventud Socialista) emerged as the strongest and most organized youth organization. However, the more spontaneous emergence of the AJR over the course of 1959 initially under the auspices of the army challenged the position of the Juventud Socialista. They were merged in April 1960 and later were relaunched as the Unión de Jóvenes Comunistas (UJC), a highly selective organization, in April 1962, after which the membership dropped from over eighty thousand in 1962 to under thirty thousand by 1964 (membership figures taken from Miguel Martín, "Nueva etapa de la Unión de Jóvenes Comunistas Cubanos," *Cuba Socialista* 4, no. 36 [1964]: 50). Members of the youth organizations could be as young as fourteen or as old as thirty-four.

8. Fidel Castro, "Discurso pronunciado en la clausura del Congreso de la Asociación de Jóvenes Rebeldes, en el Stadio Latinoamericano," *Revolución*, 5 April 1962, 5.

9. Similar ideas can be found in Guevara's texts of the 1960s, especially "¿Qué debe ser un joven comunista?" [October 1962], in Ernesto Guevara, *Obra revolucionaria* (Mexico: Ediciones Era, 1967), 356–66; and Ernesto Guevara, "El socialismo y el hombre en Cuba" [12 March 1965], in *Obras, 1957–1967*, vol. 2, *La transformación política, económica y social*, 2nd ed. (Havana: Casa de las Américas, 1977), 367–84, esp. 380. For further discussion of notions of youth in the revolutionary discourse, particularly with reference to the UJC and moral panic, see Anne Luke, "Creating the Quiet Majority? Youth and Young People in the Political Culture of the Cuban Revolution," in *Rethinking the Cuban Revolution Nationally and Regionally: Politics, Culture and Identity*, ed. Par Kumaraswami (Chichester: Wiley-Blackwell, 2012), 127–44.

10. "Zafarranchitos," *Bohemia*, 20 January 1967, 73.

11. "Zafarranchitos," *Bohemia*, 24 May 1968, 57.

12. For a full account of the relationship between Cuba and the New Left, see Kepa Artaraz, *Cuba and Western Intellectuals since 1959* (New York: Palgrave Macmillan, 2009).

13. Jorge Domínguez, *Cuba: Order and Revolution* (Cambridge, MA: Harvard University Press, 1978), 140.

14. Antoni Kapcia, *Havana: The Making of Cuban Culture* (Oxford: Berg, 2005), 90.

15. Raúl Aguiar, *El bonchismo y el gangsterismo en Cuba* (Havana: Editorial de Ciencias Sociales, 2000).

16. Gerardo Fulleda León, "Aquella luz de La Habana," *Gaceta de Cuba*, no. 4 (July-August 2005): 5.

17. Arturo Arango, "Josefina Suárez, la memoria de El Puente," *Gaceta de Cuba*, no. 4 (July-August 2005): 8.

18. Fulleda, "Aquella luz de La Habana," 4; José Mario, "La verídica historia de Ediciones El Puente, La Habana, 1961–1965," *Revista Hispano-Cubana* 6 (2002), www.hispanocubana.org. The Malecón still serves, at the time of writing, as an important public nighttime space for young people in Havana.

19. Fulleda, "Aquella luz de La Habana," 5.

20. Arango, "Josefina Suárez," 7–8; Fulleda, "Aquella luz de La Habana," 6.

21. Alexei Yurchak, *Everything Was Forever, Until It Was No More: The Last Soviet Generation* (Princeton: Princeton University Press, 2006), 164.

22. Lourdes Casal, "Literature and Society," in *Revolutionary Change in Cuba*, ed. Carmelo Mesa-Lago (Pittsburgh: University of Pittsburgh Press, 1971), 450.

23. One of the intentions of the El Puente group was to publish translations of foreign texts, including the controversial "Howl" by Ginsberg. Roberto Zurbano, "Re-pasar El Puente," *Gaceta de Cuba*, no. 4 (July-August 2005): 2.

24. Barry Miles, *Ginsberg: A Biography* (New York: Simon and Schuster, 1989), 341–52.

25. Jose Mario, "Allen Ginsberg en La Habana," *Mundo nuevo*, no. 34 (1969): 49.

26. Barry Miles explains that the term *Sicks (enfermitos)* derived from the comedy of Beat comedian Mort Sahl, which was termed "sick." *Ginsberg*, 342.

27. Enrique Jane, "El mundo de los diferentes," *Mella*, no. 340 (6 September 1965): 7.

28. Ibid., 8.

29. Aníbal Rodríguez, "La moda," *Alma Mater*, 20 July 1967, 4.

30. Yurchak, *Everything Was Forever*, 170, 173–75.

31. Miles, *Ginsberg*, 342.

32. Ibid., 367–68.

33. Jose Yglesias, *In the Fist of the Revolution* (Harmondsworth: Penguin, 1970), 271; Ian Lumsden, *Machos, Maricones and Gays: Cuba and Homosexuality* (Philadelphia: Temple University Press, 1996), 72.

34. These were initially established to house young men who were unwilling to join the workforce, but they were soon put to a different purpose, to confine homosexuals and other perceived immoral elements.

35. Dénia García Ronda, interview by author, Havana, 3 April 2003. García Ronda is a Cuban writer and academic and the assistant director of *Temas* magazine.

36. Ñico, "La minifalda" [cartoon], *Bohemia*, 9 February 1968, 74.

37. Dick Hebdige uses the anthropological concept of *bricolage* to explain how a style is created. He argues that commodities are used in a way that is meaningful to the subculture but in a different way than they are to the dominant culture, thus creating a new subcultural set of meanings. Dick Hebdige, *Subculture: The Meaning of Style* (London: Methuen, 1979), 102–6.

38. A 1963 study by Cuban psychologist Gustavo Torroella, *Estudio de la juventud cubana* (Havana: Comisión Nacional Cubana de la UNESCO, 1963), found music to be highly important in the leisure time of young people; see 112, 138, 155.

39. Clara Díaz, *Silvio Rodríguez* (Havana: Editorial Letras Cubanas, 1993), 19.

40. Ñico, "La canción protesta" [cartoon], *Bohemia*, 11 August 1967, 32.

41. Pio Serrano and L. R. Nogueras, "La canción protesta: Historia de una tragedia americana," *Caimán barbudo*, no. 7 (1966): 10.

42. Gorsuch, *Youth in Revolutionary Russia*, 3–5 and 64–65.

43. Kapcia, *Havana*, 145.

44. In interviews conducted by the author in 2003, one interviewee sang "Day in the Life," from the Beatles album *Sgt. Pepper's Lonely Hearts Club Band* of 1967, and another hummed "Fool on the Hill" from *Magical Mystery Tour* of the same year (Fernando Martínez Heredia, interview, Havana, 19 May 2003; Guillermo Rodríguez Rivera, interview, Havana, 6 May 2003). Martínez Heredia is a leading Cuban intellectual who came to prominence in the 1960s, and Rodríguez Rivera was a celebrated young poet of the sixties and a leading light in the Caimán Barbudo group of young poets).

45. Artemy Troitsky, *Back in the USSR: The True Story of Rock in Russia* (Sydney: Omnibus Press, 1987), 12.

46. García Ronda, interview.

47. Sabrina Petra Ramet, ed., *Rocking the State: Rock Music and Politics in Eastern Europe and Russia* (Boulder, CO: Westview Press, 1994), 3, www.questia.com/read/100253215.

48. Díaz, *Silvio Rodríguez*, 16.

49. Martínez Heredia, interview.

50. Ibid.

51. Leech, *Youthquake*, 8.

52. Yurchak, *Everything Was Forever*, 204.

53. Aristide, "Radiomania" [cartoon], *Bohemia*, 2 February 1968, 74. The comical treatment of radio in this Cuban cartoon, which implies that Cubans of all shapes, sizes, and ages share a passion for radio, differs distinctly from Soviet treatment of the same theme in a Soviet cartoon

of 1970, which is critical of the radio as, according to Yurchak, an "individualized practice of listening"; *Everything Was Forever,* 179.

54. Robin Moore, *Music and Revolution: Cultural Change in Socialist Cuba* (Berkeley: University of California Press, 2006), 35–44.

55. Robin Moore, "Transformations in Cuban *Nueva Trova,* 1965–95," *Ethnomusicology* 47, no. 1 (2003): 13. There were also several key female protagonists such as the performer Sara González and the composer Teresita Fernández (Moore, *Music and Revolution,* 143).

56. Clara Díaz, *La Nueva Trova* (Havana: Editorial Letras Cubanas, 1994), 18. The group of poets and artists associated with *Caimán barbudo* were linked with *nueva trova* and the new youth culture and would take part in the public gatherings at Coppelia and elsewhere. The foregrounding of youth is evidenced once again by the naming of the newly established daily national newspaper as *Juventud rebelde* (Rebel Youth), established in 1965.

57. Pedro Abreu, "Silvio, solo," *Bohemia,* 22 March 1968, 76, emphasis in original.

58. Díaz, *Silvio Rodríguez,* 25.

59. Ibid., 20.

60. Silvio Rodríguez, *Cancionero* (Havana: Letras Cubanas / Ojala, 2008), 153.

61. Díaz, *Silvio Rodríguez,* 18.

62. Moore, "Transformations in Cuban *Nueva Trova,*" 11.

63. Moore, *Music and Revolution,* 151–52.

13 In Search of an Ending

Seventeen Moments *and the Seventies*

Stephen Lovell

For a long time, historians of the Soviet Union have had little need of the sixties. Their purposes have been served admirably by the notion of the Thaw (ca. 1954–64). The sixties have connotations of personal liberation and political protest that seem absurdly inappropriate for the still straitlaced and repressive Soviet Union. In recent years, however, it has become almost a commonplace to note that the Thaw did not end with Khrushchev's ouster in October 1964. Soviet culture has been shown to retain its edginess, contentiousness, and experimentation at least until 1967. Josephine Woll justifiably claims for her history of Thaw cinema Andrei Tarkovskii's *Andrei Rublev* (1966), Larisa Shepit'ko's *Wings* (1966), and Kira Muratova's *Brief Encounters* (1967).[1] A leading historian of the Thaw phenomenon, Stephen Bittner, finds its end to be "ambiguous and uneven," located somewhere between the arrest of Joseph Brodsky and the invasion of Czechoslovakia.[2] As several contributors to the present book show (notably Nick Rutter and Rachel Applebaum), the Soviet Union's opening to the wider world was not reversed by a change in the leadership. Nor, of course, is it the case that the West in the 1960s was quite the unbuttoned place of dinner-party lore.

In short, there is every reason to believe that the sixties have potential as a new frame of reference to supplement, and perhaps even supplant, the Thaw. But a word of caution is in order. Decades, like centuries, are convenient constructs; they can be lengthened or shortened to suit the historian's design. There is a danger that whatever a particular researcher happens to find interesting or appealing will be corralled for the "sixties," while everything else will be consigned to the murky thereafter. The task of the present chapter, then, is to find a less subjective criterion for distinguishing one decade from another: to argue for a cutoff point beyond which "the seventies" begin. What I have in mind, of course, is not December 1969 or any other specific chronological marker but rather some identifiable cultural or social paradigm shift.

This is not an easy task. If the 1960s are the most mythologized decade in postwar European history, the 1970s are the grayest and the most amorphous. It is no longer true, at least in the West, that the seventies are passed over by historians.[3] But this is still widely viewed as the era that taste forgot, or when the lights went out, or when the postwar consensus broke down. There is no question in most people's minds that life was more colorful on either side of this decade. As for Soviet history, the 1970s are still largely uncharted territory, partly because the sources available to study them are less accessible, and less intensively worked over, than those for Britain or the United States, but mainly, I think, because this decade is wedged in between the rambunctious "sixties" and the dramatic "eighties." It is just too tempting to turn Brezhnev's rule, known since the Gorbachev years as the "era of Stagnation," into the "long seventies." The decade lacks powerful advocates who might turn the tide of underappreciation. Nothing written on the seventies has the flair of Petr Vail' and Aleksandr Genis's *The Sixties*.[4]

Yet the signs are that attitudes are changing. In 1996, as a graduate student in Moscow, I attended the launch of the Russian edition of *The Sixties* and naively asked Vail' whether he might consider writing a sequel on the seventies. He replied that he had not himself lived through the period (having emigrated to the United States in 1971) and did not have the deep cultural knowledge that such a book required. Now, however, a new generation of historians and cultural commentators—one that never left the Soviet Union, and whose formative years coincided with the seventies—is gaining voice, whether on the printed page or in the TV studio. Foremost among them is Leonid Parfenov (b. 1960), whose TV series and lavishly produced accompanying books have made the case for the seventies (as well as the sixties, eighties, and nineties) as "that without which we can't be imagined, still less understood." Parfenov allows the viewer to be beguiled by the artifacts and habits of Soviet everyday life, perhaps even to succumb to nostalgia, though he retains an element of ironic detachment.[5] Much less irony is evidenced in the views of the many Russians who, in opinion surveys since the fall of communism, have voted the Brezhnev era the best moment in twentieth-century Russian history to have lived.[6]

While these signs of growing interest in the seventies are welcome, as historical analysis they are of dubious value. The cultural contours of the decade disappear in a tug of nostalgia for sausage at two rubles seventy. We are left with the awkward question of the decade's distinctiveness: When *did* the sixties end and the seventies begin?

Perhaps the question is not so difficult after all. However far historians attempt to stretch the Thaw, in 1968 they reach the end of the road. The crushing of the Prague Spring is the moment when the intelligentsia shed any illusions about their political regime, and when that regime redoubled its commitment to authoritarianism and Soviet patriotism. As we learn from Christian Noack's chapter, even amateur singers came under uncomfortably close scrutiny in the post-1968 era. In this light, what is distinctive about the 1970s is the divide between "official" and "unofficial" culture, or between "here" and "there" (given that many prominent cultural figures were voting with their feet and leaving in the "third wave" of emigration). This is the line taken in a Russian volume that makes perhaps the most concerted attempt so far to crack the cultural code of the Soviet seventies.[7] The gulf between official and intelligentsia culture is likewise a leitmotif in a collection of memoirs that is tellingly entitled *Tanks in Prague, Mona Lisa in Moscow*.[8] The automatic assumption of such a volume is the primacy of the intelligentsia subculture—proscribed and semiproscribed books, the visual arts, and above all theater. Film historians can also sign up to this interpretive framework. The category of "shelved" films becomes much more significant in the late 1960s and early 1970s. Birgit Beumers, for example, devotes a section to it in her recent history of Russian cinema and another few pages to Andrei Tarkovskii, the intelligentsia director par excellence. As a counterweight, she has a section called "Mainstream Cinema Playing Safe."[9]

So perhaps what is going on in the 1970s is the de facto abandonment of earlier attempts to create a culture at once "mass" and "elite" and instead the coming of age of mass culture in a sense that would be recognizable to a Western audience, along with an entirely taken-for-granted distinction between "mass" and "elite" cultural interests. Genres would seem to become more self-explanatory, and the criteria for mass success more transparent. In 1973, about which I will say more in due course, the two box office hits were an adaptation of Mayne Reid's *Headless Horseman* (69 million tickets sold) and the screwball comedy *Ivan Vasil'evich Changes Profession* (60.7 million), which both drew about twice as many viewers as the next contender.[10]

But this picture of a neat aesthetic division of labor is complicated by the fact that the 1970s saw the full arrival of a new screen medium: TV. In the 1950s and 1960s it was largely finding its feet. There were plenty of teething troubles: technical glitches abounded, and TV was notably less prestigious than other media as a place of work for aspiring Soviet journalists. From the late 1960s, however, TV came out from the shadow of the big screen. By 1970, it was truly a national medium, having established itself as a sine qua non of Soviet domesticity.[11]

The TV Moment in Soviet Culture

Here I should put my cards on the table: my answer to the question "What were the seventies?" is going to rely heavily on a single twelve-part TV series that was first shown in August 1973. Admittedly, this series—Tat'iana Lioznova's *Seventeen Moments of Spring (Semnadtsat' mgnovenii vesny)*—is the biggest cult phenomenon in the history of Soviet (and indeed Russian) television. But that does not necessarily make it a historical milestone or an acceptable metonym for a whole era.

The series could not have achieved its remarkable success if it had not ridden the wave of a still-new medium and a brand-new TV genre: the miniseries.[12] By 1976, even the All-Union Congress of Soviet Writers could make a nod to the *mnogoseriinyi fil'm* as a respectable topic for discussion and investigation.[13] In 1971, however, when the shooting of *Seventeen Moments* began, the form was still in its infancy. The five-part Civil War drama *The Adjutant of His Excellency (Ad"iutant ego prevoskhoditel'stva)* had aired in April 1970, the crime drama *The Investigation Is Conducted by the Experts (Sledstvie vedut znatoki)* had been launched in February 1971, and the seven-part *The Shadows Disappear at Noon (Teni ischezaiut v polden'*, based on a novel by Anatolii Ivanov) had been shown in the space of a week in February 1972. But these were still thin pickings for the Soviet viewer. The big screen retained a formidable presence in the Soviet cultural market: in the late 1960s and early 1970s, cinema audiences were at their peak, and they only began slowly to tail off from the mid-1970s.[14] At an internal studio discussion of *Seventeen Moments,* more than one speaker expressed passing regret that the film had been made merely for the small screen. The director of the Gor'kii Studio recalled that there had been some debate on whether to make the film for TV or for the big screen. While it was a shame to take viewers away from the cinema, he concluded that *Seventeen Moments* would have greater "ideological" value on TV. A speaker at a later meeting briefly raised the same concern but conceded that this was a project of unprecedented scope: "Television has until now not had a single work on this scale." Lioznova herself complained of the enormous difficulties she had had producing 840 minutes of screen time in a relatively small studio that was more accustomed to the shorter and more discrete feature-film format.[15] Spy adventures had a long and distinguished history in Soviet cinema: from the postwar *The Secret Agent's Feat (Podvig razvedchika,* 1947) through to adaptations of the first two novels that featured the protagonist of *Seventeen Moments,* Otto von Stirlitz: *No Password Required (Parol' ne nuzhen,* 1967) and *Major Whirlwind (Maior Vikhr',* 1967). On general principles, it might be thought that the feature film would better suit the nail-biting genre of spy story, with its minute-by-minute suspense, than the sprawling TV epic.

Of course, a TV series has compensating advantages. With its *longue durée*, it offers far greater opportunities for individual characterization and narrative complexity than does big-screen cinema. This is not so much a matter of plot twists, of which there can be many in a one-hundred-minute feature film. Rather, TV allows different modes of time to exist simultaneously: it can accommodate the quotidian, the generational, the cyclical—and the grand historical narrative that is close to obligatory in Soviet culture. A TV series can—at least in principle—be both monumental and individual, both epic and everyday. It can infuse the relationship between the individual and the historical with new meaning.[16]

Here we find a clue to the distinctive qualities of Soviet culture in the 1970s (or post-1960s). To speak schematically, if Stalinist cinema sees the hegemony of the monumental, Thaw cinema sees a creative—but often unbalanced and aesthetically unsatisfactory—attempt to put the individual back into the grand narrative. On a second or third viewing, a quintessential Thaw film like *The Cranes Are Flying (Letiat zhuravli,*

1957) is striking for the rushed quality of its narrative. It relies heavily on emotional shortcuts like the cartoonish turpitude of the heroine's husband, Mark, during the evacuation. At the other extreme of Thaw output, in works such as Marlen Khutsiev's *I Am Twenty (Mne dvadtsat' let,* 1964) or Georgii Daneliia's *I Stroll around Moscow (Ia shagaiu po Moskve,* 1963) we find episodic creations where the viewer is denied any true narrative resolution.

If we move forward to the Soviet Union's international prizewinner of the Brezhnev era, *Moscow Does Not Believe in Tears (Moskva slezam ne verit,* 1980), we find that the narrative impetus of *The Cranes Are Flying* is combined with the long duration of a Khutsiev film. The narrative is more carefully historicized and the characters are given more space, even if the film remains a formula narrative. Other big-screen creations of the Brezhnev era exemplify even better the drive for all-encompassing narrative wholeness: notably the five-part war epic *Liberation (Osvobozhdenie,* 1968–71). But the TV series takes length—and wholeness—to a new extreme. It is the major mass-cultural innovation, and the quintessential cultural form, of the 1970s.

Introducing *Seventeen Moments*

The other asset of TV was its huge and immediate impact: its capacity to unite tens of millions of people, all seated in their respective homes, in a real-time experience. No TV event fulfilled this potential better than *Seventeen Moments.* The series had been the subject of at least one high-profile preview on the program *Kinopanorama* in June of that year.[17] It also helped that this was an adaptation of a novel by the wildly popular crime and spy writer Iulian Semenov. But nothing quite prepared viewers—or the authorities—for the impact of *Seventeen Moments.*

The first episode was shown on Channel 1 at 19.30 on Saturday 11 August; the last went out on Friday 24 August.[18] Viewing was thus an exceptionally intense experience for those who were lucky enough to catch all twelve episodes: the audience was granted only two days off over two weeks. The Soviet public was transfixed. Lioznova saw the lights going out in neighboring windows after each evening's episode finished. The series quickly generated its own folklore: Ekaterina Gradova, who took the lead female role, was mobbed in a grocery store near her home and took two hours to return to her worried husband; the divorce rate spiked after the first showing of the series as women understood the full extent of their husbands' inadequacy; there was a fashion for naming sons Iulian.[19]

Not at all apocryphal were the letters that flooded into State Television. The department directly responsible for the series received 1,653 letters on *Seventeen Moments* in August 1973 (compared with 147 letters for the entire department the previous August). The responses were overwhelmingly positive and impeccably mixed with regard to the social background of their authors. Almost a quarter were classified as "employees," 17 percent as workers, 11 percent as agricultural workers, 35 percent as schoolchildren, and 13 percent as pensioners. Almost half were under thirty, about another quarter in their thirties and forties, and another quarter over fifty. Viewers clearly relished the extended format, and many offered detailed analysis of the series. For one viewer these were "the most exciting moments of my life," while a group of collective farmers from the Chuvash Republic awarded the lead actor, Viacheslav Tikhonov, the title of "Honorary Kolkhoznik."[20] Even in September, after the series had left the air, *Seventeen Moments* elicited 664 letters. For comparison, the other well-loved series of the era, *The Investigation Is Conducted by the Experts*, drew only 321 letters—and this after the program makers had gone so far as to "kill off" one of the heroes.[21]

Letters on the series also poured into the Main Directorate of Programming. They mainly expressed a practical concern. Not only had the film been shown in the summer holiday season (when many people were away), it had occupied an inconvenient slot in the schedule: in the early evening many people were still struggling home from work, and mothers were putting their children to bed between 7:30 and 9:00. The episodes were repeated the following morning, but that was no help for the many people who had to be back at work.[22]

The authorities soon bowed to the pleas for a rerun, which was granted in December 1973. Once again, eyewitnesses reported the emptying of Moscow streets.[23] The letters poured in, accounting for more than 40 percent of the mailbag of the Department of Television Films that month. Viewers' appetite for Stirlitz had still not been satisfied: as before, there were countless requests for episodes to be shown after rather than before the evening news *(Vremia)*.[24]

The cult of Stirlitz eventually reached the summit of the Soviet system. Brezhnev did not see the series when it first came out but was by all accounts deeply impressed when his minders did show it to him and insisted on watching it repeatedly. According to a story doing the rounds of the upper *nomenklatura* on the eve of Gorbachev's accession: "Once, at the end of the film when the character Shtirlitz is told that he's been named a Hero of the Soviet Union, Brezhnev turned to the others and said: 'Has he received it yet? I'd like to hand it to him myself.' ... And so a few days later he personally awarded Tikhonov the Hero Star and the Order of Lenin, under the full impression that he was in fact Shtirlitz."[25] This story is suspiciously reminiscent of a Russian *anekdot*.[26] Yet while that generic resemblance may make us question its truth value, it only confirms the cultural resonance of *Seventeen Moments,* which has left an enormous trace in popular humor. A search for the keyword "Stirlitz" on anekdoty.ru yields more than two thousand hits.[27] Besides wordplay and double entendres (which parody the spy's imperative to avoid eliciting suspicion or creating ambiguity), Stirlitz *anekdoty* mainly embroider on the theme of the hero's absurd ability to get himself out of any tight corner.

Accounting for the phenomenal popularity of the series is not altogether straightforward. On first inspection there is nothing so very exceptional about *Seventeen Moments.* The series was a politically orthodox enterprise, neatly fitting both the Cold War context and the flourishing genre of the anticapitalist spy story. Elena Prokhorova has gone so far as to argue that the rise of the spy thriller signifies the end of the Thaw. This genre—along with the police procedurals and detective stories that Prokhorova also investigates in her dissertation—are all about the reimposition of order after the relative loosening of narrative norms in the 1960s.[28]

If the spy thriller was the quintessential post-Thaw genre, Iulian Semenov was the archetypal post-Thaw writer. Born into a well-connected Soviet family (in the 1930s his father was deputy editor of *Izvestiia* under Bukharin), Semenov had also experienced the dark side of Stalinism (with his father's arrest in 1952). While he was apparently dismayed by the change of political course in the mid-1960s, he quickly made a brilliant career.[29] After graduating in oriental studies in the mid-1950s, he was a correspondent and traveler in many of the hot spots of the Cold War: Afghanistan, Vietnam, Cuba, Nicaragua, West Germany. He married into a powerful literary and cultural dynasty: his father-in-law was the famous children's writer Sergei Mikhalkov, and his young brother-in-law was the future director Nikita. He also developed an extraordinarily close and undisguised relationship with the KGB. From the late 1960s onwards, his main patron was Iurii Andropov, who provided him with the freedom to travel the world and mine KGB contacts and archives.[30] His many links to the "organs" led to great speculation that he was a KGB informer, though there seems no reason to go that far: Andropov et al. kept him on a loose rein, knowing that he would use his considerable freedoms to the glory of their organization. Semenov was certainly prolific. He would eventually produce fourteen novels with Stirlitz as protagonist; *Seventeen Moments of Spring* was apparently written in seventeen days.[31]

Interpreting *Seventeen Moments*

Seventeen Moments—both the book and the series—has an impeccably anti-Western premise. In the spring of 1945, the Americans and the Germans are seeking a separate peace that would leave Soviet Russia out in the cold. Fascists and liberal capitalists are alike in their perfidy and hostility to communism. Stirlitz dutifully follows orders from Moscow Center, and the series even has cameos from Stalin as the wise and omniscient voice of authority.[32] The *New York Times* correspondent Hedrick Smith suggests that the first showing of the series was delayed until Brezhnev returned from America in summer 1973: a piece of such blatant anti-Americanism might have undermined détente.[33] In subsequent years, the series was supposedly used to train KGB operatives in tradecraft. Far less speculative are the accounts of police input in the making of the series. Semen Tsvigun, Andropov's deputy, took a close interest in it, and KGB consultants were listed in the credits under false names. The police even got a minor role in the series: a major in the criminal investigation department of Moscow oblast played a Gestapo man in episode 10.[34]

There is no reason to doubt that the Cold War surtext was what many of the first viewers of the series responded to. In 1973, veterans were writing letters to the newspapers praising *Seventeen Moments* for showing true heroism and reminding Soviet people they shouldn't let down their guard in an era of détente.[35] The director herself was a good Soviet patriot (and remained so to her death in 2011, to judge by the few published interviews of her later years).[36] At the internal studio discussion of the film, Lioznova defended the use of footage from Leningrad and Stalingrad as part of Stirlitz's interior monologue (even though he had not himself witnessed these events): "However brilliant the spy might be, the fate of the war was decided not by Stirlitz but by the enormous heroism of the people."[37]

But the Cold War interpretation of *Seventeen Moments* does not come close to exhausting the possibilities. From the very beginning, the series has lent itself to Aesopian readings that turn Soviet ideology on its head. Far from setting up a polar opposition between communism and fascism, the series may be seen to draw a line of equivalence between them. Much of what *Seventeen Moments* communicates on the workings of the Nazi elite might be more applicable to the Soviet *nomenklatura* of the Brezhnev era. This is a well-ordered party-state rather than the chaotic agglomeration of agencies that Nazi Germany really was. Semenov's daughter remarks in her biography of her father that the famous dossiers he provided on leading Nazis ("A true Aryan, has Nordic, stoical character . . .") were transparently a reference to Soviet bureaucratic practice.[38] Whatever view we take of authorial intention, this was unquestionably the view taken by much of the Soviet intelligentsia. Many other hints at Soviet *realia* are scattered through the series. Stirlitz's conversation with a disgruntled general in a train, for example, is reminiscent of nothing so much as the unrestrained "kitchen talk" of the Brezhnev era. More generally, members of the intelligentsia could feel that Stirlitz was one of them: a man of culture and education, but one driven by his environment to a disjuncture between word and deed, or at least word and thought. The lead role was taken by Viacheslav Tikhonov, who by the early 1970s was already the epitome of tortured *intelligentnost'* (thanks notably to the role of Andrei Bolkonskii in Sergei Bondarchuk's *War and Peace*).[39]

How exactly did *Seventeen Moments* achieve this remarkable ambiguity? How could it appeal equally to KGB officers and war veterans and to ironically minded academics? An important part of the answer lies in the form and structure of the series. *Seventeen Moments* does not do what films in its ostensible genre are supposed to do. It has with some justice been called an " antithriller."[40] As one of the speakers at a studio discussion noted, the genre was hard to pin down: it was "maybe a psychological thriller [detektiv], maybe a political thriller, maybe not a thriller at all. Most likely it's an account of that period, done seriously and in depth."[41] Usually, TV dramatizations accelerate the novels they adapt; Lioznova's *Seventeen Moments* slows Semenov down. The book is more plot driven; the interior monologues take up less time. Overall, the book is less richly textured and more simplistic in the way it delivers its key messages: after watching the restrained and subtle film, it is hard to believe that the novel contains a lurid scene where Himmler confronts Hess over film footage of the latter masturbating in the toilet.[42] It is well-attested that Semenov, a devotee of Hemingway and the spare masculine style, had his differences with the equally strong-willed Lioznova. He particularly objected to the famous wordless scene where Stirlitz and his wife (accompanied by her NKVD minder) stare across a café at each other after a fifteen-year separation.[43] It is hardly surprising that Lioznova kept Semenov away from the studio during filming. Nor is it surprising that the first viewers of the series saw it as an entity quite distinct from the book. One commentator at the Gor'kii Studio put it bluntly: "I have read Semenov's novel. It's a typical thriller, but the director has managed to raise it to the heights of a psychological film."[44]

While the slow pace of *Seventeen Moments* would become one of the series's hallmarks, it also represented an innovation. Some early audience members—whether in the Artistic Council of the Gor'kii Studio or in the general public—found themselves losing patience with it. One viewer from Leningrad complained that the narrative voice-overs meant that the actors were not acting but merely "posing in front of the camera"; another noted with some dismay the "tranquil and leisurely behavior of the fascists."[45] A similar point had been made by a studio reviewer who asked rhetorically, "What does Tikhonov do? On one occasion he kills an agent provocateur, but the rest of the time he is just thinking. He walks around, picks up some glasses, pours something into them. We see a closeup of him thinking—I suppose this is all good, but sometimes we lose a sense of proportion." As another speaker noted, such longueurs seemed inappropriate for TV: "What we have just seen is undoubtedly meant for the big screen. When you watch a film on TV, you are not as focused as in the cinema. You keep getting distracted, there's always something to prevent you from concentrating." Even after the second studio showing (of episodes 4–6), some reservations were expressed on this score. Some of the inner monologues were felt to be ponderous, and the action was in places too slow.[46]

Such impatience remained a minority response. But even those speakers at the studio meetings who took a more positive view noted the pacing of the film as one of its distinctive features and formal innovations. Feature films were not always able to deliver a detailed enough portrait of people: "We are in too much of a rush, we're afraid that the viewer will jump up and leave," and "tempo" sometimes comes at the expense of nuances of character.[47] The most consistent gripe from the studio representatives concerned not the leisurely pacing but the countdown that regularly appeared on the screen. This implied a minute-by-minute urgency that made no sense given the otherwise slow and reflective quality of the action. Not only was it unclear why individual minutes or hours mattered, there was not even any clear sense of what the eponymous seventeen "moments" were.[48]

It is true that each episode ends with a cliffhanger, but even here there is little action. The cliffhangers are rather intellectual: the most famous of them is Müller's "Stirlitz, could you please stay behind" (*A vas, Shtirlits, ia poproshu ostat'sia*), which introduces the late Soviet equivalent of the famous philosophical dialogue between Ivan and Alesha in *The Brothers Karamazov*. For the most part Stirlitz does nothing more dynamic than park his car. In the most striking instance of heroic inaction, he pulls his car into a lay-by for a thirty-minute power nap while the entire Gestapo is looking for him. In Elena Prokhorova's apt phrase, he is the "hibernating protagonist."[49] He is a thinker rather than a doer or a talker. The warmest and most natural conversation he has is with a stray dog. The only person he kills is a police informer, and he does so in a slow-motion, contemplative way.[50] Several commentators have drawn the stark contrast between Stirlitz and James Bond. Bond plays roulette with bad guys and glamorous women; Stirlitz plays chess with an old woman. To Gaby, the younger woman who is apparently in love with him, he utters the immortal line "As a chess partner you do not interest me."[51]

The title and structure of the series imply taut plotting and real-time narrative. But this impression is complicated by the slower epic time of the passing of the seasons (*spring* is just as important a word in the title as *moments*) and by Stirlitz's regular prolonged bouts of introspection. Nor does the series have much sense of final closure. In the 1970s, as Prokhorova notes, agents usually survive and continue working on enemy territory instead of dying heroically or returning to the motherland.[52]

Not only is the series slow, but it impedes the forward motion of the plot by lingering looks backward. It aches with nostalgia—a point most obviously illustrated by the wordless scene between Stirlitz and his wife. But nostalgia is also there in its very fabric: its lingering closeups, the fact that it is shot in black and white. A wistful sense of the passing of time pervades the series. The weather outside may be springlike, but the mood is distinctly autumnal. The opening scene, where Stirlitz sees birds in the air, could hardly be more different from its famous counterpart in *The Cranes Are Flying*, where young lovers gambol along the embankment of the Moscow River. Stirlitz is in the countryside rather than the city; the weather is gray rather than sunny; and he is with an old woman, Frau Zaurich.

Seventeen Moments is a distinctly middle-aged series. This fits the 1970s trend of graying protagonists.[53] In the book Stirlitz thinks of himself as an old man at forty-five.[54] In a scene with his young female admirer Gaby and Frau Zaurich, he confesses, "I like old people and children best." For Tikhonov, this was the latest point in a screen trajectory that had taken him from rural troublemaker in *It Happened in Pen'kovo* (Delo bylo v Pen'kove, 1957) to grouchy schoolteacher in *Let's Get Through to Monday* (Dozhivem do ponedel'nika, 1968).[55]

But the past to which the film gestures is not only that of the individual biography but also that of a historical epoch. As well as conforming (however loosely) to the spy genre, the series is also a contribution to the enormous Soviet cinematic response to World War II. Here too, however, we can identify it as distinctly "post-Thaw" in its approach to this central theme of Soviet historical memory. *Seventeen Moments* is the work of people (whether Semenov or Lioznova) who were still very young at the moment of the German invasion. It does not seek to capture the emotional truth of the war through a concentrated narrative of suffering, self-sacrifice, and redemption (as is the case in the landmark war films of the Thaw era). Instead, it seeks to win the viewer over to its version of events through the impression of scrupulous documentary authenticity. The regular insertion of documentary footage (especially in the early episodes), the dossiers presented on leading Nazis, and the authoritative voice-overs giving bulletins on the course of the war all remind us of the connection between the compelling fictionalized encounters in the Reichssicherheitshauptamt (RSHA) and the "objective" historical record. All this is faithful to the spirit of the book. According to his daughter, Semenov considered documents to be "sacred" and placed great emphasis on research in preparing for his books.[56] He also relied on his own experiences for historical authenticity. Not only had he been shown round Berlin in 1945 by his father, he had a journalistic posting to West Germany (during which he pestered his acquaintance Klaus Mehnert to take him to some of the key sites of the Third Reich); and he had consulted Lev Sheinin, who had been present at the Nuremberg Tribunal, for descriptions of the leading Nazis.[57] Lioznova too seems to have striven not just for flawless continuity but also for historical accuracy. No effort seems to have been spared in this cause. The director noted that making the series had been a "catastrophically complex task" and that obtaining the necessary resources had been a constant struggle. A speaker at the final studio discussion also commented on the enormous volume of work the series had required: the only roughly comparable case on Soviet TV had been *The Shadows Disappear at Noon*— but that had been seven episodes rather than twelve.[58] The series was in production for almost three years. The careful planning of each scene in advance itself took six months. Shooting began in the GDR in March 1971; other locations were Riga, Georgia, and Moscow.[59] Viewers and critics of the time were apparently won over by the grand scale of this historical reconstruction. At the first studio discussion of the series, it drew praise for its "professionalism" and "precision." In the final meeting, it was commended for its "rich and faithful" depiction of foreign locations (and this despite its staying comfortably within its foreign currency budget).[60] Later on, in a standard Soviet cinema history, *Seventeen Moments* was praised for its reconstruction of Berlin in 1945.[61] As the letters to State Television reveal, Leonid Brezhnev was by no means the only person in the Soviet Union left uncertain as to whether Stirlitz was a real person. A crew from the Pacific fleet posed the question directly to the author: "Some of us say that Colonel Isaev is a fictional hero, others that he is real. We ask you to send us the one correct answer."[62]

Yet in fact the film is a long way from achieving flawless historical authenticity. In recent years, it has become something of a field sport to point out the anachronisms in the series. We now know, if we did not already, that Stirlitz had a car better than his due, and indeed would not have had his own car at all in February 1945; that the bathroom fittings in Stirlitz's villa are Soviet, not German; that no such dossiers were compiled on leading Nazis; that the fashions are those of the 1960s and 1970s, not those of the 1940s; that the Nazi uniforms are inaccurate; and much else besides.[63]

It would be easy to write off these offenses against historical accuracy: given the resources of the Gor'kii Studio in the early 1970s, and the imperfect state of Soviet knowledge on the Third Reich, the film is still a remarkable piece of sustained and imaginative reconstruction. The problem is, however, that some of the anachronisms are too blatant to be accidental. It is curious, for example, that the camera shows Stirlitz writing a top-secret letter to Himmler in Russian. Even more curious is the fact that he has Edith Piaf singing "Je ne regrette rien" on his car radio.

The pervasiveness of anachronism in the series shows just how much, despite its claims to *dokumental'nost'*, it was a response to its own time. This was not yet another exposé of the evil and depraved Third Reich but a window on the West for a 1970s audience that craved information about the wider world. The scenes in Berlin and Bern (a.k.a. Riga) serve the purpose of constructing this imagined West. It is telling, for example, that near the very end, in the twelfth episode, Stirlitz receives his instructions from the Center in a Bern café (in fact the Riga Station in Moscow). He is propositioned by a drunk woman, but that does not distract the camera too much from this last look at bourgeois comforts.[64]

Stirlitz corresponds to Soviet stereotypes of Western behavior: he can be regarded not only as the ideal *intelligent* but as the ideal Western gentleman. He enjoys all the autonomy and professional ease of a Frankfurt man about town. He is wonderfully mobile in his car: he can go where he wants when he wants. He can cross borders at will. This is a very far cry from Stalin-era culture, with its theme of borders "under lock and key."[65]

Such displacement activities are highly characteristic of 1970s culture. Dreams of transnational Leftism were still very much alive in the 1960s, as Nick Rutter shows in his contribution to this volume, but within a few years they had given way to an acceptance of civilizational differences that allowed people to indulge passionate curiosity about other parts of the world while remaining firmly Soviet. Another cult TV phenomenon of the decade was the Soviet adaptation of Sherlock Holmes, which was also filmed in Riga. Other high-profile films of the era, such as *Teheran 43* and *Mimino,* contained extensive footage of Western cities such as Paris, London, and Frankfurt. But not all acts of displacement are analogous. There was no question, to a Soviet viewer, that Victorian England was a desirable place in which to imagine oneself; nor was there any doubt that showing double-decker London buses or the embankment of the Seine, as in *Teheran 43,* was as good as glamorizing them. None of this could be said of *Seventeen Moments,* whose action takes place at the heart of the most infamous regime in history, one that had inflicted vast suffering on the Soviet people a mere thirty years before. It is hard to picture a British film of the 1970s, or even of the 2000s, making Himmler, Müller, and Schellenberg so glamorous and sympathetic. It is still hard to imagine any Nazi on the British screen not being given a silly German accent. But here we have the lovable cynic Müller (Leonid Bronevoi), the upright Karl Wolff (Vasilii Lanovoi), the formidable Ernst Kaltenbrunner (Mikhail Zharkovskii), and of course the feline Schellenberg (Oleg Tabakov). Even Stirlitz bears some responsibility for the allure of this version of the Third Reich. At one point, he catches himself speaking of the Germans as "us." He plays his German role to such perfection that it becomes rather hard to believe in his essential Sovietness. Perhaps to correct this impression, Lioznova included the easily—and justifiably—parodied scene where Stirlitz roasts potatoes in the fire and downs vodka to mark the Day of the Red Army.[66]

Even now, almost forty years on from the first showing of *Seventeen Moments*, it is possible to be struck by the sheer weirdness of seeing Soviet heroes in SS uniforms. Mark Lipovetskii has given an amusing account of his double-take on spotting at Kursk Station in Moscow a cigarette ad featuring SS men: this, it turned out, was not neo-Nazi propaganda but yet another homage to Stirlitz.[67] But what of the first viewers of the series, for whom the dissonance between the aesthetic and the moral was surely all the greater? There is some evidence of moral discomfort. Vsevolod Sanaev, the first choice for the role of Müller, reputedly turned the role down on the grounds that he would not be seen in an SS uniform.[68] A participant in the Gor'kii Studio discussion was alarmed to find himself being made to sympathize with the fascists, even though such a thing should have been impossible.[69] The same speaker was left dissatisfied with the portrayal of Schellenberg by Tabakov, and it appears this view was more widely held among the viewing public. One viewer from Moscow said the casting of Tabakov had been a "big mistake" by the director: "Nature has endowed Tabakov with a boyish face, and it's impossible to believe that this youngster is a hardened enemy, a cunning associate of Himmler."[70]

How then can we explain this extraordinary move to put well-loved Soviet actors, including the positive hero of the series, in SS uniforms? One argument would be the need to maintain good relations with the GDR and not to demonize Germany. But although Stirlitz says he loves the German people, we see him almost exclusively in the company of leading Nazis.

Another argument (put forward notably by Lipovetskii) holds that the Third Reich and Soviet Russia have a basic affinity as authoritarian societies and as empires. Stirlitz is essentially helping the imperial cause to hold firm against Western liberal democracies. This is a nice reading, though it by no means explains everything—after all, it is precisely the relatively liberal aspects of German life that we see in Stirlitz's driving around, in his visits to Elefant, in his evenings at home in suburban domesticity.

Still another theory would identify *Seventeen Moments* as an example of "camp totalitarianism"—as the Soviet equivalent of *The Producers*. But "Springtime for Stirlitz" is ultimately an unsatisfactory reading. The *anekdoty* should not mislead us into believing that humor and irony were the dominant modes of reception among the Soviet viewing public. *Seventeen Moments* remains vastly more ambivalent and empathetic toward the enemy than anything analogous in Western Cold War culture.

There remains something remarkable about the capacity of *Seventeen Moments* to offer something for everyone. To war veterans it offered an example of military heroism and self-sacrifice, along with a warning of the perennial perfidy of the West. Just enough time—a full generation—had passed since the war for this "humanizing" of the enemy to be legitimate. As a speaker at the Gor'kii Studio noted, it was now time to stop depicting the enemy as "idiots," which only undermined the achievements of Soviet counterintelligence.[71] To the thinking person it offered a parable of the plight of the *intelligent* under the Soviet system. To younger, and some older, viewers it offered a tantalizing glimpse of an imagined West. To women it offered a model of masculinity that was often absent in real life.

In the process it bridged two key divides that had never before been so securely straddled in Soviet culture. The first was the tension between Soviet patriotism (not to say imperialism) and the fascination with the wider (especially Western) world, its freedoms and prosperity, that was a basic fact of Soviet society by the 1970s. On screen the two could perhaps be combined only through the retro aesthetic of black-and-white: the contemporary West shown in color would have been just too beguiling. Offscreen, the characteristically 1970s blend of statist patriotism and cosmopolitanism was best embodied by Stirlitz's creator. Iulian Semenov was a staunch defender of the Soviet cause in his novels but an exceptionally well-traveled Soviet citizen who found much to admire wherever he went; a man with a hard-drinking, straight-talking persona, a free spirit in the mold of his literary model Hemingway, but a writer who could move in KGB circles without feeling any cognitive dissonance. Whatever assessment we reach of Semenov's life and works, he was a figure who would have been unthinkable in the Thaw generation with which he entered maturity.

The second divide was that between the public and the private self. Stirlitz is a man with an impeccably public mission to which he has devoted his life for more than twenty years, in the process forgoing many pleasures and comforts. On the other hand, he is a man driven by his situation to protect his inner being literally with his life. If he allows anyone else into his consciousness, he is done for. Stirlitz's stream of thought is where the main action of *Seventeen Moments* takes place. There are two Stirlitzes: his face and body are that of Viacheslav Tikhonov, his soul lies in the interior monologues of Efim Kopelian's voice-over.

It is here, more or less, that Elena Prokhorova in her dissertation finds the broader significance of the miniseries in the Soviet 1970s: this medium was a way for collectivist values to be given individual meanings. To see this as the cultural manifestation of Stagnation, or as a return to aesthetic stasis or conservatism, or as the subordination of the personal to the collective, seems too negative an assessment. What we have here is evidence of a successful and viable, and distinctively Soviet, mass culture. This was a culture that had outgrown the political ideology that it ostensibly served. *Seventeen Moments* was supervised every step of the way, indeed sponsored, by the KGB, yet left room for intelligentsia and ironic readings that Andropov would no doubt have abhorred if they had occurred to him. The series sustained the fundamental Soviet oppositions between self and other, "us" and "them," but did so in ways that were vastly more humane than official Soviet discourse permitted (or, for that matter, than American Cold War discourse permitted).

Of course, not all cultural products of the 1970s were as successful as *Seventeen Moments* in performing this feat (perhaps none of them were); and not all media were as successful as TV.[72] But the TV series in general, and *Seventeen Moments* in particular, are acceptably representative of the semiotic system of Soviet culture when it put the elongated Thaw, or the sixties, behind it and reached its steady state in the early 1970s. And perhaps we shouldn't any more call this "late Soviet culture" but rather "Russian culture." The internationalism of Soviet culture had waxed and waned since its early days in the 1920s, but it had never been abandoned. The ambition to be a lodestar for progressive humanity, both in form and in content, underpinned the Soviet cultural enterprise. That ambition reached its height in the 1960s, an era of unprecedentedly intense cultural exchange and interaction across national boundaries. The prospects seemed bright around 1960, the high-water mark of Khrushchevian optimism, a moment when the USSR could hope to exert a formative influence on a revolution a few dozen miles from Florida. In due course, however, the causes for transnational optimism sharply decreased. When there was no more de-Stalinization to talk about, Soviet writers seemed to Western readers less cutting edge than blunt instrument. Mass Soviet tourism to Czechoslovakia was not doing much to foster the friendship of peoples. Even the Soviet Union's charismatic guitar poets did not travel well (unless they married French actresses).[73]

Given all these disappointments, the Soviet Union could hunker down and work on the establishment of a strong and viable—and largely televisual—national culture. It would have typological resemblances to mass cultures elsewhere—but these would be precisely resemblances rather than evidence of determinative transnational impact. The collapse of the Soviet Union, and the various upheavals (social and cultural as well as political) that accompanied it, should not blind us to the fact that the continuities from the 1970s in contemporary Russian culture are much more striking than the discontinuities. Just recently, a prequel *Isaev* (about the life of the young spy) has been made for Russian TV, while the original *Seventeen Moments* has been shown in a new color version. Mark Lipovetskii has acutely suggested that Putin is Stirlitz *après la lettre,* combining as he does commitment to the great power mission with slick Westernness.[74] So perhaps future cultural historians will speak of *Seventeen Moments* not just as emblematic of the post-Thaw seventies but as initiating a broader "age of Stirlitz" lasting from 1973 to sometime in the second or third decade of the twenty-first century.

Notes

I thank Julian Graffy and members of the Russian Cinema Research Group at the School of Slavonic and East European Studies, University College London, for valuable comments on a version of this paper.

1. Josephine Woll, *Real Images: Soviet Cinema and the Thaw* (London: I. B. Tauris, 2000).

2. Stephen V. Bittner, *The Many Lives of Khrushchev's Thaw: Experience and Memory in Moscow's Arbat* (Ithaca: Cornell University Press, 2008), 10. On the history of the Thaw metaphor and its limitations as a blanket description of the era, see 1–13.

3. For two recent high-profile accounts of Britain in that decade, see Andy Beckett, *When the Lights Went Out: Britain in the Seventies* (London: Faber and Faber, 2009); and Dominic Sandbrook, *State of Emergency: The Way We Were: Britain, 1970–1974* (London: Penguin Books, 2010).

4. Petr Vail' and Aleksandr Genis, *60-e: Mir sovetskogo cheloveka* (Ann Arbor, MI: Ardis Press, 1988).

5. A recent assessment of the Parfenov project sees it primarily as an exercise in nostalgia, which may not be entirely fair; see A. Markov and Ia. Komarova, "Nostal'giia versii 2.0? Nekotorye razmyshleniia v sviazi s tele/knizhym proektom L. Parfenova 'Namedni,'" in *Trudy "Russkoi antropologicheskoi shkoly,"* vol. 7 (Moscow: RGGU, 2010), 96–109. However, the charge of nostalgia should certainly be leveled at Parfenov's follow-up project, *Kakie nashi gody* (launched November 2010), which was a rather glib and glossy exercise in retrospection.

6. In 1995 and 1997, just over a third of respondents said that life in Russia had been best under Brezhnev; in 2002 this proportion had grown to almost half. See Boris Dubin, "Litso epokhi. Brezhnevskii period v stolknovenii razlichnykh otsenok," in *Zhit' v Rossii na rubezhe stoletii: Sotsiologicheskie ocherki i razrabotki* (Moscow: Progress-Traditsiia, 2007), 384–85.

7. K. Iu. Rogov, ed., *Semidesiatye kak predmet istorii russkoi kul'tury* (Moscow: Venetsiia-O.G.I., 1998).

8. Mariia Dubnova and Arkadii Dubnov, *Tanki v Prage, Dzhokonda v Moskve: Azart i styd semidesiatykh* (Moscow: Vremia, 2007).

9. Birgit Beumers, *A History of Russian Cinema* (Oxford: Berg, 2009).

10. Data from Fedor Razzakov, *Zhizn' zamechatel'nykh vremen, 1970–1974: Vremia, sobytiia, liudi* (Moscow: Eksmo, 2004), 904. Foreign films also did well in the 1970s. In 1973 they included an English *Jane Eyre* as well as movies from the GDR, France, Italy, and India. On the colossal impact of Bollywood, see Sudha Rajagopolan, *Leave Disco Dancer Alone! Indian Cinema and Soviet Movie-Going after Stalin* (New Delhi: Yoda Press, 2008).

11. See Kristin Roth-Ey, "Finding a Home for Television in the USSR, 1950–1970," *Slavic Review* 66, no. 2 (2007): 278–306.

12. A fine study of this genre—the only full-length study, as far as I know—is Elena Prokhorova's PhD dissertation, "Fragmented Mythologies: Soviet TV Mini-Series of the 1970s" (University of Pittsburgh, 2003). A good short treatment of *Seventeen Moments* in this context is Rodolphe Baudin, "Le phénomène de la série culte en contexte soviétique et post-soviétique: L'exemple de Semnadcat' mgnovenij vesny," *Cahiers du monde russe* 42, no. 1 (2001): 49–70.

13. *Shestoi s"ezd pisatelei SSSR* (Moscow: Sovetskii pisatel', 1978), 331.

14. See M. Kosinova, "Parametry krizisa organizatsionno-ekonomicheskoi sistemy sovetskogo kinematografa," in *Posle ottepeli: Kinematograf 1970-kh*, ed. A. Shemiakin and Iu. Mikheeva (Moscow: In-t Kinoiskusstva, 2009). The hit miniseries of the early 1970s played a key role in tipping the balance from cinema to TV: in his study of Dnepropetrovsk, Sergei Zhuk finds the authorities in 1974 sanctioning the release of Western films as a means of drawing back to the cinema young people who had been captivated by *The Adjutant of His Excellency* and *Seventeen Moments*. See S. I. Zhuk, "Zapad v sovetskom 'zakrytom' gorode: 'Chuzhoe' kino, ideologiia i problemy kul'turnoi identichnosti na Ukraine v brezhnevskuiu epokhu (1964–1982 gody)," *Novoe literaturnoe obozrenie* 100 (2009): 561–62.

15. Artistic Council, transcript of meeting, 30 November 1972, in Rossiiskii gosudarstvennyi arkhiv literatury i iskusstva (RGALI), f. 2468 (Kinostudiia im. Gor'kogo), op. 8 (1971–73), d. 353, l. 47, and transcript of meeting, 1 March 1973, in RGALI, f. 2468, op. 8, d. 354, ll. 7, 45.

16. For further reflections on the various kinds of temporality in the miniseries, see Prokhorova, "Fragmented Mythologies," 83.

17. "Tematicheskii plan na iiun'–avgust 1973," in Gosudarstvennyi arkhiv Rossiiskoi Federatsii (GARF), f. 6903 (Gosteleradio), op. 33 (Glavnaia direktsiia programm), d. 25, l. 47.

18. Checked according to the broadcast log in GARF, f. 6903, op. 33, d. 37.

19. Razzakov, *Zhizn' zamechatel'nykh vremen*, 821–82, 890; N. Ia. Tendora, *Viacheslav Tikhonov: Kniaz' iz Pavlovskogo Posada* (Moscow: Eksmo, 2008), 124.

20. Survey of viewers' letters, August 1973, in GARF, f. 6903, op. 36 (Otdel pisem tsentral'nogo televideniia), d. 22, ll. 39–41. Regrettably, these files in the Gosteleradio fond are mere "surveys" of viewers' letters; the originals have not been preserved.

21. Survey of viewers' letters, September 1973, in GARF, f. 6903, op. 36, d. 22, ll. 57, 64.

22. Survey of viewers' letters, August 1973, in GARF, f. 6903, op. 36, d. 22, ll. 58–59.

23. Klaus Mehnert, *The Russians and Their Favorite Books* (Stanford: Stanford University Press, 1983), 46.

24. Survey of viewers' letters, December 1973, in GARF, f. 6903, op. 36, d. 26, ll. 56–57, 89.

25. Anatoly Chernyaev, *My Six Years with Gorbachev* (University Park: Pennsylvania State University Press, 2000), 11.

26. It may or may not be true. What is beyond doubt is that Brezhnev handed out state awards to Lioznova and to leading actors from the film (notably Tikhonov).

27. To be precise, 2,236 as of 2 December 2010. On 23 February 2009, for comparison, the site had 1,852 Stirlitz *anekdoty*: the corpus is still growing.

28. Prokhorova, "Fragmented Mythologies," 40.

29. On Semenov's gloomy reaction to the fall of Khrushchev, see Ol'ga Semenova, *Iulian Semenov* (Moscow: Molodia gvardiia, 2006), 81.

30. The biography by Semenov's daughter is frank about the working relationship with Andropov, though she likens it—with tongue not very far in cheek—to that between Catherine the Great and Voltaire; see Semenova, *Iulian Semenov*, 86–87. Note also the memoir by a KGB general-major in Ol'ga Semenova, ed., *Neizvestnyi Iulian Semenov: Umru ia nenadolgo . . . Pis'ma, dnevniki, putevye zametki* (Moscow: Veche, 2008), 524–29, which testifies to Semenov's remarkable self-confidence in dealing with the country's top brass.

31. Semenova, *Iulian Semenov*, 95.

32. These scenes remained in the final version, even though they were quite heavily criticized in the studio discussions. In the first studio discussion, one speaker called the Stalin scene "traditionally weak" and recommended its removal. In the last discussion, the criticism became more categorical: the actor's performance was "bad," this was an "artificial figure," a "piece from another film that is out of place stylistically." But while Lioznova agreed that the scene was weak and the actor unconvincing, she herself found Stalin a "complex" figure whose significance was still "unclear" to her; evidently, she did not agree that the Soviet leader had no place in her film. See Artistic Council, transcript of meeting, 30 November 1972, in RGALI, f. 2468, op. 8, d. 353, l. 30, and transcript of meeting, 28 April 1973, in RGALI, f. 2468, op. 8, d. 355, ll. 13, 20, 27, 41–42. In any case, it seems unlikely the authorities would ever have allowed the film to be made without some recognition of the guiding wisdom emanating from the Kremlin. According to Ol'ga Semenova, her father was forced by the censors to revise his screenplay to place greater emphasis on the role of Moscow Center; Semenova, *Iulian Semenov*, 145.

33. Hedrick Smith, *The Russians* (London: Ballantine Books, 1976), 397.

34. Razzakov, *Zhizn' zamechatel'nyh vremen*, 824.

35. Marina Adamovich, "Ne dumai o 'Mgnoven'iakh' svysoka . . . ," *Iskusstvo kino*, no. 3 (2002): 84. The summary of letters to Central Television notes that many viewers commented on the "civic

value" *(grazhdanskoe znachenie)* of the series. See survey of viewers' letters, August 1973, in GARF, f. 6903, op. 36, d. 22, l. 40.

36. For example, Sergei Nekhamkin, "Tat'iana Lioznova: 'Do i posle Shtirlitsa,'" *Izvestiia*, 6 February 2003.

37. For the critique and Lioznova's defense, see Artistic Council, transcript of meeting, 1 March 1973, in RGALI, f. 2468, op. 8, d. 354, ll. 20, 38–39, 42.

38. Semenova, *Iulian Semenov*, 100.

39. It might be added that a lot of the *anekdoty* play on Stirlitz's presumed *intelligentnost'*.

40. Adamovich, "Ne dumai o 'Mgnoven'iakh' svysoka," 76.

41. Artistic Council, transcript of meeting, 30 November 1972, in RGALI, f. 2468, op. 8, d. 353, l. 14.

42. Iu. S. Semenov, "Semnadtsat' mgnovenii vesny," in *Sobranie sochinenii*, 5 vols. (Moscow: Sovremennik, 1983–84), 3:352–53.

43. On the tensions between Semenov and Lioznova, see Semenova, *Iulian Semenov*, 145–46. One of the speakers at the studio discussion of the first three episodes (30 November 1972) mentioned that the scene between Stirlitz and his wife had been controversial, though she herself liked it, seeing it as the moment when Tikhonov warmed up and overcame a tendency to "monotony" in other scenes; Artistic Council, transcript of meeting, 30 November 1972, in RGALI, f. 2468, op. 8, d. 353, l. 5. According to the Semenov novels, Stirlitz had last seen his wife twenty-three years ago in Vladivostok as he was departing with the White emigration on an assignment set by Dzerzhinskii. Semenov's main objection to the insertion of the scene in the TV series was that it violated historical plausibility.

44. Artistic Council, transcript of meeting, 28 April 1973, in RGALI, f. 2468, op. 8, d. 355, ll. 24–25. When the Brezhnev leadership decided to hand out state prizes for the series, Semenov was (apparently through oversight) omitted from the list and took vast offense.

45. Survey of viewers' letters, August 1973, in GARF, f. 6903, op. 36, d. 22, l. 41.

46. Artistic Council, transcript of meeting, 30 November 1972, in RGALI, f. 2468, op. 8, d. 353, ll. 18, 35–36, and transcript of meeting, 1 March 1973, in RGALI, f. 2468, op. 8, d. 354, l. 13.

47. Artistic Council, transcript of meeting, 30 November 1972, in RGALI, f. 2468, op. 8, d. 353, ll. 10, 14.

48. For versions of this criticism, see Artistic Council, transcript of meeting, 30 November 1972, in RGALI, f. 2468, op. 8, d. 353, ll. 5–6, 12, 29, 31, 38, 41, and transcript of meeting, 1 March 1973, in d. 354, ll. 15, 35.

49. Prokhorova, "Fragmented Mythologies," 87.

50. Note the objection to this by one of the studio reviewers: "We've gotten used to the fact that Soviet spies traditionally don't kill people": Artistic Council, transcript of meeting, 30 November 1972, in RGALI, f. 2468, op. 8, d. 353, l. 41.

51. A phrase that was disliked by one of the studio commentators: Artistic Council, transcript of meeting, 1 March 1973, in RGALI, f. 2468, op. 8, d. 354, l. 14. On the Bond comparison, see Baudin, "Phénomène de la série culte," 55; Adamovich, "Ne dumai o 'Mgnoven'iakh' svysoka," 85.

52. Prokhorova, "Fragmented Mythologies," 78.

53. As noted in Iu. Mikheeva, "Neser'eznoe kino: Sovetskaia intelligentsiia v komediiakh 70-kh," in Shemiakin and Mikheeva, *Posle ottepeli*, 279.

54. Semenov, "Semnadtsat' mgnovenii vesny," 322.

55. Though a few years later he would turn down the role of a sixty-seven-year-old Stirlitz in the film version of the novel *Bomba dlia predsedatelia* because he did not want to be made up as old ahead of his time; Semenova, *Iulian Semenov*, 147.

56. Semenova, *Iulian Semenov*, 84.

57. Mehnert, *Russians and Their Favorite Books*, 47; Semenova, *Neizvestnyi Iulian Semenov*, 17.

58. Artistic Council, transcript of meeting, 1 March 1973, in RGALI, f. 2468, op. 8, d. 354, l. 45, and transcript of meeting, 28 April 1973, in RGALI, f. 2468, op. 8, d. 355, l. 10.

59. The day-by-day log of the shooting of the series is at RGALI, f. 2468, op. 8, d. 851.

60. Artistic Council, transcript of meeting, 30 November 1972, in RGALI, f. 2468, op. 8, d. 353, ll. 18–19, 23, and transcript of meeting, 28 April 1973, in RGALI, f. 2468, op. 8, d. 355, l. 8.

61. S. Drobashenko, *Sovetskoe kino 70-e gody: Osnovnye tendentsii razvitiia* (Moscow: Iskusstvo, 1984), 67–68.

62. Semenova, *Neizvestnyi Iulian Semenov*, 21. The relationship between the characters of *Seventeen Moments* and their real-life prototypes continues to exert a good deal of fascination over the Russian public. See, for example, a recent, laughably thin attempt to show that Müller, the chief of the Gestapo, was actually working for the Soviets; Valerii Shambarov, *Semnadtsat' mgnovenii Gestapo-Miullera* (Moscow: Eksmo, 2005). Not too many fictional characters would, like Stirlitz, be paid the compliment of a full-length biography (pieced together from the series of Semenov novels); see Pavel Gor'kovskii, *Rasshifrovannyi Isaev* (Moscow: Eksmo, 2009).

63. Some of these inaccuracies were picked up by the first viewers of the series; see survey of viewers' letters, August 1973, in GARF, f. 6903, op. 36, d. 22, l. 41. Recent publications in this vein include K. A. Zalesskii (author of a five-volume encyclopedia of the Third Reich), *Semnadtsat' mgnovenii vesny: Krivoe zerkalo Tret'ego Reikha* (Moscow: Veche, 2006), and Klim Degtiarev, *Shtirlits bez grima: Semnadtsat' mgnovenii vran'ia* (Moscow: Eksmo, 2006); even Tendora, *Viacheslav Tikhonov*, has a chapter in this vein.

64. One internal reviewer objected to the length of this scene; see Artistic Council, transcript of meeting, 28 April 1973, in RGALI, f. 2468, op. 8, d. 355, l. 7.

65. Thanks to Julian Graffy for elaboration of this point.

66. As Klaus Mehnert notes, Semenov too was remarkably free of hostility toward the Germans; see Mehnert, *Russians and Their Favorite Books*, 172.

67. Mark Lipovetskii, "Iskusstvo alibi: 'Semnadtsat' mgnovenii vesny' v svete nashego opyta," *Neprikosnovennyi zapas*, no. 3 (2007): 131.

68. Tendora, *Viacheslav Tikhonov*, 131. Faina Ranevskaia apparently turned down the role of Frau Zaurich on the grounds that it was not convincing; S. Sekirinskii, "'Semnadtsat' mgnovenii vesny': istoriia i sovremennost' v teleseriale 70-kh," in *Istoriia kino/ Istoriia strany*, ed. S. Sekirinskii (Moscow: Znak, 2004), 351.

69. Artistic Council, transcript of meeting, 28 April 1973, in RGALI, f. 2468, op. 8, d. 355, l. 23.

70. Survey of viewers' letters, August 1973, in GARF, f. 6903, op. 36, d. 22, l. 41.

71. Artistic Council, transcript of meeting, 1 March 1973, in RGALI, f. 2468, op. 8, d. 354, l. 5, similarly l. 36.

72. It is worth noting that the most high-profile new TV series of autumn 1973 was a six-part adaptation of the socialist realist classic *How the Steel Was Tempered*, which in November elicited more than three thousand letters; see "Tematicheskii plan na iiun'–avgust 1973," in GARF, f. 6903, op. 36, d. 25, l. 23.

73. I allude here to the chapters in this volume by Gonçalves, Jones, Applebaum, and Djagalov.

74. Lipovetskii, "Iskusstvo alibi," 146.

Index

Page numbers in *italics* indicate illustrations, photos, or tables.

Contributors

Rachel Applebaum received her PhD in Russian and Eastern European history from the University of Chicago in 2012. In 2012–13 she is a Visiting Assistant Professor of Modern European History at Lafayette College. She is currently writing a book on socialist internationalism in the Eastern bloc.

Rossen Djagalov is a Tutor in the Committee on History and Literature at Harvard University. He received his PhD in comparative literature from Yale University in 2011. His dissertation was entitled "The People's Republic of Letters: Towards a Media History of Socialist Internationalism."

Robert Edelman is Professor of Russian History and the History of Sports at the University of California, San Diego. He is author of *Serious Fun: A History of Spectator Sports in the USSR* (1993) and *Spartak Moscow: A History of the People's Team in the Workers' State* (2009).

João Felipe Gonçalves is a Postdoctoral Fellow at the Center for Latin American Studies at the University of Chicago and the author of *Rui Barbosa: Pondo as idéias no lugar* (Rio de Janeiro, 2000).

Anne E. Gorsuch is Professor of History at the University of British Columbia. Her publications include *Youth in Revolutionary Russia: Enthusiasts, Bohemians, Delinquents* (2000) and *All This Is Your World: Soviet Tourism at Home and Abroad after Stalin* (2011).

Polly Jones is Fellow and Tutor in Russian at University College, University of Oxford. She is editor of *The Dilemmas of De-Stalinization: Negotiating Cultural and Social Change in the Khrushchev Era* (2006) and *The Leader Cult in Communist Dictatorships: Stalin and the Eastern Bloc* (2004). Her monograph *Myth, Memory and Trauma: The Stalinist Past as Soviet Culture, 1953–69* is forthcoming.

Lilya Kaganovsky is Associate Professor of Slavic, Comparative Literature, and Cinema and Media Studies at the University of Illinois, Urbana-Champaign. She is the author of *How the Soviet Man Was Unmade* (2008), and articles on gender and masculinity in Soviet and post-Soviet literature and film. Her current projects include a book on Soviet cinema's transition to sound and, together with Masha Salazkina, a coedited volume on sound, music, and speech in Soviet and post-Soviet cinema.

Diane P. Koenker is Professor of History at the University of Illinois at Urbana-Champaign. She is the author of *Republic of Labor: Russian Printers and Soviet Socialism, 1918–1930* (2005) and *Club Red: Vacation Travel and the Soviet Dream* (2013).

Stephen Lovell is Professor of Modern History at King's College London. His publications include *The Soviet Union: A Very Short Introduction* (2009) and *The Shadow of War: Russia and the Soviet Union, 1941 to the Present* (2010).

Anne Luke lectures in the faculty of Social Sciences at Birmingham City University in the UK. She researches and publishes on the history, culture, and politics of youth and the lives of young people in the Cuban Revolution.

Sabina Mihelj is Senior Lecturer in Media, Communication and Culture at Loughborough University, UK. She is the author of *Media Nations: Communicating Belonging and Exclusion in the Modern World* (2011) and coeditor of *Central and Eastern European Media in Comparative Perspective* (2012).

Christian Noack is Associate Professor with the European Studies group at the University of Amsterdam. He has recently published "Building Tourism in One Country? The Sovietization of Vacationing, 1917–41," in *Touring beyond the Nation: A Transnational Approach to European Tourism History*, edited by Eric G. Zuelov (2011), and "Andere Räume: Sowjetische Kurorte als Heterotopien," in *Mastering Russian Spaces: Raum und Raumbewältigung als Probleme der russischen Geschichte*, ed. Karl Schlögel (2011).

Susan E. Reid is Professor of Russian Visual Culture in the Department of Russian and Slavonic Studies, University of Sheffield. Recent publications include *Pleasures in Socialism: Leisure and Luxury in the Eastern Bloc*, coedited with David Crowley (2010), and "Who Will Beat Whom? Soviet Popular Reception of the American National Exhibition in Moscow, 1959," *Kritika* (2008). She is completing a book provisionally entitled *Khrushchev Modern: Making Oneself at Home in the Soviet 1960s*.

Nick Rutter is completing a PhD in history at Yale University. His dissertation is entitled "Fete of the Future: The World Youth Festival, 1945–1975." He is author of "Western Wall: The Iron Curtain Recast in 1951," in *Cold War Crossings: International Travel and Exchange in the Soviet Bloc, 1940s–1960s* (forthcoming 2013), edited by Patryk Babiracki and Kenyon Zimmer.

Lewis H. Siegelbaum is Jack and Margaret Sweet Professor of History at Michigan State University. He is the author of the award-winning *Cars for Comrades: The Life of the Soviet Automobile* (2008), and he most recently edited *The Socialist Car: Automobility in the Eastern Bloc* (2011).

Lightning Source UK Ltd.
Milton Keynes UK
UKHW021828141219
355318UK00024B/804/P